n Foreign Policy
76:
Speeches and Documents

R E. BLANCHETTE

ton Library

ton Library No. 118
by Gage Publishing Limited
tion with the Institute of
Studies, Carleton University

f reprints, original works, and new
of source material relating to Can-
d under the editorial supervision of
te of Canadian Studies of Carleton
, Ottawa.

f the Institute

Canadian Cataloguing in Publication Data

Main entry under title:

Canadian foreign policy 1966-1976

(The Carleton library; no. 118)
Sequel to Canadian foreign policy 1955-1965.

Bibliography: p.

ISBN 0-7715-5664-0 pa.

1. Canada—Foreign relations—1970-　　　—Sources.*
2. Canada—Foreign relations—1945-1970—Sources.*
I. Blanchette, Arthur E. II. Carleton University. Institute of Canadian Studies. III. Series.

FC602.C36　　　327.71　　　C80-094377-5
F1034.2.C36

31, 769

Contents

VII. INTERNATIONAL DEVELOPMENT

Editorial Note

VIII. THE ENVIRONMENT

Editorial Note

Preface

With the publication of this volume, the Carleton Library now documents a span of thirty years (1945-75) in the field of Canadian foreign relations.* In order to maintain consistency, the same editorial principles and techniques were used in this volume as in its two predecessors. Again, the editor was faced with an abundance of material and severe winnowing was necessary to avoid bulkiness. As with the two previous volumes and for much the same reasons, some subjects had to be omitted altogether. To compensate for these omissions, a list of books for further reading has again been provided. When possible, the same chapter sequence has been followed as in the past, but readers will notice some changes. The chapters on the UN, NATO, and the Commonwealth, are somewhat shorter. These subjects received relatively less government attention as the decade advanced. Continental defence is dealt with under the topic of the United States. Three new chapters appear, reflecting new subjects or emphases: environmental affairs, international development, and the foreign policy review of 1968-70. The chapter on the provinces is considerably longer, owing to the growth of provincial activity in the external sector.

The decade witnessed no change in the political party at the helm of Canadian affairs. The Liberal Party has been in office since 1963. The

---

* See R. A. MacKay, *Canadian Foreign Policy, 1945-1954*, Carleton Library No. 51 (Toronto: McClelland and Stewart, 1971), and A. E. Blanchette, *Canadian Foreign Policy, 1955-1965*, Carleton Library No. 103 (Toronto: McClelland and Stewart, 1977): both volumes are still available from Gage Publishing Limited. Henceforth these volumes are referred to as R.A.M. and A.E.B. The two volumes covering the 1955-1975 period were planned as an integrated work. They are thus closely related and could be used as one book, since they frequently provide an account not only of the origin and evolution of a given foreign policy problem but also of its outcome.

former Prime Minister, L. B. Pearson, retired in 1968 and was succeeded by Mr. Pierre-Elliott Trudeau, who led the Liberals to victory and a majority government in June of that year. The former Secretary of State for External Affairs, Mr. Paul Martin, became Government Leader in the Senate, and Mr. Mitchell Sharp took over the External Affairs portfolio. He was followed in office by Mr. Allan J. MacEachen in mid-1974. Mr. MacEachen placed particular emphasis on international development, to which he gave much strength and impetus.

In the area of international trade, Mr. J. L. Pépin became Minister in 1968. His imagination, industry, zest, and good humour made him one of Canada's best trade ministers. He was succeeded in office in 1972 by Mr. Gillespie, who was followed by Messieurs Jamieson and Chrétien. Mr. Jamieson moved to External Affairs in 1976.

On the official level, the Department of External Affairs was headed until 1970 by Mr. Marcel Cadieux as Under-Secretary of State for External Affairs. He was followed by Mr. A. E. Ritchie, previously Ambassador to the United States. Mr. Ritchie was succeeded by Mr. Basil Robinson, who was Under-Secretary from 1974 to 1977. He is now Northern Pipeline Commissioner. Prime Minister Trudeau paid particular attention to external affairs after assuming office. His views were paramount, notably in the field of overall policy, defence, and development. His special assistant and advisor on international relations, Mr. Ivan Head, was particularly influential in the foreign policy sector since 1968. Deputy Minister of Industry, Trade and Commerce since 1964, Mr. J. H. Warren moved to London as High Commissioner in 1971 and to Washington as Ambassador in 1975. He was followed as Deputy Minister by Mr. James Grandy in 1971.

Many changes occurred in the provincial cast during the decade. In Alberta, Premier Lougheed came to office in 1971. He has vigorously defended his province's interests, particularly in the field of energy. The late Premiers Johnson and Bertrand of the *Union Nationale* Party in Quebec came to office in 1965 and 1967 respectively. In 1969, the *Union Nationale* was followed by the Liberal Party under Mr. Robert Bourassa, whose government took a somewhat softer stand on federal/provincial relations. Mr. Bourassa's victory at the polls coincided with President de Gaulle's departure from the political scene in France. The Bourassa Government was in turn succeeded by that of Mr. René Lévesque's *Parti Québécois* as a result of the provincial elections of November 15, 1976.

Finally, the name of one non-Canadian actor on the stage must be mentioned: Charles de Gaulle, who was President of the French

Republic during the first four years of the decade under consideration. De Gaulle's policy of favouring Quebec and circumventing Ottawa abroad, notably in France and Francophone Africa, probably
caused more anguish and received more concentrated attention in
Ottawa than any other development at the time.

For reasons outlined below, during the ten-year span under review,
Canada was not as prominent on the international scene as previously, except in the sectors of aid, law of the sea, and environment.
Nevertheless, this is a fascinating period to study. The problems with
France alone make for lively reading. Old questions such as the
opening of diplomatic relations with Peking and the Vatican were
solved. New fields of diplomacy, *viz.*, energy questions, food/popula-
tion problems, and so on, were opened up.

Largely as a result of constitutional concerns, national unity problems, economic difficulties such as inflation and unemployment, Canada became less outward-looking during the decade. Certain international developments also contributed to this development—for instance, the settlement of issues by the great powers in the style of
Kissinger, while lesser powers such as Canada were left on the side-
lines. Yet the main exponents of Canadian foreign policy in the mid
to late 1940s, L. S. St. Laurent, L. B. Pearson, C. D. Howe, N. A.
Robertson, Brooke Claxton, and others would all recognize today the
landmarks and milestones of their day.

The quest for collective security has not been abandoned. Canada
still supports the UN, albeit perhaps with somewhat less enthusiasm
than thirty years ago. Canadian forces in NATO, although reduced in
size, continue to contribute to the defence of Western Europe. Our
approach to trade remains multilateral and, along with the United
States, we have been one of the few proponents of free trade at a time
when major trading blocs are being established. Support for international monetary stability continues to be a tenet of Canadian foreign
policy. These broad principles were laid down thirty years ago. If they
have remained basically the same, the emphasis has changed a good
deal—particularly over the last ten years. This has partly been the
result of the domestic conditions mentioned above, but also of
changed international circumstances and the advent of new subjects of
diplomacy.

The enhancement of direct Canadian interests, the preservation of
national unity and national sovereignty, concern for social justice and
human rights, energy and food problems, worry about a deteriorating

physical and human environment now receive more government attention and emphasis. The roles of helpful-fixer/honest-broker and of peace keeper were viewed as Canada's prime contributions to collective security and world peace. However, the main external concerns of much of the two decades following World War II have shifted more to the background. Western Europe is viewed as being in a better position to defend itself now than thirty years ago. As a result, the UN and NATO loom rather less prominent on the horizon of Canadian foreign policy than even a decade ago. At the same time many changes in relationship have occurred over the past three decades with regard to individual countries important to Canada. Relations with the United States, Europe, and Japan have become increasingly important and complex. Relations with Africa and Asia, virtually non-existent in 1945, now occupy a substantial band in the external spectrum. The Commonwealth as an institution, however, has receded somewhat as an element of foreign policy, owing largely to the increase in bilateral relations among individual members. Nevertheless, from some points of view, the wheel has come full circle. In the late 1930s, Secretary of State for External Affairs Mackenzie King was justifying Canada's few foreign-policy ventures in terms of the extension abroad of interests at home. Some thirty years later, his successors, Mitchell Sharp and Paul Martin, were echoing much the same thoughts.

Psychologically there are some similarities in outlook and approach between both periods. Domestic problems, then as now, were urgent and worrisome. Policy makers understandably concentrate on what is most pressing: the Depression in the 1930s; national unity, inflation, and unemployment today. However, the parallel is not entirely accurate. Canada in the 1970s has wide and varied interests abroad and many previously domestic concerns have now assumed an international character—for instance, resources and energy. In the 1930s, Canada had virtually no international presence. Indeed, at one time, Prime Minister Bennett considered abolishing the Department of External Affairs as an economy measure.

Acknowledgments

The editor is again indebted to Professor Michael Whittington of Carleton University for helpful advice and also to Mr. James Marsh, Publications Editor of the Carleton Library series, whose services—invariably courteous and effective—were invaluable. Special thanks are due to Professor Michael Gnarowski, General Editor of the Carleton Library series, for his encouragement and support in helping to bring this volume to completion. Mention should be made of the competent help of the reference staff of the library of the Canadian Embassy in Washington, Mesdames Kilkenny, O'Neill, and Sutherland, under the able direction of Mrs. Merle Fabian. Mr. A. F. Hart, Director, and Professor D. M. Page, Deputy Director, of the Historical Division in the Department of External Affairs, read the manuscript, which was much improved as a result of their counsel and help. Mr. F. McEvoy, also of the Historical Division, proved to be a thoroughgoing ferret in tracking down elusive information.

Without the patient, able, and painstaking co-operation of Miss Elisabeth Keiller, this book would never have met the Carleton Library series deadline.

The editor of this volume is now on posting for the Department of External Affairs as Canadian Ambassador to Tunisia. He is of course responsible for the selection of documents presented in this book, which are entirely in the public domain. The views expressed in the various chapter introductions, explanatory notes and other editorial linkage are also his and do not necessarily reflect the views of the Department of External Affairs. Again it is hoped that they will help to ease the flow of the text and fill such gaps as a book of documents must inevitably contain.

Arthur E. Blanchette
Tunis, October 1, 1980

Abbreviations for main sources

CHCD **Canada, House of Commons Debates**

CTS **Canada Treaty Series**

SS **Statements and Speeches published by the Department of External Affairs**

DEA **Department of External Affairs**

DND **Department of National Defence**

QP **Queen's Printer (Department of Supply and Services)**

**To Ed Ritchie
and Basil Robinson**

I. The United Nations

˜ Although Canada was elected to the Security Council for the third time in 1967, the United Nations was somewhat less significant in Canada's external relations during the 1966-76 decade than during the preceding one. Government attention had focussed on the constitutional and parliamentary issues of the time, on problems of inflation and unemployment, and on such international difficulties as France and Quebec in the context of "*La Francophonie*", and on the growing tendency for great-power settlements outside the context of the UN. There was, furthermore, a general disillusionment with peace keeping after the eviction of UNEF by Egypt shortly before the Six Day War during June 1967 in the Middle East.

The UN itself was beset by a number of serious difficulties during the decade. By 1965, it was on the verge of insolvency as several powers—notably the U.S.S.R., France, and others—had begun as a matter of principle to refuse to pay their assessed share of authorized expenditures in respect of activities they opposed. By the mid-1960s, an amount of $140,000,000 was owing to the UN; its net cash reserves had dwindled to less than $15,000,000; its Working Capital Fund was all but exhausted; its debts amounted to some $45,000,000, in addition to outstanding bonds in the value of $150,000,000 issued to finance peace-keeping operations. (Some $87,000,000 remains to be paid.) The peace-keeping aspect of the UN's financial crisis was eased somewhat in the 1970s when some of the countries concerned (France and Albania) began to make payments of their share of the UN budget that now goes to reimburse states which purchased the bonds, including Canada. Although the Security Council established UNEF II, China, Albania, Libya, Iraq, and Syria have refused to pay their share of expenses owing to political objections to the presence and role of the Force.*

---

* Article 19 of the Chapter, depriving defaulting countries of their voting rights, has not been invoked since the majority of members prefer to avoid a confrontation on the issue.

The UN became the scene of a potentially far more serious problem as the decade advanced: the growing estrangement between the developed and less-developed countries of the world. Contributing to this confrontation were the large increase of UN membership during the 1960s as a result of the liquidation of former colonial empires, notably in Africa; the long festering of certain intractable problems such as in the Middle East; the intolerable racial situation in Southern Africa; and, especially, the "revolution of rising expectations" among the less-developed countries of the world. Most of the latter are to be found south of the 30th parallel of north latitude; hence the "North-South" appellation applied to the split.

Increase in membership also led to verbosity and inefficiency. As the Secretary of State for External Affairs, Mr. Mitchell Sharp, put it in his address to the General Assembly on September 29, 1968: "The UN is drowning in a sea of words", and also in a plethora of "unwieldy boards and committees". He urged remedial action, but such exhortations went unheeded. The UN has continued to talk interminably, presumably on the assumption that talking may prevent shooting. Sharp also urged streamlining the UN's structure, an identification of its priorities, and the avoidance of confrontation in its activities. Little progress in these areas has been achieved.*

Nevertheless, the UN was not without some notable successes. The problem of Chinese representation was finally solved in Peking's favour in 1971. Progress was made in the field of disarmament with the signing of the Nuclear Non-Proliferation Treaty in 1968 and the Seabed Disarmament Treaty in 1971. Some order was put in the UN aid structure when its multifarious activities in this field were brought together under the United Nations Development Program (UNDP) in 1966. United Nations interest in environmental problems led to several important conferences, such as that at Stockholm on the Environment in 1972; on Global Population Problems at Bucharest in 1974; and on Human Settlements ("Habitat") at Vancouver in 1976. Conferences on the Law of the Sea continued.**

---

* A discussion paper entitled "Where is the United Nations Heading?" is available from DEA in Ottawa. It was presented as a contribution to the Annual Meeting of the UN Association in Canada, May 11-15, 1977, in Winnipeg. It examines the major challenges facing the UN today and also describes Canada's contribution to the United Nations.

** These aspects of UN activity are documented in Chapter VIII below; those on aid and development, the North-South debate, and the UN Conferences on Trade and Development, in Chapter VII. These topics were dealt with

By 1975, the UN had become almost totally radicalized and its primary characteristic became that of confrontation: between the developed and less-developed countries; the Arabs and the Israelis; the Chinese and the Russians; the oil exporters and the oil importers; and racial antagonists. All in all, the situation was lively and provocative, but it was not particularly happy or promising.˜

1. Canada as a Member of the Security Council

Statement by the Secretary of State for External Affairs, Mr. Paul Martin, at the University of Western Ontario, London, Ontario, February 17, 1967.

Today, I propose to speak in particular of Canada's role as a member of the Security Council. At the last session of the General Assembly, Canada was elected to the Security Council for the third time in 19 years, and will serve during 1967 and 1968.

Election to the Council is based, according to the United Nations Charter, on "the contribution of members of the United Nations to the maintenance of international peace and security and to the other purposes of the organization", as well as on the principle of equitable geographical distribution. It is true that the candidates for election to the Council are now chosen on the basis of geographical groupings, but the fact remains that the contribution a country can make to the work of the United Nations is an important factor in each group's choice of candidates. For example, it is not without significance that the other candidates elected with Canada this year were India, Brazil, Denmark and Ethiopia—all nations which have played an important part in the activities of the United Nations.

The Security Council has not always lived up to the high hopes which were placed in it at San Francisco 22 years ago. As you know, some degree of co-operation between the great powers is essential if the Council is to carry out its Charter function of primary responsibility for the maintenance of international peace and security. But for many years the suspicions and animosities which clouded relations between the U.S.A. and the U.S.S.R. reduced the Council to virtual

---

in Chapter 1 on the United Nations in the preceding volume. Separate chapters have been set aside for them in this one, owing to their growing importance.

paralysis. In its early years, for example, the Council used to hold more than 100 meetings annually. In the decade of the Fifties, it never held more than 50 meetings annually, and in 1959, when Canada was last on the Council, it held only five meetings. Since 1960, it has shown more vigour. It has been especially successful in limiting and then stopping the outbreaks of violence in Kashmir and Cyprus.

What are the issues which are likely to come before the Council in the months ahead? The trouble spots are obvious. The situation in the Middle East, the situation in Rhodesia, the situation in Southeast Asia, the question of South Africa's racial policies, the continuing dispute between India and Pakistan over Kashmir, the unresolved problem of the relations between Greek and Turkish Cypriots—these are the kinds of situation or dispute that immediately come to mind.

Last year the Council spent 40 per cent of its time on the question of Israel's relations with Syria and Jordan, and a quarter of its time on the situation in Rhodesia. The year before it spent much of its time dealing with the situation in Kashmir and the situation in the Dominican Republic, but was not required to consider the situation in the Middle East at all. So, to some extent, the Council is a prisoner of events.

Over 60 items remain on the Security Council's agenda, and all are potentially relevant to the maintenance of international peace and security, even though many of them are dormant. To take the most obvious example, the situation in Vietnam remains on the Security Council's agenda although it has not been discussed for over a year because there is no basis for agreement within the Council as to what the United Nations can or should do to bring peace to that unhappy country.

While it is true, therefore, that the Council usually reacts to rather than shapes events, it is equally true that constructive use of the Council depends on the seriousness with which governments regard their obligations under the Charter. It is no service to international peace to treat the United Nations as a substitute for the task of direct negotiation, or to use its machinery for the purpose of publicizing charges which it is impossible to verify. Indeed, I would urge that, before a subject is given consideration by the Security Council, the Council should satisfy itself that the question is one which does in fact endanger international peace, and that the parties concerned have themselves examined all peaceful means for the settlement of the dispute before placing it on the agenda.

Whatever the subject under discussion, however, Canada will take a position which is consistent with our record of strong support for the principles of the United Nations Charter and for the strengthening of the organization.

We shall act independently and according to our best judgment—keeping in mind, of course, our special relations with our allies on the Council, our Commonwealth ties and our interest as a nation which looks both across the Atlantic and across the Pacific oceans. We shall have in mind our responsibilities as members of the International Control Commissions in the states of Indochina and as participants in the United Nations Emergency Force in the Middle East and in the United Nations Force in Cyprus. These responsibilities will shape our attitudes but certainly not limit our determination to participate actively in the search for solutions to the disputes concerned.

We shall be conscious also of the importance of finding common ground between the permanent members of the Council without sacrifice of principle. It is true now—as it was in 1945—that the ability of the permanent members of the Council to work together is an important condition for the maintenance of peace. In the intervening years, the smaller powers have performed many of the arbitration, conciliation and peace-keeping functions which it was thought in the beginning would be the primary responsibility of the permanent members. Yet they have only been able to do this insofar as some consensus, tacit or otherwise, has been in existence between the permanent members. The main exception to this rule was the United Nations intervention in Korea, but I do not think we should look upon that episode as a significant precedent for the future.

Of course, we must expect that there will continue to be situations which involve fundamental differences of opinion, or of interest, between the U.S.A. and the U.S.S.R. and in these situations there cannot be any doubt as to where Canada will stand. Nevertheless, it will be our purpose to work with the other non-permanent members of the Council to find ways and means of permitting the United Nations to function effectively, and therefore to emphasize its capacity to act as a third party and impartial presence.

We shall also be concerned during our term on the Council to see if we can improve the procedures for organizing peace-keeping operations.* Since we last served on the Council in 1959, Canada has participated in United Nations Forces in the Congo and in Cyprus, helped to provide air support for observers on the borders of Yemen,

---

* See SS 67/12 of April 26, 1967, by Mr. Martin, for a detailed account of Canada's experience and conclusions with respect to peace keeping between 1948 and 1967.

and provided the commander for the Observation Mission sent to the border between India and Pakistan in the fall of 1965.

A. PEACE KEEPING

~War broke out in the Middle East during early June 1967, soon after the Egyptian government insisted on the withdrawal of UNEF. It is known as the Six Day War because of its duration. Short as it was, it was disastrous without parallel for the losses that it inflicted upon Egypt and its allies. Israeli forces quickly reached the Suez Canal and Sharm el Sheik on the Red Sea at the entrance to the Gulf of Aqaba. They took the Golan Heights in Syria, which dominate the Upper Jordan Valley and Lake Tiberias in northeastern Israel. They occupied the enclave between Jerusalem and the Jordan River (the "West Bank"), thus rounding out Israel's borders pretty much as they are today.

A further outbreak of hostilities occurred in October 1973. It resulted in a somewhat better showing militarily on the Arab side and also in the beginnings of Arab "oil diplomacy" with its energy-crisis connotations with which we are familiar today. UNEF was reconstituted in late 1973 and a Canadian contingent formed part of the force. Canada was active in the UN Special Committee on Peacekeeping Operations throughout the decade.

After lengthy negotiations in which the United States Secretary of State, Dr. Henry Kissinger, was the driving force, Israeli forces withdrew from the east bank of the Suez Canal in 1975 and traffic has resumed between the Mediterranean and the Red Seas. The negotiations conducted by Dr. Kissinger have yet to be concluded and Israel continues to occupy the bulk of the territory acquired in 1967.

At the end of the decade, Canadian policy towards a settlement in the Middle East envisaged a situation where "the manner in which legitimate Palestinian concerns would be represented in the course of the search for a peace settlement is a matter for agreement by the parties involved. The same principle clearly applies to the declared aspiration of the Palestine Liberation Organization to establish an independent national authority in the region. If the emergence of any Palestinian entity were to be envisaged at some stage, it would be essential that this should be the result of agreement among the parties involved, which, of course, include Israel". The full text of this important policy statement is given below.

Thirty years after the creation of Israel a lasting peace in the Middle East—regrettably—is still far from certain.

Cyprus, likewise, continues to be a peace-keeping problem. Basic Canadian policy regarding Cyprus is documented in the previous volume and has not changed. Between March 1964 and January 1975 some 17,000 Canadians served with UNFICYP at a net cost to Canada of more than $25,000,000, exclusive of other forms of assistance such as humanitarian relief. Turkish armed forces now occupy some 40% of the island as a result of the events of the summer of 1974. A solution is still not in sight.*~

2. Canadian Policy Regarding the Middle East

Statement in the House of Commons by the Prime Minister, Mr. L. B. Pearson, June 8, 1967. (Extracts)*

What is the basis for such a political settlement and a more enduring peace than an armistice along with a state of war? We must not forget that in the almost 20 years since 1948 there has been an armistice but there has also been a state of war. I think I can only outline what I think is a possible basis, and there is nothing original in it.

There will have to be certain military withdrawals, after a cease fire, by negotiation and agreement. If the military status quo, or something approaching it, is to be restored there must be certain political guarantees which will produce stability. This will require understanding on both sides and some firm and agreed decisions by the United Nations Security Council to back them up. That cannot be done unless the four permanent members of the Security Council can get together. I leave hon. members to form their own opinions about the ease with which this can be accomplished, notwithstanding the encouraging sign the other night when at least they agreed on a cease fire resolution. But to bring the Israeli forces back behind the borders of last week, without doing anything about the situation in the gulf of Aqaba, would not provide for peace but merely a temporary absence of hostilities.

* See Mr. MacEachen's statement of July 7, 1975, to the United Nations seminar at Mount Allison University, Sackville, New Brunswick, for a detailed account of Canada's participation in UNFICYP.

* See also his statement, CHCD, May 24, 1967.

So, I suggest secondly, that regardless of the legal controversy, which can be sent to the International Court for decision, there should be no exercise by those who claim the right of sovereignty, whether that claim is valid or not—and I am not attaching any judgment to that—to interfere with any innocent passage through the strait of Tiran and the gulf of Aqaba to Elath, which should be recognized by all as an Israeli port.

The third point is that something should be done about the right of Israeli ships, which right was exercised by all other ships until a day or so ago, to navigate the Suez Canal. There have been decisions by the Security Council of the United Nations affirming that right, but in practice the affirmation has not meant very much to Israel.

The fourth point is the establishment once again, in spite of our somewhat disillusioning experiences in the last few weeks, of a United Nations presence in force between the armies that have been fighting, and a presence which will operate on both sides of the border. There has been a great reluctance on the part of Israel to allow United Nations truce observation groups to operate on her territory. This is one respect in which I think she should change her policy and on which agreement should be reached.

Mr. Diefenbaker: Was it reluctance or refusal?

Mr. Pearson: She turned down the request that they should operate on Israeli soil, just as the United Arab Republic could have turned down the request that UNEF operate on her soil. This UN supervision could be done by enlarged observer groups, as we have already discussed in the House, under UNTSO, constituted and operating in accordance with effective and agreed arrangements to be worked out by the United Nations. That must be done.

I had an interesting exchange with the Secretary General of the United Nations about the withdrawal of the Canadian contingent from UNEF on such short notice. The Secretary General wrote me—and this letter has been made public—and paid great tribute to the work of the Canadians in this force and to the work of Canada in the interests of peace keeping. He said:

Canada has thus given unstinting and vital support to UNEF both at the headquarters of the United Nations and in the field. Irrespective of the circumstances of the withdrawal of UNEF and the consequences of that withdrawal, ten and a half years of succesful service to peace is a historic achievement.

U Thant went on:

> Canada's large role in that achievement and your government's unfailing understanding of the requirements of UN peace-keeping operations are widely recognized and appreciated here.

I replied to that letter the other day; I think this communication has also been made public. I thanked the Secretary General for his generous references to the men of our force and said this, which I hope will commend itself to members of the House of Commons:

> Despite current difficulties faced by the United Nations in the peace keeping field, I am hopeful that it will be possible to profit from the experience gained in UNEF and to use the lessons learned, to develop, in due course, within the framework of the United Nations, more effective machinery "to save succeeding generations from the scourge of war", in the words of the charter.

Then I went on:

> In the continuing effort that must be carried on to plan for United Nations peace keeping forces organized and established in a way which will avoid the disturbing experience we have just gone through in the disbanding of UNEF, the United Nations can count on our full support. Recent events show that the work of the United Nations in the field of peace keeping is not less, but more important than ever and that this work must include advance planning, so that United Nations peace-keeping forces in the future will have a clear and strong basis on which to operate.*
>
> The next point relates to what I have been saying about a United Nations presence. I would also hope that there could be a demilitarized zone on both sides of the border and that effective steps—I know they have been attempted, and the men of these observer groups have served with great courage and devotion—will be taken to prevent infiltration, terroristic acts and provocation on both sides.
>
> There is one other element of a settlement which has to be dealt with and in some ways is the most difficult and complex of all. It is the refugee question.

---

* UNEF was not reconstituted until after the next outbreak of hostilities in 1973. Defence in the late 1960s was based on the White Paper of 1964, which placed great emphasis on peace keeping. Withdrawal of UNEF thus caused greater impact than might otherwise have been expected.

When the fighting ended in 1948 there were about 750,000 Palestinian Arabs who left their homes. I will not go into the pressures which were on them to leave but they left their homes and became refugees. There are one and a quarter million of them now, after nearly 20 years. They are maintained by the United Nations.

A real opportunity has never been given to these refugees to decide whether they could or would be willing to locate in other countries, and perhaps a sufficient effort has never been made to get at least some of them back to their homes in Israel. Of course the two things would go together. They have been tragically used as pawns in the game of Middle East politics, and unless a much more effective effort is made to deal with this situation than has been possible in the past, it will not be too easy to be optimistic about the other elements of the settlement.

Those are the five or six elements of a political solution. Whether they could be successfully worked out in a political settlement I do not know because there is an issue which goes even deeper than any of the ones I have mentioned, the issue of deep fear and hostility on both sides, the Arab side and the Jewish side. Until that fear is removed somehow I do not think there will be peace in that area. Yet if it could be removed and at least a mutual acceptance on both sides could be built up, there is no doubt in my mind that the Arab states would be among the first and most important beneficiaries of that change through the help and co-operation that they could get from Israel.

3. Canadian Participation in the United Nations Emergency Force for the Middle East

Statement by the Secretary of State for External Affairs, Mr. Mitchell Sharp, in the House of Commons on November 14, 1973.

An uneasy cease fire now prevails on the Middle Eastern battlefield, which for 15 days, from October 6 to October 22, and again until October 26, witnessed the most furious and bloody fighting in that beleaguered area in modern times. The most sophisticated and destructive equipment was unleashed in the Sinai desert and on the Golan plateau. The biggest tank battles since the Second World War raged on the ground, while dozens of aircraft were struck down from the skies every day, and in the surrounding waters several naval encounters took place near the harbours of the Eastern Mediterranean. Peaceful navigation and trade were interrupted to the point where even some of the governments of that oil-rich region were forced to ration gasoline. Casualties mounted rapidly, and even now we are uncertain as to their extent, although the total must be unbearably high, especially in relation to the results achieved.

The mounting fury of the fight was possibly the only reason why it so abruptly ceased. The great powers who were supplying arms in increasing quantity to each side fortunately realized that they were being drawn into a dangerous confrontation, with the Soviet Union talking of unilateral intervention on the scene, while the United States placed its own forces on an increased state of alert. It was at this crucial stage that the United Nations Security Council agreed to the establishment and dispatch of an emergency force to supervise a cease fire and separate efforts to prevent a recurrence of the fighting.

Given the circumstances as I have just recalled them, there could be no doubt in anyone's mind that never had an emergency measure of this nature been so evidently and urgently necessary. While Canada did not seek participation in the emergency force, we were determined that, once we were invited, it would be a success, and I am sure this is a point of view that would be supported by all parties in the House. We were asked at an early stage by the Secretary-General of the United Nations to contribute in a vitally important role. Just two and a half hours ago the Secretary-General of the United Nations was on the telephone to me urging the importance of Canada's participation and urging our participation in certain of these vital functions upon which the whole of UNEF depends.

After due consideration, the Government decided to accept the request and communicated this decision to Parliament. In accordance with the practice followed in the past when a Canadian contingent has been contributed to a peace-keeping force, as opposed to the sending of peace observers, we are asking Parliament to approve the Government's decision. Leaders of all parties represented here indicated, in response to my announcement of October 30, that they supported a Canadian contribution to peace keeping under the United Nations in the Middle East if it appeared there was a useful role for us to play. Spokesmen for all parties took the same view as I did, that no one could say no to such a request.

The conception of peace-keeping or peace-observation forces under the United Nations, which owes so much of its development to a great Canadian, our former Prime Minister and a Member of this House, the Right Honourable Lester B. Pearson, is firmly supported by this Government, as it has been by previous Canadian Governments of all political stripes. We did not, however, accept the call to join a new UNEF without careful consideration. Experience over the years, some of it rather disappointing, has led us to look for certain criteria that, in our judgment, should be met if a peace-keeping operation is to be effective and if Canadian participation in it is to be worth while. We have no illusions that, in this imperfect world, the criteria for an ideal peace-keeping operation will ever be met in full. These criteria must, however, be constantly reiterated and promoted if peace keeping is to be made a more effective instrument rather than a source of disillusionment to a world community hungry for peace.

The criteria Canada seeks to apply when considering participation in a peace-keeping operation include certain points of a political nature, as well as others of a more technical kind. A fundamental point is the existence of a threat to international peace and security. There is no doubt of that in this case. Ideally, peace keeping should be directly linked to agreement on a political settlement among the parties to the conflict. At least there should be reasonable expectations that the parties will negotiate a settlement. The peace-keeping force must be responsible to a political authority, and preferably that authority should be the United Nations. The sponsoring authority should receive reports and have adequate power to supervise the mandate of the force. The parties to the conflict must accept the peace-keeping force and Canadian participation in it must be acceptable to all concerned. Further considerations are that the peace-keeping force must have a clear mandate, including such things as freedom of movement, and that there must be an agreed and equitable method of financing the operation.

Some of these criteria were not met when we participated in the International Commission in Viet Nam, or in Cyprus in 1964, or in the UNEF of 1956. After our departure from Viet Nam, I made it clear that certain features of the operation made it impossible for the Commission to operate effectively. One major impediment was the absence of a political authority to which it could report.

The United Nations may not be the only possible sponsoring body, but we have not yet found better auspices under which to work at peace keeping. It is, therefore, a matter of satisfaction that in the Middle Eastern situation the emergency force should be put under the authority of the UN. To be precise, it is under the command of the United Nations, vested in the Secretary-General, and under the authority of the Security Council.

In 1964, the House debated the dispatch of a Canadian contingent to Cyprus under great pressure of time and in circumstances that did not allow for the application of rigorous conditions. The island was on the brink of civil war, with intervention threatened from neighbouring countries, and peace-keeping troops had to be sent as quickly as possible. For nine years, the United Nations force in Cyprus has kept conflict from breaking out and it must therefore be counted, to that extent, as a success. It has not, however, led to a settlement of the underlying problems. The absence of a direct link between a peace-keeping force and a negotiated settlement is a weakness, perhaps an unavoidable one, in the Cyprus situation.

Another weakness of the Cyprus peace-keeping operation is the absence of equitable financial arrangements. This time we are determined that the treatment accorded Canada should be equivalent to that accorded to other contributing countries. The Secretary-General has stated that his preliminary estimates of the United Nations' own direct costs for UNEF, based upon past experience and practice, are $30 million for the six-month period authorized by the Security Council. These costs are to be considered expenses of the United Nations organization and are to be borne by the members of the United Nations as apportioned by the General Assembly, presumably in about the same proportions as each country's share in the United Nations annual budget. Canada's share of that budget is currently 3.08 per cent. I might point out to the House that, even if we did not participate in this peace-keeping operation, we should, of course, still pay our share of the peace-keeping costs. It is worth recalling that Canadians have been participating for many years in the United Nations Truce Supervision Organization in the Middle East, and that UNTSO continues to exist and to perform a useful role on the ceasefire lines. Our previous experience in the Middle East in 1956, which was the first major United Nations venture in peace keeping, is naturally very much in our minds at this time. Sadly, we seem to be back where we were 17 years ago. In fact, the request to Canada to participate in the 1973 UNEF is due in great part to the fact that we have special skills and experience, not only in peace keeping generally but in peace keeping in the Middle East, and in the role that is now assigned to our contingent.

The original request from the Secretary-General for Canadian participation on October 27 was in terms of Canada supplying the logistic component of the force. That role has been assigned to us precisely because of the effective way in which Canada discharged it from 1956 to 1967, and the skills that our troops demonstrated in doing their job.

Two aspects of our previous experience are relevant to the new task assigned to Canada in the same area. First, the way in which UNEF had to terminate its peace-keeping function in 1967 and evacuate the Middle East gave rise to a great deal of discussion, both at the United Nations and in Canada. From that unhappy episode certain lessons have been drawn.

There is no point in participating in a peace-keeping operation unless our participation is acceptable to all, and especially to the sovereign state upon whose soil the force is to be deployed. I can assure the House that we did not accept this task until the Secretary-General had given us formal assurance that the presence of a Canadian contingent would be acceptable to all parties, and especially to Egypt, since UNEF will be deployed on Egyptian territory. In addition, I confirmed the Egyptian agreement personally with the Foreign Minister of Egypt when I met him a few days ago in Washington.

Part of the difficulty encountered with the original UNEF in 1956 was that it did not come under the authority of the Secrutiy Council and did not have the unqualified backing of the great powers. Nor was the mandate of the force so clearly set out and accepted by the parties concerned.

The Secretary-General, in his report to the Security Council on October 26, 1973, set out as essential conditions that the Force must have at all times the full confidence and backing of the Security Council, and that it must operate with the full co-operation of the parties concerned. This report was approved by the Security Council and we felt more assured that the 1973 UNEF was to be on a sounder basis than that of 1956. It is on that basis that we acceded to the Secretary-General's request of October 27 and accepted our assignment on the force.

There is now a renewed opportunity for the parties involved to employ the respite that UNEF provides to tackle their basic differences. The principles of a just and lasting settlement have been set out since 1967 in Security Council Resolution 242, but until now no progress has been made in implementing that resolution and no negotiations based on its principles have taken place. Resolution 338 of October 22, 1973, which is the basis for the present cease fire, also deals with the problem of a peaceful settlement. It calls for an immediate beginning to the implementation of Resolution 242 in all its parts and for the beginning of negotiation between the parties under appropriate auspices.

UNEF is not charged with the basic problems involved in a Middle

East settlement. Its tasks are limited to supervising the implementation of the cease fire, the return of the parties to their October 22 positions and the use of its best efforts to prevent a recurrence of fighting. These will be the tests of UNEF and they will be acid tests. Should the parties to the recent conflict fail to comply with the Security Council resolutions and not allow UNEF to operate effectively, the gleam of hope that the cease fire and Resolution 338 offer will be threatened with quick extinction.

As I have said, the framework for peace exists in the resolutions adopted by the Security Council. The problem, in our view, has never been so much one of interpretation as of implementation of these resolutions. I further indicated in the House last week, in reply to a question, that, in our view, such provisions of Resolution 242 . . . as those calling for the withdrawal of Israeli forces from occupied territories and the establishment of secure and recognized boundaries for all states in the region had to be taken together. Naturally, such matters as the drawing of boundaries may prove to be a long task, but is it beyond our imagination to devise means of starting the implementation of the various provisions simultaneously?

The so-called Rogers Plan in 1970 provided for partial implementation of Resolution 242, by a simultaneous reopening of the Suez Canal to navigation and a withdrawal by Israeli forces from the east bank of the canal. While that plan failed, the idea of balance is still a valid one. In fact, the whole basis of Resolution 242 is a balance of obligations and commitments. The problem of Palestinian refugees is one of the items in that balance. The resolution affirms the necessity "for achieving a just settlement of the refugee problem", and this problem should be at least broached simultaneously with the other matters I have mentioned. Canada has not forgotten these refugees. We are the third-largest contributor to the United Nations agency which looks after their needs and we have just increased by $550,000 our contribution for the current year.

The main thing now is quickly to get around to negotiating "under appropriate auspices" as Security Council Resolution 338 has it. To us, it would seem that the United Nations offers appropriate auspices. Others have mentioned the great powers, or some of them. We should hope that they would exert their influence to stimulate the parties to begin negotiations. To the Canadian Government any auspices would seem appropriate that provide a means whereby talks can begin on the essential aspects of the problem.

4. Status of the Palestinians—Canadian Policy

Statement by the Secretary of State for External Affairs, Mr. Allan J. MacEachen, to the United Nations General Assembly, New York, November 20, 1974. (Extracts)

We consider it essential to any lasting and comprehensive settlement that there be respect for the sovereignty, the territorial integrity and the political independence of Israel and of every other state in the Middle East. We remain opposed to any attempt to challenge the right of Israel or the right of any other state in the region to live in peace within secure and recognized boundaries free from threat and acts of force.

The important issue we are now examining, concerning the status of the Palestinians and their role in efforts to achieve a negotiated peace, has figured prominently in this tragic history. From the outset, Canada has recognized that the Palestinians represent a major interested element in the Middle East situation. Security Council Resolution 242, firmly subscribed to by Canada since its adoption in 1967, called for a just settlement of the Palestine refugee problem. Canada has given and continues to give substantial financial support to the United Nations Relief and Works Agency. Recent developments, including this debate, testify to the growing acknowledgement that cognizance must be taken of the need for the Palestinian people to be represented and heard in negotiations involving their destiny. Canada is fully in accord with the view that any enduring peaceful settlement of the Arab-Israeli dispute must take account of the legitimate concerns of the Palestinians.

We have noted with satisfaction that there have been, within a relatively short space of time, territorial adjustments on two fronts in the form of the existing disengagement agreements. We may also be witnessing a fundamental change of appreciation of existing realities on the part of both sides to the dispute. On the one hand, Arab governments appear more disposed to recognize Israel's right to exist. Israel, for its part, has reaffirmed its intention to pursue the search for peace with its Arab neighbours, and to this end has indicated greater recognition of the fact that Palestinian concerns will have to be taken into account in some way if real peace is to be achieved.

This said, ... it will be clear that the question is how legitimate Palestinian concerns are to be brought to bear in efforts to reach a just and durable settlement. Canada has firmly resisted giving advice on what form Palestinian representation should take in future negotiations. The claim of the Palestine Liberation Organization to represent the Palestinians is thus one that, in our view, is not for Canada to decide. It is a question that remains to be resolved by the parties directly involved in the course of their continuing efforts to work towards an agreed peace, and Israel, in our view, is an essential party in deciding the question.

The manner in which legitimate Palestinian concerns are to be represented in the course of the search for a peace settlement is a matter for agreement by the parties involved. The same principle clearly applies to the declared aspiration of the Palestine Liberation Organization to establish an independent national authority in the region. If the emergence of any Palestinian entity were to be envisaged at some stage, it would be essential that this should be the result of agreement among the parties directly involved, which, of course, include Israel. In this respect, the establishment, evolution and existence of any such entity should in no way prejudice the continued existence of the state of Israel.

B. DISARMAMENT

˜General and complete disarmament has continued to elude the powers. The pattern of piecemeal progress by sectors established with the Partial Nuclear Test Ban Treaty in 1963, documented in the previous volume, continued to prevail. The important Nuclear Non-Proliferation Treaty (NPT) came into being in 1968. A number of Canadian ideas were reflected in that Treaty as it finally emerged.* The NPT was opened for signature in July 1968. By September of that year, some eighty states had signed it, including Canada. Today the total is much greater, of course, but a number of countries with nuclear or near-nuclear capacity, such as China, France, certain Middle Eastern and South Asian states, among others, have not yet done so.

Canada continued to play an active role in UN disarmament bodies, although without the intensity characteristic of the previous decade, when disarmament was the deep and abiding concern of the former Secretary of State for External Affairs, Mr. Howard C. Green.

Canada's uranium exports were governed throughout this period by the guidelines announced in the House of Commons by Prime Minister Pearson on June 3, 1965. They stipulated that exports would be for

---

* See the Press Release issued by the Department of External Affairs on August 17, 1965, for background.

peaceful purposes only, subject to verification and control. This did not, however, prevent India from exploding a nuclear device in 1974, an event which led to a considerable tightening of previous policy as announced by Prime Minister Trudeau and by Secretary of State for External Affairs Jamieson on June 17, 1975, and December 22, 1976, respectively.⁻

5. Nuclear Non-Proliferation Treaty: The Canadian Position*

As one of the four Western members of the ENDC, Canada has from the start been actively involved in the formulation of the NPT. It has strongly supported the principle of and has attached high priority to the treaty. It believes that the treaty will be an important factor in maintaining stability in areas of tension, in creating an atmosphere conducive to nuclear-arms control and generally enhancing international stability.

Basic Formula

Canada considers that it will effectively prevent proliferation without prejudicing the right to legitimate collective defence arrangements.

Safeguards Article

Canada believes that effective safeguards are essential to the effectiveness and durability of the treaty. It would have preferred that safeguards be applied equitably to all parties, but it realizes that the Soviet position has made this impossible. However, with the U.S. and British undertakings to accept safeguards voluntarily on their peaceful nuclear activities, it acknowledges that all parties to the treaty but one will be effectively subject to safeguards on their peaceful nuclear programmes.

---

* From *External Affairs*, October 1968, pp. 425-26. See SS 68/11 of March 13, 1968, for a detailed outline of the Canadian position by General E. L. M. Burns, Canadian Representative to the Eighteen Nation Disarmament Committee. See also SS 67/22 of June 18, 1967, for a useful comparative study of the Canadian and United States approaches to nuclear arms control. See CTS 70/7 for the complete text of the Treaty. In September 1971, during the Conference of the Committee on Disarmament, Canada called for a halt to all testing.

Peaceful Uses of Nuclear Energy

Canada does not believe that the NPT will inhibit the development of the nuclear programmes of signatories for legitimate peaceful purposes or interfere with international trade in nuclear material and equipment. On the contrary, it believes that the treaty will tend to enhance such development and trade. It has strongly supported the provision that will prohibit non-nuclear states from conducting nuclear explosions for peaceful purposes, since it maintains that military and civil nuclear explosive technologies are indistinguishable and that the development of the latter would inevitably accord a non-nuclear state a nuclear-weapon capability. It has, however, been insistent that, in return for surrendering their nuclear-explosion option, non-nuclear states should be guaranteed access to peaceful nuclear-explosive services from the nuclear powers under appropriate international procedures and on a bilateral basis or through an international body. While this principle is contained in Article V, Canada thinks it should be further elaborated in a separate agreement.

Nuclear-Arms Control

Canada believes the nuclear parties have made an important commitment to achieve further progress rapidly towards effective measures of nuclear-arms control. Canada supports the right of groups of states to establish nuclear-free zones.

Procedural Questions

Canada considers that the procedural provisions will enable the treaty to be implemented smoothly and will, at the same time, give it sufficient flexibility for adaptation to changing circumstances.

In sum, Canada considers the treaty to be a major contribution to international peace and security and to represent the optimum reconciliation of many divergent national objectives, interests and concerns in respect of the threat of the further proliferation of nuclear weapons. It hopes that, in the near future, there will be a sufficient number of ratifications to enable the treaty to come into force.*

---

* Disarmament is of course a serious and complicated subject, but certain simplifications are possible. Having once been the victim of long and tedious hours of discussion on what in the early 1930s constituted offensiveness in a weapon, years later Mr. Pearson related the following story:

6. Strategic Arms Limitation Talks (SALT)

Statement by the Secretary of State for External Affairs, Mr. Allan J. MacEachen, at the Thirtieth Session of the General Assembly of the United Nations, New York, September 22, 1975.

The SALT talks have been of major importance in promoting a climate of strategic stability and political détente. But they have not halted the competition in nuclear armaments. Nor have they achieved steps of actual nuclear disarmament. The problems involved are infinitely complex, but the need for solution is pressing. We urge the United States and the Soviet Union to conclude their present negotiations and to proceed without delay to achieving steps of nuclear disarmament. We also urge the nuclear-weapons powers to re-examine the technical and political obstacles to an agreement to end nuclear-weapons testing.

Efforts to curb the proliferation of nuclear weapons must be accompanied by efforts to ensure that the further dissemination of nuclear technology is devoted solely to peaceful purposes. The Conference to Review the Non-Proliferation Treaty reaffirmed the treaty's vital role as the basic instrument of the non-proliferation system. It made it clear, that all parties, both nuclear-weapons states and non-nuclear-weapons states, must meet their obligations fully under the treaty. This is essential if the dangers of proliferation are to be averted.

I have been associated in one form or another with disarmament conferences since I went to the first Geneva Disarmament Conference in the early 30s as a very junior secretary in the Canadian delegation. At that time, with junior secretaries from other delegations, we had the answer to all the questions. We often used to meet for dinner after the day's sessions, at a café in Geneva, the Bavaria, where we exchanged views on the follies and misdemeanours of our elder delegates, and how, if we were only given the chance, we could have solved all these matters. I remember one night when we had been sitting during the day in a committee where our seniors had been arguing as to what constituted an offensive weapon and a defensive weapon in connection with naval disarmament—if a gun was 8.4" calibre, it was offensive and, if it was 7.2", it was defensive. We agreed that this was all pretty silly and that the answer to this particular question was a simple one that could have been discovered within 15 minutes of the opening of the meeting—namely that the offensiveness or defensiveness of a weapon depended on whether you were in front of it or behind it. There was nothing else to be said about it.

The review conference also reaffirmed the role of the treaty as the basis for wider co-operation in the peaceful uses of nuclear energy. Canada will fulfill its obligations under the treaty to facilitate, to the extent it is able, international co-operation in the exchange of nuclear technology and materials for peaceful purposes, particularly between the advanced and developing countries. The need for such co-operation has clearly been increased by the change in world energy costs. However, I should, at the same time, stress that we have an obligation to ensure, to the maximum extent possible, that the co-operation we enter into does not in any way contribute to the proliferation of nuclear weapons or to the manufacture of nuclear explosive devices for whatever purpose.

Preoccupation with the dangers of nuclear weapons must not blind us to the growing threat from use of conventional force. Urgent and closer attention must now be given to the search for arms control and the reduction of forces in order to promote regional stability and mutual security. Now that the Conference on Security and Cooperation in Europe has been concluded, we look for substantial progress from the negotiations in Vienna on the reduction of forces in Central Europe.*

The basic responsibility for reducing the dangers and burdens of armaments rests primarily with the major military powers. But we must recognize the various constraints under which they operate if we wish effective arms-limitation and disarmament agreements. Advances in military technology often complicate efforts to find the technical and military basis for agreement and satisfactory means of verifying commitments. Agreements must promote or be compatible with the security interests of participating states. Disarmament negotiations are unlikely to succeed unless political conditions are conducive to progress.

But this is no argument for inaction in this Assembly. It is no argument for accepting the present and totally unsatisfactory rate of progress in achieving disarmament measures. The General Assembly must continue as the forum of international concern and as a spur to action in the field of disarmament.

---

* See the U.S.A.-U.S.S.R. Interim Agreement on the Limitation of Strategic Offensive Weapons, May 1972, as regards the first phase of the SALT talks, known as SALT I. The SALT II talks got under way in February 1974 and are still continuing. They too are concerned with arms limitation. At their conclusion, the talks would then move to SALT III — that is, from limitations to reduction. Canada is not a party to these talks. Owing to the sensitivity of the subject, very little information about them has been released to the public.

7. Canada's Uranium Policy

Text of the Press Release issued by the Prime Minister's Office, Ottawa, June 3, 1965. (Extracts)

As the House is aware, the Government has been reviewing its policy with respect to the export of uranium.

World requirements for uranium for peaceful purposes will increase very greatly in the years to come. Canada holds a substantial portion of the known uranium reserves of the world and in the future may well be the largest single supplier for the rest of the world. It is vital that the Canadian industry be in the best possible position to take advantage of expanding markets for the peaceful uses of this commodity.

As one part of its policy to promote the use of Canadian uranium for peaceful purposes the Government has decided that export permits will be granted, or commitments to issue export permits will be given, with respect to sales of uranium covered by contracts entered into from now on only if the uranium is to be used for peaceful purposes. Before such sales to any destination are authorized, the Government will require an agreement with the Government of the importing country to ensure, with appropriate verification and control, that the uranium is to be used for peaceful purposes only.

Canada has been a member of the International Atomic Energy Agency since its inception and successive governments have vigorously supported the principle of safeguards on uranium sales. This policy is a fundamental part of Canada's general policy to work internationally to avoid the proliferation of nuclear weapons.

As to the commercial aspects of the policy, two general principles will apply, designed to facilitate exports and to ensure that the requirements of both export and domestic consumers are met in an orderly way.

First, the Government recognizes that countries constructing or planning to construct nuclear reactors will wish to make long-term arrangements for fuel supply. Accordingly, the Government will be prepared to authorize forward commitments by Canadian producers to supply reactors which are already in operation, under construction or committed for construction in other countries for the average anticipated life of each reactor, generally calculated for amortization purposes to be 30 years.

Second, and in addition, the Government will be prepared to authorize the export for periods of up to 5 years of reasonable quantities of uranium for the accumulation of stocks in the importing country.

Within the terms of the policy I have outlined, the Canadian Government will actively encourage and assist the Canadian uranium industry in seeking export markets. The commercial aspects of the policy will, of course, be reviewed from time to time in the light of changing conditions.

Finally, in order to avoid any reduction in the current level of employment and production in the industry in Canada, the Government will purchase uranium for stockpiling to the extent that current sales prove insufficient to achieve this objective during the next 5 years. These purchases will be made at a price of $4.90 per pound of Uranium Oxide. Purchases will be made only from companies which have previously produced uranium, and will be limited in the case of each company willing to sell at $4.90 to the amount necessary to maintain an appropriate minimum level of employment and production for that company.

As soon as the details of the stockpiling program, including arrangements for eventual disposal, have been discussed with the uranium industry and decided upon, they will be announced to the House and Parliament will be asked to approve the necessary expenditure for the current fiscal year.

8. Canada's Obligations as a Nuclear Power

Statement by the Prime Minister, Mr. Pierre-Elliott Trudeau, to the Canadian Nuclear Association, Ottawa, June 17, 1975. (Extracts)

We have three obligations as a nuclear power. Those obligations form the basis of Canada's nuclear policy.

The *first* of these obligations finds its origin in the character of Canadians, and in those circumstances of wilderness and weather that contributed to that character. We are a society that has not forgotten its frontier origins. We are a people who have experienced the torment of need, who understand the benefits of sharing. It is inconsistent with that experience and that understanding that we should now deny to the less-developed countries of the world the opportunity to gain a hand-hold on the technological age. It is inconsistent with the character of Canadians that we should expect those hundreds of millions of persons living in destitute circumstances in so many parts of the world to wait patiently for improvement while their countries proceed painfully through the industrial revolution.

It would be unconscionable under any circumstances to deny to the developing countries the most modern of technologies as assistance in their quest for higher living standards. But, in a world increasingly concerned about depleting reserves of fossil fuels, about food shortages, and about the need to reduce illness, it would be irresponsible as well to withhold the advantages of the nuclear age—of power reactors, agricultural isotopes, cobalt beam-therapy units.

All these devices Canada has. All these devices the world needs. If we are serious in our protestation of interest and our desire to help, if we are honest when we say that we care and intend to share with those less well-off than ourselves, if we are concerned about the instability of a world in which a fraction of the population enjoys the bulk of the wealth—in any of these events we cannot object to the transfer of advanced technology. Technological transfer is one of the few, and one of the most effective, means available to us of helping others to contribute to their own development. It forms one component of the program for action for a new international economic order adopted by the United Nations and endorsed so enthusiastically by the vast majority of the countries of the world. It remains as a cornerstone of Canada's economic-assistance policy and the programs under that policy that we operate in the UN, in the Commonwealth, in L'Agence francophone, in the Colombo Plan, and elsewhere.

Unless the disadvantaged countries are given the opportunity to pass out from the medieval economic state in which many of them find themselves and into the twentieth century of accomplishment and productivity, the gap between rich and poor will never narrow. In that process, we must help them to leapfrog the industrial revolution. Nuclear technology is one of the most certain means of doing so. In instances, therefore, where electric power from nuclear sources is cost-effective, where the advantages of nuclear science are of demonstrable benefit, we should be prepared to share our knowledge and our good fortune. That is why Canada chose, 20 years ago, to assist the world's most populous democracy in overcoming its desperate problems of poverty. We can be proud, as Canadians, of our co-operation with India. The decision taken by Prime Minister St. Laurent to enter a nuclear-assistance program with India was a far-sighted and generous act of statesmanship. It goes without saying, of course, that our nuclear transfers should be subject to safeguards always; and that is my next point.

The *second* of the three obligations underlying the Government's nuclear policy arises out of the dangerous nature of the improper uses to which nuclear materials can be put either by accident or design. For that reason the Canadian Government is obligated to Canadians and to all persons everywhere to assure that nuclear devices, materials or technology from Canadian sources not be used for explosive or illegal purposes. This is done through the application of safeguards.

Familiarity with nuclear processes and confidence in their peaceful benefits must never blind us to the destructive capability of a nuclear explosive device or the politically destabilizing effect that can be caused in certain circumstances by the mere existence of such a device. For these reasons, this second obligation must be regarded as no less important than the first. For, no matter how sincere is our commitment to equality throughout the world, no matter how successful is our progress towards it, our achievements will be Pyrrhic should nations be unable to avoid the inhumanity of nuclear-weapons usages or threats.

Canada is not envious of any country that is able to achieve new scientific plateaus for the benefit of its people nor, to my knowledge, is any other industrialized state. If a newly independent nation is able to leap in a single generation from the stage of steam to the age of the atom, Canada applauds. If that leap was accomplished through Canadian assistance, we are proud. But the vault must be genuine, and the new plateau must be firm. Nuclear projects have proved their benefit to man in dozens of ways—ways well known to most of you—but no one has yet demonstrated convincingly that there are practical, economic, peaceful benefits of nuclear explosions. Not Americans, not Russians, not Indians. If at some time in the future such benefits be demonstrated, then they should be made available on an internationally accepted basis, under appropriate safeguards, and through a UN agency, to all countries declared by international experts able to benefit. Canada is opposed to any peaceful nuclear explosions not conducted in accordance with the provisions of the NPT. In doing so, we are not imputing motives; we are attempting to avoid the subjunctive.

These are the reasons why Canada signed the Non-Proliferation Treaty, why we voiced such criticism of the Indian test, why I seize every opportunity to garner the support of world leaders for a tightening and an extension of safeguards and controls. These are the reasons why we shall continue to do so.

In the past several months, I have argued the importance of a strengthened safeguards regime with some 40 heads of government—

around a conference table, as at the Commonwealth meeting in Jamaica, and across a desk, as with each of the nine leaders I have visited in Europe and the several that have come to Ottawa. The Secretary of State for External Affairs addressed the Non-Proliferation Treaty Review Conference in Geneva last month—and was the only foreign minister to do so.* Senior government officials have travelled tens of thousands of miles in an effort to tighten existing safeguards and to broaden both the scope of their impact and the breadth of their application by supplier countries. We have raised the standard of our safeguards—with full support for the International Atomic Energy Agency, which administers them—to the point that they are the toughest in the world (and we are constantly on the alert for ways to make them more practical, more effective). We impose, as well, still another constraint—we refuse to engage in nuclear co-operation without an explicit exclusion of explosive uses.

I do not pretend that the present international regime for the inspection and detection of nuclear cheating is foolproof. I am painfully aware that the NPT is yet far from universally supported. I am deeply conscious of the responsibilities that devolve on Canada as a world leader in the peaceful application of nuclear energy. But to those who contend that there is an incompatibility between these two obligations I have mentioned—assisting the less-developed countries and preventing nuclear proliferation—I remind them that the statute of the International Atomic Energy Agency, the world's nuclear policeman, charges the Agency to spread "throughout the world" peaceful applications of the atom "bearing in mind the special needs of the under-developed areas". Canada is an active member of the IAEA and does its utmost to ensure the successful attainment of those two objectives.

These, then, are the first two of the obligations that form the foundation of Canada's nuclear policy—an obligation to the have-not countries of the world and an obligation to the people of the world. The *third* obligation is to our own people. This obligation takes several forms: the provision of safe sources of energy, the preservation of the environment, the fostering of a competitive Canadian industry in all its stages—of exploration, mining, processing, fabrication, design and sales.

Tonight, I'd like to emphasize for a moment one aspect of that obligation—to Canadian industry—and the several ways in which it is discharged. One method is through the repeated declaration of the Canadian Government of its conviction of the fundamental worth and

---

* See SS 75/13 of May 7, 1975, for the text of his remarks.

demonstrated superiority of the CANDU reactor over any other design. Another is the decision of the Federal Government to assist financially in constructing first CANDU units within each province. Still another is the wide range of research, developmental and marketing programs funded and pursued by Atomic Energy of Canada Limited and supported abroad by all the facilities of the Department of Industry, Trade and Commerce and the Department of External Affairs.

The success of the CANDU conception is attracting increasing attention world-wide because of its safety record, its respect for the environment, its reliability, its efficient fuel utilization, and its economy of operation. The remarkable performance of the Pickering installation will lead, I have little doubt, to the adoption of this Canadian-developed technology in a large number of countries abroad.

The Government is no less interested in safe, tamper-proof facilities than it is in assurance that reactors cannot purposely be diverted to non-peaceful ends. We must protect ourselves against accident and criminal elements. A contribution of significant proportion has recently been made by Canadian industry in the design of a spent-fuel shipping-cask incorporating novel shielding and physical properties.

As nuclear-generated power-plants have increased in number world-wide, partly in response to higher fossil-fuel costs, partly out of concern for continuing security of oil and gas supply, the demand for continuing security of oil and gas supply, the demand for uranium has undergone a startling change. After a depression in world uranium prices lasting almost 15 years, there has suddenly occurred a dramatic shift from a buyer's to a seller's market. During the 1960s, exploration programs necessary for the location of new mineral formations had slowed down and, in many instances, ceased altogether. Throughout this period, federal funds ensured the preservation in Canada of a nucleus of the uranium-production industry. As demand-pressure grew in the 1970s, however, it became apparent that further help was needed to ensure adequate exploration. Federal response was twofold. Funds were provided a year ago to the Crown corporation Eldorado Nuclear Limited to permit it to re-enter the uranium-exploration field. More recently, the Federal Government initiated a uranium-reconnaissance program to permit a systematic general exploration of Canada in order to point up promising areas for detailed exploratory studies. The Government expects that the change in world price and the federal stimulus to exploration will serve to attract from Canadian sources fresh equity investment in the Canadian uranium industry, a growth industry with special incentives and benefits for Canadian investors.

9. Nuclear Relations with India

Statement by the Secretary of State for External Affairs, Mr. Allan J. MacEachen, in the House of Commons, May 18, 1976.

I should like to inform the House today that the Government has decided that further nuclear co-operation with India is not possible. The decision has been difficult. It has challenged the Government, as indeed it has challenged all thinking Canadians, to review a number of fundamental principles.

Canada's nuclear co-operation with India began in the context of the Colombo Plan. It has as its basis the belief that nuclear power could be vital to the equitable economic growth of a number of developing countries. The energy crisis, and the serious dislocations it has brought with it, have tended to reinforce this belief and the genuine success achieved by Indo-Canadian co-operation in the development of nuclear power for energy, agriculture and medicine has proved the practicality of this approach.

India's detonation of a nuclear explosive device in 1974 made it evident that Canada and India had taken profoundly differing views of what should be encompassed in the peaceful application of nuclear energy by non-nuclear-weapon states.* Canada is one of the earliest and most vigorous proponents of the Nuclear Non-Proliferation Treaty. A basic element of the treaty, which guides Canadian policy in the field of nuclear exports and safeguards, is that it recognizes no technical distinction between nuclear explosives for peaceful and non-peaceful purposes.

Canada has foregone the possible benefits of developing so-called peaceful nuclear explosions on the basis that, pursuant to the NPT, nuclear-explosive services would be available from a nuclear-weapon state at such time as need and feasibility were demonstrated. India, however, does not accept what it views as discrimination between the nuclear powers and other states, and insists that all countries should be free to use all phases of nuclear technology for whatever they view as peaceful purposes.

Notwithstanding these differences, both countries agreed to explore

---

* See the statements made by the Secretary of State for External Affairs, Mr. Mitchell Sharp, in the House of Commons on May 18 and May 22, 1974, at the time of the nuclear explosion. See also AEB, pp. 277-79 for background.

together a negotiated termination of nuclear co-operation. These negotiations had, earlier this spring, reached a point where both sides decided that governmental decisions were required. The decision now taken by Cabinet takes into full account the issues that I raised when I spoke in the House on March 23. Canada has insisted that any co-operation in the nuclear field be fully covered by safeguards that satisfy the Canadian people that Canadian assistance will not be diverted to nuclear-explosive purposes. This Canadian objective could not be achieved in these negotiations.

Both sides have made a concerted effort in good faith to reach a basis for agreement. However, the Canadian Government has decided that it could agree to make new nuclear shipments only on an undertaking by India that Canadian supplies, whether of technology, nuclear equipment or materials, whether past or future, should not be used for the manufacture of any nuclear-explosive device. In the present case, this undertaking would require that all nuclear facilities, involving Canadian technology, in India be safeguarded. We should be prepared to reach agreement with India on this basis only. In view of earlier discussions, however, we have concluded that the Indian Government would not be prepared to accept [such] safeguards.

In making this statement regarding our nuclear co-operation with India, I should like also to refer briefly to the other aspects of our relationship. There is no question but that our nuclear differences are profound; nevertheless, nuclear affairs form only one part of what has been a broad and important relationship. The decisions reached by the Government concerning one aspect of our relations are not intended to preclude the pursuit of other elements of mutual interest in our overall links with India. The Canadian Government remains prepared to review these elements and to pursue our common objectives in both bilateral and multilateral fields because we believe that our ties with this important developing Commonwealth nation must not be allowed to lapse through any lack of will on our part.

Editorial Note

As regards the General Welfare, Human Rights, and the Structure of the United Nations, documented in the two preceding volumes, Canadian policy remained basically unchanged between 1965 and 1975. It is therefore not repeated here. A series of important international legal instruments came into force in early 1976: the International Covenant on Economic, Social and Cultural Rights, the International

Covenant on Civil and Political Rights, and the latter's related Optional Protocol. These instruments reaffirm principles contained in the Universal Declaration, define new ideals for the attainment of other basic social rights, and establish procedures designed to promote compliance with their provisions. After thorough consultations with the provinces, which share jurisdiction in human rights matters, Canada acceded to the two Covenants and the Optional Protocol on May 19, 1976.

II. NATO

The decade under review was a complex one both for NATO itself as well as for Canada in the context of the Alliance. Early in 1966 France withdrew her land and air forces from the NATO command structure (her sea forces had been withdrawn in 1963), although she remained a member of the Alliance. This decision caused a great deal of turmoil and readjustment, including the transfer of the military (SHAPE) and political (Council) components of NATO to Brussels, as well as the removal of Canadian and United States bases and installations from French soil. Fortunately, détente between East and West was easing tensions at the time and adaptation to the French decision proceeded more smoothly than anticipated.

Détente, along with Western Europe's growing power and prosperity, increasingly prompted Canada toward the end of the 1960s to question whether the European members of the Alliance should increase their contributions to NATO and whether maintenance of Canadian contributions at current levels was really in Canada's best interests, especially at a time of mounting domestic economic difficulty.

Shortly after the election in April 1968 of Mr. Pierre-Elliott Trudeau as leader of the Liberal Party and its victory at the polls in June of that year, the new government undertook a broad review of Canada's foreign and defence policies. Canadian contributions to NATO were carefully scrutinized and reductions took place, as documented below, notably in the White Paper *Defence in the '70s*, published under the signature of the then Minister of National Defence, Mr. Donald Macdonald, in August 1971. Contributions to NORAD (dealt with in the next chapter) remained basically unchanged.

The Soviet invasion of Czechoslovakia in 1968 was sharply decried by the NATO countries and ranks were closed on the occasion. In the long term, the invasion was generally viewed as an aberration, however deplorable. It was not allowed to interfere with détente, which made possible considerable progress in hitherto contentious areas: the Berlin settlement in 1971; the negotiations between NATO and the

Warsaw Pact countries for Mutual and Balanced Force Reductions (MBFR), which have been going on for some years in Vienna; the meetings between the Soviet Union and the United States which began at Helsinki in 1969 with respect to the limitation of nuclear weapons through the Strategic Arms Limitation Talks (SALT); the Conference on Security and Cooperation in Europe (CSCE) at Helsinki between 1972 and 1974.

Canada's commitments and contributions to NATO in the mid-1970s remained much as they had been decided upon in the 1969 defence review—that is, a modest land and air force in Europe (five thousand men), the protection of Canadian sovereignty, the defence of North America, surveillance of the Arctic and maritime approaches to Canada. The level of Canada's defence forces has remained basically unchanged since the early 1970s at about seventy-eight thousand regular personnel and twenty-two thousand reservists. The Secretary General of NATO and some NATO powers have been publicly critical at times of the size of Canada's contribution to the Alliance. Yet, in the words of John Holmes:

> It is ironical that those Western European (including British) ministers who do so much huffing and puffing about something called "Europe", about "its" rights and "its" interests and "its" voice, feel no shame in reprimanding a non-European country of middle size for not being willing to go on defending Europe indefinitely.*

Today, as the Alliance reaches the end of its third decade, it is having to face altogether different types of challenges arising particularly from the growth of Communist Party strength in Italy, Portugal, and elsewhere in Western Europe. A former Canadian Cabinet Minister was fond of saying at the time of the formation of NATO that: "There is less chance of rape when there are 15 in the bed." The prospect lately (1975-76) has been less one of rape than of seduction.⁻

10. Canada and NATO—Implications of France's Withdrawal

Statement to the House of Commons Standing Committee on External Affairs, on April 4, 1966, by the Secretary of State for External Affairs, Mr. Paul Martin.

---

* J. W. Holmes, *Canada: A Middle-Aged Power*, Carleton Library Number 67 (Toronto: McClelland and Stewart, 1976), p. 14.

Article XIII of the North Atlantic Treaty permits signatories to opt out in 1969, the twentieth anniversary of its conclusion. The year 1969, for this good reason, has been regarded as the year for stocktaking. It was with this in mind that, in December 1964, I proposed on behalf of the Canadian Government, at the NATO ministerial meeting, that the North Atlantic Council should undertake a review of the future of the alliance. Although this proposal was approved by the 14 other members of the NATO alliance, nevertheless the idea was not pursued because the President of France had begun to articulate his nation's dissatisfaction with the NATO organization and no one wanted to precipitate a premature confrontation.

It is now less than a month since the French Government first formally informed their NATO allies of their decision to withdraw from the integrated defence arrangements.

My view and that of the Government of Canada is that NATO has served a useful purpose. I take it from the reaction the other day to the Canadian position on the French announcement that this view, generally speaking, reflects the opinion of the political parties in Parliament. We have only to cast our minds back to the immediate postwar period; Europe was then unsteadily extricating itself from the morass left by the Second World War and Stalin was pressing in every way to extend his influence through Western Europe to the Atlantic. The picture has now changed, as President de Gaulle has said. It is not unreasonable to ask: "Is the alliance still necessary? Is General de Gaulle right in advocating the end of the integrated military organization of the alliance? Is the strategic concept of the alliance still valid? Is it time to leave the defence of Europe to the Europeans?" These are questions that are being asked at the present time, and they are fair questions. Naturally, by virtue of my own responsibilities, I have been asking myself some of these questions. It may be helpful if I began what I have to say on the situation in NATO resulting from the French action by summarizing the main elements of the position now taken by our NATO ally, France. These comprise:

(1) a decision to withdraw French forces from NATO's integrated military structure and French officers from the integrated head-quarters, these decisions to take effect on July 1, 1966;

(2) a decision to require the removal from France of the two integrated military headquarters known as SHAPE and the Central European Command. France has proposed that the removal be completed by April 1, 1967;*

* SHAPE moved to Brussels in 1967.

(3) a decision to require the withdrawal from France of foreign forces and bases. France has proposed that the United States and Canadian bases be withdrawn by April 1, 1967;

(4) France has indicated a wish to retain its forces in Germany, while transferring them from NATO to French command.

(5) France intends to leave its forces in Berlin, where they are established on the basis of occupation rights and where there is a tripartite command.

(6) France has indicated a willingness to negotiate arrangements for establishing, in peacetime, French liaison missions with NATO commands.

(7) France has indicated a readiness to enter into separate conversations with Canada and the United States to determine the military facilities which the respective governments might mutually grant to each other in wartime.

(8) France intends to remain a party to the North Atlantic Treaty and to participate in the activities of the NATO Council. This, as I understand it, is the position taken by the Government of France.

It is only fair to note that these positions have been previously stated, in one form or another, by the President of the French Republic during the last two years.

This last element of the French position is naturally welcomed by the Canadian Government as an indication of France's desire to continue its formal association with the other parties to the Treaty. It will, I need hardly add, be the concern of the Canadian Government to encourage French participation to the greatest extent feasible.

It is evident that some of the French objectives can be attained by unilateral action; for example, the withdrawal of French troops from SACEUR's command and of French officers from the combined headquarters. Some other objectives will require negotiations over modalities and the timing—for example, the withdrawal of NATO headquarters and of foreign bases from French territory. Finally, some proposals depend on working out arrangements with other members of the alliance and will involve negotiations on substance—for example, the presence and role of French troops in Germany and the liaison arrangements which might be established between French and NATO commands.

It must be clear to the members of the Committee that the French proposals raise a host of problems, the range of which has not been fully determined. They raise questions with political, military, financial, and legal implications. We are examining these questions with our allies, informally with the 14 other than France and, where appropriate, with France and the 14. We are, as well, engaged in an examination of the contractual situation, and the documentation in that connection is now being carefully examined by our legal officers.

The first French *aide-mémoire* also sets out briefly the reasons which, in the view of President de Gaulle, justify the position which he takes. The following arguments are listed:

First, he argues that the threat to Western Europe has changed and no longer has the immediate and menacing character it once had; he says that the countries of Europe have restored their economies and recovered their earlier strength; he argues that France is developing an atomic armament which is not susceptible of being integrated within the NATO forces; that the nuclear stalemate has transformed the conditions of Western defence; and that Europe is no longer the centre of international crises.*

These are observations with which I imagine we are all more or less in agreement. But do they, singly or jointly, justify the conclusion drawn by the French Government that integrated defence arrangements are no longer required for the defence of Western Europe?

Let me examine each of the French arguments in turn:

First, the threat to Western Europe. Over the years the Soviet Union has steadily strengthened its military forces in Eastern Germany and in the European area in general. These forces are now stronger than at any time since the end of the Second World War. While I recognize that the likelihood of an actual attack has diminished, the effectiveness of NATO's defence arrangements has been, and remains, a factor in this favourable turn of events. Moreover, it is considered prudent to base defence policy on the known capabilities of a possible enemy rather than on his declared intentions, or even his supposed intentions as we may rightly or wrongly assess them. To avoid any possible misinterpretation, I also want to make clear my conviction that NATO countries should avoid provocation of the Soviet Union. On the contrary, Canada strongly favours the promotion of better understanding between the Soviet Union and the Western

---

* During March 1966, Carleton University conducted a lecture series on "The Communist States and the West". Mr. Martin concluded the series by speaking on "Canada's Role in East-West Relations", in which he analysed at length the nature of the Soviet threat to Europe and the West. See SS 66/10 of March 11, 1966, for the text of his remarks on that occasion.

countries. But, as the Cuban experience of 1962 demonstrated, progress towards better relations may be greater when it is clear that
there is no alternative to accommodation.

Secondly, Europe's recovery. It is, of course, true that the European countries have greatly strengthened their positions in every way.
We applaud this development. We know that the generosity of the
United States, through the Marshall Plan, greatly contributed to this
happy consequence. We have, in fact, been assuming that this would
in time enable the Western European states to take on increasing
responsibility for European defence, possibly within the framework of
new co-operative arrangements among the European members of the
alliance. The French action may have set back this prospect, as it has
the immediate effect of dividing the countries of Europe over what
their defence policies should be.

Thirdly, it is a fact that France has developed an independent
nuclear force. But, as we see it, this is not an argument against the
integration of other forces. The United Kingdom has demonstrated
that the acquisition of a strategic nuclear force does not require the
withdrawal of other national forces from the unified command and
planning arrangements.

Fourthly, it is true that a nuclear stalemate had developed in place
of the earlier United States nuclear monopoly. But this is not new. It
has been the case for ten years. Moreover, this fact has not diminished
the need for unified planning, if the European countries are to make
an effective contribution to the defence of Europe.

Fifthly, I also acknowledge that Europe is not at present the centre
of international crises. But, until there is a political settlement in
Central Europe, it will remain an area of potential crisis, particularly
if the arrangements which have brought about stability in the area
should be upset.

In my judgment, and in the judgment of the Canadian Government, the arguments presented in the French *aide-mémoire* do not
support the conclusion that unified command and planning arrangements are no longer necessary for the defence of Western Europe.

It is striking that all of the other members of NATO have joined in
reaffirming their belief in the need for unified command and planning arrangements in a declaration, the text of which I communicated
to the House of Commons on March 18.* I expect members of the

---

* See SS 66/11 of March 18, 1966, for the text. See also Mr. Martin's
  statement (CHCD), June 16, 1966, regarding some of the practical results of
  France's withdrawal.

External Affairs Committee and the Defence Committee will be interested to know that the strongest support for the integrated military arrangements has come from the smaller members of the alliance, who consider that the only way to assure their defence is by pooling their contributions in a common effort. It seems to me that, if the principle of an alliance is accepted, the experience of the last two world wars and the requirements of modern weapons demonstrate the need for unified command and joint planning. Indeed, one of the most remarkable successes of the postwar world has been the development within NATO of effective peacetime arrangements for military cooperation.

I have explained why we and other members of NATO are not persuaded by the French arguments. I wish now to examine the implications of the actions which have been taken by the French Government.

Providing NATO itself does not disintegrate (and I see no danger of that happening), the immediate military consequences of the French action are thought to be manageable. France has already withdrawn from NATO command, during the last six years, most of its previously integrated forces. The net loss in forces available to NATO from the announced withdrawal, while significant, will not be too serious, particularly if workable arrangements can be devised for maintaining French troops in Germany. But the loss for practical purposes of French land and air space has strategic implications for the defence of Western Europe, which will have to be carefully studied.

Even more worrying to my mind are the possible political implications. These consequences are, of course, still quite uncertain, so that it is possible to speak only in the most general and cautious terms. But it is obvious that the French actions may weaken the unity of the alliance. This would, in turn, jeopardize the stability of Central Europe, which has been built on allied unity and particularly on French, British, and American solidarity in Berlin and in Germany. I do not want to elaborate, but it is possible to anticipate that French bilateral relations with some of the NATO allies, particularly those who carry the larger burdens, will be put under strain. The balance of forces within the alliance will of necessity be altered. Finally, France's example could stimulate nationalist tendencies which have been encouragingly absent in Western Europe since the last war.

The Canadian Government is not unsympathetic to many of the considerations which underlie the French wish for change. We know that circumstances in the world have changed since NATO was established. We have long believed that members of the alliance, particularly those such as France which have spoken of the need for change, should present concrete proposals to encourage consultation within the alliance.

It is reasonable to look towards a greater acceptance of responsibility by Europeans for the defence of Western Europe. However, any North American move to disengage militarily from Europe will be dangerously premature until the European countries have made the necessary political and institutional arrangements to take over the responsibilities involved. It follows, at this time of uncertainty about NATO's future, that Canada should avoid action which would create unnecessary strain or otherwise impair the solidarity of the alliance. This need not and should not preclude us from making adjustments, in the interest of economy and efficiency, in the manner in which we contribute to European defence. And we should seek to ensure that there is a constructive evolution in the organization of the alliance; and we should take advantage of the actions taken by the Government of France to do exactly what we ourselves proposed in the fall of 1964, which is to engage in serious examination of the state of the alliance.

Insofar as the Canadian bases in France are concerned, the Government of France has taken unilateral action. It appears to be a final decision. At any rate, it has stated that it would like to see the Canadian bases withdrawn by April 1, 1967, although I express the hope, and have no doubt, that the French Government will be prepared to negotiate mutually acceptable arrangements, including compensation and dates for the withdrawal of the bases. Since the objective of sending Canadian troops to Europe was to contribute to the integrated defence arrangements from which France is withdrawing, this Government has accepted the logic that Canadian forces in France cannot outstay their welcome. They will have to be moved elsewhere.

I referred earlier to the determination of other members of NATO to preserve the effective arrangements which have been worked out for joint planning and unified command. This is only prudent, and Canada fully shares this determination. This will provide a continuing defence against the Soviet military capacity still directed at Western Europe. It will help preserve the precarious stability in Central Europe. Moreover, under the present integrated defence arrangements, there being no German general staff, Germany has placed all its troops directly under NATO commanders. The dismantling of the existing structure would lead to the reversion of all European forces to national command.

Inevitably, our attention in the near future will be taken up with handling the immediate consequences of the French action. But we shall not lose sight of the need for NATO to adjust to the changing circumstances since the alliance was concluded. Indeed, the adjustments which the French action will require of the existing military arrangements provide opportunities, which we intend to take to examine with our allies the possibilities for developing improvements in the NATO structure and to consider how the alliance should develop in the long run, and also to consider what reductions and what savings can be effected without impairing the efficiency of the Organization, or of our contribution to it.

Although I am speaking about NATO, I wish to emphasize that—to the extent this depends on Canada—we will not allow our disappointment to affect Canada's bilateral relations with France. The Canadian Government has been working steadily to improve and intensify our relations with France. For our part we will not interrupt this process. Differences over defence policy need not impair the development of our bilateral relations in the political, economic, cultural, and technical fields.

For instance, we are sending an economic mission to France within the course of a few weeks, which will be representative both of government and of business, designed to encourage further trade relations between France and Canada. There certainly will be no interruption between these and other contacts that we have established and continue to establish with France. These are matters which can and should be kept separate from defence arrangements within NATO. In all this, we assume that the French Government agrees that this is a desirable approach, and we have no reason to doubt that this is their view.

I want to conclude this part of my statement by referring again to the objectives which the Canadian Government intends to follow in the situation created by the French action.

In NATO, our policy will be, firstly, to seek, in consultation with our allies, including France as far as possible, to limit the damage to the unity and effectiveness of the alliance, and to recreate a relationship of mutual confidence among all the members; secondly, to help preserve the essential features of NATO's existing system of unified command and joint planning for collective defence; thirdly, to continue to maintain an appropriate contribution to NATO's collective defence system; fourthly, to take every opportunity to examine with our allies possibilities for developing improvements to the NATO structure and to consider the future of the alliance in the long run.

With regard to France, the Government will, firstly, negotiate, either bilaterally or multilaterally as appropriate, fair and reasonable arrangements for those adjustments which may be required as a result of French withdrawal from NATO's integrated defence arrangements; secondly, leave the door open for the eventual return of France to full participation in the collective activities of the alliance, should France so decide. Finally, we will continue, notwithstanding NATO differences and with the co-operation of the French authorities, to develop our bilateral relations with France.

11. Mutual and Balanced Force Reductions

Declaration adopted by Foreign Ministers and Representatives of Countries Participating in the NATO Defence Programme, June 1968.*

Meeting at Reykjavik on 24th and 25th June, 1968, the Ministers recalled the frequently expressed and strong desire of their countries to make progress in the field of disarmament and arms control.

Ministers recognized that the unresolved issues which still divide the European continent must be settled by peaceful means, and are convinced that the ultimate goal of a lasting, peaceful order in Europe requires an atmosphere of trust and confidence and can only be reached by a step-by-step process. Mindful of the obvious and considerable interest of all European states in this goal, Ministers expressed their belief that measures in this field including balanced and mutual force reductions can contribute significantly to the lessening of tension and to further reducing the danger of war.

Ministers noted the important work undertaken within the North Atlantic Council by member governments in examining possible proposals for such reductions pursuant to Paragraph 13 of the "Report on the Future Tasks of The Alliance", approved by the Ministers in December 1967. In particular, they have taken note of the work being done in the Committee of Political Advisers to establish bases of comparison and to analyse alternative ways of achieving a balanced reduction of forces, particularly in the central part of Europe.

Ministers affirmed the need for the Alliance to maintain an effective military capability and to assure a balance of forces between NATO and the Warsaw Pact. Since the security of the NATO countries and the prospects for mutual force reductions would be weakened by

---

* From *External Affairs*, DEA, Ottawa, August 1968, pp. 323-24.

NATO reductions alone, Ministers affirmed the proposition that the overall military capability of NATO should not be reduced except as part of a pattern of mutual force reductions balanced in scope and timing.

Accordingly, Ministers directed permanent representatives to continue and intensify their work in accordance with the following agreed principles:

a) Mutual force reductions should be reciprocal and balanced in scope and timing.

b) Mutual reductions should represent a substantial and significant step, which will serve to maintain the present degree of security at reduced cost, but should not be such as to risk destabilizing the situation in Europe.

c) Mutual reductions should be consonant with the aim of creating confidence in Europe generally and in the case of each party concerned.

d) To this end, any new arrangement regarding forces should be consistent with the vital security interests of all parties and capable of being carried out effectively.

Ministers affirmed the readiness of their governments to explore with other interested states specific and practical steps in the arms-control field.

In particular, Ministers agreed that it was desirable that a process leading to mutual force reductions should be initiated. To that end they decided to make all necessary preparations for discussions on this subject with the Soviet Union and other countries of Eastern Europe and they call on them to join in this search for progress towards peace.

Ministers directed their permanent representatives to follow up on this declaration.

12. Mutual and Balanced Force Reductions

Statement by the Secretary of State for External Affairs, Mr. Mitchell Sharp, to the North Atlantic Assembly, Ottawa, September 27, 1971. (Extracts)

NATO is the most important forum in which North Atlantic countries can work toward the reduction of East-West tension. The alliance has become increasingly effective as a forum for consultations on defence and arms-control questions and many other political issues. One of the most compelling reasons for Canada to remain a member of NATO is the important political role that the alliance is playing—and that we can play as a member—in reducing and removing the underlying causes of potential conflict by negotiation, reconciliation and settlement. We continue to attach great significance to this aspect of the alliance's activities.

It is the Canadian view—shared by other members of the alliance—that we should carefully and prudently take advantage of changes in the East bloc and a greater receptiveness on the part of Eastern European countries to try to deal with them on a business-like basis. We have already gone a considerable distance in this policy—for example, through the visit of our Prime Minister to the Soviet Union in May of this year. We are now preparing for the return visit of Mr. Kosygin, the Chairman of the Council of Ministers of the Soviet Union, next month. We have no illusions about the difficulties in resolving major differences in these contacts, but there are benefits to be reaped, not only by the NATO country concerned but also by the alliance as a whole. The sum of all the bilateral contacts can have an important impact on the development of détente.

Mutual balanced force reductions is a long-standing NATO objective in the struggle to reduce tensions in Europe and one to which Canada attaches great importance. Reductions of the forces confronting each other could provide continuing security for both sides—and I emphasize "both sides"—while lowering defence costs. The Brezhnev speeches of March and May this year may signal a breakthrough. Certainly the indications that the Soviet Union is serious about force-reductions negotiations must be followed up. Canada supports NATO efforts to probe Soviet intentions bilaterally. We also think that a representative of the alliance could supplement bilateral contacts by discussing with the Soviet Union and others the possibilities of moving to negotiations as soon as possible, on the basis of agreed principles. We were gratified that NATO ministers, at their meeting in June, endorsed the explorer idea and that this and other ideas will be examined at the high-level meeting in Brussels next week. The MBFR issue is very complex, involving as it does the forces of many countries in several parts of Central Europe, but the rewards would be commensurate with the effort required to reach agreement.* It goes with-

---

* Owing to the confidential nature of the negotiations, there is very little solid information available in the public domain about the MBFR negotiations.

out saying that Canada is no more prepared than any of its allies to concede tangible security for unsubstantial promises. Yet we are encouraging our NATO colleagues to move forward on this issue, taking advantage of real opportunities in the search for a mutually acceptable agreement.

Berlin

Canada was not a party to the four-power talks on Berlin, but we participated actively in the alliance consultations that have accompanied them. We welcome the agreement on the first stage which emerged after months of hard bargaining. It is our hope that the second stage of the negotiations—between the appropriate German authorities—will be completed soon. Until then, Canada, in concert with its allies, does not think that the time has come to shift from bilateral to multilateral discussions on the possibility of a conference on European security. We are not dragging our feet by insisting on a satisfactory conclusion to the Berlin talks as a prerequisite for a security conference; we are simply recognizing that failure to achieve East-West agreement on Berlin would indicate that the climate was not ripe for the resolution of wider European problems. Once a Berlin agreement has been achieved, however, we see considerable value to be derived from a conference on European security, provided such a meeting was properly prepared and had good prospects of success. Any conference of this kind should involve not only all the members of NATO and the Warsaw Pact but interested neutral countries in Europe. While awaiting a Berlin agreement, the alliance must pursue its studies of the procedural and substantive problems of a conference against the day when a conference is a reality.

13. Conference on Security and Co-operation in Europe—Final Report*

Statement by the Secretary of State for External Affairs, Mr. Allan J. MacEachen, in the House of Commons, on December 2, 1975.

The document I have just tabled, the Final Act of the Conference on Security and Co-operation in Europe (called from the outset by its

---

* See Legault, Albert, "La Nouvelle Politique de Défense du Canada", *Le Devoir*, November 25 and 26, 1969, for background.

initials CSCE), was signed at Helsinki on August 1 by the heads of government of the states of Europe and of Canada and the United States. It is intended to establish the basis for the development of future relations between their countries and peoples. It is, therefore, an entirely forward-looking document; it does not look back to the past.

Many Canadians have been erroneously led to believe that, by signing the Final Act of the CSCE, Canada and its allies did something that sanctified the status quo in Europe. It is true that the Soviet Union, for the last 30 years and during the course of the CSCE itself, sought to gain acceptance of the political and geographical situation in Europe. But, throughout the conference, the NATO allies worked to avoid a document that could be pointed to in years to come as a surrogate peace treaty for the Second World War. Not one word of the Final Act justifies the claim that it constitutes recognition of Soviet hegemony in Eastern Europe or of the postwar de facto borders.

Canada entered the negotiations with a specific set of concerns. We wanted to play a part in the conference commensurate with our interests in Europe. In this we succeeded. We wanted to see incorporated in the Final Act measures to assist the freer movement of people and ideas. This goal has been achieved. Worthy of special note in this regard is the strong text on the reunification of families sponsored by Canada.

We sought the development of a confidence-building measure involving advance notification of military manoeuvres and, after difficult negotiations, such a measure was worked out. Finally, Canada had important economic and environmental interests to safeguard and advance; and the appropriate texts in the Final Act meet our requirements in this respect.

The Final Act provides for a meeting at senior-official level in Belgrade in 1977 to review progress in implementation and possibly to organize a resumed conference. It is the policy of the Government to ensure that, for its part, the Final Act is implemented as soon and as completely as possible. Copies are being sent to all Federal Government departments and agencies concerned, to provincial governments and to non-governmental organizations whose co-operation is essential to the carrying out of Canada's responsibilities under the Final Act. Copies are now available to the public through the outlets of Information Canada.

Domestically, we are examining what changes should be made in our present practices to meet the moral commitments we have accepted. In our bilateral relations we are using the document to provide guidance in communiqués, agreements and treaties. Multilaterally, consideration is already being given to the matter of implementation in two United Nations bodies, the Economic Commission for Europe and UNESCO.

A. A NEW DEFENCE POLICY, 1969

~ On May 29, 1968, shortly after assuming office, Prime Minister Trudeau issued a policy statement in which he said:

> We wish to take a fresh look at the fundamentals of Canadian foreign policy to see whether there are ways in which we can serve more effectively Canada's interests, objectives, and priorities. . . . We shall take a hard look, in consultation with our allies, at our military role in NATO and determine whether our present military commitment is still appropriate to the present situation in Europe.

This reassessment took place between May 1968 and June 1970. It covered both defence and foreign affairs. The defence conclusions emerged in April 1969 about a year before the foreign policy review. They are dealt with in the immediately following pages, since they affected primarily Canada's commitment to NATO. (The foreign policy review is documented in Chapter X). The defence review in particular engendered a good deal of controversy both within and outside government circles. Opinion in the Cabinet was apparently divided on the issue.* A compromise ensued. Canada would remain a member of the Alliance, but contributions would be reduced.

With the wisdom of hindsight, Mr. Sharp had this to say in 1973 about the NATO review (SS 73/14 of May 2, 1973):

---

* See SS 69/4 of March 1, 1969, for the views of the Secretary of State for External Affairs, Mr. Mitchell Sharp, outlining the importance of NATO. See also SS 67/9 of March 15, 1967, and SS 67/35 of November 13, 1967, for the views of his predecessor who considered that "strong allied forces continued to be required in Europe"; that "Canada should continue to contribute forces to NATO in Europe and to co-operate in the defence of North-America". Bruce Thordarson's *Trudeau and Foreign Policy* (Toronto: Oxford University Press, 1972) goes into this aspect of the question in considerable detail.

Looking back five years, I am free to admit that we in the Government were a bit "ham-handed" in the way we handled the NATO issue, but it was fortunate that we made our mistakes early and had time to profit from them. The intention was clear: we wanted to involve the public in the decision-making process. We actively sought the views of the academic community, of Members of Parliament, of groups like the CIIA (Canadian Institute of International Affairs). We invited the House of Commons Committee on External Affairs and Defence to make a report. I personally spoke throughout the country explaining NATO and the terms for Canadian membership. In the end we reached a reasonable and acceptable decision to continue in NATO but to reduce the numbers of our troops in Europe.

14. A New Defence Policy for Canada

Statement to the Press by the Prime Minister, Mr. Pierre-Elliott Trudeau, on April 3, 1969.

A Canadian defence policy, employing in an effective fashion the highly skilled and professional Canadian Armed Forces, will contribute to the maintenance of world peace. It will also add to our own sense of purpose as a nation and give renewed enthusiasm and a feeling of direction to the members of the armed forces. It will provide the key to the flexible employment of Canadian forces in a way which will permit them to make their best contribution in accordance with Canada's particular needs and requirements.*

The Government has rejected any suggestion that Canada assume a non-aligned or neutral role in world affairs. Such an option would have meant the withdrawal by Canada from its present alliances and the termination of all co-operative military arrangements with other countries. We have decided in this fashion because we think it necessary and wise to continue to participate in an appropriate way in collective security arrangements with other states in the interests of Canada's national security and in defence of the values we share with our friends.

Canada requires armed forces within Canada in order to carry out a wide range of activities involving the defence of the country, and

---

* For further background see *Fifth Report to the House of Commons* respecting Defence and External Affairs Policy, March 25, 1969, prepared by the Standing Committee on External Affairs and National Defence.

also supplementing the civil authorities and contributing to national development. Properly equipped and deployed, our forces will provide an effective multi-purpose maritime coastal shield and they will carry out operations necessary for the defence of North American airspace in co-operation with the United States. Abroad, our forces will be capable of playing important roles in collective security and in peace-keeping activities.

The structure, equipment and training of our forces must be compatible with these roles, and it is the intention of the Government that they shall be. Our eventual forces will be highly mobile and will be the best-equipped and best-trained forces of their kind in the world.

The precise military role which we shall endeavour to assume in these collective arrangements will be a matter for discussion and consultation with our allies, and will depend in part on the role assigned to Canadian forces in the surveillance of our own territory and coast-lines in the interest of protecting our own sovereignty. As a responsible member of the international community, it is our desire to have forces available for peace-keeping roles as well as for participation in defensive alliances.

Canada is a partner in two collective defence arrangements, which, though distinct, are complementary. These are the North Atlantic Treaty Organization and the North American Air Defence Command. For 20 years NATO has contributed to the maintenance of world peace through its stabilizing influence in Europe. NATO continues to contribute to peace by reducing the likelihood of a major conflict breaking out in Europe, where, because the vital interests of the two major powers are involved, any outbreak of hostilities could easily escalate into a war of world proportions. At the same time, it is the declared aim of NATO to foster improvements in East-West relations.

NATO itself is continuously reassessing the role it plays in the light of changing world conditions. Perhaps the major development affecting NATO in Europe since the Organization was founded is the magnificent recovery of the economic strength of Western Europe. There has been a very great change in the ability of European countries themselves to provide necessary conventional defence forces and armaments to be deployed by the alliance in Europe.

It was, therefore, in our view entirely appropriate for Canada to review and re-examine the necessity in present circumstances for maintaining Canadian forces in Western Europe. Canadian forces are now committed to NATO until the end of the present year. The Canadian force commitment for deployment with NATO in Europe beyond this period will be discussed with our allies at the meeting of the

Defence Planning Committee of NATO in May. The Canadian Government intends, in consultation with Canada's allies, to take early steps to bring about a planned and phased reduction of the size of the Canadian forces in Europe.

We intend, as well, to continue to co-operate effectively with the United States in the defence of North America. We shall, accordingly, seek early occasions for detailed discussions with the United States Government of the whole range of problems involved in our mutual co-operation in defence matters on this continent. To the extent that it is feasible, we shall endeavour to have those activities within Canada which are essential to North American defence performed by Canadian forces.

In summary, Canada will continue to be a member of the North Atlantic Treaty Organization and to co-operate closely with the United States within NORAD and in other ways in defensive arrangements. We shall maintain appropriate defence forces, which will be designed to undertake the following roles:

a)   the surveillance of our own territory and coastlines—i.e., the protection of our sovereignty;

b)   the defence of North America in co-operation with United States forces;

c)   the fulfilment of such NATO commitments as may be agreed upon; and

d)   the performance of such international peace-keeping roles as we may, from time to time, assume.

The kind of forces and armaments most suitable for these roles is now being assessed in greater detail in preparation for discussion with our allies.*

15. Defence in the 1970s

Extracts from the White Paper on Defence, issued under the signature of the Minister of National Defence, Mr. Donald S. Macdonald, Ottawa, August 1971.

WHY DEFENCE POLICY WAS REVIEWED

Important international and domestic changes have occurred since the

---

* See SS 69/15 of September 19, 1969, for a detailed account of the force structure which emerged. See also Mr. Trudeau's speech of April 12, 1970, to the Alberta Liberal Association (Document No. 79 below).

review of defence policy which culminated in the White Paper issued in 1964. These changes have required a fundamental reappraisal of Canadian defence policy by the Government.

International Developments: The most significant changes on the international scene with consequences for Canadian defence policy have occurred in the nature of the strategic nuclear balance between the United States and the Soviet Union, and in the state of East-West political relations both in Europe and directly between the two super powers. These changes, together with the emergence of China as a nuclear power and the growing economic strength of Europe and Japan, have resulted in a loosening of the bipolar international system. This trend is emphasized by the announcement that President Nixon of the United States will shortly be visiting the People's Republic of China, indicative of a major change in policy for both countries. On the other hand, the prospects for effective international peace keeping, which were viewed with some optimism in 1964, have not developed as had been hoped.

National Concern: There have been developments within Canada of particular importance to the employment of our defence forces. Defence responsibilities required re-examination as a result of Government decisions to regulate the development of the North in a manner compatible with environmental preservation, and with legislation enacted to prevent pollution in the Arctic and the Northern inland waters. Other relevant developments included the extension of Canada's territorial sea, the establishment of fisheries protection and pollution control zones on the Atlantic and Pacific coasts, and the heightened pace of exploration for offshore mineral resources. Finally, the threat to society posed by violent revolutionaries and the implications of the recent crisis—although the latter occurred well after the defence review began—merited close consideration in projecting Canadian defence activities in the 1970s.

THE BASIS FOR DEFENCE POLICY IN THE 1970S

Defence as Part of National Policy

Defence policy cannot be developed in isolation. It must reflect and serve national interests, and must be closely related to foreign policy, which the Government reviewed concurrently with defence. In the course of these reviews the principle that defence policy must be in phase with the broader external projection of national interests was underlined. In addition, internal aspects of national defence were also considered; these included aid of the civil power and assistance to the civil authorities in the furtherance of national aims.

National Aims: In the foreign-policy review general national aims were defined as follows:

- that Canada will continue secure as an independent political entity;
- that Canada and all Canadians will enjoy enlarging prosperity in the widest possible sense;
- that all Canadians will see in the life they have and the contribution they make to humanity something worthwhile preserving in identity and purpose.*

Policy Themes: To achieve these aims, the themes of Canada's national policy were more specifically defined as seeking to:

- foster economic growth,
- safeguard sovereignty and independence,
- work for peace and security,
- promote social justice,
- enhance the quality of life,
- ensure a harmonious natural environment.

The first concern of defence policy is the national aim of ensuring that Canada should continue secure as an independent political entity —an objective basic to the attainment of the other two national aims. In the policy themes flowing from the national aims, the Canadian Forces have a major part to play in the search for peace and security and also have an important and growing role in safeguarding sovereignty and independence. Accordingly it is to these two themes of national policy that the activities of the Canadian Forces are most closely related. However, defence policy can and should also be relevant to the other policy themes, and the contribution of the Department of National Defence to national development will be examined in this context.

---

* Some of these themes are reminiscent of debates in the House of Commons during the 1930s. See, for instance, CHCD, February 19, 1937.

Peace and Security

The Changing Scene: One of the most important changes in international affairs in recent years has been the increase in stability in nuclear deterrence, and the emergence of what is, in effect, nuclear parity between the United States and the Soviet Union. Each side now has sufficient nuclear strength to assure devastating retaliation in the event of a surprise attack by the other, and thus neither could rationally consider launching a deliberate attack. There have also been qualitative changes in the composition of the nuclear balance. Of particular importance to Canada is the fact that bombers, and consequently bomber defences, have declined in relative importance in the strategic equation.

Greater stability in the last few years has been accompanied by an increased willingness to attempt to resolve East-West issues by negotiation, although it is still too early to judge the prospects for success. Formal and informal discussions are in progress between the U.S. and the U.S.S.R. on a long list of subjects, involving problems around the globe. Of overriding importance are the current Strategic Arms Limitation Talks (SALT) where signs of agreement are emerging. Other negotiations of major importance are the Four Power Talks on Berlin in which the U.S. and U.S.S.R. are joined by Britain and France in an effort to resolve one of the main issues still outstanding from the Second World War. The Federal Republic of Germany has initiated a series of negotiations fundamental to the future prospects for East-West relations, which have already yielded important agreements with the U.S.S.R. and Poland. In addition, the Government hopes it will be possible to open negotiations on Mutual and Balanced Force Reductions (MBFR) in Europe in the near future.

At the same time the nations of Western Europe are growing more prosperous and are co-operating more closely, and the likelihood has increased that the European Economic Community will be enlarged. The European members of the North Atlantic Treaty Organization (NATO) are now able to assume a greater share of the collective Alliance defence, particularly with respect to their own continent. The North Atlantic Alliance remains firm but within it there is now a more even balance between North America and Europe.

Change has been even more rapid in the Pacific area where Japan's phenomenal economic growth continues and where China's military and political power is substantially increasing. Primarily as a result of these developments in Europe and Asia, but also as a consequence of change in other parts of the world, there has been a return to a form of multi-polarity in the international system. Although the U.S. and the U.S.S.R. continue to have overwhelming military power, and in particular nuclear power, the relative ability of these two countries to influence events in the rest of the world has declined in recent years.

One other development in the international field of particular importance to Canada should be noted. In 1964 there was considerable optimism in this country concerning the scope for peace keeping. In the intervening years the United Nations Emergency Force was compelled to leave the Middle East. Little progress has been made towards agreement on satisfactory means of international financing of peace-keeping forces. And amidst the tragedy of the Vietnam conflict, the effectiveness of the International Commission for Supervision and Control in Indo-China has further diminished. Additional observer missions were created and operated for a short time on the borders of West Pakistan and India following the border clash of 1965 and in Nigeria in 1969, but no substantial peace-keeping operation has been authorized since 1964 when the UN Force in Cyprus was established. For many reasons the scope for useful and effective peace-keeping activities now appears more modest than it did earlier, despite the persistence of widespread violence in many parts of the world.

Sovereignty and Independence

Canada's sovereignty and independence depend ultimately on security from armed attack. In this sense, the contribution of the Canadian Forces to the prevention of war is a vital and direct contribution to safeguarding our sovereignty and independence. Defence policy must, however, also take into account the possibility that other challenges to Canada's sovereignty and independence, mainly non-military in character, may be more likely to arise during the 1970s. They could come both from outside and from within the country, and to deal with them may in some ways be more difficult. While deterring war is not an objective Canada alone can achieve, and is therefore one which must be pursued through collective security arrangements, the other challenges to sovereignty and independence must be met exclusively by Canada. The provision of adequate Canadian defence resources for this purpose must therefore be a matter of first priority.

THE DEFENCE OF NORTH AMERICA

The Nuclear Deterrent System

The only direct external military threat to Canada's national security today is that of a large-scale nuclear attack on North America. So long as a stable strategic balance exists, the deliberate initiation of nuclear war between the U.S.S.R. and the U.S. is highly improbable; this constitutes mutual deterrence. It is far from being the theoretically ideal means of maintaining peace, but the Government, while continuing to participate in the arms-control deliberations, remains convinced that there is nothing to replace it at present. Therefore, Canada must do what it can to ensure the continued effectiveness of the deterrent system.

The Government concluded in its defence review that co-operation with the United States in North American defence will remain essential so long as our joint security depends on stability in the strategic military balance. Canada's objective is to make, within the limits of our resources, an effective contribution to continued stability by assisting in the surveillance and warning systems, and in the protection of the U.S. retaliatory capability as necessary. Co-operation between Canada and the U.S. in the joint defence of North America is vital for sovereignty and security.

Canada's Contribution

This paper indicates what in the Government's view would be the most appropriate and effective contribution, taking into account political, strategic, economic and military factors. Given the resources available for defence, and the almost limitless demands on them, the contribution will be directly related to the surveillance and control role for the Forces.

In air defence, Canada's part in the past has been one of contributing to the provision of interceptor aircraft, surface-to-air missiles, radars, communications and associated headquarters. These activities, conducted since 1958 under the NORAD agreement, have had three main benefits for Canada:

- they have helped to assure the protection of the U.S. deterrent against what was at one time the main threat, that of Soviet bomber attack;
- they have provided for a defence which would take place beyond the settled areas of Canada; and
- they have enhanced Canada's control over its own territory.

In maritime defence, Canada contributes forces through arrangements with the United States and assumes responsibility for ocean areas adjacent to Canada's shores. These arrangements have had two main benefits for Canada:

- they have provided surveillance over contiguous ocean areas against surface and subsurface vessels, and provided warning of a build-up of potentially hostile forces; and
- they have provided the capability necessary to cope with hostile activity.

THE NORTH ATLANTIC TREATY ORGANIZATION

There were two main reasons for the decision to review the level of our force contribution in Europe. Economic circumstances in Europe had undergone a marked change in the nearly twenty years since Canada first stationed peacetime forces in Europe. Under the protective shield of NATO, Western Europe had succeeded in transforming the shattered economies of 1945. Since then its GNP has grown to about $600 billion per year for a population which exceeds 300 million people, and in many countries there is a high level of employment. In considering the defence implications of this phenomenal recovery, Canada concluded that its European partners were now able to provide a greater proportion of the conventional forces needed for the defence of their own region of the Alliance.

The second reason for review was that other national aims—fostering economic growth and safeguarding sovereignty and independence—dictated increased emphasis on the protection of Canadian interests at home. In addition, Government-wide financial restraints, and the resulting need for compatibility of roles and equipment for our home and overseas-based Armed Forces, dictated the need for some adjustment.

The Government reaffirmed Canada's adherence to the concept of collective security, and announced that Canada would continue to station significant though reduced forces in Europe as part of the NATO integrated force structure. Forces based in Canada for emergency deployment to Europe were not reduced. The Government reached its decision after an exhaustive examination of all factors bearing on national security. The decision did not suggest an overall reduction in NATO-wide defence, although Canada hopes that East-West negotiation will render this possible in the future. What Canada was seeking was a redistribution of effort for the defence of the European part of the Treaty area. The reductions were preceded by full consultations and implemented over a two-year period to permit internal adjustments to be made by members of the Alliance.

The decision reflected the Government's judgment that Canadian security continues to be linked to Western Europe and that Europe is still probably the most sensitive point in the East-West balance of power. It is the area from which any conflict, however limited, might most readily escalate into all-out nuclear war engulfing Canadian territory.

Canada's military contribution in Europe reinforces its political role in the important negotiations in progress, or in prospect, designed to lead to a resolution of some of the tension-producing issues which persist from the Second World War. It would be wrong to believe that the situation in Europe is frozen or to conclude that there is no prospect of altering the NATO/Warsaw Pact military confrontation. Success in any of these initiatives, however, ultimately depends on the receptiveness of the other side.

Canadian membership in NATO can thus be justified solely on security and political grounds. Canada has in addition a direct interest in the economic well-being of Western Europe and in the preservation of trading relations with this second ranking Canadian market. In connection with the further development and probable enlargement of the European Economic Community (EEC) Canada is engaging in important negotiations with certain of our allies who are current and prospective members of the EEC. The community of interest we share with these countries through common NATO membership should be a positive factor in these negotiations.

Forces Stationed in Europe

The reduction in the strength of the Canadian Forces assigned to Allied Command Europe forecast in April 1969 has now been effected. The land element has been co-located with the air element in Southern Germany, with headquarters in Lahr, giving our forces in Europe a distinctive Canadian identity. Their combined strength is approximately 5,000 instead of the 10,000 formerly stationed in Europe. The Government has no plans for further reductions.

INTERNATIONAL PEACE KEEPING

Canada's experience has provided it with an exceptional insight into the successes and failures of past and present international peacekeeping practices. The experience has all too often been frustrating and disillusioning. Some operations have been severely hampered by inadequate terms of reference and by a lack of co-operation on the part of those involved. Other detrimental factors have been the absence of political support of some of the great powers, and insufficient international logistic and financial resources. Certain operations have tended to become "open-ended" in the absence of a political settlement between the parties to a dispute.

Benefit can be derived from these efforts, regardless of how disappointing some of them may have been. The Government continues to support the concept of peace keeping and will seek to utilize Canada's experience, to develop guidelines, within the United Nations and elsewhere for effective peace-keeping operations. The Government will consider constructively any request for Canadian participation in peace-keeping ventures when, in its opinion, based on the lessons of the past and the circumstances of the request, an operation holds the promise of success and Canada can play a useful role in it.

It is, of course, impossible to predict when a request will next be made and to foresee the size and scope of any future operations. Many of the conflicts likely to arise in this decade will have their roots in subversion and insurgency, and will not therefore lend themselves easily to resolution through the use of internationally constituted peace-keeping bodies.

Indo-China and the Middle East are two areas where the establishment of some kind of peace-keeping or truce supervisory operation might form part of an eventual settlement. If asked to participate in such an operation, a major factor affecting the Government's decision would be the existence of realistic terms of reference. They would have to reflect a consensus by all parties on the purposes which the operation was intended to serve and the manner in which it was to discharge its responsibilities.

A new requirement may also develop for the supervision of arms-control agreements, involving the use of specialized personnel capable of inspecting, for example, installations on the seabed or the deployment of military forces.

In keeping with the Government's intention to give positive consideration, when warranted, to requests for Canadian participation in international peace keeping, the Government intends to maintain its capability to respond quickly. A battalion group of the Canadian Armed Forces will remain on stand-by, and Canadian Forces personnel will continue to receive training to prepare them for service within peace-keeping bodies.

16. NATO in 1973: How It Serves Canadian Interests

Statement to the Canadian Parliamentary Association by the Secretary of State for External Affairs, Mr. Mitchell Sharp, Ottawa, April 17, 1973.

The purpose of my remarks tonight is to outline some of the reasons why we believe participation in NATO serves Canadian interests.

The commitment to assist each other in the event of an attack is enshrined in the North Atlantic Treaty, which was signed in 1949, with Canada one of the original signatories. Although France no longer participates actively in the integrated military structure of NATO, it has remained a member of the alliance and its forces engage in exercises and planning for joint military operations. At present we contribute forces to the three major areas of the alliance—in Europe itself, in the Atlantic, where our maritime forces are earmarked for assignment to SACLANT in the event of an emergency, and in North America, through the NORAD Agreement (although this is not formally part of the North Atlantic Treaty). In all three spheres, our contribution is modest in the overall scale, but well respected because of its high calibre and professional qualities.

These forces of all the members of NATO, including U.S. nuclear strength, constitute the Western component of the present system of balanced mutual deterrence. Pending greater progress towards disarmament or a more effective world collective security system under the United Nations, the present balance of deterrence is our best safeguard for peace. In short, NATO's primary security purpose is deterrence.

Its second main purpose is to pursue all realistic avenues of détente. At NATO headquarters in Brussels, there is a highly effective mechanism for inter-allied consultation on a whole range of international political and defence questions of common interest. It is headed by the North Atlantic Council, which meets at least twice a year at ministerial level; but the Council is permanently in session and can be convened in a matter of hours to deal with crises as they arise. Canada and the 14 other nations are represented at senior ambassador level. The Council is assisted by a complex network of committees, including a Committee of Economic Advisers, a Committee of Political Advisers and a Science Committee.

In addition to their traditional functions, these committees now have to adapt themselves to new forms, as well as to the increased pace of consultations, in order to provide the necessary co-ordination of Western positions on subjects on the agenda of the Conference on Security and Co-operation in Europe and Mutual Balanced Force Reductions preparatory talks in Helsinki and Vienna. Specialized NATO sub-committees, drawing on legal, economic, political and cultural expertise from capitals, are busily engaged in elaborating NATO's positions on these and many other issues for use in the negotiations themselves. It is clear that a full and careful preparation of these negotiations is necessary in order to ensure their success.

NATO has also embarked on a program to stimulate co-operation in another area of non-military activity. Comprising nearly all the major industrial states of the world, NATO has successfully promoted an exchange of views and experience on environmental and ecological problems under the auspices of the NATO Committee on the Challenges of Modern Society. You will be aware that Canada was host to the plenary session of this committee last week. It was generally agreed that this had been a very useful meeting.

In *Foreign Policy for Canadians*,* a primary aim of Canadian policy was defined as follows: "Canada should continue secure as an independent political entity". For a country of Canada's size and geographical location, membership in the alliance provides a high degree of security at a relatively low cost in terms of resources devoted to defence. Even though we contribute forces to all three areas of the alliance, the proportion of our gross national product devoted to defence is considerably lower than that of several other members.

In defence, as well as in political terms, participation in the wider collective defence arrangements of NATO is helpful in projecting our national identity. The Canadian land and air forces in Europe are now combined in one headquarters and, although relatively small, have achieved a deservedly high reputation for effectiveness. They represent in European eyes the visible evidence of Canada's continuing commitment to the alliance.

Participation in NATO's common defence effort does not prejudice the Government's freedom of decision or involve an automatic commitment as to the means of providing mutual support. Article V of the NATO treaty requires that each member take "such action as it deems necessary" in the event of aggression in the treaty area. We can be satisfied that Canadian troops in Europe cannot be ordered into action by SACEUR without a fully conscious decision by the Canadian Government to authorize him to do so. Similarly, our maritime forces in the Atlantic are only "earmarked" for assignment to SACLANT in an

---

* See Chapter X.

emergency. Canadian Government authority must be given before they can be deployed in action.

Given Europe's continuing preoccupation with security, the continued presence of Canadian forces has important political overtones. It is evident that Canada's forces in Europe do not play a critical part in the overall strategic equation. However, as a symbol of the credibility of the North American commitment, they remain very important from a political standpoint. This is particularly true in the case of the Federal Republic of Germany because of its special situation. The other smaller members of the alliance, such as the Netherlands and Norway, who are less than sure about the political consequences or the adequacy of integration of defence arrangements among Europeans, are most anxious to retain intact the United States and Canadian commitment to Europe. The Norwegian Foreign Minister, who was visiting Ottawa last week, expressed his Government's special appreciation for Canada's participation in NATO and for contingency plans we have made to send additional forces to that country as a reinforcement measure in the event of an emergency.

Participation in NATO can also have certain direct benefits for Canadian industry. In the NATO program for satellite communication facilities, in which some significant sums will be expended in the coming years, we have obtained recognition that the bids of Canadian manufacturers for all the projects related to this program will be evaluated free of import taxes and duties. It took some bargaining, of course, and it could eventually be accepted as a principle because governments rather than private agencies were the parties to the arrangements. This is a useful illustration of the special advantages we seek to derive from the security relationship with Europe and the kind of concession we are given. There is a good deal more in the way of technological "spinoff" for Canada, of course, by way of access to European systems in the space and communications fields.

Other illustrations worth mentioning are the possibilities for co-operation with our European allies in the defence production field, which are currently being pursued on many fronts. There are also many co-operative arrangements with them in the field of training whereby Canada extends the use of Canadian training facilities on a full-recovery basis to Britain and the Netherlands. Others are under discussion. All these bring regional economic benefits to Canada at some facilities which might otherwise be closed down or remain dormant.

Participation in NATO provides a means of strengthening our relations with the countries of Western Europe. To the extent that most, if

not all, of the European members of NATO attach considerable importance to the alliance as a guarantee of their security, Canadian support for and active participation in the political and military activities
of the alliance can help create a favourable attitude towards Canada
on the part of the individual European governments. This can, in
turn, influence the position of the same governments when, as members of the EEC, they are required to take action which could affect
Canadian interests. A good example of this inter-action was the West
German Government's initiative in making a direct reference to Canada's economic interests in the communiqué issued by EEC heads of
government last year. This step was prompted, we have good reason
to believe, by the importance the Germans continue to attach to
maintaining a Canadian presence in Europe.

As you know, Canada is making a special effort to develop a
satisfactory relationship with the newly enlarged European Economic
Community.* Important Canadian economic interests are at stake,
particularly with the situation arising out of the admission of Britain.
To the extent that we continue to play a positive and constructive role
in NATO, I am convinced that our participation in the alliance cannot
but assist us in establishing a good working relationship with the EEC.

NATO strength and solidarity can take much of the credit not only
for maintaining peace but also for the progress made to date on East-
West issues. The West German Government itself has acknowledged
that its *Ostpolitik* could not have succeeded without the backing of its
allies. The road to the opening of the negotiations in Helsinki on the
CSCE and in Vienna on MBFR required an unstinting diplomatic effort
on the part of all concerned, and deliberate and careful consultation
in NATO. There is a strong conviction in Europe, which we share, that
NATO solidarity will need to be maintained throughout the negotiations which have already been initiated.

Our membership in NATO is our admission-card to the consultations
and negotiating tables of the alliance. This is particularly important at
the present time, when Canada is directly participating in two separate
but related negotiations which have opened a further phase in the
lowering of tensions and increasing security in Europe and in the
world. The first of these is the Multiple Preparatory Talks in Europe,
which have been under way in Helsinki since November last year,
with some 35 countries participating. Canadian interests are closely
engaged in the CSCE agenda items, and it is worth singling out the
economic and freedom-of-movement issues to illustrate the range and

---

* See Chapter VI.

importance of the CSCE issues for Canada's foreign and domestic policy aims.

The second set of negotiations in which we are directly participating is the exploratory talks on Mutual and Balanced Force Reductions, which have been under way in Vienna since late January. The main participants in this negotiation are the countries of NATO and the Warsaw Pact which maintain forces in Central Europe. We expect this to be a difficult negotiation, but it seems to us that it would be illusory to expect détente to flow from the CSCE negotiations if parallel steps are not taken to reduce the tensions stemming from the present confrontation of forces in Central Europe.

This is why we regard the CSCE and MBFR as parallel sets of negotiations which we hope will lead to further progress in East-West détente. Needless to say, they present an unprecedented opportunity for Canadian co-operation with the countries of Europe, and in particular with our fellow members of NATO, where consultation on the Western position in these negotiations is proceeding apace.

Canada is determined to maintain and strengthen its traditional ties with the countries of Western Europe. This policy will serve Canadian interests not only because of the direct benefits arising from improved bilateral relations with the individual countries but also because it will serve to underline our separate identity and offset somewhat the preponderant influence of the United States.

NATO provides a unique forum in the shape of the Council, where almost every day Canada has an opportunity to express its national point of view on policy matters of key importance to the European members as well as to the United States. Through our participation in the Council and the NATO committees, we have frequently found ourselves siding with the Europeans on issues where the views and interests of the super-powers may diverge from those of the smaller and middle-size members of the alliance. There is no shortage of occasions when we have the opportunity to express a distinct Canadian point of view, whether this be in the Council at ambassadorial level or at the ministerial sessions.

III. Canada—United States Relations

˜ Relations with the United States ebbed and flowed throughout the decade. In the late 1960s they were still troubled by the war in Viet Nam and by the unsettled situation of China in the world community.* These issues were largely solved in the early 1970s and Canadian/American relations might have been expected to become somewhat more buoyant as a result. To the contrary, they reached their low point on August 15, 1971 when Canada found—much to its dismay—that it was definitely included in the provisions of the "Nixon Doctrine". This policy measure was designed to correct United States balance-of-payments problems and to bring about a more equitable international monetary system. Canada, in its relationship with the United States, had become *un pays comme les autres*.**

Things turned out to be not quite so bad as anticipated. The 10 per cent surcharge on exports to the United States lasted only until mid-December. The shock was eventually overcome. However, it led to several changes in Canada's approach to the United States and to world affairs, the effects of which are still being felt. The "Third Option" aimed at "lessening the vulnerability of the Canadian economy to external shocks, especially those from the United States" is one of them. The contractual link recently established with the European Economic Community is another, as are current vigorous attempts to increase Canadian trade and other relations with such alternate areas as Japan and Latin America. The decision to reduce energy exports to the United States is yet another. The principle of continen-

---

* See A.E.B., Chapter VI, The Far East, for background.

** Canada was exempted from the provisions of the U.S. interest equalization tax measures of July 1963 and from the mandatory regulations of 1968 regarding direct capital investment. The Canadian Government again sought an exemption in 1971, on the grounds that with a floating rate of exchange market forces had been at play for some time and that there were no obstacles in Canada to imports from the United States. The appeal was rejected.

talism, which sometimes has characterized Canada's approach to its relations with the United States in the past, particularly with regard to resources, has been less in evidence recently.

Nevertheless, the ties between the two countries have continued to be closely interwoven, indeed almost inextricably so. Each is the other's best trading partner. Tourism continues to grow, as do cultural and other public affairs exchanges. The arrangements of NORAD in the field of defence, renewed in 1968 and again in 1973, still prevail. Both countries continue to support NATO and are virtually the only ones in the world still upholding the principle of free trade. The Automotive Parts Agreement of 1965 has brought benefits to each partner, as has the Air Transport Agreement of 1966. Solutions are being found to environmental problems, particularly water and oil pollution.

The difficulties resulting from the acquisition of the Mercantile Bank by the National City Bank of New York, the status of *Time* and the *Reader's Digest* in Canada, were dealt with and solutions found.* Considerable concern was voiced over the possible impact of the United States' export incentive plan of late 1971 known as DISC (Domestic International Sales Corporation). This was viewed as being contrary to the principles and obligations of GATT and strong protests were lodged. Countervailing measures and incentives were introduced in Canada. Again, fortunately, the consequence of the DISC arrangements were not so severe as anticipated. The size of United States investments in Canada and their impact on the Canadian economy led to the Foreign Investments Review Act in 1974, which gives the Government authority to screen investments from abroad.**

---

* Owing to space considerations it is not possible to document these questions. For further information, see Peter C. Newman, *The Distemper of Our Times*, Greywood Publishing Limited, Winnipeg, pp. 208-09, 379-83, and 455-61. Pages 455-61 give the texts of diplomatic notes exchanged between the two governments about the Mercantile Bank. See also Mr. MacEachen's speech of March 20, 1975, to the World Affairs Council and New England Trade Center, Boston, Mass., regarding the final outcome of the *Time* and *Reader's Digest* cases.

** The report (Proceedings No. 33) of the House of Commons Standing Committee on External Affairs and National Defence, published on August 17, 1970, provides much useful background on Canada – United States relations generally and on investments in particular. See also *Canada – United States Relations*, report by the Senate Standing Committee on Foreign Affairs, Ottawa, QP, December 1975, and its second report, August 1978, on "Canada's Trade Relations with the United States".

Generally, an *ad hoc* approach has characterized the management of Canadian relations with the United States. The only step taken to try to achieve an overall management approach occurred in 1965. It took the form of the Heeney-Merchant Report (June 28, 1965), from the names of its authors: two former ambassadors in Washington and Ottawa respectively, who had been asked by Prime Minister Pearson and President Johnson to prepare a report on how the two countries should consult and deal with each other. It strongly urged an approach characterized by what became known as "quiet diplomacy". This approach was considered by many, especially in the academic world, as being out of tune with the times. The report does not appear to have been put into effect.

In his speech to the Winnipeg Branch of the Canadian Institute for International Affairs on January 23, 1975, Mr. MacEachen dealt with the management of Canadian relations with the United States. His remarks on that occasion are well worth noting.

The two countries are becoming increasingly interdependent and the issues between them accordingly greater in number and complexity. In these circumstances, relations are likely to become more, not less, difficult. As interaction increases, conflicts of interest and differences of view are bound to develop. Both governments are becoming increasingly involved in a wide range of domestic social and economic activities many of which turn out to have foreign policy implications. Two years ago federal financial assistance was extended under the Department of Regional Economic Expansion programme to the Michelin Tire Corporation to locate in Nova Scotia. This was regarded by many in the United States as an attempt to subsidize an export industry, and as a consequence the United States applied countervailing duties on this Canadian export. This is a striking example of how a domestic programme, in this instance, one designed to remedy regional economic disparities, can become an issue in our relations with the United States.

Although this new period in our relations with the United States will be complex and at times difficult, our approach to it should be positive. The fact is that fundamentally the relationship is a healthy one. We must remember that Canada and the United States continue to share similar views, and cooperate closely, on a whole range of important international issues.

To respond to this evolving situation there is a new pattern developing in the management of our relationship which, in my view, will help to promote harmony and is in keeping with the new character of that relationship. It consists of analysis of the particular national interest to be served, followed by consultation, discussion or negotiation with a view to reaching a mutually acceptable settlement of the particular problem. One of the most important ingredients in this process is that of regular consultation and discussion.

In this connection I want to emphasize the importance of advance consultation. It seems to me that the sensible way of doing business is to notify the United States whenever possible of our intentions in advance of our taking major decisions on matters affecting United States interests and where appropriate to provide an opportunity for advance consultations. Naturally, we would expect the United States authorities to treat us in the same way whenever they are about to take action which would affect our interests. This practice corresponds to the more mature and complex stage that our relationship has now reached. It would help to diminish fears and misunderstandings on both sides. In short, it is an important way of keeping our relations with the United States in a healthy condition.

All in all, despite the increasing complexity and rising range of problems in our relationship with the United States, it is without doubt much more comfortable to share a boundary with the bald eagle than the brown bear.˜

A. ECONOMIC RELATIONS

17. Canada–United States Economic Relations in the Mid-1960s*

Statement by Mr. Mitchell Sharp, Minister of Finance, University of Rochester, Rochester, New York, May 5, 1966. (Extracts)

I propose to discuss two major developments of this period. The first was the Canada–United States Automotive Agreement and the events that led up to it. The second was the effect upon American-Canadian economic and financial relations of the measures taken by the United States to deal with its balance-of-payments problems.

Since the Automotive Agreement had its origin in efforts by Canada to improve its balance-of-payments position, it is possible to say that much of the drama, the suspense and the change of these past three years to which I have referred arose from the concern of both our countries with their respective balance-of-payments positions.

---

* See also SS 66/4 and SS 66/5 of January 27 and February 2, 1966, for Mr. Sharp's statements in the House of Commons on this subject.

Lest there be confusion about words, let me explain briefly the nature of our balance-of-payments problem and how it differs from that of the United States.

Our problem is one that does not exist for the United States at all. It is that of a large and persistent deficit in what are defined as current payments. These relate to purchases and sales of goods of all kinds, and of services such as tourism, transportation, insurance and the like, together with interest and dividends and certain transfer payments. This deficit has only once fallen below half a billion Canadian dollars in the last 11 years, and was over $1 billion last year. Scaled up to the dimensions of the United States economy, this would represent a deficit approaching $15 billion, or substantially more, in one year, than your entire gold reserve. The structure of the Canadian economy is such, however, that it attracts a substantial volume of foreign investment capital (particularly from the United States). Provided that the flow of such capital remains unimpeded, it can normally be counted upon to offset much, if not all, of Canada's current-account deficit, though of course the inflow of capital adds to Canadian indebtedness in one form or another, incurs a continuing economic cost in the shape of interest or dividend payments to the foreign investor, and is all ultimately repayable or repatriable.

The United States, by contrast, earns a healthy surplus each year in respect of current transactions as I have described them (and a substantial part of that surplus is attributable to transactions with Canada). It is a function both of the structure of the U.S. economy and of the pre-eminent financial and political role of the United States in the world that the flow of capital is outwards from this country. It takes the form of investment as well as foreign aid, and in recent years it has generally exceeded the current-account surplus earned by the United States.

To any extent that Canada does not succeed in covering her current-account deficit by attracting capital, she has to meet the shortfall by payments of gold and foreign exchange out of reserves. The United States, on the other hand, can and does finance the excess of its capital outflow over its current-account surplus with its own currency, and in so doing has provided most of the very necessary liquidity to the world's monetary system in the post-war period. Problems only arise, as they have done recently, when major creditors of the United States rightly or wrongly judge themselves to be oversupplied with reserve dollars and exercise the option inherent in the system to switch back into gold.

In the year 1962, our current-account deficit was $874 million. Of this deficit, no less than $580 million was accounted for by trade in automotive vehicles and parts. The deficit in the automotive sector had increased by nearly 25 per cent within a 12-month period.

The previous Government, in November 1962, had taken certain steps to correct this situation. Specifically, it allowed Canadian automotive producers to bring into Canada free of duty automatic transmissions and engines, on the condition that and to the extent that they expanded their exports of automotive parts.

After reviewing the results of this somewhat limited programme, the present Government decided to extend the plan and to allow Canadian motor-vehicle producers to import any type of part they needed and, indeed, to import motor vehicles free of duty in step with whatever increase they achieved in their exports to the United States or to other countries. We felt that this would provide a stronger incentive to our producers to specialize, that they would become more efficient and that, in consequence, they would be able to compete more effectively on world markets.

The new plan was only beginning to take effect when one of the automotive-parts manufacturers on your side of the border cried "foul". This producer lodged a complaint with the United States Bureau of Customs alleging that our incentive plan was simply a device to subsidize exports. He asked the United States Government to apply countervailing duties, that is to say additional duties equal to the subsidy which he claimed was being given to Canadian producers by the Canadian Government.

It was obvious that this put the whole programme into jeopardy. Whatever the outcome of that complaint, it would be months before the application for countervailing duties could be finally disposed of. Meanwhile no United States importer could run the risk of having to pay retroactively the duty that might be assessed.

It seemed to us that this situation had arisen because of a real lack of understanding of what we were trying to do. The root of the Canadian problem—and this is true of other industries as well as the automotive industry—is that we have a very small domestic market. So long as production in Canada is geared exclusively to supplying only this market, our producers are not in a position to achieve the full economies of scale. As a result, their unit costs are higher, they are not able to compete effectively with foreign producers, and the Canadian consumer often has to pay higher prices.

It is not simply that Canadian plants are often smaller than plants in the United States. Even when our plants are the same size as yours, they tend to produce a much greater range of products. In the automobile industry one of our largest assembly plants customarily produced as many as 600 different models of passenger-car and truck. Even the most complex assembly operation in the United States would not attempt to produce more than 250 models, and most United States assembly plants would concentrate on a much smaller range of products. This holds true for parts production as well.

The obvious solution for a country in this position is to specialize — to limit itself to doing the things it can do best and produce a selected range of vehicles and parts for both the home market and for export. The remaining types of parts and vehicles needed to provide consumers with a range of choice can then be imported.

A solution along these lines did not seem unreasonable, given the fact that all our large motor-vehicle producers had plants on both sides of the border and many of our parts producers were subsidiaries of United States manufacturers.

The Canadian Government made soundings in Washington to see if we couldn't find a way of doing this that would avoid any danger of running foul of United States law. The United States Government expressed sympathy with the Canadian position. Officials met to explore the possibilities and, in a surprisingly short time, draft proposals were placed before the two Governments suggesting a free-trade agreement covering most types of motor vehicle — cars, trucks and buses — and the parts needed to produce them.

In a few more weeks of intensive negotiations an agreement was reached in January last year by the two Governments and signed and placed by the President before Congress, where it was ratified in October 1965. The Agreement is now in full effect.

The Agreement provides basically for the removal of tariffs between the two countries on motor vehicles and original equipment parts, although there are one or two limitations.

For our part, we have extended duty-free treatment to imports from all countries but we have limited the right to import vehicles free of duty into Canada to our motor-vehicle producers. To qualify as a Canadian producer, a manufacturer must manufacture vehicles in Canada. He must also continue to spend at least the same amount each year on Canadian labour and materials as in 1964 and must continue to assemble in Canada at least the same proportion of vehicles as he did in that year. Firms that were not in production in 1964 can qualify for free entry if they meet similar conditions.

Why did we think these provisions were necessary? We were concerned to avoid too drastic and too rapid changes in the structure of the industry in Canada. We wanted to retain a certain basic volume of assembly work in Canada. We also wanted to ease the problems that would otherwise face some of the numerous parts manufacturers in Canada. Moreover, without these safeguards, Canadian consumers would have been free to buy their cars and trucks in the United States and the future of both parts production and assembly production in Canada would have been highly uncertain. This was recognized by the United States when we negotiated the Agreement.

We have also sought certain additional commitments from our vehicle producers to ensure that we will not only retain basic automotive production facilities in Canada but that production of Canadian automotive products will expand with the growth in the North American market. We hope that we shall be able to correct some of the imbalance that at present exists between Canada's share of production and consumption within that market.

Accordingly, the Canadian Government asked Canadian vehicle manufacturers for firm assurances that they will increase their purchases of Canadian labour and materials between 1964 and 1968 in step with their domestic sales. The Canadian producers have also undertaken to make further purchases of Canadian labour and materials over and above these amounts.

I hope that this brief account of one of the major developments in Canadian-American economic relations in the past three years justifies my assertion about drama and suspense in the relations between our two countries. I trust, too, that I have successfully conveyed some idea of the significance of this Agreement to both our countries.

What is happening is an integration of the North American automotive industry, but an integration that provides time for the Canadian industry to adjust to more competitive conditions and, equally important, one which also provides the basis for a relative shift in output in Canada to compensate for the historically slower development of the Canadian industry and the Canadian market. It is not perhaps the kind of free-trade agreement that the purists would have advocated; it is not something that you would find in the textbooks. But it is an important step forward. Indeed, in this imperfect world and given the particular circumstances of Canadian-American relations, it is really a remarkable achievement.

I believe that this Agreement is bound to benefit consumers on both sides of the border. It is possible now for producers to plan their production operations on a more rational basis and to achieve higher levels of efficiency in both their Canadian and American plants.

The net effect on our balance of payments remains to be seen. Certainly, there has already been an enormous increase in the two-way flow of trade in automotive products between our two countries. This will increase as the programme goes forward. One should not focus just on the future course of our automotive deficit with the United States, since many of our exports in this sector go to other countries. On a world-wide basis, I should look for a significant improvement in Canada's import-export performance in this sector. At the very least we have already restrained the rapid growth in the automotive deficit.

It would, of course, be a mistake to read too much into the Agreement. There is no other North American industry quite like the automotive industry and, therefore, the Automotive Agreement, at least in its present form, should not necessarily be looked on as a pattern for other industries. However, there can be no doubt that the successful working of the Agreement will encourage efforts to find new ways and means by which Canadian and United States industry can participate more equally in the North American market. Such solutions could go beyond the conventional processes of mutual tariff cutting; the search will also lie in the direction of finding selective measures that take account of the unique structural features of industrial and corporate relations in particular industries.

As I have already said, the Automotive Agreement had its origin in efforts by Canada to increase its industrial efficiency and thus improve its current-account balance. A new dimension has been added to the Canadian problems by the recent emergence of the United States balance-of-payments problem. Canadians, at least until recently, had not given much thought to the possibility that the United States might ever have to limit its export of capital.

Let me describe what happened when the United States began taking defensive action.

I think we may fairly say that the first major measure adopted by the United States to deal with its balance-of-payments problem, the Interest Equalization Tax, was announced, in mid-1963, without full appreciation of the interdependence of our two countries. As you know, the tax, in essence, was designed to reduce the return of U.S. loan capital placed abroad or, conversely, to increase the cost to the borrower by roughly one per cent.

The reaction to this announcement in Canadian financial circles was one of shocked surprise, quickly followed by serious weakness in the markets. Canadian official reserves of gold and foreign exchange declined by more on the single day of the announcement than on any one day during the Canadian exchange crisis of 1962. It was fairly obvious that the tax would be counted the more successful the less its yield—in other words, even supposing that Canada could bear the added cost of borrowing in the U.S. market, the volume of such borrowing was also in question. Clearly the situation was critical. A team of senior Canadian officials went immediately to Washington. As a result of their discussions with the U.S. authorities, a joint announcement was made that new issues of long-term Canadian securities in the United States would be exempted from the provisions of the tax. That crisis was ended.

The basis on which Canada successfully gained the exemption of its own long-term borrowings from this tax is twofold; first, these Canadian borrowings do not contribute to the U.S. balance-of-payments deficit, and second, there would be no net gain to the United States from reducing them. Roughly speaking, every dollar of capital invested in Canada by U.S. residents flows back into the States more or less immediately in payment for at least a dollar's worth of goods or services imported by Canada from the States. Without any deliberate action on Canada's part, measures such as the Interest Equalization Tax would reduce the U.S. payments surplus in respect of goods and services approximately in proportion to the reduction in U.S. capital outflows. The undertaking given in return for the exemption of long-term Canadian new issues from the Interest Equalization Tax was that Canada would not make use of the exemptions to a greater extent than was necessary to meet its current-account deficit; in other words, that it would not thereby build up its exchange reserves.

The Interest Equalization Tax (IET), and the exemption of long-term new Canadian issues from it, became law in the fall of 1964. Both in anticipation of the enactment and for some time after it, there was naturally a press of Canadian borrowers coming to the U.S. market with issues that had been deferred in the earlier months of uncertainty. A situation of some strain developed in the market, which was, of course, no more in the interest of Canadian borrowers than of the United States authorities. My predecessor as Minister of Finance, therefore, agreed, towards the end of the year, to assist in alleviating this pressure by requesting major Canadian borrowers to defer further offerings of securities in the U.S. market for the time being.

At the beginning of the following year, i.e. at the beginning of 1965, President Johnson announced another defensive action, namely voluntary guide-lines. They were aimed at reducing the extension of short-term credit abroad by U.S. financial institutions, and at encouraging non-financial corporations both to reduce their net transfers of capital abroad and improve their current-account earnings.

These February 1965 guide-lines also applied to non-financial corporations. The 400 or so major industrial and commercial corporations concerned were each asked to achieve a target improvement in their individual foreign payments positions, by any combination of higher exports, lower imports, increased repatriation of earnings, reduced capital outflows for investment, and so forth. Canada was specifically excepted from this target, for the very good reason that any improvement in the position of those corporations *vis-à-vis* Canada would have had to be reflected in increased Canadian borrowings under the exemption from the IET. Canada was not excepted, however, from a request that these corporations should, where possible, repatriate any cash balances they might be holding abroad.

Nor was Canada exempted from any of the provisions of the companion programme of guide-lines applying to banks and other financial institutions, administered by the Federal Reserve. The most important element was the request that banks should limit to a very moderate rate indeed the growth in their short-term credits abroad. Almost equally important to Canada was the request that non-bank financial institutions should observe a similar guide-line in respect of their short-term foreign assets.

The prospect for Canada in 1965, therefore, after these guide-lines were announced, was one of a fairly substantial draining away to the United States of short-term capital at least; and this did, in fact, occur.

The request was certainly complied with, but I don't think we can say that the market, this time, took it in its stride. Considerable doubt and uneasiness was apparent. For two years running, Canadian borrowers had been "warned off" the U.S. market, however understandably and politely, at about the same time of the year and despite the freedom of access implicit in the exemption from the IET. How real and how permanent was that freedom, therefore? (Fortunately, the situation was somewhat clarified soon after.)

Last December saw the introduction of new programmes of guide-lines to reinforce those of February. For the first time, a quantitative limit as well as the interest penalty involved in the IET was placed upon purchases of long-term foreign securities by U.S. investors. (I realize that this limit, like all the guide-lines, is, in fact, voluntary; but it is no more than realistic to suppose that it will be observed, and can be regarded as having almost mandatory force.) At the same time, the programme for non-financial corporations was extended to another 400 companies and reinforced by a specific target for the limitation by each of their direct investment abroad, inclusive of the reinvestment of foreign earnings. The target was to be global in each case, and it was made clear by the U.S. authorities that it was not expected to be allowed to jeopardize specific commitments such as those made in Canada by the U.S. auto manufacturers; but Canada was *not* exempted from the target.

As Minister of Finance I have made it plain to the U.S. authorities and to the Canadian public on several occasions since this last measure was announced that I question both its wisdom and its likely efficacy in relation to Canada, primarily for the same reasons that would defeat any other move by the United States to reduce the outflow of U.S. capital to Canada, i.e. the immediate impact upon the U.S. current-account surplus with Canada. But I will not abuse your hospitality by arguing the point here. What is crucial to the developments that I have been outlining to you is that this measure placed a significant measure of restriction upon the only remaining substantial source of financing for Canada's current-account deficit. If, in these circumstances, the quantitative limitation of new long-term borrowings in the U.S. had indeed been applied to Canadian securities, then I'm afraid we should have had, all too soon, the chance to see demonstrated in practice the interrelation between the United States trade surplus and the outflow of U.S. capital to Canada. I think the outcome would have been at the very least discomforting to the United States; I know that it would have been savagely detrimental to the continued expansion of the Canadian economy.

Fortunately, I am able to report that the machinery of consultation and co-operation between our two countries ensured that this point was fully taken by your own authorities, and that this quantitative guide-line was not applied to Canadian long-term new issues. In return, Canada's original undertaking to stabilize its exchange reserves around the level prevailing at the time the Interest Equalization Tax was first announced was reinforced by an assurance that the Canadian Government would, as necessary, buy or sell its own securities in the U.S. market in order to achieve this.

I wish I could report that all doubts and uncertainties have finally been dispelled by this arrangement, and that the balance-of-payments relation between Canada and the United States has been clearly set upon a course of mutual understanding and support. I am afraid, however, that there have been further moments of concern and misconstruction. Views expressed by members of the U.S. Administration as to the responsibilities of United States international corporations operating abroad have been reported out of context and interpreted as suggestions that they should change their commercial and competitive practices and place the interests of the United States ahead of the interests of the countries in which they operate.

If the quite sharp reaction in Canada to what American ministers were thought to have said has come to the attention of the American public at all, I imagine that it may well have been put down in large part to offended national dignity. I can assure you that, on the contrary, very real and practical considerations underlay the concern expressed.

At the conclusion of the last meeting of the United States – Canada Cabinet Committee on Trade and Economic Affairs held in March 1966, the United States clarified the intention of its guide-lines by including the following in the communiqué:

> The United States members made clear that the U.S. Government was not requesting U.S. corporations to induce their Canadian subsidiaries to act in any ways that differed from their normal business practices as regards the repatriation of earnings, purchasing and sales policies, or their other financial and commercial activities. United States members re-emphasized the view that United States subsidiaries abroad should behave as good citizens of the country where they are located. Where U.S. companies were in doubt as to these views, the U.S. Government would ensure that any misunderstandings would be dispelled.

Canada has now issued a set of guide-lines of its own, regarding the way in which we expect the Canadian subsidiaries of foreign corporations to conduct themselves, amounting, in sum, to an expectation that they will act as good corporate citizens of Canada.

These Canadian guide-lines are intended to clear the air and resolve doubts and confusion that may have existed in the minds of managements of foreign subsidiaries in Canada. It should not detract from their effectiveness in this respect that they contain nothing that has not been stated before, at one time or another, and nothing that is in conflict with the aims of your own balance-of-payments programme. I should suggest, too, that they represent the very minimum that the United States or any other major nation itself expects of corporations operating within its own borders but owned or controlled abroad.

Canada's current-account deficit is not the overnight result of a wild international spending spree by Canadians; it is a part of the present structure of the Canadian economy. Successive measures taken by the

United States have nearly all threatened to reduce that deficit for us, either directly or by cutting off the capital by which it is financed, despite the fact that our deficit represents a surplus for the United States. It is hardly surprising that Canadian political and financial circles have become so sensitive to each and every new move and statement made here in the United States in connection with your balance of payments.

In this respect our Canadian balance-of-payments problem is similar to the American balance-of-payments problem. No country, small or large, is able any longer to treat its external accounts merely as the fortuitous result of internal economic and financial developments. The rest of the world is not prepared to acquiesce automatically in the major adjustments in their own economies which are required to accommodate large deficits or surpluses thrown up by the internal policies of one country. There is general insistence that all countries so order their internal affairs that the interests of their trading partners are given due consideration. This means that for countries whose external accounts are in equilibrium, balance-of-payments considerations are a constraint upon internal policies. For countries whose external accounts are not in equilibrium, balance-of-payments considerations must be elevated to the level of positive policy objectives. Both Canada and the United States are in the latter category.

It is significant that we should both find ourselves faced with the necessity of making balance in our international payments an objective of deliberate policy in spite of the fact that our basic balance-of-payments positions are fundamentally different. We, in Canada, have a large and persistent current-account deficit which other countries are being asked to finance. You in the United States have a large and continuing current-account surplus, and supply by far the major part of long-term capital needs in the world, partly from the proceeds of short-term borrowings from other countries. In spite of the fundamental strength of your position in comparison with ours, you, as well as we, are regarded by an important part of the world as having an unsatisfactory balance-of-payments relation with them. In these circumstances, neither of us can regard ourselves as being in a satisfactory balance-of-payments equilibrium.

18. A New Look at the Canada—U.S. Automotive Agreement

Statement by Mr. Jean-Luc Pépin, Minister of Industry, Trade and Commerce, to the Canadian Automotive Parts Manufacturers' Association in Toronto, October 23, 1968. (Extracts)

As you are aware, we shall again very shortly be discussing the Canada-U.S. Automotive Agreement with the United States Government.* Our neighbors seem to think that Canada has done a little too well out of the Agreement. We in Canada take the view that we have still a long way to go before we have—as indicated in the second objective of the Agreement—a fair and equitable share of the total North American market for automotive products. It will be important to try to bridge this difference of approach during the forthcoming discussions.

Tonight I should like mainly to review what has been achieved and better define the important job which still lies ahead.

"In the beginning" (1964) it was found that the automotive industry, even though it was already one of the most important segments of our economy, appeared to be well below the achievement of its potential sales capabilities. It was considered essential that a plan be devised which would enable the industry to expand its output to a level more in keeping with the market requirements.

As you all know, this concern led the Government to enter into "the" Agreement with the United States in an attempt to eliminate the barriers to trade in automotive products between our two countries.

The Agreement is now working well and, while all the objectives have not yet been fully realized, we have made good progress towards them.

What did the Canadian automotive industry look like in 1964?

The industry was competing with difficulty in its own domestic market, supplying only about half of it: vehicle production was 671,000 units. Average monthly employment in the industry was 69,000 workers. The annual exports in vehicles and automotive parts from Canada amounted to a mere $90 million. Our total automotive trade with the U.S. was only $818 million, and 86 per cent of this was imports. And, closer to home, the factory value of parts shipments was only $627 million.

Where do we stand now?

The industry as a whole has benefited substantially, through the immediate expansion of production which followed the Agreement and the movement which has taken place towards the combination of

---

* See *An Econometric Analysis of the Canada-United States Automotive Agreement: The First Seven Years*, available from The Economic Council of Canada, Ottawa, for a detailed study of the agreement and its results.

the markets of the two countries. You, the auto-parts manufacturers, have been very much a part of this success.

I have been informed that, of the many representations which were made to Ottawa in opposition to this Agreement, one small group of parts manufacturers was most outspoken. "This trade agreement has caused our doom," the group said. "We cannot compete and we are unquestionably faced with closing up shop." It is interesting to note that many of these very manufacturers have since greatly expanded their production and have built new factories.

Another success story relates to the manufacture of automotive frames. Prior to 1964, no frames were made in Canada at all. Today there are two manufacturers. Their production represents, annually, a multi-million-dollar activity, and is currently undergoing a major expansion.

The Canadian automotive industry's overall position is reflected in press comments. I quote:

> Vehicle *production* rises 76 per cent over 1964 to 1.1 million units.
>
> Average monthly *employment* has increased by more than 15,000 workers, with a similar increase in related industries.
>
> Canadian automotive *exports* have risen from $99 million in 1964 to $2.5 billion in 1968 ... an increase of 2,400 per cent.
>
> Total automotive *trade* with the U.S. has risen from $818 million to $5.3 billion between 1964 and 1968.

And, closer to home:

> Annual factory value of parts shipments rises 71 per cent (from 1964 level of $627 million) to $1 billion.

These are impressive achievements, and I do not wish for a moment to minimize them. However, we must not permit any complacency to creep back into the industry.

FUTURE

Impressive as the results have been to date, there is a big job yet to be done. There are rewards available to you through the full achievement of the objectives of the Agreement by way of a still more competitive industry.

As you know, the Economic Council, in its recent review, has predicted for 1975 a vastly expanding Canadian economy, including a much greater market for consumer products. This should further increase the demands that will be placed upon the automobile and parts industry.

What are the needs of the future?

The Economic Council has given us a preview of what could be the picture in 1975: A *gross national product* of at least $100 billion – up from the 1967 level of approximately $65 billion. *Exports should attain* about $25 billion, possibly rising at an average annual rate of over 10 per cent. Personal *transportation* equipment could be the third most important consumer expenditure item (having surpassed clothing and footwear). Consumer expenditure in this sector will have risen from the 1967 level of $2.6 billion to almost $5 billion.

What's in this for you?

Are you making appropriate plans to get the maximum share of this greatly expanding domestic market? Are you making serious efforts to obtain a more equitable share of the total North American market?

We, industry and government, have a responsibility to create the conditions that will facilitate the achievement of these goals. A good economic environment can be fostered by government action, but employers and employees must do the work of industrial growth.

Problems of the Future

Looking ahead, what are the practical problems and hindrances that your group and the entire automotive industry must overcome? Let's mention three: (1) *Investment and growth financing*; (2) *management*; (3) *marketing*.

Investment and Growth Financing: The Canadian automotive industry has invested in the order of $1 billion between 1964 and 1968. It took that much to bring you where you are today.

If I freely interpret the Economic Council's hopes for 1975, I venture to say that it will take *at least* another $1 billion in new investment by 1975, just to enable you to stand still! That's right – $1 billion just to maintain the portion of the North American market which you now have.

In order to achieve a more equitable share of the market, therefore, the Canadian automotive industry investment must be greater – considerably greater! For example, just to have the value of Canadian production match our consumption, a further investment in excess of $2 billion could be required.

The present need for expansion and modernization is not unlike the situation the industry faced back in 1964 (departing, of course, from a higher level). The need for greater product specialization and plant improvement which was emphasized by the Agreement will most certainly continue into 1975, if not permanently. I'm sure that you fully appreciate this and that you will take the necessary steps to meet this challenge as you have done in the past.

To date, the next investment required has largely been met by the industry itself and I am hopeful this trend will continue. In order to complement the industry's efforts in this regard, the Adjustment Assistance Board was formed to provide financial assistance and tariff remission on production machinery to help *all* parts manufacturers to compete in the new market.

As you are all well aware, this Board has been under the capable direction of Dr. V. W. Bladen, whose close association and understanding of the automotive industry is well known. I hardly need to mention his outstanding contribution to both government and industry down through the years.

Since 1965, the Adjustment Assistance Board has granted 73 loans totalling about $60 million. Its tariff-remission activity has granted remissions of approximately $5 million on automotive production machinery and equipment. A further 24 remission applications are still under consideration.

We feel this is proof positive of the Government's efforts to complement those of the industry itself, proof also of the Government's concern in assisting manufacturers to be as competitive as possible by obtaining the most modern equipment available.

As you may be aware, Government programs, including the activities of the Adjustment Assistance Board, are now under review in Ottawa to assess their current status and future relevance. In this regard, the industry's views and recommendations expressed through the Association and its executive have been most welcome and are receiving close consideration.

One more word on marketing. There are many rumours regarding suggestions for a broadening of the Auto Agreement to include a wider range of products. In this regard, we recognize your industry's concern about certain of these suggestions and your views have been helpful in the Government's continuing assessment of this matter.

I wish to assure you that the Government will carefully weigh *all* the ramifications of any proposed changes or additions to the Auto Agreement—always keeping in mind the significant role which has been and will continue to be played by the parts manufacturing industry in the success of the Agreement and in the economy of the country. I presume this is judgment and thoroughness—and, remember, politicians too have to be good managers!

19. The "Nixon Doctrine", August 15, 1971

Transcript of the Press Conference given by Mr. Mitchell Sharp, Acting Prime Minister, East Block, August 16, 1971. (Extracts)

Mr. Sharp: The President of the United States yesterday made a statement which contained four main points. First of all, he announced a wage/price freeze, 90 days; he announced a number of budgetary and tax measures to stimulate the United States economy; he announced the application of a temporary import surcharge up to a maximum of 10% applying to all dutiable imports not already subject to quantitative limitations by the United States; then he announced that the United States had informed the International Monetary Fund that it no longer will freely buy gold for settlement of international transactions; in other words, the United States dollar is not any longer convertible at a fixed price of gold.

As far as Canada is concerned, we recognize that the United States has a very serious problem; a very serious problem quite different from our balance-of-payments problem. It is running a big deficit on overall account; the United States dollar has been weak. They also have the internal problem of inflation, which has been rather more serious even than it has been in Canada; and they have problems of unemployment not unlike problems that we have here in Canada too. We are prepared to co-operate with the United States in trying to bring about a better international monetary system. It is as much in our interest as it is in the interest of the United States, that there should be some basis for international transactions. The United States is a great trading nation and so are we, proportionately even more important in terms of trade's contribution to our gross national product. Therefore, as far as the Canadian government is concerned, we are very anxious to co-operate with the United States in trying to work out better monetary arrangements, throughout the world. Indeed, the Minister of Finance, Mr. Benson, is the Chairman this year of the Group of 10, which is the group of the 10 most important finance ministers in the world and maybe he will want to call a meeting to discuss this very question that has been laid before the world so dramatically by President Nixon.*

As to the particular measures, we are very concerned about the proposal to apply a surcharge on duty with respect to imports not subject to quantitative restrictions into the United States. We made a preliminary estimate of the impact of this upon Canada and it appears that something in the order of 25% of our exports to the United States would be affected by this surcharge. It is very difficult to be precise at this point, but since none of the goods that are freely entering the United States will be subject to the surtax, we can take off a high proportion of our exports for that reason; for example, newsprint is not subject to the surcharge. We can also eliminate our exports to the United States under the Automotive Agreement, since these are not subject to duty and they are exempted. We can also exempt, or at least include, in the exemptions, our exports of oil, since these are subject to quantitative import restrictions into the United States. However, even the 25% is serious. I should make another qualification, that it isn't necessarily 10% in all cases: it is a maximum of 10% subject to a limitation in the Trade Agreement Act of the United States, whereby the result in duty cannot be returned to a level higher than it was before the Trade Agreement process began. So, in some cases, the surcharge will not be as high as 10%.

In his statement, the President made clear that the purpose of this import surcharge, which as I have just said, would apply to something like 25% of our exports to the United States, was to bring about a correction of unfair exchange rates and bring about modifications in discriminatory tariff and non-tariff barriers against the United States. Now, we have had a floating dollar since May of 1970; the Canadian dollar itself has appreciated substantially in value since that time (by some 7%); we do not restrict imports from United States. In the President's own terms, and I would quote from his speech yesterday, he said: "This import tax is a temporary action, not directed against any other country, but an action to make certain that American products will not be at a disadvantage because of unfair exchange rates. When the unfair treatment is ended, the import tax will end as

---

* See SS 71/23 of September 21, 1971 for a more detailed account of the impact on Canada of the "Nixon Doctrine"; also the Prime Minister's statement of August 20, 1971, with background analysis in *External Affairs*, Vol. XXIII, No. 9, September 1971, pp. 326-35.

well." In the President's own terms, the import surcharge should not apply to Canada; and this will be the burden of representations that will be made by the Canadian government to the United States administration within the next few days. A delegation will be leaving some time this week, I hope as soon as it can be arranged, which will be led by a Minister or perhaps more than one Minister and will make representations along these lines as well, of course, as engage in consultations with the United States on the other measures upon which we are very anxious to co-operate.

Q. What is going to happen to the Canadian dollar?

A. Well, judging by what happened on the market today, it is very difficult to tell. The Canadian dollar fluctuated a bit in relation to the United States, but the fluctuations were not large. At one time, the Canadian dollar was strong and other times, it was weaker and I think it ended today a little stronger. But these were very small fractional changes.

Q. Do you foresee any problem that the dollar will rise to parity, that it will go even higher than last week?

A. Well, I don't think that, anymore than U.S. Commerce Secretary Connolly would want to speculate about the future value of the American dollar. This is something that only time will tell, there are factors on both sides. The American actions are designed to strengthen the position of the American dollar and these could offset the obvious weaknesses that have appeared.*

---

* See also Mr. Trudeau's press conferences on the occasion of his visits to Washington, March 25, 1969, and December 7, 1971, the texts of which are available from the Library, Canadian Embassy, Washington. The first is the famous "On sleeping with an Elephant" press conference. It covered such subjects as oil exports to the United States, the implications for Canada of President Nixon's "Safeguard" Anti-Ballistic Missile System, the state of Canadian negotiations with Peking regarding recognition, etc. The second dealt with the "Nixon Doctrine" and temporary U.S. surcharge on imports. The surcharge was lifted on December 19, 1971, after agreement in the Group of Ten (meeting in Washington) that the U.S. dollar would be devalued by 7.9% in terms of gold. The officials, finance ministers, and sometimes the heads of government of the world's main capitalist countries now meet in so many distinct economic groups that it is hard to keep track of them: *The Group of Five* (Britain, France, West Germany, Japan, the U.S.A. – that is, the largest economies); *The Group of Seven* (The Big Five plus Canada and Italy); *The Group of Ten* (the Seven plus Belgium, the Netherlands, and Sweden). Actually Switzerland is now a member of the Group of Ten, which makes it 11!

Q Mr. Sharp, of the $4 billion of Canadian exports which will be possibly adversely affected by the tax surcharge . . .

A. No, I didn't. I said a quarter.

Q. Twenty-five percent.

A. Twenty-five percent, and the figures for 1970 . . . our exports to the United States were in the order of $10.6 billion, so we're talking about something between two-and-a-half and three billion dollars.

B. FOREIGN OWNERSHIP AND TRANSNATIONAL CORPORATIONS IN CANADA

20. Foreign Ownership and the Multinational Corporation*

Statement by Mr. Robert H. Winters, Minister of Trade and Commerce, at the Forty-Second Canadian Purchasing Conference, Montreal, July 10, 1967.

Significant as tariff reduction and trade liberalization negotiations have been in the past, and will continue to be in the future, there is another fact of economic life which I believe will be of increasing importance to the international economic environment of the years ahead: the rise of the multinational company with operations in more than one country. These corporate giants, whose interests are far flung, will, I believe, have great influence on the development of world trade and production in this latter third of the twentieth century. Being in a position to rationalize production in many countries, these supranational companies can provide unequalled opportunities for the ever more rapid economic progress of mankind.

In this modern world, in which the dimensions of space and time and geography are so rapidly shrinking, a narrow nationalist approach is outmoded. In this era of jet travel, it takes hours to transport men and goods over distances that once took months, or even years, to cross. Events on the other side of the planet enter our living-rooms and our awareness within moments of their happening.

---

* See *Foreign Ownership and the Structure of Canadian Industry*, report of the Task Force on the Structure of Canadian Industry, Privy Council, Ottawa, January 1968. This is known as the "Watkins Report", from the name of the chairman of the Task Force, Prof. Mel Watkins, University of Toronto. See also Mr. Pearson's statement of May 19, 1966, to the American Society of Newspaper Editors, Montreal, for further background.

Multinational companies have long existed. But never before have they occupied such a prominent place in the economic affairs of so many nations. The list of companies producing goods and services in half a dozen or more countries is today a long one. Some 200 American corporations have such an international scope of operation; some 30 European; and some Canadian. And rare is the country which has not within its borders a subsidiary of one of the multinational giants.

In Canada alone, the subsidiaries of foreign corporations number in the thousands. But before turning to look at these Canadian subsidiaries let me briefly touch upon the advantages and strengths of the multinational corporation in the world economy.

In essence, these international giants can streamline and expedite the exchange of capital and manpower, of machines and men, of ideas and innovations. Research done in one country can be made rapidly available to many. Managerial techniques and skill and training acquired in one country can be utilized and shared among others.

In part, the strengths of multinational companies can be matched by consortia of smaller companies—particularly in the field of exporting. In my opinion, much more use can be made of this technique, and we are at present studying areas in which further government action might facilitate this channel for developing collective strength by a number of smaller companies concerting together for specific purposes.

Well-managed multinational companies discharging their responsibilities as good corporate citizens have great potential and promise. But they bring with them many problems as well. These giant corporations, and the governments of the nations within whose boundaries they operate, have to adjust to the new concepts and techniques dictated by this product of our changing times. The subtle and difficult problems of the degree of decentralization essential to a worldwide operation must be solved.

National governments will have to update many of their traditional policy concepts. What, for example, do capital flows between nations represent in the era of the multinational company? As one economist has observed, in dealing with these giant international corporations, "it matters less how much capital actually crosses national frontiers, than whether or not this capital has an effect on the 'domestic' sector within the economy".

Exports, too, take on a new meaning as, increasingly, international transactions take place within the framework of a single multinational firm, and as the international operations of a company with headquarters within one nation have a substantial impact on the trading performance of many other nations.

Fiscal policy must be flexible as the incentives or disincentives provided to multinational firms become an increasingly important element in a nation's tax structure. And monetary policy, when capital is acquired more through complex intercorporate linkages, and less on the open market, will have gradually to be reformed to fit the changing circumstances.

National policies cannot ignore the importance of multinational companies. It can make the economic climate favourable or unfavourable for them depending upon whether the government deems them to be harmful to the nation or whether it wishes to utilize their advantages. But, before this can take place, we should gain much more knowledge of the impact of these multinational firms on national economies. And because this question is of particular importance to Canadians, this is what we have set out to do.

The enormous contribution of foreign capital to Canada's economic development cannot be overstated. There is no doubt about the fact that foreign direct investment in Canada has enabled us to achieve a relatively high standard of living much more quickly than we could otherwise have done.

Foreign Capital

Reliance upon foreign capital is by no means new to Canadians. It is deeply rooted in the basic structure of our economy and, since before Confederation, has been an essential feature of our development. Spread over great geographical areas, the utilization of Canada's natural resources has taken tremendous amounts of capital, management initiative and know-how to develop. But because of Canada's sparse population, the domestic supply of these essential nation-building resources has fallen well short of requirements, particularly in times of rapid development. Such a period characterized the Canada of a century ago. In fact the need for foreign capital to maintain the rapid rate of growth was one of the prime reasons for Confederation itself. One important motive leading the British North American colonies to unite was the need to provide a broader, credit-worthier base for foreign borrowing.

The importance of foreign capital to the Canadian economy today can be seen in the magnitudes involved. The most recent estimates indicate foreign interests have a total stake of $33 billion in our economy. Their net investment, allowing for Canadian assets abroad, exceeds $20 billion—nearly twice the total annual value of our exports.

Half this foreign investment is in ownership of Canadian enterprises. It is heavily concentrated in the areas of manufacturing and of mineral production. Foreign-owned companies now account for three-fifths of Canada's manufacturing and mining and three-quarters of our petroleum and natural-gas industries. More than three-quarters of the foreign ownership is in the hands of residents of the United States.

This subject is, therefore, of great interest to Canadians. A committee of the Federal Cabinet has been assigned to the task of searching out and presenting further information. And the Department of Trade and Commerce has, as a result of continuing studies started early last year, undertaken to contribute data for their work. This occasion today provides me with an opportunity to comment briefly upon some of the results of the Department's work.

One primary interest was with the corporate behaviour of foreign-owned subsidiaries in Canada as the activities of these firms—both real and imagined—have been the subject of much debate in recent years.

Three basic fears about the presence of foreign ownership in the national economy have been raised. *One* is that they will create a charge against the country—in the form of repayment of debt and payment of interest and dividend—of unmanageable proportions. While recognizing that any inflow of capital creates a debt (and in our case it is substantial), I must point out that interest and dividends paid abroad amount to only about two per cent of our gross national product—a third of what it was during the 1930s. And, on a *per capita* basis, Canadians invest much more heavily in the United States than Americans do here.

Secondly, it is stated these multinational corporations are used, or could be used, as instruments of political control by a foreign government. There is not time for me to dwell at length on this suggestion. Let me say, however, that what foreign capital does in Canada is a matter for the Government to determine. It is up to us to state the rules of the game and we have done so. But my examination of the situation has led me to believe that, by and large, foreign subsidiaries in Canada conduct themselves as good corporate Canadian citizens. It may be, as Raymond Vernon, Professor of International Trade and Investment at the Harvard Business School, has suggested, more accurate to say that: "As a general rule, the subsidiaries of multinational corporate groups have a special sense of their 'foreignness' and of their vulnerability to criticism and hostility on the part of the local community. Partly for that reason, the subsidiaries of such groups ordinarily appear to be among the better-behaved members of any local business community. Usually, they seem both sensitive and responsive to the formal requirements of national law, to a degree which national enterprises seldom match." I don't disagree with that statement.

Thirdly, it has been suggested that the criteria under which these multinational companies operate are not in the best national economic interest of Canada—that the national economic good is ill-served by an organization which, it is feared, would be prepared to sacrifice national interest to its overall corporate advantage. Here, again, it is the responsibility of the Government to see that this does not happen. But, as part of its programme, the Government must state what criteria are to be followed to make sure the national interest is served.

This we have done through the enunciation of 12 "Guiding Principles of Good Corporate Behaviour in Canada". I stated these principles in a letter to foreign-owned subsidiaries in Canada some 15 months ago. Corporate reaction was requested and from 363 larger foreign-owned companies I asked for some detailed figures concerning their operations and financing so that we might study trends and patterns of corporate behaviour.*

Foreign Subsidiaries

This programme seemed to be welcomed, and the response to it has been impressive. Of the 3,300 companies to which I wrote, more than 2,500 have replied. Many of those not replying are now dormant, are simply nominees, have been merged with other companies or are of a type which could not contribute to our study. Of the 363 major subsidiaries, all but 17 have replied. And I was most gratified to note, the other day, that the Canadian and American Chambers of Commerce recently approved "Fifteen Precepts for Successful Business Operating Procedures in Canada and the United States" substantially embodying the 12 guiding principles we propounded.

---

* SS 67/26 of August 29, 1967, provides an analysis of replies received to Mr. Winters' letter of March 31, 1966, about the Principles.

Many of you, or, at least, many of the companies you represent, will have studied these principles, so there is no need for me to reiterate them here today. Many more of you will have followed the extensive coverage given the results of this survey by the Canadian press. And you will, I am sure, have given some attention to the 75-page report recently released by the Department of Trade and Commerce on 266 of these larger foreign-owned subsidiaries—accounting for two-fifths of all non-financial business done by large firms in Canada.

If you want a detailed analysis of their implications, I am afraid you will have to wait until the Cabinet committee has completed its work. I should say, however, that nothing uncovered so far by the Department or by any independent researchers would indicate there is validity to the charge that foreign ownership *per se* acts against our national interests. Of course, it doesn't prove that every last foreign subsidiary is pure as the driven snow in every particular. But no matter how much work is done, no matter how many studies are produced, there will always be those who maintain that foreign-owned companies as a class are serious offenders against the national interest. We intend to keep the matter under review and point out areas where improvement in corporate conduct is indicated. But our studies to date do suggest that the standard is much better than some people would have us believe.

For example, some have argued that foreign subsidiaries do less than their share of exporting—a claim which, if widely proven, would be of very serious concern to me, as Minister of Trade and Commerce. Some companies do have their sales policies determined at head office and do not export from Canada. But the majority of subsidiaries do export now and some of the remainder indicate they intend to do so. The statistics we now have are the best proof of their performance. We shall continue to encourage the few stragglers, as indeed we do for Canadian-owned companies.

The major foreign-owned subsidiaries, accounting for one-third of this nation's total exports, sell roughly the same proportion of their goods and services abroad as does the whole economy—close to 20 per cent of total output. Many instances were cited where the parent firm had been of invaluable assistance in developing export business for the subsidiary.

Further, these firms show a moderate surplus on their commodity trade with the outside world—just as the overall economy shows a trade surplus. And their overall current and capital receipts just about balance; these subsidiaries are thus paying for themselves without involving an external financing burden for the economy as a whole.

Another expressed fear is that foreign subsidiaries to too great a degree look outside our borders for their sources of materials. I have already expressed my concern about the purchasing policies of all companies in Canada—both domestic and foreign-owned—and, indeed, of individual citizens. The question is whether the conduct of foreign-owned companies varies greatly from that of Canadian-owned companies in this area. Evidence indicates that it does not.

For the first five months of 1967, compared with the same period last year, the healthy 16.5 per cent advance achieved in exports has been about matched by a similar increase in imports. It is this which gives a new urgency to the development and utilization of economic sources of supply in Canada. And it would not be regarded as good corporate behaviour for foreign subsidiaries to discriminate against competitive Canadian suppliers.

In fact, of these larger subsidiaries' total expenditures in 1965 (some $13.5 billion), roughly 40 per cent went to pay Canadian wages and salaries and another 40 per cent to purchases of Canadian goods and services. That amounts to nearly $11 billion spent in Canada.

In their replies to my letter, nearly every company indicated a widespread and purposeful effort toward domestic sourcing. Many companies reported substantial increases in Canadian content in the products they produce. And I was pleased to learn that many of these firms find Canadian suppliers competitive, providing prices and services at a level sufficient to offset the alleged advantages of purchasing from traditional foreign sources of supply.

Greater Domestic Participation

Recognizing the positive contribution of foreign capital to Canada's economic development does not, of course, mean we must not seek greater domestic participation in the expansion of our economy. Canadians will reap a larger share of the proceeds of industrial development to the extent that we participate more fully in the creation and ownership of Canadian industry. The proportion of our new development which we can carry out with Canadian resources is determined first by the rate of growth and secondly by how, and how much, we Canadians choose to devote our resources to industry-building pursuits.

It will not be increased by keeping out foreign capital. On the contrary, it will be diminished. Any reduction of foreign funds into Canadian enterprise would run the risk of slowing up Canada's development, with all the well-known consequential results. The surest way to achieve greater Canadian ownership is to foster, not impede, our economic development; and then to encourage the use of the proceeds from this growth in expanding our own capital resources and developing new enterprise.

Foreign ownership is part and parcel of the growing trend toward the large multinational corporation. This is a fact of life which, if accepted and used properly, can bring great benefits. Whether or not it is used wisely in the economic programme of the nation depends upon the extent to which the Government defines the rules of the game. In the final analysis, it does not matter very much who owns the capital—it is the use to which it is put that counts, and this is a field in which the Government can be the determining influence.

21. The Issue of Foreign Investment

Statement by Mr. Jean-Luc Pépin, Minister of Industry, Trade and Commerce, to the Chamber of Commerce, Victoria, May 8, 1972.

British Columbia, like the rest of Canada, has generally welcomed, as we shall continue to welcome, the addition from the outside of capital, technology, and management to help develop Canadian resources.

Partly because of that "open-door" policy, Canadians have come to enjoy...and take for granted...many advantages—including our high standard of living.

Quite naturally, concern over our ability to direct our own economy has risen along with the degree of foreign ownership.

Most Canadians remain ambivalent on the subject, but, according to one recent survey, almost 44 per cent of us view American ownership of Canadian companies as having an adverse effect on our economy. This compares with 41 per cent two years ago, and 34 per cent three years ago.

Strangely enough, while Ontario is normally considered Canada's centre of "economic nationalism", the same survey found that the greatest anxiety actually exists in British Columbia, where 53 per cent of the public said U.S. ownership was a "bad thing" (University of Windsor, International Business Studies research, sample 5,000 Canadians).

The Federal Government shares this concern—hence the thorough examination, hence the announcement of May 2.

Screening, Another Step

Canada has, in the past, adopted a number of measures to maintain and foster Canadian control.

Foreign investment in banks and other key financial institutions, broadcasting facilities, newspapers and magazines is subject to specific laws effectively keeping them under Canadian control.

On the positive side, the present Government has set up the Canada Development Corporation, which will play an active role in developing strong Canadian-controlled businesses. The previous Government had set up the very successful Panarctic (Panarctic Oils Limited).

The tax reform of last year contained several measures deliberately designed to reach the same objective. I refer, for instance, to the 10 per cent limit on investment abroad by Pension Funds, and to small-business tax advantages available to Canadians only.

Now another step is taken: the screening of takeovers.*

The Policy

Foreign companies seeking to buy out or take over an existing Canadian business above a certain size will be screened.

The purpose will be to examine the proposals; to approve those that, on balance, will bring "significant benefits" to Canada; to negotiate with the proposed acquirer in those cases where he can reasonably expect to make a greater contribution to Canadian development; and to refuse to allow those takeovers that would not bring significant benefits to Canada.

Five factors will be taken into account:

1. the effect of the acquisition on the level and nature of Canadian economic activity and employment;
2. the degree and significance of participation by Canadians;

---

* See *Foreign Direct Investment in Canada*, QP, Ottawa, 1972, known as the Gray Report since it was prepared under the direction of the Honourable Herb Gray, MP.

3.   the effect of the acquisition on Canadian productivity, industrial efficiency, technological development, product innovation and product variety;

4.   the effect of the acquisition on competition within Canadian industry or industries; and

5.   the compatibility of acquisition with Canadian industrial and economic policies.

Some commentators have expressed regret at the generality of these factors. We couldn't help it. Right or wrong, criteria would have had to be too general; if made specific, they could be counterproductive (e.g. money inflow).

Why the Executive Branch?

Some have wondered why screening by the executive branch and not an independent tribunal?

The question to be answered in the screening process is not a legal one at all; it's basically an economic one—with social and political considerations.

Two ways of doing it were left—screening by a board or commission, or by a department. In both cases, the Minister and Government are "responsible", with different degree of autonomy for the instrument. We compromised—there will be an office of takeovers in the department, with a "registrar" leading it.

The office will use the knowledge and judgment of the nine specialized branches of Industry, Trade and Commerce and of other departments, Energy, Mines and Resources, Finance, etc. Had we set up a semi-independent commission, it would have had to create another centre of competence, bringing about costly and unnecessary duplication.

Why Not More Than Takeovers?

Why not extend the screening process to all forms of foreign investment, for example?

It was not judged to be politically practical and economically realistic—in principle by some, or at this time by others.

There was also the problem of administration. The complexities of screening 150 cases a year for "significant benefits" should be easy to imagine.

And there is no single way to increase the control by Canadians on their economy; just a few weeks ago, for example, my Department announced support for management training and for export marketing which will be used mostly by Canadian-owned firms.

How Important Is the Decision to Screen Takeovers?

It has been observed that takeovers represent a fairly small portion of foreign investment, only between 5 and 20 per cent, annually.

I suggest that the establishment of the principle and of the apparatus for the screening of takeovers is a major development. The "standards" applicable to the screening of takeovers will sooner or later influence all foreign ownership. I call that the "exemplary value" of the new system.

Some have argued that the takeover law means little, because foreign firms can still enter the country directly and run a Canadian company out of business. Yes, but this would be done by direct competition, which means that the new company has out-performed, to the advantage of Canadian consumers, the existing Canadian operation. In most cases, there will be room for both.

The Interim Period

Questions have been raised over a possible flood of foreign takeovers occurring before the policy becomes law.

I hope this will not happen. Foreign investors are now well aware of the Government's intentions. Even in recent months, the Government has been voluntarily informed of many proposed acquisitions; I trust that companies contemplating important takeovers during the interim period will keep the Government advised.

While there will always be a wide range of opinion among Canadians about the actual balance between the benefits and costs of foreign investment, there is certainly no disagreement with the proposition that foreign direct investments should work in our best interests. The main purpose of the screening process will not be to block—though there will be some refusals—but to optimize the Canadian interest.

22. Foreign Investment and Energy—Areas of Vital Concern to the U.S. and Canada

Statement by the Secretary of State for External Affairs, Mr. Allan J. MacEachen, to the Center of Inter-American Relations, New York, March 19, 1975. (Extracts)

The United States' large-scale involvement in Canada has been a major postwar phenomenon and had reached the levels I have just cited by the early seventies.* Consequently, we needed to reassess the impact of such a high degree of economic dependence upon a single country, as well as the attendant and similarly lop-sided socio-cultural interaction between our two societies.

This was very much on our minds during the Canadian Government's 1970 foreign policy review; and the impact of an economic relationship with the United States, which is too exclusive, was placed in even sharper focus by the economic measures adopted by the United States administration in August 1971. Two things became gradually apparent to us.

The first is Canada's excessive vulnerability to the impact of the United States—which, some Canadians felt, even undermined the rationale for the existence of Canada as a distinct political entity.

The second conclusion we reached was that, if the Canadian mouse so frequently found herself crowded in bed by the American elephant (to quote Prime Minister Trudeau's metaphor), it was largely because she had failed to seek out other bedpartners. Or, if I may be allowed to coin my own phrase, Canada had puritanically opted for strict monogamy in a polygamous world! We now realize the importance of the European Community. We are seeking to exploit the tremendous opportunities offered by Japan. We should do more in strengthening our relations with developing countries, with Eastern Europe, and with China and the countries of the Pacific basin.

Accordingly, we have sought to pursue in recent years national economic policies that would help to secure greater control over our own economic destiny; and we have devised a diplomatic strategy to diversify our international relations. For example, the Prime Minister of Canada returned only this weekend from a European tour that enabled him to explore areas of mutual interest, both bilateral and multilateral, with the leaders of five member-states of the European Community.

But I want to stress that our foreign policy seeks to supplement, and not to supplant, Canada's long-standing relations with the United States. Similarly, the ultimate goal of our economic policies is to strengthen the Canadian economy and enable us to become more

---

* A reference to the book value of direct foreign investment in Canada of some $26.5 billion in the early 1970s, of which the U.S.A. accounted for roughly 80 per cent.

mature, capable of holding our own in a more balanced, healthier relationship with the U.S.A. For the basic fact of Canada's geopolitical situation is that its links with the United States will always remain the single most important dimension of its foreign policy. Nor do we deplore this fact; despite the greater national awareness of recent years, the Canadian Government is very conscious of the quite extraordinary advantages resulting from Canada's proximity and traditionally close relations with the United States.

Let us consider one specific area of mutual interest and concern—it has to do with investment. I am aware that concern is being voiced in the United States about our foreign-investment review measures. Equally, we are very conscious that Americans are at present by far the largest group of outside investors in Canada. I should like, therefore, to explain the background to, and the nature of, our foreign-investment review measures.

The rapid growth in direct foreign investment in Canada is largely a post-1950 phenomenon. In the period 1950-1970, the book value of direct foreign investment rose from $4 billion to $26.5 billion. Ten per cent of this total investment is held by residents of Britain. Another 10 per cent, roughly, is held by other European countries and Japan. The United States accounts for about 80 per cent.

It is estimated that close to 60 per cent of our manufacturing industries, about half of our mining and smelting, and just over three-quarters of our petroleum and natural gas industries are controlled by residents of other countries. In certain sectors such as chemicals, automobiles, computers, transportation equipment and machinery, the degree of foreign control runs from 80 per cent to over 90 per cent. In fact, the degree of foreign control of industry is much higher in Canada than in any other industrialized country.

Canada's traditional policy towards foreign investment has been an open and receptive one. Unlike many countries, we did not have machinery to monitor and check investment flows. Indeed, Canada encouraged foreign investment as much as possible, recognizing that it was absolutely essential for its economic development.

Today, Canadians are much more aware than they were in the past of both the costs and the benefits of foreign investment. They want to minimize the costs and maximize the benefits to Canada. At the same time, they recognize that, as in the past, foreign investment has an important and necessary contribution to make to future economic growth.

It is against this background that the Foreign Investment Review Act was conceived. It represents an effort to establish more effective control over the economic environment and to obtain greater benefit for Canada, but on a basis that recognizes our need for foreign investment and our obligations to our economic partners in the international community.

The Foreign Investment Review Act applies across the whole economy and provides the Canadian Government with the authority to screen:

1. acquisitions of control of Canadian businesses by foreigners;
2. investments from abroad to set up new businesses; and
3. expansion of existing foreign-controlled firms into unrelated businesses.

The first part of the Act, concerning foreign acquisitions or takeovers, came into effect in April 1974. The other provisions, dealing with the establishment of new foreign-controlled businesses and expansion of existing foreign-controlled firms into unrelated business, have not yet been brought into effect. It may be noted that the powers and interests of the provincial governments are a factor of importance in this context.

The test that any foreign investment faces is whether it is, in the judgment of the Government, likely to be of significant benefit to Canada. The assessment is made on the basis of five criteria:

1. the impact on economic activity, including such factors as employment, the processing of Canadian resources, and the development of exports;
2. the degree and significance of Canadian participation in ownership and management;
3. the effect on productivity, efficiency, and technological development;
4. the effect on competition; and
5. the compatibility with national and provincial industrial and economic policies.

These criteria indicate that the Government is seeking to encourage improved economic performance. That is the main thrust of the review process.

Each case is reviewed on its own merits, every effort being made to be fair and reasonable to the potential investor. The record on the handling of applications supports this view.

Since the coming into force of the Act in April 1974, 121 certified takeover applications have been considered. Of this number, 52 have been allowed, nine disallowed, and 15 withdrawn. The remainder are still under review.

Our policy is to strike a balance between our continuing need for direct foreign investment and our desire, indeed our need, to exercise greater control over our economic environment. Foreign investment is still welcome in Canada; but we want to ensure that this investment will bring significant benefits to our economy. For we believe Canada can offer significant benefits to foreign investors.

I should like now to turn to another field of great and common concern to the United States and Canada: energy, specifically oil and natural gas. I should like to explain the background and direction of Canadian policy in this field.*

First, let me speak about our imposition of a tax on Canadian oil exports to the United States. Although there is now a greater understanding of the Canadian position on the part of the United States Government, there continues to be much public confusion on this matter. When the export charge was instituted in October 1973, Canada was criticized for taking unfair advantage of the sharp rise in world oil prices that began at that time, and of the United States dependence on imported oil. What critics failed to realize is that our self-sufficiency in oil is more apparent than real. We are importers as well as exporters of oil in more or less equal proportions. About half our production is exported to the United States and the other half supplies that part of Canada west of the Ottawa Valley. Consequently, our Eastern provinces are totally dependent on imported oil purchased at world prices. With the increase in world prices, we could hardly continue to export oil to the United States at less than the going price. Also, one of the cardinal principles of our energy policy is that sales abroad must be at world prices. This is essential for an economy that relies to a large extent on the export of natural resources. Consequently, we imposed a tax on oil exports that reflects the difference between the domestic price and the world price. It is intended to ensure that we receive fair market value for our oil. As the domestic price moves upwards in line with the Government's objective of encouraging further exploration and energy conservation, the export charge will be correspondingly reduced.

A problem that has concerned people in the United States is the future volume of oil exports. It recently became evident that the extent of Canada's known reserves was not as great as had been

---

* For background see *Canadian Annual Review of Politics and Public Affairs*, edited by John Saywell, University of Toronto Press, 1974, pp. 90-97, "Federalism and Oil".

previously estimated and that, at the current rate, production would be depleted within a short time. At the same time, it also became apparent that alternate sources, in particular the Athabaska oil-sands, would probably come "on stream" at a slower rate, and a much higher cost, than we had assumed. The Canadian Government, therefore, decided, in the absence of new supplies becoming available, to gradually phase out oil exports over the next ten years—which means, in effect, oil exports to the United States.

We recognize that this policy involves some difficulty for the United States. The decision to phase out our oil exports gradually reflected our awareness of the problems posed for some areas of the United States. But I think you will agree that it would be both economically and politically unsound for the Canadian Government to continue to supply markets beyond its borders at the expense of domestic requirements.

We also recognize, however, that there is a special problem for the oil-refineries in the northern Mid-West states—the so-called "northern tier" . . . which are completely or mainly dependent on Canadian oil. We remember that these refiners were the first customers for our oil in the Sixties. We certainly want to minimize the impact on them of changes in our export capability. We have told the United States Government that we are ready to explore possible ways of alleviating this problem, and indeed discussions are under way. We feel that some accommodation should be made for these refiners.

Natural gas poses another potential problem in our bilateral relations.

On January 1 of this year, the Canadian Government raised the export price of Canadian gas to $1.00 a thousand cubic feet. This step was taken because it was found that Canadian gas was substantially under-priced in United States markets. The Canadian position is that gas exports should be priced in a competitive relationship to other energy commodities in the United States. Also, it has to be understood that inordinately low prices lead only to wasteful use and future shortages. The United States Government has recognized the need for a rise in price. The two governments appear to have adopted similar policy objectives.

The question of volume of export is more difficult. At present Canada sells about 1 trillion cubic feet of natural gas a year to the United States, which amounts to about 40 per cent of Canadian production. The problem is that, given the availability of known reserves, Canada could experience shortages in the near future unless other sources can be brought into production. The National Energy Board is studying this and will be reporting to the Government.*

This whole situation shows how complex and, at times, difficult our bilateral relations have become. In these circumstances, it is all the more important that both sides strive to maintain what is fundamentally a healthy, friendly and mutually beneficial relationship. It is essential that, as appropriate, prior notification, discussion, consultation and negotiation play a central role in the management of relations between the United States and Canada. To this end, it is vital that each country have an accurate understanding of what the other is trying to accomplish, and that each have the opportunity to put forward its own concerns for consideration by the other. That is why I have sought to explain to you Canadian policies on foreign investment and energy, two areas of vital interest to Canada and the United States.

C. DEFENCE

23. NATO and North American Air Defence

Statement to the House of Commons Standing Committee on External Affairs on March 7, 1968, by the Secretary of State for External Affairs, Mr. Paul Martin. (Extracts)

The principal threat to North America, now and for the foreseeable future comes from the growing Soviet arsenal of intercontinental ballistic missiles. Defence against these ICBMs is both technically difficult and enormously expensive, but some progress in missile defence has been achieved in recent years. Members of the Committee will be aware that the United States has recently announced its intention to deploy what it calls a "thin" ABM system directed against China.

The position of the Canadian Government on the proposed missile defence system was stated by the Prime Minister on September 22 at a press conference in these terms, and I quote: "We have no intention at this time of taking part in any such ABM system."

---

* Earlier the problem tended to be just the opposite: Canadian concern about United States controls on imports of Canadian oil. See speech by Energy Minister Greene in Denver, Colorado, May 12, 1970, for background and details.

That is, the "thin" ABM system which was announced by the United States at that time. He went on:

> Naturally, we are keeping the matter under careful review. We do not wish to commit the Government to any particular course of action in the future as to what might be the best solution to the security problem that Canada will face.

While the principal danger to North America comes from the ICBMs, there is also, as the Minister of National Defence has pointed out, a substantial threat from manned bombers. The existing Soviet long-range bomber fleet is not large and it is assumed the number will diminish somewhat over the next decade. But nevertheless it continues to be there, and continues to be a substantial threat. In spite of this diminishing trend, these bombers will continue to pose a serious threat to North America throughout the next decade.

Given this situation, the Government believes it would be irresponsible to ignore such a threat, particularly when it is technically and financially practical to defend against it. For these reasons, the Government will, of course, have to continue to co-operate with the United States in the defence of the continent against bombers.

There are those who would like to think that, by keeping to ourselves, we in Canada could avoid both becoming a target in our own right and being involved in an attack on the United States. Apart from any obligation we might feel to contribute to the defence of North America, this view ignores the fact that Canada is located geographically along the main path which any Soviet—and indeed Chinese—attack against the United States would be likely to follow. Even if there was no intention of attacking Canada, there would always be the possiblity that an accident or miscalculation would result in nuclear weapons coming down on Canadian territory, as well as the danger from fall-out resulting from nuclear explosions over targets in the United States.

Apart from this, it is difficult to imagine that in attacking the United States an enemy would allow Canada to remain as a willing— or even unwilling—asylum for the United States population as well as a reservoir of food, arms, electric power and industrial capacity.

We cannot prudently do otherwise than assume that a potential attacker would expect Canada to be sympathetic to the United States and thus likely, in the event (God forbid) of a nuclear attack, to lend assistance if we were capable of doing so. He would never believe he could ignore this possibility, and I think he would be right. Now I must say that my own view is that the dangers of aggressive war are remote (perhaps one could say unlikely), but no government is worthy of the trust given to it by the people of the country which it serves if it does not realistically examine the situation in the world in which it finds itself, and we have had within the last six months at least one situation that must have caused any government to realize that there are some precautions that it must take in its own security interests.

There are, of course, several ways in which Canada could play a useful part in North American air-defence arrangements. One possibility would be for us to provide from our own resources the portion of the continental air-defence system which needs to be located in Canada. This would be a very large portion of the whole and would necessitate an outlay of financial and personal resources which we believe to be beyond our capacity.

Another possibility would be to leave the entire burden for North American bomber defence to the United States, but give them unlimited access to Canadian air-space and Canadian bases for both training and operational purposes. This would keep the cost to Canada to a minimum but it would tend to erode our sovereignty as well as any influence we could otherwise have on the development of air-defence policies—policies which would inevitably have a significant impact on us.

A third possibility is to share the task of North American bomber defence with the United States on an appropriate basis. This co-operative approach is the one which has been followed in all our defence relations with the United States since the beginning of the Second World War, and, in the view of the Government, is the one which makes the most sense as far as continental air defence is concerned, given the disadvantages of the other alternatives.

I would just like to say by way of parenthesis at this point that the arrangements for continental defence made between the Government of Canada through the Department of National Defence and its opposite number in the Government of the United States are not part of the NORAD structure. The NORAD structure does not involve a commitment of Canadian resources. It involves simply participation in a common command structure and in the planning process.

To preserve basic Canadian interests while participating in joint defence activities with a partner as powerful as the United States, it has been necessary to develop certain principles to govern our approach to specific problems. Over the years there has been mutual understanding that co-operative defence projects in either country should:

a) be agreed to by both Governments;
b) confer no permanent rights or status upon either country and should be without prejudice to the sovereignty of either country;
c) be without impairment to the control of either country over all activities in its territory.

In addition to these three principles, it has been found that, for a variety of reasons, the actual provision of the necessary manpower and equipment can best be handled through individual national contributions made on an *ad hoc* basis as requirements are defined.

Of course, if forces from the two countries are to be employed, it is essential to have satisfactory arrangements to ensure that they can be effectively utilized in time of need. One way of doing this is to co-ordinate respective national command and control elements. This formula was employed in the North American air-defence field prior to 1958 but it was found to be inadequate in circumstances where an immediate reaction to minimum warning of attack is essential.

If co-operation between the air-defence forces of both countries is to be effective, it is necessary to have a single air-defence plan, previously approved by the national authorities of the two countries, and an integrated command and control system. For the past ten years these requirements have been satisfactorily met by NORAD. We ourselves are now in the process of negotiation and consideration of this matter.

One of the major advantages of the NORAD arrangement, which was entered into by the previous Administration in the summer of 1958, apart from making the most effective use of the available air-defence forces of both countries, has been the opportunity it has provided for Canada to play a role in the formulation of continental air-defence policy. Canada has provided the Deputy Commander in Chief and senior operations officers in the NORAD headquarters, as well as the Commander of the Northern NORAD Region and the Commanders of two NORAD divisions, including one in the United States. Plans are jointly drawn up by officers of the two countries and must be approved by both Canadian and United States authorities. United States thinking naturally plays a major part, but it is not by any means exclusive. The authority of the Commander in Chief NORAD in all respects is jointly determined by the two Governments. It is also perhaps worth noting again that the NORAD system is exclusively defensive in nature and cannot possibly be used for any purpose apart from the defence of North America.

The NORAD Agreement will lapse on May 12 unless it is renewed. The Government is currently, as I said a moment ago, giving careful consideration to this Agreement.

To the United States, partnership for the defence of our respective homelands is an important manifestation of the basic friendship between the two countries, which enables us to speak frankly and to differ with the United States in other areas where such vital interests are not at stake. If we are seen to be doing our part in the defence of this continent, we are in a stronger position to express our views on other issues where we may disagree. In summary, I would like to make the following points. Canada is involved in a threat to this continent from manned bombers which no responsible government can ignore. In this situation, there are three choices open to us:

a) We could accept responsibility for providing all of the facilities and undertake all of the activities required in Canada for effective continental bomber defence. In our judgment this is beyond the financial capacity of this country.

b) We could permit the United States to assume controlling responsibility for the entire task both in the United States and Canada. This would involve a surrender of sovereignty which this Government is not prepared to contemplate.

c) We can share the task of continental defence on an appropriate basis.

This third choice provides for effective defence within our means, while fully protecting Canadian sovereignty. The NORAD arrangement is based on the principle of shared responsibility for continental air defence, but by itself renewal of the Agreement would not be a commitment of specific forces and equipment.

As I said earlier:

"This is achieved through *ad hoc* arrangements between the two Governments as the need arises."

Based upon what I would think anyone would agree to was an elementary principle—namely, that in our own defence interests we have to have arrangements made with our neighbour for continental defence and the defence of our own country.

24. Renewal of the NORAD Agreement, March 30, 1968

On March 30, notes were exchanged in Washington between representatives of the Canadian and U.S. Governments for the purpose of renewing the NORAD agreement for a period of five years. The original agreement, which was concluded in 1958, was due to expire on May 12 of this year.*

The U.S. note was signed on behalf of the Secretary of State by Mr. John M. Leddy and the Canadian reply was signed by Mr. A. E. Ritchie, Canadian Ambassador in Washington.

The renewal was made subject to the provision that a review of the agreement might be undertaken at any time at the request of either party and that it might be terminated by either government after such a review, following a period of notice of one year.

The exchange of notes also stipulates that the agreement would not involve in any way a Canadian commitment to participate in an active ballistic missile defence.

The following are the texts of the two notes.

U.S. Note

Excellency,

I have the honor to refer to discussions in the Permanent Joint Board on Defence and elsewhere regarding the mutual interest of the United States and Canada in the continued co-operation between the two countries in the strategic defense of the North American continent. In particular, these discussions have concerned themselves with the North American Air Defense Command established on August 1, 1957, in recognition of the desirability of an integrated headquarters exercising operational control over assigned air defense forces. The principles governing the organization and operation of this Command were set forth in the Agreement between our two Governments dated May 12, 1958. That Agreement provided that the North American Air Defense Command was to be maintained in operation for a period of ten years.

The discussions recently held between the representatives of our

---

* The Agreement was extended without alteration for a further two years from May 12, 1973. See CTS 1971/17. See also SS 73/11 of April 13, 1973, for an analysis of the military considerations behind the renewal, as outlined by the Minister of National Defence to the House of Commons Standing Committee on External Affairs and National Defence. See also the text of Prime Minister Trudeau's press conference, Washington, D.C., March 25, 1969, regarding his talks with President Nixon on defence, particularly as regards anti-ballistic missile (ABM) policy.

two Governments have confirmed the need for the continued existence in peacetime of an organization, including the weapons, facilities and command structure, which could operate at the outset of hostilities in accordance with a single air defense plan approved in advance by the national authorities of both our countries. In the view of the Government of the United States, this function has been exercised effectively by the North American Air Defense Command.

My Government therefore proposes that the Agreement on the North American Air Defense Command effected by the exchange of Notes, signed at Washington, D.C. on May 12, 1958, be continued for a period of five years from May 12, 1968, it being understood that a review of the Agreement may be undertaken at any time at the request of either party and that the Agreement may be terminated by either Government after such review following a period of notice of one year.

It is also agreed by my Government that this Agreement will not involve in any way a Canadian commitment to participate in an active ballistic missile defense.

If the Government of Canada concurs in the considerations and provisions set out above, I propose that this Note and your reply to that effect shall constitute an agreement between our two Governments, effective from the date of your reply.

Accept, Excellency, the renewed assurances of my highest consideration.

> For the Secretary of State
> John M. Leddy

March 30, 1968.

Canadian Note

Sir,

I have the honour to refer to your Note of March 30, setting out certain considerations and provisions concerning the continuation of the Agreement between our two Governments on the North American Air Defence Command effected by the exchange of Notes of May 12, 1958.

I am pleased to inform you that my Government concurs in the considerations and provisions set out in your Note, and further agrees with your proposal that your Note and this reply, which is authentic in English and French, shall constitute an agreement between our two Governments effective today.

Accept, Sir, the renewed assurances of my highest consideration.

(Signed) A. E. Ritchie

March 30, 1968.

D. THE THIRD OPTION

25. Canada and the United States—The "Third Option"

Statement by the Secretary of State for External Affairs, Mr. Mitchell Sharp, to the Canadian Institute of International Affairs, Toronto, November 18, 1972. (Extracts)

Let me now turn to our relations with the United States. Here I think the present state of play may be somewhat clearer, because the Government's position has been placed on the record with considerable care recently.

To begin, I hope that, if you have not done so already, you will obtain a copy of the special issue of *International Perspectives* that appeared on October 17. This issue was entirely devoted to my article entitled "Canada-U.S. Relations: Options for the Future". The article represents some of the main assessments and conclusions of a series of studies that had been in progress for about a year in the Government, to which both my Cabinet colleagues and officials of the Department of External Affairs contributed. If you wish to acquaint yourselves with the Government's basic approach to Canada-U.S. relations, I urge you to read this article.*

The studies on which the article is based were begun in the mood of questioning that followed the announcement of President Nixon's new economic policy in August 1971. I shall try to summarize the main lines of its argument. In the face of the inherent pull of continental forces, the article identifies three options for Canada in the future development of our relations with the United States. They are:

a) Canada can seek to maintain more or less its present position in relation to the United States with a minimum of policy adjustments; or

---

* Available from either QP or DEA, Ottawa. See also the "Report on Canada – United States Relations", July 27, 1970, printed in *Proceedings*, No. 33, House of Commons Standing Committee on External Affairs and National Defence.

b) Canada can move deliberately towards closer integration with the United States;

or

c) Canada can pursue a comprehensive long-term strategy to develop and strengthen the Canadian economy and other aspects of its national life and in the process to reduce the present Canadian vulnerability.

The first option—maintaining the present position in relation to the United States with a minimum of adjustment—would involve pursuing the same general trade and industrial policy to which we are accustomed. There would continue to be a large degree of laissez-faire in our economic policy. The multilateral, most-favoured-nation approach would continue to rule in trade policy. We would go on trying to get better access to United States markets, to maintain some form of special relation with the United States. Industrial development would continue to be export-oriented to a considerable degree. Exports generally would still be dominated by commodities and semi-processed goods. No doubt we should continue trying to diversify our exports while avoiding so far as possible any greater degree of dependence on United States markets. We should try also to obtain more employment in Canada through a greater degree of processing of Canadian commodities. But this would be essentially a pragmatic option. We should deal with the issues as they arose, and not concern ourselves greatly about where the broad tendency of our policy was leading us, or whether the various parts of our policy were guided by a single sense of direction and purpose.

How well would this option work for us in practice? That would depend on the relative success we had in maintaining our position in United States and other markets. The costs of this option would vary accordingly. But suppose we take an optimistic view. Suppose the United States does not turn protectionist, and suppose an open world-trading system brings Canada success in other markets as well. We might pursue this option for some time with apparent success. But the fact is that the continental pull has a momentum of its own. Therefore there is a risk that, in pursuing this purely pragmatic course, we should be drawn more and more into the United States orbit. And remember, even this is on optimistic assumptions. In appearance, we should be following a policy intended at least to maintain, if not improve, our present relative position. But in fact, we might be falling behind.

The second option would be closer integration. This could mean many things. It could mean more arrangements like the Auto Pact, confined to particular industries. These arrangements, we know, have advantages. But they create difficulties too. They could put us at a bargaining disadvantage both with the United States and with other trading partners. We might come to the conclusion that something more extensive was necessary—a free-trade area or even a customs union. Either of these would lock us permanently into arrangements with the United States that, in themselves, might appear to be to Canada's material advantage. But would they increase our independence?

In fact, were we to pursue this option, we might be forced to the conclusion that the only way we could compensate for the overwhelming economic power of our partner would be to opt at the same time for some form of political union. In this way, we should seek to obtain maximum direct influence over the economic decisions that affected us.

I have pursued the logic of this option to the point where its difficulties will be plain to you. It has undoubted attractions in material terms. There is a sort of parallel in it to the movement towards European unity. But the parallel breaks down on examination. There is a world of difference between the internal balance which can result from economic and political union of a number of European societies, which positively desire to overcome old enmities through union, and the internal balance which would result from the union of two North American societies, one of which is so immensely powerful that the other must struggle to maintain its distinctiveness.

And all of this is without asking whether either Americans generally or Canadians generally would want union. I should not try to predict what the reaction might be in the United States. In Canada, I should expect almost any form of closer integration to arouse more opposition nowadays than proposals of this kind have in the past; and I should expect the opposition to come from all parts of the country.

The third option would be to decide that, over time, we should work to lessen the vulnerability of the Canadian economy to external shocks, especially those from the United States. Our purpose would be to recast the Canadian economy to make it more rational and more efficient as a basis for Canada's foreign trade. The basic nature of the economy would remain unchanged. The option would mean encouraging specialization, rationalization and the emergence of strong Canadian-controlled firms. Our domestic base, a prosperous nation of 22 million, should be adequate to produce efficiency in all but the most complex and capital-intensive industries. We should still depend for a great deal of our national wealth on our success in exporting goods and services. But we should deliberately broaden the range of foreign markets in which we could successfully compete. We might also find that Canadian firms could provide a higher proportion of our domestic needs—not because we were deliberately trying to reduce our dependence on imports but simply because they were the most competitive suppliers. There would be no question of retreating from our fundamentally liberal trading policies into protection, or of abandoning the most-favoured-nation principle in trade agreements with the United States or other countries.

This option would require close co-operation of government, management and labour. It would require, as well, the close co-operation of all levels of government. Since the option involves a deliberate strategy, some degree of planning would be involved. But, considering the wide range of government involvement in the economy already, I doubt whether this option would radically alter relations between government and business. Working out the required consensus between the Federal Government and the provinces would require close consultation, but I see no reason why this need lead to friction. On the contrary, the basic harmony of federal and provincial objectives in industrial development could widen the area of federal-provincial co-operation.

Much the same could be said of the cultural dimension. The kinds of policy instruments required to support an independent and flourishing national culture already exist. What may be necessary is the extension of policies that have already proven their worth to sensitive new areas created by the age of mass communication.

These, then are the three options. Now that you know what they are, I can make some general comments on them.

First, options are not policies. They provide a framework within which policy decisions can be taken. They can give a basic orientation to policies. But they are not policies themselves. Within the limits of any one of these options, quite a wide range of different practical measures could be adopted. Depending on circumstances, quite different policy "mixes" could be consistent with the option in question. All the option gives you is the sense of direction in which you want to be heading.

Even this may overstate the case. There is a real difference between the first option on the one hand and the second and third on the other. The first is not really a strategy at all. It is reactive. It involves waiting on events. It means facing individual issues as they arise, and deciding these issues on their own merits, not in relation to some larger purpose. In this sense, it does not pretend to tell you where you are going. The second and third options, by contrast, involve choosing a goal, acting rather than reacting, and judging individual issues in relation to the goal chosen. In the case of the second option, the goal would be integration with the United States in some form; in the case of the third option, the goal would be an economy and culture less vulnerable to the continental pull.

All three options are, of course, abstractions. Like all abstractions, they tend to simplify complex matters. But the distinctions they draw between the various courses open to Canada are basically valid and useful. None of these options is a straw man, set up only for the sake of being knocked down. Nor is this a case of three alternatives, of which two are plainly unacceptable extremes and the third merely a compromise with no virtue other than the fact that it is a compromise. On the contrary, each option has a perfectly respectable argument that can be made for it. Each has to be thought through in its own right. And you will find that the article on Canada – United States relations tries to pursue the logic of each option in a detached and dispassionate way; it gives a fair picture of the implications in all three cases.

The Government has given these options careful consideration. The published article on Canada – United States relations in fact represents the distillation of a number of discussions in the Cabinet and studies by officials. This process has been going on for the better part of a year. The Government's conclusion is quite clear: our choice is Option Three. We believe that Option One, the pragmatic option, runs a serious risk over time of weakening Canada's relative position. We believe that Option Two, the option of integration, is unacceptable for a variety of reasons. In the Government's view, the best choice for Canada is Option Three: to pursue a comprehensive long-term strategy to strengthen the Canadian economy and other aspects of our national life and in the process to reduce the present Canadian vulnerability.

The Third Option, then, demands some additional comments. To begin, let me repeat: an option is not a policy: it only gives a sense of direction to policies. Some of these policies already exist. Others remain to be worked out in the mutually supporting fields of fiscal and monetary affairs, trade, competition and foreign ownership, science and culture. Under Option Three, we shall have a permanent test for each policy instrument we devise; what will it do to strengthen our economy and reduce its vulnerability? And we shall be compelled to examine each policy instrument in relation to the others, because each will be intended to support and reinforce the others. The proof of the pudding will be the kind of industrial strategy we pursue, the kind of energy policy we adopt, and so on. But the result will not be anything it would be sensible to call "Canada's United States policy". The emphasis of the Third Option is on Canada—on decisions that have to be taken in this country by Canadians—rather than matters to be negotiated with the United States. Deciding about Option Three means deciding what sort of Canada Canadians want to have. To borrow the language of the foreign policy review, it means ensuring our continued freedom to develop in our own way through a judicious use of Canadian sovereignty.

Thus the option is in no way an anti-American option. It implies no hostility to the United States. It assumes continuing friendship. Its object is to lessen Canadian vulnerability over time. This means two things: that, especially in an age of interdependence, it will be impossible to make Canada totally invulnerable to continental pressures and unrealistic even to try; and, second, that whatever success we have will be achieved not overnight but over time. So there will be no sudden break in the pattern of Canada's relations with the United States. Nor, even in the long run, will the relation cease to be unique in the world in its closeness and complexity. It is entirely consistent with this option that Canada and the United States will go on being each other's best customer by a wide margin. There may even be particular areas of our exports where the United States market will become relatively more important than is the case even today. But this will not be a factor of increased dependence; it will be a factor of the competitive success of export-oriented Canadian firms too well established to create fears of increased Canadian vulnerability. The economic relation between Canada and the United States will continue self-evidently to be a special relation in its scale and intimacy, but perhaps less so in the sense of demanding special arrangements to ensure that it functions well.

This, then, is how the Government proposes to approach Canada's relations with the United States. Obviously I have been speaking about a complex process that could only unfold over a period of months and years. Many policy decisions will be involved. Some of these decisons have already been taken; others are matters for a relatively remote future. But some are matters of immediate concern. I think you can count on seeing this reflected in the program the Government presents to Parliament at the opening of the new session.

E. AIR AND WATER POLLUTION

26. Transboundary Water Problems—Niagara*

Text of letter dated April 11, 1968, from Mr. A. D. P. Heeney, Chairman, International Joint Commission, to Mr. Marcel Cadieux, Under-Secretary of State for External Affairs.

International Joint
Commission

Commission
Mixte Internationale

April 11, 1968

Dear Mr. Cadieux,

I have the honour to report to you the development by the International Joint Commission of a new and promising procedure in the discharge of the Commission's growing responsibilities in the field of transboundary air and water pollution between the United States and Canada. I refer to the "pilot" public international meeting conducted by the Commission at Niagara Falls, New York, on January 16 and 17, 1968, with regard to the pollution of the Niagara River.

The Commission has long served as the chosen instrument of the two Governments to deal with transboundary pollution. Article IV of the 1909 Boundary Waters Treaty, which established the Commission, contains a solemn pledge that "the waters herein defined as boundary waters and waters flowing across the boundary shall not be polluted on either side to the injury of health or property on the other". One of the earliest References to the Commission, on August 1, 1912, requested an investigation into the extent of boundary waters pollution. The Commission reported on September 10, 1918, that the entire stretch of boundary waters, with the exception of the Great Lakes beyond their shore waters, was polluted and that conditions existing in the Detroit and Niagara Rivers especially were in clear contravention of the treaty. The Commission recommended in its 1918 report that it

---

* On January 16 and 17, 1968, the International Joint Commission held a public meeting in Niagara Falls, New York, to review progress in both countries toward the control of the pollution of the Niagara River. In the following letter to the Under-Secretary of State for External Affairs, the Commission reports on the results of the meeting and on its intention to take similar action in other areas where transboundary pollution has become a source of concern.

be given jurisdiction to regulate and prohibit such pollution; but although the two Governments considered this suggestion and even went so far as to exchange drafts of a convention on the subject, nothing further was done until 1946.

In that year the two Governments asked the Commission to conduct a new investigation into the pollution of the Great Lakes connecting channels, comprising ultimately the St. Mary's and St. Clair Rivers, Lake St. Clair, and the Detroit and Niagara Rivers. In its report of October 11, 1950, the Commission recommended that the continuing problem of pollution of these waters be dealt with by adoption of criteria specified as "Objectives for Boundary Waters Quality Control", and in addition that the Commission be vested with supervisory jurisdiction to oversee the achievement of these "Objectives". The two Governments accepted these recommendations as a means of complying with their treaty undertakings, and in the ensuing years the "Objectives" have served as a model for the formulation by Federal, State and Provincial authorities of their own water quality standards. For its part the Commission has kept abreast of abatement progress through regular reports from international advisory boards appointed by the Commission for this purpose and has taken followup action when required.

In recent years the Commission's responsibilities in the field of transboundary pollution have increased significantly in scope and complexity. For example, on October 7, 1964, the two Governments asked the Commission to investigate the pollution of Lake Erie, Lake Ontario and the International Section of the St. Lawrence River. On September 23, 1966, the Commission was given a new Reference charging it with the responsibility of inquiring into the extent of air pollution across the international boundary, beginning with the Port Huron—Sarnia and Detroit—Windsor areas but extending ultimately to other areas where the Commission may determine there is a serious problem. When the Commission has concluded its comprehensive investigations now under way pursuant to these two References, it will have to consider what remedial measures to recommend to Governments and in particular whether it should propose a continuing supervisory role for itself and if so on what terms.

It is in this context that the Commission's experience of the last few months with pollution of the Niagara River may prove instructive.

The Niagara River has long been seriously polluted. The Commission in 1918 reported that the waters below the Falls showed "an intense pollution from shore to shore and from the surface to the bed of the stream". In 1950 the Commission found "progressive overall degradation" of the waters in the connecting channels from pollution sources culminating in heavy industrial and municipal waste discharges on the upper Niagara River. The current and still unsatisfactory condition of the river is described in the October 1967 Summary Report of the Commission's Lakes Erie-Ontario Advisory Board, a copy of which is attached for your information. As if to highlight the continuing seriousness of the situation described in this Summary Report, the Commission has just learned from its Advisory Board that the 1968 spring flushout of the Buffalo River has carried an unusually heavy discharge of oils and other concentrated wastes into the Niagara River, causing a substantial number of duck kills.

The condition of the Niagara River below the Falls, particularly discolouration of the water and occasional distressing odours, is offensive to local residents on both sides of the border and also to the three million tourists who annually visit the Falls from every State and Province in the two countries and from many foreign countries. Their concern, which is often given sharply critical voice, is symptomatic of broad and growing public insistence on restoring the quality of our common North American natural environment. This popular pressure, of relatively recent growth, has brought new urgency to the pollution-control efforts of Federal, State and Provincial authorities in both Canada and the United States, and at the same time has cast into clearer relief the special contribution that has been and can continue to be made by the International Joint Commission.

On the United States side, where the principal sources of the pollution of the Niagara River are located, there has been a recent profusion of new laws and regulations by both Federal and State Governments. The 1965 New York State Pure Waters Program, funded by a billion-dollar bond issue, includes stream standards and abatement schedules which have been submitted to and approved by the Federal Water Pollution Control Administration pursuant to Federal law. For the Niagara River, the approved standards are based upon the Commission's 1950 "Objectives" and in some respects are more demanding.

Section 206 of the Federal Clean Water Restoration Act of 1966 provides in addition for direct federal enforcement measures to be taken in the case of pollution from United States sources which endangers the health or welfare of persons in a foreign country, but this section is applicable only to a foreign country which extends reciprocal rights to the United States. Moreover, the law as written purports to confer on the foreign country the status of a "State water pollution control agency", which makes its enforcement procedures something less than truly international.

Section 206, however, explicitly subordinates its procedure to the provisions of the 1909 Boundary Waters Treaty.

In Canada the primary responsibility for pollution control resides in the Provincial authorities. The Ontario Water Resources Commission Act of 1957 empowered the OWRC to deal comprehensively with industrial and municipal waste, and it has issued regulations and directives thereunder. Ontario and New York officials have worked closely together on the Niagara River to compare stream data and water quality objectives with a view to concerting their efforts along the international boundary.

It is here that the Commission has been able to play a role that is perhaps especially useful; namely, that of bringing together the pollution-control authorities in the relevant jurisdictions on both sides of the border and working with them towards the common objective of a satisfactory environment. Nothing better illustrates this function than the composition of the Commission's Lakes Erie-Ontario Advisory Board; chaired on each side by an official of the respective federal pollution-control agencies, its membership includes also the Deputy Commissioner in charge of New York's Pure Waters Program and the General Manager of the Ontario Water Resources Commission. It is these knowledgeable and responsible officials who submitted the Summary Report attached to this letter.

In the past the Commission has usually acted on Board reports by issuing citations to particularly delinquent industries and municipalities or by conferring privately wth responsible pollution-control authorities to urge acceleration of abatement programs. This time the Commission decided to go further and to draw on an aroused public opinion as a spur to pollution-control efforts. In late October the Commission released the Summary Report and announced that an international meeting open to the public would be held in January to review the adequacy and effectiveness of existing programs and to consider ways of ensuring that these programs are successful.

The response was gratifying. The Commission heard testimony or received written statements from 26 persons, including Federal, State, Provincial and local elected representatives, officials of pollution-control agencies at all levels of government, industry spokesmen and interested private citizens and associations; 30 additional representatives of these various groups registered their attendance. Because of the nature of the problem, a great deal of time was devoted to close questioning of the New York State representative about the detailed functioning of the Pure Waters Program. But the two volumes of transcript and associated papers, on file with and available for inspection at the Washington and Ottawa offices of the Commission, also disclose far-reaching discussion of many matters not dealt with in the Summary Report: emerging evidence of degradation of Lake Ontario at the mouth of the Niagara River, future problems of thermal pollution associated with nuclear and conventional power plants, the difficulties of coping with major oil spills of the *Torrey Canyon* type, and a variety of other questions. The Commission expects to be considering these issues in the course of its investigation of Lakes Erie-Ontario and the International Section of the St. Lawrence River, and will at the appropriate time have specific recommendations to make to the two Governments.

As to present conditions on the Niagara River itself, the Commission has reached the following major findings and conclusions:

Findings

1. International pollution, caused principally by sources on the United States side, exists in the Niagara River to the detriment of water uses in both countries including public water supply, fish and wildlife, recreation and aesthetic enjoyment.

2. The Commission's 1950 water quality "Objectives" are not met in various portions of the river. Furthermore, in some respects the "Objectives" are inadequate and should be up-dated to reflect advances in the state of the art and to produce truly satisfactory water quality.

3. New York State, as the jurisdiction with primary enforcement responsibility, has developed a comprehensive Pure Waters Program including detailed effluent requirements and timetables on the Niagara River, and these standards have in turn been approved by the United States Secretary of the Interior.

4. Barring major inflation or diversion of available financial resources, the abatement program established for the Niagara River should—if effectively enforced—bring the quality of its waters progressively into satisfactory condition by the end of 1972.

5. It is essential that sufficient flexibility be maintained to augment existing abatement programs so as to meet new demands on or threats to water quality as they arise.

Conclusions

1. New York State is providing a constructive example of the initiatives that can be taken to meet growing public demand for restoring the quality of our natural environment. It is essential that the United States Federal Government join in this effort by appropriating the authorized federal share of the cost of these programs.
2. The lessons learned from this public international meeting will be helpful to the Commission's Advisory Boards in completing the task assigned to them of recommending improvements to the Commission's 1950 "Objectives".
3. There is at present no occasion for the convening of an enforcement conference on the Niagara River under Section 206 of the U.S. Clean Water Restoration Act of 1966. At the same time the two Governments should continue to consult together about harmonization of national laws or other means of fulfilling the pledge contained in Article IV of the Boundary Waters Treaty of 1909.
4. The Commission intends to augment its monitoring of the achievement of water quality objectives on the Niagara River in two ways. First, it will ask its Lakes Erie-Ontario Advisory Board to review with the New York State authorities on a regular basis the detailed composition of the effluent discharged by each industrial and municipal plant covered by an enforcement order, to compare these data with the effluent criteria and timetables established for each such plant, and to advise the Commission as to which if any of such plants are doing less than possible to meet the established schedules and to improve pollution control in the interim. Second, the Commission intends to hold another comprehensive public international meeting no later than July 1, 1970, to assess the progress of abatement programs and to advise the two Governments at that time whether the forecast completion date at the end of 1972 will be met.

A more general and "institutional" conclusion drawn by the Commission is that the technique of enlisting informed public support for abatement measures, through such procedures as the release of special Advisory Board reports and the convening of public international meetings, greatly strengthens the hand of the Commission in exercising the supervisory jurisdiction with which it has in the past and may in the future be entrusted by the two Governments. Thus the Commission is pleased to be able to report its development of a procedure which promises to add new effectiveness to its functions in the field of both air and water pollution.*

This communication has been reviewed and approved by the Commission as a whole at its meeting of April 8-11, 1968. An identical letter is being sent by the Chairman of the United States Section to the Under-Secretary of State.

Yours sincerely,
(signed) A. D. P. Heeney,
          Chairman.

27. Transboundary Water Problems – The Garrison Diversion

Statement by the Secretary of State for External Affairs, Mr. Allan J. MacEachen, to the CIIA Branch, Winnipeg, January 23, 1975.

I would like to discuss briefly one outstanding issue between Canada and the United States which shows how our new relationship should be managed. It concerns a project of particular interest to this province—the Garrison Diversion Unit.

It involves, as you know, a huge complex of canals, dams and reservoirs designed to irrigate some quarter of a million acres in North Dakota with water from the Missouri River system. The problem for Canada arises from the fact that as envisaged at present the return flows from the irrigation project will drain primarily into the Souris River flowing northward into Canada and also into the Red

---

* It is not possible to cover all aspects of Canadian-American transboundary water problems in a book of this size. (This document has been provided mainly as an illustration of the range and complexity of the subject and of the work of the IJC.) Basically, there are five main questions involved: the reduction of pollution in the Great Lakes–St. Lawrence River system; the East and West Coast oil tankers problem; the Garrison and Chicago Diversions; the proposed flooding of the Skagit Valley. The Canadian position on the Chicago Diversion has been documented in the preceding volume. The Garrison Diversion is dealt with below. See the IJC's report of January 1971 for a comprehensive analysis of pollution in the Great Lakes–St. Lawrence River system. See also CTS 72/12 for the text of the Great Lakes Water Quality Treaty with the United States. As regards the Skagit Valley problem, see *Canadian Annual Review of Politics*

River. The potential consequences of this are serious. We would be faced with increased flooding and with the prospect of large-scale pollution that would cause damage to health and property in Canada. Because of this Canada has raised objections to the project on the basis of the Boundary Waters Treaty of 1909 which provides that neither country will pollute waters flowing into the other to the injury of health or property.

Since 1969, the Governments of Canada and the United States as well as the Governments of Manitoba and North Dakota have exchanged information and held numerous discussions on the issue. We have particularly welcomed working closely with the Government of Manitoba on this subject and have appreciated the continuing support and participation of the Manitoba authorities in our dealings with the United States. I think that this issue provides an excellent illustration of federal-provincial co-operation in dealing with an international problem.

At the technical level, the enormous amount of information exchanged has meant that the Canadian authorities have been kept fully informed on all technical aspects of the project including its timetable and progress. The United States side has been kept fully informed of the technical analysis which supports the Canadian case against the project. At the political level the various exchanges have kept each side fully aware of the other's intentions, strategy and concerns.

What has been the value of this practice of regular consultation and exchange of information? It has allowed a fluidity of approach to the positions of both sides which has meant that the hardening of positions on considerations not central to the issue involved has been avoided. It has also precluded the kind of conflict that can arise when positions are taken on the basis of misinformation. The tactic of confrontation at the political level has been avoided. The political position of both parties depends on answers to highly technical questions of water quality, water management and agricultural techniques. If confrontational tactics had been indulged in, the whole issue could have escalated to the political level long before the essential technical

---

and Public Affairs, edited by John Saywell, University of Toronto Press, particularly the 1973 and 1974 editions. As regards tanker pollution, see Mr. MacEachen's speech to the World Affairs Council and New England Trade Centre, Boston, March 20, 1975.

work had been done and a political deadlock with little room for manoeuvre could have resulted.* It is also worth noting that those portions of the project which directly affect Canada have not so far been constructed.

---

* In the same speech, Mr. MacEachen had the following to say about the effects of United States legislation on Canadian trade with Cuba. This following brief extract is given to indicate the outcome of this problem which began nearly two decades ago. (See A.E.B., pages 209, 230-32.)

"Another kind of issue on which some progress has to be made with the United States is the problem posed by the United States Trading With the Enemy Act and in particular the United States Cuban Assets Control Regulations administered under the Act. This Act which serves to deter Canadian companies which are subsidiaries of United States firms from conducting normal export business with Cuba clearly has extra-territorial effect. You will be aware of the recent cases illustrating this problem. Although Canada is not the only country affected, the extent of United States business interests in Canada makes it a particular factor in Canada– United States relations. Clearly Canada cannot accept extra-territorial application of the laws of any other nation. This problem has been discussed periodically by successive Canadian and United States governments without a resolution satisfactory to Canada. If consultation is to be used in this instance, as I think it should be, it would be our objective that the outcome would be that the companies doing business in Canada would not be deterred by United States law or by corporate policy made in the United States from doing normal export business. Indeed, I have initiated discussions with United States authorities with a view to finding a satisfactory solution to the problem.

"You will be aware that amendments to the Anti-Combines Investigation Act are currently before the House of Commons. When passed these amendments will enable the Restrictive Business Practices Commission to issue directives prohibiting Canadian companies from obeying foreign laws and orders."

IV. The Far East

˜ Three areas again dominated the scene of Canada's relations with the Far East: Indochina, China, and Japan. Much the same pattern prevailed as during the previous ten years. ˜

A. INDOCHINA

˜ The war in Vietnam reached its height during the late 1960s. An armistice was concluded in January 1973. Hostilities ceased finally in 1975 with Hanoi's victory over Saigon. In 1973, Canada again accepted the task of supervising the peace, but this time laid down fairly stringent conditions before doing so. These conditions were not met and Canada withdrew from the International Commission for Control and Supervision, as the new peace-keeping body was named, during July 1973.

The Canadian position vis-à-vis the war evolved a good deal over the years: from general sympathy and understanding of the United States' position in the early and mid-years of the decade to increasing skepticism and aversion as the war ground on. It is impossible in a volume of this size to fully document the evolution of Canada's outlook. Therefore, only the highlights are given in the following pages. As a guide for further reading, here is a list of the more important statements, speeches, and related documents, regarding Canadian policy and initiatives:

1965
ss 65/8 of March 8.
Press Release, DEA, April 30, giving Canada's general approach to Vietnam at that time.
House of Commons Standing Committee on External Affairs and National Defence, June 10, which provides a comprehensive survey of the war, North Vietnam's four conditions for a settlement, and useful historical background to the conflict.

1966
ss 66/1 of January 24.
ss 66/14 of April 4, which also includes an exchange of letters between Prime Minister Pearson and President Ho Chi Minh.

1967
ss 67/2 of February 3.
ss 67/10 of April 10.
ss 67/13 of April 27.

1968
ss 68/9 of March 18, which describes the results of the visits to Hanoi of Mr. Ormond W. Dier, Canadian Commissioner to the ICSC at the time. See also the account given below of the Seaborn visits to Hanoi in 1964-65.

1970
ss 70/8 of May 1, regarding the invasion of Cambodia.¯

28. Call for Bombing Pause in Vietnam

Statement by the Prime Minister, Mr. L. B. Pearson, on accepting the 2nd Temple University World Peace Award at the Founder's dinner of the University's General Alumni Association, Philadelphia, April 2, 1965. (Extracts)

When a savage war broke out between the two Vietnams, the whole problem of peace keeping entered a very difficult stage. What had been a Vietnamese war against a colonial power became a Communist attack against a Vietnamese state.

In this tragic conflict, the U.S. intervened to help South Vietnam defend itself against aggression and at the request of the Government of the country that was under attack.

Its motives were honourable; neither mean nor imperialistic. Its sacrifices have been great and they were not made to advance any selfish American interest. U.S. civilians doing peaceful work have been wantonly murdered in this conflict.

The Government and the great majority of the people of my country have supported whole-heartedly U.S. peace keeping and peace-making policies in Vietnam. We wish to be able to continue that support.

After the outbreak of armed conflict in the South, the Vietnam Commission, on which my country was represented, became virtually powerless.

The problem became not one of peace keeping by an International Commission, but of peace making by warring states. Unless that peace making takes place, the war in Vietnam might well become a far wider and more terrible conflict.

Obviously the situation cannot be expected to improve until North Vietnam becomes convinced that aggression, in whatever guise, for whatever reason, is inadmissible and will not succeed. I hope that this conviction is growing in Hanoi, though I admit there are no signs of that at the moment. I hope they also realize that the only alternative to a cease fire and a mutually acceptable settlement is chaos and disaster, and that North Vietnam would be a primary and tragic victim of that.

On the other hand, no nation—particularly no newly independent nation—could ever feel secure if capitulation in Vietnam led to the sanctification of aggression through subversion or spurious "wars of national liberation", which are really wars of Communist domination.

On the other hand, the progressive application of military sanctions can encourage stubborn resistance, rather than a willingness to negoti- ate. So continued and stepped-up intensification of hostilities in Viet- nam could lead to uncontrollable escalation. Things would get out of hand.

A settlement is very hard to envisage in the heat of battle, but as the battle grows fiercer, it becomes even more imperative to seek and to find one.

What are the conditions for such a settlement? First, there must be a cease fire; they must stop fighting.

Aggressive action by North Vietnam to bring about a communist "liberation" (which means communist rule) of the South must end. Only then can there be negotiation with any chance of success. In this connection, continued bombing action against North Vietnam beyond a certain point may not have this desired result. Instead of inducing authorities in Hanoi to halt their attacks on the South, it may only harden their determination to pursue, and even intensify, their present course of action. Modern history has shown that this is often the result and one that we don't intend when we take massive retaliatory action.

The retaliatory strikes against North Vietnamese military targets,

for which there has been great provocation, aim at making it clear
that the maintenance of aggressive policies toward the South will
become increasingly costly to the Northern regime.

After about two months of air strikes, the message should now have
been received "loud and clear". The authorities in Hanoi must know
that the United States, with its massive military power, can mete out
even greater punishment. They must also know that, for this reason,
the cost of their continued aggression against South Vietnam could be
incalculable.

If, however, the desired political response from Hanoi has not been
forthcoming, and it hasn't yet, the response which would indicate a
change in policy, this may result from a desire to avoid what would
appear to Hanoi to be the public humiliation of backing down under
duress. And the Northern communist regime is probably also under
pressure from another direction to avoid the public abandonment of a
policy which fits the Communist Chinese doctrine of "wars of national liberation".

If, then, a series of increasingly powerful retaliatory strikes against
North Vietnam does not bring about this preliminary condition of a
cease fire, surely we must give serious consideration to every other
way by which a cease fire might be brought about.

There are many factors in this situation which I am not in a
position to weigh or even know. But there does appear to be at least a
possibility, in my view, that a suspension of air strikes against North
Vietnam *at the right time* might provide the Hanoi authorities with an
opportunity, if they wish to take it, to inject some flexibility into their
policy without appearing to do so as the direct result of military
pressure.*

If such a suspension took place for a limited time, then the rate of
incidents in South Vietnam would provide a fairly accurate way of
measuring its usefulness and the desirability of continuing it. I am
not, of course—I would not dare—propose any compromise on points
of principle, nor any weakening of resistance to aggression in South
Vietnam. Indeed resistance may require increased military strength to
be used against the armed and attacking communists. I merely suggest
that a measured and announced pause in one field of military action
at the right time might facilitate the development of diplomatic resources which cannot easily be applied to the problem under the

---

* See *Mike III, pp. 138-44, for President Johnson's reaction to this
suggestion (Toronto, University of Toronto Press, 1975).*

existing circumstances. It could at least, at the very least, expose the intransigence of the North Vietnam government if they remained intransigent.

Obviously, the objectives of any lasting settlement cannot be defined in detail at this stage. But I think that few would quarrel with President Johnson's view which he expressed the other day—that an honourable peace should be based on "a reliable arrangement to guarantee the independence and security of all in Southeast Asia". Both sides should examine the substance of a possible, rather than a perfect, settlement.

29. The Ronning Missions to Hanoi

Statement to the House of Commons on July 8, 1966, by the Secretary of State for External Affairs, Mr. Paul Martin. (Extracts)

My right honourable friend [Mr. Diefenbaker] spoke of Mr. Ronning's two visits to Hanoi. I should like to underline certain aspects of this initiative which may have been lost sight of in the great volume of publicity which Mr. Ronning's visits have generated.

First, I have said that this was a Canadian initiative and that it was carried out by Mr. Ronning on the instructions of the Canadian Government, and not on the instructions in any way of any other government. I reiterate this today because the impression has been created in some quarters that Mr. Ronning's mandate may have been something other than it was.

Second, I should like the House to understand that the assignment we have taken on is essentially in the nature of a good offices assignment. It is inherent in such an assignment that we should be concerned to understand the positions and attitudes of all the parties, and that we should do our best to interpret and clarify the positions and attitudes of one side to the other. That, broadly speaking, has been the form which Mr. Ronning's assignment has taken.

Third, I would like to restate the ultimate object of this initiative. It has seemed to us that, if a beginning is to be made in the long and patient process which we hope will lead to ultimate peace in Vietnam, we must find a basis on which both sides would be prepared to see such a beginning made. The mere calling of a conference, desirable as that is, does not meet this essential objective, as we have learned in our discussions with both sides. This is the only potentially useful channel through which there has been contact with both sides in a long time. I will not say it is the only channel, but it is the only channel which has access to both sides. I regard this as a tribute to our country as well as to Mr. Ronning himself.

I do not wish to give the House a misleading impression of our results so far. We have not achieved any spectacular results and I think I can quite frankly say that we have had no illusions as to the pace at which progress was likely to be possible.

As I have explained previously to the House, we regard the two visits which have now been made to Hanoi—there may be others—as phases of a continuing effort. Over how long a period of time this effort may extend I cannot say. What is significant is that we have had a fair hearing and on both occasions with the top personalities of the North and the South and, of course, with the Government of the United States. I can say that if the channel we have established remains open, and if its potential usefulness is not called into question by any of those concerned, I do not think, in a situation where a failure of communication may be crucial, we can discount the significance of such a channel for the time when the circumstances for the solution of the Vietnam conflict are ripe.*

30. Bases of Canada's Policy on Vietnam**

On January 17, 1967, a delegation of professors from the University of Toronto called on the Prime Minister and the Secretary of State for External Affairs to deliver and discuss a letter commenting on Canadian policy on Vietnam. Text of letter and reply.

The fact that the cruel devastation of Vietnam has been going on for such a long time does not render the continuing rain of explosives and chemicals more acceptable.

The fact that so many have already pleaded so often for an end to this terror does not make the suffering of the uncountable victims more bearable, nor does it make the situation less dangerous. Indeed, with each escalation, the possibility of Chinese intervention and a world war becomes more real.

We call upon the Canadian Government to demand, unequivocally, an immediate, unconditional and permanent end to the United States

---

* Mr. Chester Ronning, a Far Eastern specialist, had recently retired from the Canadian Foreign Service after a highly distinguished career.

** From *External Affairs,* Ottawa, DEA, April 1967, pp. 131-135.

bombings of North and South Vietnam, and the earliest possible withdrawal of U.S. military forces from the area.

We further call upon the Canadian Government to reveal all military production contracts related in any way to the Vietnam war, and to consider following the example of Sweden in refusing to sell arms to the U.S. until this intervention ceases.

Prime Minister Pearson's Reply

In the course of the discussion, the Prime Minister undertook to reply formally to the professors' letter in detail. The text of his reply reads as follows:

I need hardly tell you that the situation in Vietnam is one to which the Government attaches great importance in the formulation of Canadian foreign policy. That importance reflects not only the implications of the problem for world peace and the international processes of change by peaceful means but also the concern which the Government shares with responsible citizens at the toll the hostilities are taking in terms of human suffering as well as of wasted resources and lost opportunities for human betterment. On these points, I think, there can be few differences of opinion.

The real problem, of course, for governments no less than for individuals, is in translating hopes and convictions into constructive action. Constructive action, in turn, depends on a realistic assessment of the nature of the situation which it is desired to change and of the likely consequences of any given action, whether public or private, in relation to the problem. Therefore, at every stage, we must ask whether any particular step is likely to advance the issue any distance towards a solution—or even towards a more satisfactory state of affairs. Any answer to this question becomes doubly difficult in the context of problems where the direct involvement and the direct responsibility for action rest essentially with others.

Let me be more specific. I realize, as the public debate over Vietnam here and elsewhere over the past few years has shown, that it is possible to arrive at different assessments of the rights and wrongs of the various positions represented in the conflict. This is inevitable, and in the long run useful, in a free society, always provided, of course, that the differences of opinion are genuine and based on the fullest possible range of facts. But whatever the view one might hold about the origins and development of a situation such as we face in Vietnam today, I believe that the right and proper course for the Canadian policy maker is to seek to establish that element of common ground in which any approach to a solution must ultimately rest.

This is precisely the direction in which we have attempted to bring Canadian influence to bear—the search for common ground as a base for a solution to the Vietnam crisis by means other than the use of force. We have spoken publicly about our belief that a military solution is neither practicable nor desirable and we have encouraged the two sides to enter into direct contact to prepare the ground for formal negotiations at the earliest practicable time.

Public Diplomacy Not Enough

In what might be called a process of public diplomacy, the parties themselves have gone some distance over the past year or so in defining their positions. This open exchange of propositions is, of course, useful in settling international problems, but it must, I think, be accompanied by other, less conspicuous, efforts, since public positions are generally formulated in maximum terms. One aspect of these quiet efforts could be an attempt to develop a dialogue with the parties, stressing to them the urgency of seeking more acceptable alternatives to the means being used to pursue their objectives; another might be an attempt to find channels by which the parties could, in quite confidential ways, move out beyond their established positions, abandoning where necessary, tacitly or explicitly, those aspects of their positions where compromises must be made in the interests of a broader accommodation.

As I have said, I am convinced that the Vietnam conflict will ultimately have to be resolved by way of negotiation. But I do not think that a Geneva-type conference (or, indeed, any other conference) will come about simply because the Canadian Government declares publicly that this would be a good idea. It will come about only when those who are at this time opposed to such a conference can be convinced that it would be in their best interests to attend and negotiate in a genuine desire to achieve results. And, in the process, confidential and quiet arguments by a responsible government are usually more effective than public ones.

Similarly, when it comes to making channels, or "good offices", available to the parties to enable them to make contact with each other, I think that too many public declarations and disclosures run the risk of complicating matters for those concerned.

In short, the more complex and dangerous the problem, the greater is the need for calm and deliberate diplomacy. That may sound like an expression of timidity to some of the proponents of political activism at Canadian universities and elsewhere today. I can only assure them, with all the personal conviction I can command, that, in my view, it is the only way in which results can be achieved. Statements and declarations by governments obviously have their place and their use in the international concert, but my own experience leads me to believe that their true significance is generally to be found not in initiating a given course of events but lies rather towards the end of the process, when they have been made possible by certain fundamental understandings or agreements reached by other means.

Need of Reciprocal Commitments

As far as the bombing of North Vietnam is concerned, there is not the slightest doubt in my mind that this is one of the key elements, if not the key element, in the situation at the present time. You may recall that I was one of the first to suggest publicly that a pause in these activities might provide openings for negotiations. Subsequently, I have repeatedly stressed that I should be glad to see the bombing stopped, Northern infiltration into the South stopped, and unconditional peace talks begin. This has been and will remain, in broad outline, the Canadian Government's position—a position which we have adopted not in a spirit of timidity but in a sense of reality, because we believe it corresponds to the facts and because we believe that a negotiation involves reciprocal commitments. Any other position taken by the Government, I am convinced, would be unhelpful.

In your letter you also called upon the Government to reveal all military production contracts related in any way to the Vietnam war, and to consider refusing to sell arms to the U.S.A. until the intervention in Vietnam ceases. While I can appreciate the sense of concern reflected in your suggestions, I think it might be helpful if I were to try to put this question in a somewhat broader perspective than the problem of the Vietnam war alone.

Defence-Production Relations with U.S.

Relations between Canada and the U.S.A. in this field are currently covered by the Defence Production Sharing Agreements of 1959 and 1963, but in fact they go back much farther and find their origins in the Hyde Park Declaration of 1941. During this extended period of co-operation between the two countries, a very close relationship has grown up, not only between the Canadian defence industrial base and its U.S. counterpart but also between the Canadian and U.S. defence equipment procurement agencies. This relationship is both necessary and logical not only as part of collective defence but also in order to meet our own national defence commitments effectively and economically. Equipments required by modern defence forces to meet even limited roles such as peace keeping are both technically sophisticated and very costly to develop and, because Canada's quantitative needs are generally very small, it is not economical for us to meet our total requirements solely from our own resources. Thus we must take advantage of large-scale production in allied countries. As the U.S.A. is the world leader in the advanced technologies involved, and because real advantages can be gained by following common North American design and production standards, the U.S.A. becomes a natural source for much of our defence equipment. The U.S.-Canadian production-sharing arrangements enable the Canadian Government to acquire from the U.S.A. a great deal of the nation's essential defence equipment at the lowest possible cost, while at the same time permitting us to offset the resulting drain on the economy by reciprocal sales to the U.S.A. Under these agreements, by reason of longer production runs, Canadian industry is able to participate competitively in U.S. research, development and production programmes, and is exempted from the "Buy American" Act for these purposes. From a long-term point of view, another major benefit to Canada is the large contribution which these agreements have made and are continuing to make to Canadian industrial research and development capabilities, which, in turn, are fundamental to the maintenance of an advanced technology in Canada.

In this connection, I should perhaps point out that the greater part of U.S. military procurement in Canada consists not of weapons in the conventional sense but rather of electronic equipment, transport aircraft and various kinds of components and sub-systems. In many cases, the Canadian industries which have developed such products to meet U.S. and continental defence requirements have, at the same time, been able to develop related products with a civil application, or have been able to use the technology so acquired to advance their general capabilities. For a broad range of reasons, therefore, it is clear that the imposition of an embargo on the export of military equipment to the U.S.A., and concomitant termination of the Production Sharing Agreements, would have far-reaching consequences which no Canadian Government could contemplate with equanimity. It would be interpreted as a notice of withdrawal on our part from continental defence and even from the collective defence arrangements of the Atlantic alliance.

Contract Revelation Unfeasible

With regard to your specific request that we reveal all military production contracts related in any way to the Vietnam war, there is, so far as I am aware, no way in which the Canadian Government—and perhaps even the U.S. Government—could ascertain the present whereabouts of all items of military equipment purchased in Canada by the U.S.A. Such equipment goes into the general inventory of the U.S. armed forces and may be used for such purposes and in such parts of the world as the U.S. Government may see fit. The converse is true of equipment which is purchased in the U.S.A. by the Canadian Government. This long-standing arrangement—which is sometimes known as the "open border"—reflects the collective defence relationship of Canada and the U.S.A. and is an important element in the broadly based co-operation of the two countries in the defence field. It would not in my judgment be consistent with that relationship for the Canadian Government to seek to impose the sort of restriction which you suggest, nor am I convinced that, by taking such a step, we would be contributing in any practical way to achieving a political solution to the Vietnam problem.

31. The Seaborn Visits to Hanoi in 1964 and 1965

Statement in the House of Commons on June 17, 1971, by the Secretary of State for External Affairs, Mr. Mitchell Sharp.

The attention of the House has been drawn to the publication this week by the *New York Times* of a series of documents describing the involvement of the United States in Indochina up to 1968.* In these documents are several references dealing with the activities of an officer in the Department of External Affairs serving on the International Commission for Supervision and Control in Vietnam in 1964-65. I should like to give the House the facts about his activities, which he carried out on instructions from the Canadian Government.

On June 10, 1966, my predecessor, the Honourable Paul Martin,

---

*The "Pentagon" Papers.

Secretary of State for External Affairs, in a statement before the Standing Committee on External Affairs, said:

> I informed the House on Monday that our role in Vietnam has not been supine and that we have attempted to use the channels available to us by virtue of our Commission membership to establish contact with North Vietnam. Our commissioner in Saigon, over the past eight months, prior to May 31 made several trips to the capital of North Vietnam, Hanoi.
>
> During these visits he has had discussions with the local leaders and officials in an attempt to assess the North Vietnam Government's position. I asked him to go to Hanoi on May 31 and to see someone senior in the Government of Vietnam, the Prime Minister or the Foreign Minister, and this he did.
>
> This is the most recent contact that he has made and, although his report is not an encouraging one, I want to say that we have not abandoned the probing process. Mr. Seaborn, who is our Commissioner, is an officer of considerable experience and ability. He is well qualified for an important assignment of this delicate nature. He had an interview with the Foreign Minister on May 31, in which he expressed Canada's concern, and our willingness to play a helpful role if possible.
>
> He sought clarification of the North Vietnam Government's position including its reaction to the recent pause in the bombings. Naturally I cannot go into any greater detail about it at this time; but I should like to say that the Foreign Minister stated repeatedly that the four conditions which had previously been outlined by the Prime Minister of North Vietnam on April 8, taken as a whole, represented the Hanoi Government's approach to a settlement.

I should now like to give a full account of the nature of our Commissioner's mission to Hanoi during the time he was in Vietnam in 1964-65. In the spring of 1964, following a meeting between the U.S. Secretary of State, Dean Rusk, and the Prime Minister, the Right Honourable Lester B. Pearson, and the Secretary of State for External Affairs, the Honourable Paul Martin, the Canadian Government agreed that the new Canadian Commissioner on the ICC in Vietnam might be instructed to probe what was in the minds of the leaders in Hanoi and help to dispel any misunderstanding they might have as to the future course the United States intended to follow—that is, that the Americans were not thinking of pulling out of Vietnam and were prepared to increase their commitment there if this were considered necessary.

Canada's motive in agreeing to this special mission for the Canadian Commissioner was a try to promote a peaceful settlement to the conflict in Vietnam. Thus the Canadian Government considered it entirely consistent with, and indeed reinforcing, our role in the ICC. I should like to emphasize that the Commissioner acted at no time as a direct representative of the United States Government or President but only as a part of a Canadian channel of communication. It was clearly understood, of course, that messages to be conveyed in this way would be passed via Ottawa, that Canada did not associate itself with the content of the messages, and that Canada would be free to add its own comments to any message passed in either direction. Our only commitment was that there would be faithful transmission of messages in both directions. The Canadian Government's purpose in agreeing to participate in this channel of communication was to provide an opportunity to reduce misunderstandings between the United States and North Vietnam, and was founded on a strong desire to ensure the return of peace to Vietnam and to Southeast Asia. This position was understood by both the Americans and the North Vietnamese throughout.

In the course of his tour of duty in Vietnam, Mr. J. Blair Seaborn, who was the Canadian Commissioner at the time, made six visits to Hanoi. Not all of these were occasioned solely by his special mission. Canadian members of the ICC maintain contact on a regular basis with the authorities of both South and North Vietnam. On his first two visits to Hanoi, the Commissioner was received by the North Vietnamese Prime Minister Pham Van Dong on June 18 and August 13, 1964. During his first interview with the North Vietnamese leader, Mr. Seaborn explained his mission and the Canadian Government's purpose, which was to establish the Canadian Commissioner's credentials with the North Vietnamese as an authoritative channel of communication with the United States. At the same time, he conveyed the first of a series of messages from the United States Government. Mr. Seaborn reported to the North Vietnamese that United States policy was to see to it that North Vietnam contained itself and its ambitions within the territory allocated to its administration by the 1954 Geneva Agreements. He added that United States policy in South Vietnam was to preserve the integrity of that state's territory against guerilla subversion. He stated that the United States had indicated that it was not seeking military bases in the area and was not seeking to overthrow the Communist regime in Hanoi. The Commissioner informed the North Vietnamese Prime Minister that the United States considered itself fully aware of the degree to which Hanoi controlled and directed the guerilla action in South Vietnam and that the United States held Hanoi directly responsible for that action. He also made it clear that the United States considered the confrontation with North Vietnamese subversive guerilla action as part of a general confrontation with this type of violent subversion in other less-developed countries. Therefore the United States regarded its stake in resisting a North Vietnamese victory in South Vietnam as having a significance of world-wide proportions. The Commissioner mentioned examples of United States policy of peaceful co-existence having benefited Communist regimes, such as Yugoslavia and Poland. The Commissioner also reported that American public and official patience with North Vietnamese aggression was growing extremely thin and he feared that, if the conflict in the area should escalate, which he did not think was in anyone's interest, then the greatest devastation would result for the Democratic Republic of Vietnam itself. Mr. Seaborn reported that he was convinced that Pham Van Dong understood the importance and the context of the message he conveyed, and the seriousness with which the United States viewed the situation in Southeast Asia. To that extent it was judged that the initial purpose of this first contact had been successfully accomplished.

The second visit, despite its timing, was not occasioned by the incidents of August 2 and 4 in the Gulf of Tonkin and the air strikes against North Vietnamese territory on August 5. These occurred after Mr. Seaborn had arranged to travel to Hanoi on August 10 on Commission business. On August 8 the Canadian Government agreed to relay to Mr. Seaborn a further message from the United States Government repeating many of the points made in the previous message and making clear that, "if the DRVN persists in its present course, it can expect to suffer the consequences." This message was based on the talking points that were published in the *New York Times* on June 13, 1971. This message was transmitted to Pham Van Dong on August 13, 1964. Despite its severity, the Canadian Government believed that, because of its importance and in the interests of peace, it should be transmitted faithfully in accordance with our undertaking to the United States. According to our Commissioner's report, the North Vietnamese Premier was clearly angered by it and said that if war came to North Vietnam it would come to the whole of Indochina. Nevertheless, he said he wanted the Canadian channel kept open. Neither the United States nor North Vietnam, however, took any initiative to make use of it in the following weeks.

The Commissioner's third trip to Hanoi on regular Commission business was planned for November 1964, but we were asked by the United States Government to delay it to permit the preparation of a further message to the North Vietnamese. This message, which was relayed to Saigon on December 3, had nothing to add to the earlier message beyond the statement that "the time is ripe for any message Hanoi may wish to convey", and the Commissioner was instructed by the Canadian Government to deliver passively so passive a message. It was conveyed, therefore, to the head of the North Vietnamese liaison mission for the ICC. This was the only North Vietnamese official whom Mr. Seaborn saw during this third visit, from December 10 to 18, 1964. There was no response to the American invitation for communication from the North Vietnamese and in January 1965 the State Department told us that it was unlikely that the United States would have anything to communicate to Hanoi "in the near future".

American air attacks on North Vietnam began in February 1965 following a major Communist assault on American facilities at Pleiku and on February 27 Mr. Seaborn was instructed by the Canadian Government to go to Hanoi to discuss a new message with the North Vietnamese Prime Minister. He went on March 1, but Pham Van Dong would not receive him and the Commissioner saw Colonel Ha Van Lau, the head of the liaison mission, on March 4. At that time the Commissioner conveyed to him the substance of a general statement of United States policy and objective, which was also being made available to the North Vietnamese Government through the United States Embassy in Warsaw. Mr. Seaborn concluded, following this meeting, that the North Vietnamese were unlikely to use the Canadian channel of communication with the United States.

On May 28, 1965, following the suspension of bombing from May 12 to 17, the United States asked if the Canadian Government would instruct Mr. Seaborn to pass a further message to North Vietnam saying that "the United States continues to consider the possibility of working toward a solution by reciprocal actions on each side", and seeking clarification of whether American recognition of North Vietnam's "Four Points" of April 8 was regarded by Hanoi as a precondition to any discussions. Mr. Seaborn went to Hanoi for the fifth time on May 31 and saw both Ha Van Lo and North Vietnamese Foreign Minister Nguyen Duy Trinh. He reported his impression that the North Vietnamese were not interested in talking to the United States at that time. The fact that Mr. Seaborn had seen the North Vietnamese Foreign Minister was reported to the House by my predecessor, the Honourable Paul Martin, on June 7, 1965.

Mr. Seaborn visited Hanoi for the last time from September 30 to

October 4, 1965. We had told the United States Government in advance that we had serious doubts about the usefulness of giving him special instructions and on this occasion he carried no message. His only official contact this time was at a low level in the North Vietnamese liaison mission and he detected no sign of interest in discussions or negotiations. Shortly thereafter Mr. Seaborn returned to Canada at the conclusion of his normal posting in Vietnam.

It has been suggested that the Canadian Government knew, or should have known, that some of the messages it conveyed amounted to statement of an American intention to bomb North Vietnam. The Canadian Government knew of no such intention on the part of the United States. The messages we carried were couched in general terms and related to the possible consequences for the North Vietnamese Government of continued activities in South Vietnam.

It has been implied that the Canadian Government should not have carried any such messages on behalf of the United States. It was the view of the Government of that time that this was entirely consistent with its role as a member of the ICC, and indeed that it was implicit in the role that Canada should endeavour to promote a dialogue between the main parties to the conflict. The North Vietnamese made it abundantly clear to Mr. Seaborn that they did not regard our activity as in any way improper or inconsistent with our ICC role.

It has also been implied that when the bombing of North Vietnam began the Canadian Government should have made some public protest on the basis of what it is now claimed that it knew about American intentions. The Canadian Government had no information that would have justified such a protest at that time. Canada, along with many others, accepted the United States Government's version of the Gulf of Tonkin incident.

We were not allied to the United States in its operations in Indochina and were not fully informed by the United States on its various plans and intentions. Throughout, the record is clear that the Government of that day acted in good faith and in a manner consistent with our responsibilities to the International Control Commission.

32. Conditions for Canadian Participation in the ICCS

Statement by the Secretary of State for External Affairs, Mr. Mitchell Sharp, in the House of Commons, January 5, 1973.

Canada has a special interest in this matter, and not only because we are close neighbours of the United States. We have been involved, during the past 18 years, in the thankless task of supervising an earlier settlement, and of trying without success to make that supervision effective. Beyond that, we have been given clear indications of the possibility of our being asked to accept a further role. It has been indicated to us that Canada would be acceptable to all the parties as one of the members of a new international body which it is expected that the present negotiations will create when and if they are successful. Canada has not yet been formally invited to participate in this new international presence; indeed, I anticipate that no such invitation will be addressed to any of the potential members until an agreement is concluded. We have, however, been asked to consider the possibility, and we have done so most carefully.

Having our past experience very much in mind, in our discussions with the American authorities and in communications with the other parties to the Paris negotiations, as well as in public statements, the Government has developed a number of conditions and criteria on which it would base its judgment on whether Canada should participate in a new international commission for Vietnam.*

The first condition, and indeed the ultimate one, is that the provisions for the operation of the new organization, when taken as a whole, should be workable and offer real prospects of being effective. Moving from the general to the particular, we have also stipulated that all the present belligerent parties, the United States, the Republic of Vietnam, North Vietnam and the Viet Cong, should be bound by the agreement the implementation of which the new commission would observe and report upon. In this same category, we have required that there should be a "continuing political authority" that would assume responsibility for the settlement as a whole and to which the commission, or any of its members, would have access through reports or consultations. We should prefer it if such an authority could be provided for the original agreements but, failing that, we consider that it could be established by the international conference which, as we understand it, will be convened 30 days after the cease fire.

We have also insisted that the proposed new commission should have the freedom of movement and observation within the demilitarized zone and in South Vietnam necessary to achieve a proper exer-

---

* See also SS 73/5 of February 26, 1973, for the text of Mr. Sharp's statement to the opening session of the International Conference on Vietnam, which took place in Paris.

cise of its functions. Moreover, we have required that Canada should be invited to be a member of the new commission by all of the parties concerned.

In addition to these specific and essential considerations we have, from our broad experience in Vietnam, put forward a number of other suggestions and requests. The extent to which they were met would also constitute elements in our assessment of the viability of the operation as a whole. As an additional condition, we have stated that, if all the essential criteria I have already mentioned were satisfied except that which relates to the existence of a "continuing political authority", we should be prepared to consider serving on the commission for a minimum of 60 days, during which we should assess the outcome of the international conference with particular reference to the establishment of a "continuing political authority". If no such authority were created or if, once created, it ceased to exist, Canada would have to reserve the right to withdraw at any time, even after the initial two-month period. In any event, the Government could not accept a commitment beyond two years, although some other formula for opting out on shorter notice might be acceptable.

We have also said that we assumed that the necessary logistic support for the new commission would be available from the outset to make its operation substantive and effective or even possible.

The Government has also urged that unrealistic demands should not be placed upon the new commission in the initial stages particularly, and that no unrealistic expectations should be vested in it. For example, the commission should not be expected to begin functioning in any part of Vietnam before a cease fire has been established locally by the belligerents themselves.

In respect of the international conference, it has been our view that it should be free to establish its own relation with the commission or indeed with other provisions of the agreement or its protocols. The Government has also taken the view that participants in the new commission should pay the salary and allowances for their own personnel but should not otherwise be expected to contribute to the general overhead and expenses of the organization. This was an idea originally put forward, that the members of the commission should also pay part of the infrastructure. We took the strongest exception to it. Should Canada decide to participate it would signify its acceptance by a formal unilateral communication to the parties. At the same time, the Government would also communicate any reservations it may have in respect of the documents embodying the settlement, or in respect of the commission, or Canada's participation in it.

When all the texts are available, the Government will examine them in the light of these criteria, conditions and viewpoints and make its own determination on the viability of the operation and on the existence of a suitable role for Canada. The Government is conscious of the fact that there are several possible forms of response open to it between a simple refusal to take part at all and a full and unconditional involvement. The Government's assessment of the relevant texts will also take into account the importance of contributing to a scaling-down of hostilities in Vietnam and to the disengagement of American forces and the return of their prisoners of war. It is conceivable that the result of this examination might suggest a participation limited to certain aspects of the agreement or a participation for a limited period rather than an outright refusal or an unqualified undertaking to serve. If so, the parties concerned will be so advised and, if they found this acceptable, Canada could take part on a limited basis.

Also drawing on our experience, we are conscious of the dangers of allowing ourselves to be frustrated as a member of the new international organization through the possible application of a rule of unanimity. One way in which this risk could be minimized would be by regarding the new body not as a diplomatic conference held under the normal rules of confidentiality but as an international forum where the proceedings are normally open to the public. Consequently, we should not regard the new commission's proceedings as confidential or privileged in any way unless there was in any particular instance a unanimous decision of all the members to the contrary. We should instead consider ourselves free to publicize the proceedings in any way we saw fit to ensure that our view of events and, if necessary, the difference between our view and that of others was publicly available.

In putting forward our conditions, it was, of course, not our desire or intention to raise unnecessary difficulties or to seek any special position for ourselves. The fact is that Canada is in an excellent position to judge from its own experience what is necessary to a successful operation in international supervision, whether or not we become members of the proposed commission. Some of Canada's experience has been positive. Some of it, notably in Vietnam, Laos, and Cambodia, where for 18 years we have tried to make international supervision work, has been profoundly disappointing. From that disappointment, we have learned a good deal, and it is in the light of what we have learned there that we have arrived at the position I have just described, which we believe essential to the success of the operation in which we may be invited to participate.

Because of the possibility that we shall be invited to accept a new supervisory role in Vietnam, and because of our long involvement in the Vietnam problem, Canada, apart from the fact that it shares the interest of the whole world in the settlement of the Vietnam war, has a particular interest in current developments there and in the negotiations which we all hope will bring an end to the conflict. This House embodies that interest, and I think it would be fitting that the House make known its view of the situation. For that reason, we have proposed the motion which appears on the Order Paper. It is in terms which I believe deserve the support of all sides of the house. I conclude by saying this, Mr. Speaker, that it is directed to all parties in the Vietnam conflict.

33. Canada Withdraws from the ICCS

Statement in the House of Commons by the Secretary of State for External Affairs, Mr. Mitchell Sharp, May 31, 1973.

Speaking in the House on March 27, I said that the Government had decided to extend Canadian participation in the ICCS until May 31 and that before that date the Government would decide whether to remain or to withdraw.

At that time I said that we would withdraw our contingent by June 30 unless there had been a substantial improvement in the situation or some signs of an imminent political agreement between the two South Vietnamese parties.

The decision is a serious one and the Government so regards it. Canada has a reputation, I believe, for responsibility in international affairs. We have served in more peace-keeping and peace-observer roles than any other country and we remain ready to serve wherever we can be effective. We have also, in the course of this varied and extensive experience, including 19 years in Indochina, learned something about the conditions that are necessary to success in peace-keeping and peace-observer activities.

The House will recall the efforts that the Government made to establish conditions which would help to improve the prospects for the successful functioning of the International Commission of Control and Supervision provided for in the Paris agreement on Vietnam. I shall not repeat them now. The record of Canada's approach to the question of participation in the ICCS up to the end of March 1973 is to be found in a White Paper that I shall table at the conclusion of this statement.*

Stated briefly, what we sought to ensure was that the new International Commission would be an impartial, fact-finding body, supported by the parties to the peace agreement, with sufficient freedom of access to enable it to ascertain the facts about any alleged breach of the agreement and reporting quickly not only to the parties to the agreement but also to the international community as a whole. While we did not achieve all our purposes. I think it is fair to say that we helped to effect some improvements, at least in form.

What we could not ensure, and what the ICCS could not ensure, was peace in Vietnam. That depends on the parties to the peace agreement and not on the ICCS. Nor can Canada alone ensure that the ICCS fulfills its function of peace observing and reporting as provided for in the peace agreement. That too depends on the parties to the agreement and on the other member delegations of the Commission.

Notwithstanding our hesitations and doubts, we accepted membership for a trial period of 60 days. At the end of that first 60 days our hesitations and doubts had been reinforced but we were urged by many countries to show patience. So we agreed to another two-month period, which is now coming to an end.

By and large, there has been no significant change in the situation that would alter the view we formed at the end of the first 60 days, notwithstanding the strenuous efforts of the Canadian contingent to support the functioning of the International Commission.

Let me repeat that our attitude results from Canadian experience in the old ICCS and the Canadian conception of the functioning of a peace observer body. We are not criticizing the peace agreement. We welcomed that agreement; we regard it as a good agreement that provides as sound and honourable a basis for peace as was negotiable. If the parties will set themselves to applying it, as we hope they may yet do, it can bring lasting peace to Vietnam. We hope that the efforts of Dr. Kissinger and Mr. Le Duc Tho to achieve a stricter observance of the agreement will be crowned with success.

We have come to the conclusion, however, that the Canadian conception of the functioning of the International Commission has not

---

* Apart from the White Paper, see also SS 73/10 of March 21, 1973, in which Mr. Sharp describes to the House of Commons (CHCD, 21.3.1973) the results of a visit to Vietnam; SS 73/8 of March 22, 1973, also by Mr. Sharp regarding the difficulties and obstacles facing the ICCS.

been accepted and that it would be in the interest of all concerned if we were to withdraw. Nor do we believe that Canadian withdrawal would have any significant effect upon the prospects for peace in Vietnam. That depends upon the parties to the peace agreement and not upon the ICCS. It is only if the parties are co-operating in a strict observance of the agreement and are willing to use the ICCS as a means of reinforcing the agreement that the Commission can perform its function with any hope of success.

Throughout our tenure on the ICCS, we have sought above all else to be objective. We have represented none of the contending parties. We have been as insistent in calling for and participating in investigations of alleged violations by the United States and the Republic of Vietnam as we have with regard to alleged violations by the Democratic Republic of Vietnam and the other South Vietnamese Party. If the RVN or U.S.A. has been at fault, we have said so. If the other parties were to blame for cease-fire violations, we also have said so. I assure the House that we have no need to listen mutely now or later to any charges that we have acted partially; we can be proud of our objectivity in the Commission and of our attempts to see this impartiality as an integral part of Commission activities.

I also said, in my statement to the House on March 27, that Canada would be prepared to return to Vietnam to participate in the international supervision of an election clearly held under the terms of the Paris agreement and therefore with the concurrence and participation of the two South Vietnamese parties. It went without saying that our participation would not be necessary if a replacement were found for Canada on the ICCS. I am not convinced that there is much chance that an election will take place as provided for in the agreement but, if it should (and we should want to examine it carefully to make sure it was this kind of election), and if no replacement had been found for Canada, we should consider sympathetically a request to return temporarily to the ICCS for this purpose, in the light of the circumstances then prevailing and our assessment of the chances for effective supervision.

The peace agreement itself anticipates the replacement of the named members of the ICCS—Canada, Hungary, Indonesia and Poland—or any of them. I have also said that we should be prepared to remain on the Commission until June 30 so that a replacement could be found. We have since learned that the discussions which took place recently between Dr. Kissinger and Mr. Le Duc Tho will be resumed in June. We want to give those discussions every chance of success and we would certainly wish to do nothing that would complicate them in introducing what might seem to be too short a deadline for agreeing on a replacement for Canada on the Commission.

In recognition of that possible difficulty, we are prepared, if the parties to the agreement so wish, to stay for a period beyond June 30 but not later than July 31. Canada's decision to withdraw is firm and definite, but the additional flexibility should give the parties adequate time to find a replacement for the Canadian delegation. Should a successor be named and be ready to take its place before July 31, we should, of course, be prepared to hand over our responsibilities at any mutually convenient earlier time. We shall, of course, continue to function as we have been doing during the remaining period of our stay on the Commission.

B. CHINA

˜After lengthy negotiations, which were conducted largely by the Canadian and Chinese Ambassadors in Stockholm, Canada recognized Peking in 1970. The Peking Government was admitted to the United Nations in 1971 and assumed China's seat on the Security Council. Canadian relations with China remained much as they were during the previous decade, with particular emphasis on the grain trade. Prime Minister Trudeau visited China in 1973.*˜

34. Establishment of Diplomatic Relations with the People's Republic of China

Statement in the House of Commons by Mr. Mitchell Sharp, the Secretary of State for External Affairs, on October 13, 1970.

I am pleased to announce the successful conclusion of our discussions in Stockholm with representatives of the People's Republic of China, reflected in today's joint communiqué which records our agreement on mutual recognition and the establishment of diplomatic relations. The joint communiqué of the Government of Canada and the Government of the People's Republic of China concerning the establishment of diplomatic relations between Canada and China is as follows:

---

* See his press statement, issued at Peking, October 13, 1973, for an account of the results of the visit. The trade agreement between both countries (CTS 1973/31 of October 13, 1973) was renewed on October 13, 1976.

1. The Government of Canada and the Government of the People's Republic of China, in accordance with the principles of mutual respect for sovereignty and territorial integrity, non-interference in each other's internal affairs and equality and mutual benefit, have decided upon mutual recognition and the establishment of diplomatic relations, effective October 13, 1970.

2. The Chinese Government reaffirms that Taiwan is an inalienable part of the territory of the People's Republic of China. The Canadian Government takes note of this position of the Chinese Government.*

3. The Canadian Government recognizes the Government of the People's Republic of China as the sole legal government of China.

4. The Canadian and Chinese Governments have agreed to exchange ambassadors within six months, and to provide all necessary assistance for the establishment and the performance of the functions of diplomatic missions in their respective capitals, on the basis of equality and mutual benefit and in accordance with international practice.

Officials from my department and from Industry, Trade and Commerce will be leaving for Peking very shortly to begin administrative preparations for the opening of a Canadian embassy in Peking. We hope to have the embassy in operation within two or three months.

The establishment of diplomatic relations between Canada and China is an important step in the development of relations between our two countries, but it is not the first step, nor is it an end in itself. We have opened a new and important channel of communication, through which I hope we will be able to expand and develop our relations in every sphere. We have already indicated to the Chinese, in our Stockholm discussions, our interest in setting up cultural and educational exchanges, in expanding trade between our two countries, in reaching an understanding on consular matters, and in settling a small number of problems left over from an earlier period. The Chinese have expressed the view that our relations in other fields such as these can only benefit from the establishment of diplomatic relations between our two countries. They have also agreed in principle to discuss through normal diplomatic channels, as soon as our respective embassies are operating, some of the specific issues we have raised with them.

---

* This "Canadian" formula was later used by other countries. ss 72/21 of October 14, 1972, gives useful background to the negotiations which led to recognition and also provides a summary of the recent history of Sino-Canadian relations.

Status of Taiwan—Canadian Explanatory Note

As everyone knows, the agreement published today has been under discussion for a long time. I do not think it is any secret that a great deal of this discussion has revolved around the question of Taiwan. From the very beginning of our discussions the Chinese side made clear to us their position that Taiwan was an inalienable part of Chinese territory and that this was a principle to which the Chinese Government attached the utmost importance. Our position, which I have stated publicly and which we made clear to the Chinese from the start of our negotiations, is that the Canadian Government does not consider it appropriate either to endorse or to challenge the Chinese Government's position on the status of Taiwan. This has been our position and it continues to be our position. As the communiqué says, we have taken note of the Chinese Government's statement about Taiwan. We are aware that this is the Chinese view and we realize the importance they attach to it, but we have no comment to make one way or the other.

There is no disagreement between the Canadian Government and the authorities in Taipeh on the impossibility of continuing diplomatic relations after the Government of Peking is recognized as the Government of China. Both Peking and Taipeh assert that it is not possible to recognize simultaneously more than one government as the Government of China. Accordingly, the authorities on Taiwan and the Canadian Government have each taken steps to terminate formal diplomatic relations as of the time of the announcement of our recognition of the Government of the People's Republic of China.

C. JAPAN

~Canadian relations with Japan remained excellent and, as previously, centred mainly in trade. The balance generally continued to favour Canada as commercial exchanges between the two countries rose. Japanese exports to Canada are labour-intensive—e.g., cameras, appliances, automobiles, etc—while Canadian exports to Japan are basically raw materials. Japanese investments, particularly in Western Canada, continued. Fisheries questions were dealt with at the annual meetings of the International North Pacific Fisheries Commission established by virtue of the International Convention for the High Seas Fisheries of the North Pacific Ocean (June 12, 1953).*~

---

* See A.E.B. pp. 334-40 for background.

35. Canada and Japan

Statement by the Secretary of State for External Affairs, Mr. Paul Martin, to the Canada-Japan Trade Council, Calgary, October 31, 1966.

I think it would be appropriate for me to take this occasion to review some of the questions discussed at the Canada-Japan Ministerial Committee meetings earlier this month.

Japan is a major economic power and the only industrially developed country in Asia. It has a leading role in working with friendly nations to achieve a world community in which peace and economic welfare are firmly established in a way they have never been before.

I fully expect our own relations with Japan to assume increasing importance within this international context.

There are several specific reasons on which I base my expectations:

1.   Our direct contacts with Japan, official and unofficial, are increasing rapidly in volume and variety.
2.   There are opportunities for futher substantial increases in trade between the two countries.
3.   Both Canada and Japan are major trading nations and have many common interests and preoccupations with respect to trade and economic arrangements in the world as a whole.
4.   Canada and Japan assign a high priority to economic assistance to developing nations and they are associated in agencies which co-ordinate and concert international efforts in this field.
5.   We have an identity of interests and attitudes with respect to several of the problems creating the greatest political tension in the world today.

Aid to Developing Countries

The Canada-Japan Ministerial Committee reviewed the expanding programmes of both countries in the field of development assistance. The Ministers of both Governments stressed the urgent need for accelerated economic development in the developing areas.

I reported an increase in the Canadian programme, which will reach a level of about $300 million this year. Subject to economic and other relevant circumstances, our programme will continue to expand. We are making good progress towards the aid target of 1 per cent of national income. In April of this year, Japan formally pledged itself to do the same.

We paid special attention to plans for the second United Nations Conference on Trade and Development, to be held next fall. We agreed that it was vital to ensure the success of that Conference. It is clear that special efforts to promote a more rapid expansion of trade and industrial growth of the developing countries are also essential ingredients in the development process. It will be very important to focus attention on particular issues, on which practical results might be achieved.

It has been the Japanese experience, as it has been our own, that international discussions (notably in UNCTAD) are leading to an improved understanding of the magnitude and complexity of these development problems and of the directions in which more vigorous national and international efforts might proceed.

It is our hope that discussions in the "Kennedy Round" of tariff negotiations will make an important contribution to the expansion of trade in products of special interest to developing countries.

Canadian and Japanese Ministers were particularly interested in prospects for the newly created Asian Development Bank. This is likely to be an institution of major importance. Japan has taken a primary part in planning the operations of the Bank and has contributed $200 million, a sum equal to that of the U.S.A. Canada has also made a substantial subscription of $25 million to this new institution. This is over and above the significant Canadian aid programme under the Colombo Plan for countries in this area.

International Trade and Economic Relations

Canada and Japan have common interests also in fields affecting their own well-being as major world traders. They have a vital interest, for example, in reducing international trade barriers.

The "Kennedy Round" provides the first real opportunity for broad tariff and trade negotiations between Canada and Japan within a multilateral context. It could thus constitute a major step in further strengthening the trade relations between Canada and Japan and increasing and diversifying trade in both directions.

Both delegations at the Ministerial meeting emphasized the importance of obtaining significant improvements in access to each other's markets in the tariff negotiations. There will be difficulties, of course, in achieving agreement, but we hope, nevertheless, that there may be sufficient flexibility in the Japanese position to permit successful negotiation.

Canada and Japan also participate in the Organization for Economic Co-operation and Development, along with the United States and the countries of Western Europe. They support its objective of expanding world trade on a non-discriminatory basis, of achieving the highest sustainable rate of economic growth and of contributing to sound economic expansion in developing countries.

I believe that our views on another subject of current interest to the chief trading nations—that of trade with Communist nations—are close to those held by the Japanese. We believe, of course, that there are good economic and political reasons for engaging in this trade, provided that respective interests are reasonably balanced.

Canadian Trade with Japan

Trade between Canada and Japan is, of course, at the centre of many of our discussions with Japanese representatives. It is very satisfying that this trade is already extensive and that there are reasonable prospects for its continuing to increase fairly quickly. Exports and imports will total about $600 million this year.

In large measure, of course, the two economies are complementary. There has been an impressive increase in trade between the two countries during the period 1954-1965. Canadian exports to Japan increased more than three times and imports from Japan increased 12 times. Japan has become our third largest single export market and our fourth largest supplier. We should hope that, in addition to other factors stimulating trade, Expo '67 and the World Exposition in Osaka in 1970 would make their contribution to expansion.

Possibilities of Improvement

It is natural that, with trade being conducted at very high levels by nations with as strong a desire for commercial expansion as Canada and Japan, there should be areas requiring discussion, some difficulties, and various promising possibilites of improvement.

I believe that there are four points with respect to which we might look for improvement or solution to some problems: (1) rate of growth; (2) make-up of our trade; (3) barriers to trade; (4) capital investment.

Rate of Growth

In spite of the impressive increase in our trade with Japan during the last 10 years, it has recently been growing at a slower rate than our trade with the United States and some of our other major trading partners.

This may be owing primarily to a period of stagnation in Japan's domestic growth during 1965 and we are looking forward to a resumption of a higher rate of growth in our trade with the currently more favourable conditions in Japan.

Make-up of Canada-Japan Trade

We are concerned that our exports to Japan are largely composed of raw materials with little if any processing, whereas our imports from Japan are made up of highly manufactured goods.

Canada values its traditional exports to Japan, such as wheat, primarily foodstuffs and industrial materials, and we are glad to provide a continuing and dependable source of supply for many of the essential requirements of the Japanese economy. However, we are also interested in more rapidly developing our trade in manufactured goods, and we have found it particularly difficult to increase our manufactured exports to Japan, despite the fact that we have made striking progress in doing so in other highly competitive markets, such as the United States.

I think it natural that we should not want to see this situation continue indefinitely. Canadian representatives have expressed the view that both countries have a large potential for increased trade. They have also expressed the wish that this trade should increasingly take the form of exchanges of processed goods.

In some instances, of course, the reason for Canadian difficulties in selling manufactured goods lies in highly competitive production in Japan. In other instances, high tariffs or quantitative import restrictions have adversely affected exports. It is in this latter field that we should hope progress could be made.

Barriers to Trade

The Ministerial meeting gave a good deal of attention to what representatives of the two countries considered to be the main barriers or restrictions to trade moving in either direction. It is some indication of the friendly spirit of the meeting that we could discuss frankly and in very specific terms the views of the two sides on these problems.

Canadian representatives described tariff barriers, quantitative restrictions and a variety of technical and administrative obstacles encountered by Canadian exporters. We naturally laid stress on our hope that ways would be found to overcome these obstacles, both in the multilateral context of the "Kennedy Round" and in our bilateral discussions with Japan.

On the Japanese side, emphasis was placed on the difficulties which they have encountered in exporting to Canada, in particular the effects of the voluntary export restraint system.

We recognize that there are difficulties for the Japanese in applying export restraints of this kind, but have pointed out in our conversations with them that this system has unquestionably allowed a greater volume of sensitive imports into Canada than would have been feasible if Canada had had to set up import quotas. We have also pointed out that, in practice, Canada accords more liberal terms of access of imports of sensitive goods from Japan than does any other industrialized country.

Furthermore, the percentage of Japanese exports to Canada affected by these measures has rapidly decreased and now amounts to only 10 to 15 per cent of Japanese sales here. We are prepared to agree to the lifting of the remaining restraints as soon as they are no longer necessary to prevent disruption of Canadian markets—for example, in 1966 Canada agreed to the removal of transistor radios and certain textile items from the list of restraints.

I should add that there has been no question of restraints at all on an important range of exports from Japan developed during the last few years, where sales have increased very rapidly—including such sophisticated products as cars, motorcycles and cameras. I believe the recent Ministerial meeting was useful in clarifying the facts of our point of view on this whole problem.

Capital Investment

The Canadian representatives pointed out that we very much welcomed Japanese investment, which had been particularly evident on the West Coast. There had, however, been some disadvantageous features about the flow of funds between the two countries.

One of our concerns is that Japan's controls have encouraged the flow of borrowed funds rather than equity capital into Japan and that investment authorizations are too often subject to lengthy delays. Thus Canadian companies investing in Japan have all too often been unable to secure what we would regard as an appropriate voice in the control over their investments in Japan. This is in striking contrast to the position of Japanese investors in Canada, who are free to invest here in any form they wish.

The Canadian delegation expressed the hope that the remaining restrictions on Canadian investment in Japan would be lifted as soon as possible and also that Japanese investors in Canada would take into account the desirability of increasing the degree of processing in their exports from Canada. The Japanese are now fully aware of our views on this matter and we are confident that they will be giving thought to these problems.

36. The State of Canada's Trade with Japan

Statement by Mr. Jean-Luc Pépin, Minister of Industry, Trade and Commerce, to the Japanese Press Club, Tokyo, January 24, 1972.

The mission that I am leading here is the largest economic mission Canada has ever sent anywhere in the world.

What are our objectives? We are here, as you expect, to promote Canadian products and to increase our exports to your market. Of course we want to increase the volume of our exports, but we also want to improve their quality. By this I mean the degree of fabrication of these exports. We want to continue to sell you industrial materials and foodstuffs. We also want to diversify our range of exports to include more manufactured goods.

To achieve these objectives it is important that Canadian businessmen learn more and more about the Japanese market, get to know better and better, on a firsthand basis, the techniques of doing business here. On the other hand we want to talk to your Government and business leaders about some obstacles which appear to stand in the way of Canadian exports to Japan and we want to contribute to the resolution of these problems.

My officials and I will also be talking to your Government about recent international trade developments, about our community of interests in trade liberalization, about Canada's and Japan's roles in the evolving international trade scene.

What is the state of trade between our two countries? It is large and growing fast.

In 1965, two-way trade totalled $456 million and Canada had a surplus of almost $100 million. By 1970 it had more than doubled, reaching $1.3 billion. The trade surplus for Canada had kept pace, attaining over $200 million. As we entered 1971, most Canadians, and I suspect most Japanese, had come to expect that a large excess of Canadian exports to Japan over Japanese exports to Canada was a normal feature of trade between our two countries.

This situation changed dramatically last year. In 1971 Japan's sales to Canada increased by a record 38 per cent, while Canadian exports to Japan actually declined. Canadian imports from Japan leaped by more than $217 million, to over $800 million, while Canadian exports to Japan decreased slightly, to about $792 million. So in one year Japan moved from a deficit of $209 million to a possible surplus of about $10 million. The actual decrease in Canada sales was due, experts say, to a temporary slow-down in the Japanese economy. That slow-down has not affected your exports to Canada. Major increases occurred in your exports of cars, motorcycles, steel pipes and tubes, double-knit fabrics, to name just a few. In the case of automobiles, Japan doubled its sales and presently supplies 15 per cent of the total Canadian market for automobiles.

This shift in our bilateral trade might be permanent or it might be temporary. We hope that our export decline is temporary; you hope that your export leap is permanent. As I have said on many occasions, when we had a surplus, Canada does not seek a bilateral balancing of trade with any country, Japan included. Now that the shoe (granted it is a small one) is on the other foot—our foot—now that you have the surplus and we have the deficit, I do not intend to change my tune. We do not seek a balancing in our two-way trade. What we do seek, however, is a better balance in the terms of access to each other's market. We want the freedom to sell in your market. Sincerely, we do not feel that this is yet the case. I will come back to this point in a moment.

But first let me look at the content of the trade between our two countries.

Canada has been one of Japan's most important sources of industrial materials and foodstuffs—73 per cent of Canadian exports to Japan are in this category. We are in this position because we are stable and competitive suppliers. This trade has been good for Canada and it has certainly been good for Japan. We want it to continue on a mutually advantageous basis.

In the other direction, Canada has been a major market for Japanese manufactured products—97 per cent of our imports in 1971 were in this category. Your performance in Canada is a tribute to your marketing skills, but I submit it is also an indication of the openness of the Canadian market. Look again at the products you sell in

Canada. Automobiles, trucks and motorcycles, TV sets, tape-recorders and radios, steel products, snowmobiles and textiles. Most of these items compete directly with Canadian products in the Canadian market.

At the very mention of the word textiles I know you expect me to say something about Canada's textile policy.

Textile products are still an important part of your exports to us, although they are becoming less so as Japanese sales to Canada of automotive, steel and electronic goods increase. Of the 15 leading imports categories from Japan last year, textiles made up only 10 per cent of the total.

Textiles are recognized internationally as a "problem sector" of world trade. In this situation Canada does maintain some trade-restraint arrangements with Japan. But they are selective. Canada's textile policy very carefully sets out the criteria for the imposition of trade controls in this sector: imports must be causing or threatening serious injury, and the manufacturer seeking safeguards for particular products must demonstrate that he will become internationally viable through rationalization plans which he must present to the textile board. We have not asked for restraints over broad categories of goods. Restraints on individual products are removed when they are no longer needed. In the longer term, we look to a solution to the textile problem by an orderly opening-up of markets by all countries. We support efforts in the GATT to this end.

The other major industrialized countries have for many years enforced much more restrictive policies on textiles than has Canada. Per capita, Canada buys ten times more textiles from Japan than does the EEC or the U.K., almost double the per capita imports of the U.S.A. and triple those of Sweden. In value, Canada imports roughly as much from Japan as does the entire European Community—a market approaching 200 million people.

As I was saying, with a very few exceptions all your goods enter Canada without limitation and, in most cases, in direct competition with Canadian products. In turn, we should like to have the fullest opportunity to compete with Japanese products in Japan. That is what I meant when I referred to a better balance in the terms of access.

You buy from us copper, nickel and iron as ores and concentrates; you buy lumber and wood-pulp. But you do not buy our manufactured products. Only 3 per cent of Canadian exports to Japan are end-products, and, if I may speak frankly, as we do among friends, this is an unsatisfactory situation. There is a short-term and a long-term explanation to this.

Both Canada and Japan are coming through a difficult period. Both of us have experienced an economic slow-down. In Japan this has resulted in a decrease in the rate of growth. In Canada it has also resulted in high unemployment, a situation aggravated by the fact that Canada has the fastest-growing labour force among the industrialized nations. In order to provide jobs for this fast-increasing labour force, we feel we must expand further our manufacturing sector. But simple economic recovery from a temporary slow-down and fuller employment is not enough. Each country—yours and mine—has wider obligations and consequently wider objectives, economic, social and political. Canadians have a new desire, a determination to ensure a sophisticated, up-to-date, mature economy. There are some good economic reasons for this; we need job opportunities in all parts of Canada; we need to hedge against sharp fluctuations in commodity markets; we need to provide career opportunities for our bright young people; we need to participate in the more rapidly expanding sectors of international economic activity—the high technology industries. I know you will understand this in Japan.

We want to produce and specialize in the things we do well. This means we need markets not only for our industrial raw materials but for our manufactured products too—markets not only in the U.S., but overseas as well.

In searching for these markets we obviously look to Japan. The "economic miracle" for which you deserve praise has created here a large and rich domestic market. Apart from supplying raw materials and foodstuffs, we have not been able to penetrate it. As I have said, less than 3 per cent of our total exports to Japan were in the form of end-products. This compares badly with our performance in other markets. As a simple example, about 45 per cent of our total exports to the U.S.A. are fully manufactured. In the Philippines, over 60 per cent of our sales are in manufactured form.

In the process of solving our problems of distances and climate, and of developing our natural resources, we have created a body of original technology and products. We know we have competitive products to offer. What we do not have is success in selling in your market, and the question then is why not. There may be several reasons. It may be our fault, it may be your fault, or both. As Mr. Fujino, the President of Mitsubishi, said in the course of his economic mission to Canada last summer, Canadian businessmen do not try hard enough in Japan. He said that they should become more market-oriented, and that they should better familiarize themselves with Japanese business customs and consumer tastes. Mr. Tanaka, your Minister of Trade and Industry, said the same thing in our Ministerial meeting in Toronto last September. We acknowledge that there may be a lot of truth in that, which is why we have included a large group of businessmen in the present mission to Japan.

But I think there are other reasons for our lack of success in selling our manufactured products to Japan. Specifically, I am concerned that Japan's import rules and practices seriously restrict Canadian sales opportunities. We recognize that considerable progress has been made by Japan in the dismantling of direct import controls, and we are looking forward to further progress. In our view much remains to be done. For example, although most Japanese imports are no longer under direct quantitative restrictions, each and every import transaction still requires an import licence or a form of administrative approval. We are also concerned that in a number of cases import items of interest to Canada have been liberalized but that at the same time tariffs have been increased, and we are concerned that other items of special interest to Canada remain under quantitative restriction. We wish to discuss these matters. I am sure that the exchanges I am having with Mr. Tanaka and other ministers through this week, and the discussions our Canadian businessmen are having with leading Japanese industry representatives, will be most useful in providing a mutual understanding of each other's point of view.

Both Canada and Japan are major trading nations. There are natural areas of co-operation between our two countries. In technology, for example, there is much to gain through bilateral co-operation. As a matter of fact, at the Canada-Japan Ministerial Meeting in September, it was agreed that a Canadian science and technology mission would visit Japan in 1972. Plans are proceeding for this mission.

Foreign investment also offers opportunities. For our part, we welcome Japanese investment in Canada, particularly where this investment is directed towards new enterprises. As you may be aware, the matter of foreign investment in Canada has been under Government review. While a policy statement has yet to be made, you can expect that it will not be aimed at restricting foreign investment but rather at ensuring optimum returns to the Canadian economy.

Canadians have some equity investments in Japan. I have noted Japanese progress in dismantling restrictions on foreign investment and I hope that you will continue this policy in order that we can maximize the benefits that accrue from the exchange of capital.

In the multilateral sphere we have much to gain by co-operation;

we have even more to lose if the trading world is allowed to take on a protective colouring. Canada and Japan agreed last September in Toronto, and more recently at the GATT meeting in Geneva, that work should go forward towards a major new round of international trade negotiations. Prospects in this direction seemed dim a year ago, but I think this has changed. The recent dramatic shocks to the international trade and monetary system seem to have revived a willingness among the major trading nations to enter into early negotiations. We welcome recent Japanese pronouncements in this regard.

V. The Commonwealth

˜ Five major developments dominated the Commonwealth scene between 1965 and 1975: the racial situation in Southern Africa; the problem of Rhodesia; the Civil War in Nigeria; Britain's accession to the European Economic Community; and the Indo-Pakistani War, which led to the creation of Bangladesh. It is symptomatic of the dwindling impact of Commonwealth affairs in Canada that Canadian Governments during the period were generally content to follow the leadership of others regarding many of these questions. Indeed, as for some of them, leadership came less from within the Commonwealth than from outside. Even Britain's accession to the European Economic Community, which in Canada ten years before had sparked a good deal of opposition and bitterness as well as a serious questioning of the viability of the Commonwealth,* attracted much less attention in 1973 when Britain joined. Was it that the Commonwealth now appeared to be inconsequential? It will be interesting to see whether the next volume in this series will include a separate chapter on the Commonwealth.

This does not mean to say that from the Canadian point of view the Commonwealth was inactive or futile during the decade. The Colombo Plan continued to provide the major outlet for Canadian aid overseas. The Commonwealth Caribbean was an important focal point of Canadian external relations. After initial expressions of scepticism, Prime Minister Trudeau became a strong supporter of Commonwealth Prime Ministers' meetings. He made sustained efforts to modernize and streamline them, to guide them into new and more useful channels of activity, especially in the field of comparative administration and the technique of government.

New Commonwealth institutions came into being in the field of

---

* Documented in A.E.B. See Chapter VI of this volume regarding its economic implications for Canada.

education and development, notably the Commonwealth Foundation in 1966, designed to increase professional exchanges, the Commonwealth Fund for Technical Cooperation in 1971, which provides technical assistance for economic and social development, the Commonwealth Youth Programme in 1973, the Programme for Applied Studies in Government for middle and senior ranking public servants. The Commonwealth Secretariat gathered strength and experience. The Commonwealth Scholarship Programme continued unabated. Canada contributed to all these throughout the decade. Only in the military training assistance sector did Canadian aid programmes decrease or cease altogether, and that at the request of the countries concerned.

Nevertheless, the fact is that the Commonwealth today is no longer the focal point that it was in Canadian external relations even ten years ago.⁻

37. The Commonwealth – a Canadian Approach

Excerpts from a Press Conference by the Prime Minister, Mr. Pierre-Elliott Trudeau, Ottawa, January 5, 1971.

I am going to Singapore as the leader of one government to meet the leaders of other governments. We will have many things to discuss having to do with the Commonwealth and the many facets of the Commonwealth and of world problems. There is one issue which perhaps seems to dominate the speculations – the issue of the sale of arms to South Africa, just as a couple of years ago it was the issue of Rhodesia. There is always some issue which seems to be the most exciting one, in the sense that people can speculate on whether it is going to lead to disaster or not. But there are many many other things we are going to be doing in Singapore. There are many many things that the Commonwealth is performing and many more that it can perform.

One item that I suggested be put on the agenda was to use to the utmost this occasion of heads-of-state and heads-of-government meeting from various continents so that they could exchange techniques of improving, shall we say, the Parliamentary democratic system. This to me is very fundamental; it is as important as any other issue. Arms sales to South Africa is very important for some countries who want to proceed with the sales and very important for those who don't want to see it proceeded with. But to me it is just one item on the agenda.

The value of the Commonwealth as I see it is to be able periodically to sit down at the head-of-state or head-of-government level and to discuss issues which transcend continents, transcend colour, transcend racial origin, economic basis and so on. It is a forum wherein free men try to find ways to progress in a difficult world and to me there is no single issue so important that it is worthwhile breaking up the Commonwealth.

I was just fascinated at the last Commonwealth meeting by the possibilities of learning from other heads of government the techniques with which they govern their countries, how they meet the challenge of a moving democracy in a technological age or, in other cases, in societies which are just reaching their economic takeoff. And every time I meet a prime minister or a head of state I am always fascinated to know, for instance, how he holds his cabinet together, how his cabinet works, how he renews the membership, how he assures ethnic or regional representation, how the parliamentary system is prevented from bogging down in the particular countries with the particular sets of parliamentary rules that they have, how the more-developed countries can meet the challenge of an increasing number of questions to be dealt with in a seemingly non-expanding amount of parliamentary time available to them, how parliaments in Commonwealth countries with a federal form of constitution, like Australia, meet the conflicting problems between state and Commonwealth relations or federal and provincial relations. All these questions are absolutely fundamental not only to the techniques of governing but to the coherence of modern societies.

To me, to be meeting for ten days with people who in their countries are faced with similar problems and who are obviously trying to find answers to them, to me, this is too valuable an experience to miss the opportunity of exchanging techniques and exchanging ideas. How do they plan? How do they make the plan applicable? How do they shuffle their cabinets? How do they set the priorities, especially when there are two levels of government? How far in advance do they try to get their legislative timetable set up? How do they ensure the co-operation of the opposition parties? And so on, and so on. To me, this is the stuff that you cannot learn in any text-book; it is the stuff that is not taught in any political science seminar in any university of which I know; it is certainly not put in books.

Governments everywhere are facing the challenge of credibility, of relevancy. Will they be able to meet the tremendous turmoils which are shaking every country? Will representative democracy wither away and be replaced by either authoritarian or totalitarian systems, or, at the other end, by mob rule? You see, these questions are fundamental to all of us. They have much more far-reaching consequences than specific issues of what we will do next year about Rhodesia. These have to do with whether societies will survive in a democratic form or not, and this, I repeat, is something which I have been interested in not only in the Canadian Government, but I never fail to meet an important person in another country who can give me some clues as to how they are solving this relevancy gap and credibility gap.

If the Commonwealth were to be of no other use to me than that, I would think it indeed of great value, provided the people there are willing to not only discuss crisis issues but techniques of government.*

A. RHODESIA

˜Southern Rhodesia declared its independence unilaterally on November 11, 1965. The Smith Government is still in office in Salisbury (1977) despite international ostracism, sanctions, mounting guerrilla activity, and general opposition to its position and policies. However, the independence of Angola and Mozambique, following upon Portugal's withdrawal from Africa, and particularly the presence of a substantial Cuban expeditionary force in Angola, have caused the Rhodesian Government—under pressure from Britain, and the United States —to begin to negotiate with the principal Rhodesian African leaders about the timing and other modalities of African majority rule. The course of the negotiations will likely be long and arduous. ˜

38. The Use of Sanctions against Rhodesia

Statement on April 4, 1966, by the Secretary of State for External Affairs, Mr. Paul Martin, to the Standing Committee of the House of Commons on External Affairs and National Defence.

The Rhodesian declaration of independence in 1965 has precipitated an African crisis which could have the greatest implications for the Commonwealth. The illegal regime in Rhodesia is attempting to per-

---

* The Commonwealth heads of government agreed that this subject should be on the agenda of the next Prime Ministers' Meeting, which was held in Ottawa in 1973. See SS 71/6 of February 2, 1971, for the full text of the Final Communiqué of the Singapore conference.

petuate a system whereby the white settlers, who are one-sixteenth of the population, maintain effective political domination over the black majority, who are fifteen-sixteenths of the population.

This has naturally placed a severe strain on relations within the multi-racial Commonwealth and between the West and African states.

I should emphasize at the outset that Rhodesia is British territory. The illegal declaration of independence on November 11, 1965, has not been accepted by Britain and the British Government remains responsible for this territory and for the conditions to govern Rhodesian independence. Negotiations between the British and Rhodesian Governments went on for several years before the illegal declaration of independence last November by Mr. Smith. The negotiations were broken off by the Rhodesians. It then fell to the British Government to decide how to restore a legal situation in Rhodesia, and the decision was to employ economic measures rather than force. Throughout, Britain has clearly had the primary responsibility for Rhodesia. It is the colonial power.

At the same time, in view of Rhodesia's importance to race relations in Africa, and, in view of the multi-racial nature of the Commonwealth, Britain has fully recognized that the Rhodesian question is a matter of legitimate and strong Commonwealth concern. At the 1964 prime ministers' conference, there was an extensive discussion of Rhodesia and a lengthy reference to the question in the communiqué, which includes a statement of the view of Commonwealth prime ministers that independence should take place on the basis of majority rule and that a unilateral declaration of independence would not be recognized. The issue was discussed in 1965 and again referred to in the communiqué in which the Commonwealth prime ministers reaffirmed—all of them—that they were "irrevocably opposed" to any unilateral declaration of independence (UDI).

Up to last November, Canada had normal relations with the Rhodesian Government, and the Canadian Government had already sent a confidential message to the Rhodesian Government some time before the 1965 conference pointing out the grave consequences of a unilateral declaration of independence. This warning was repeated again in the succeeding months.

I myself received representatives of the Government of Rhodesia during the last two and a half years prior to UDI and explained our position, as have other governments in and outside the Commonwealth.

After the unilateral declaration of independence, many Commonwealth countries reacted very strongly, as had been generally anticipated. Various African governments argued that Britain should use force in putting down the illegal Smith regime, as Britain had already done in dealing with civil disorders and revolts in other colonies and dependencies. The Council of Ministers of the Organization of African Unity passed a resolution early in December calling on all member states to sever relations with Britain if the Smith regime was not "crushed" before mid-December. Following this resolution, various countries, including two Commonwealth members, Ghana and Tanzania, withdrew their missions from London. In an attempt to minimize the damage of this breach, Canada assumed the role of protecting power for Britain in Tanzania and for Tanzania in Britain. Ghana has since restored diplomatic relations. It is a matter of great significance to Commonwealth unity when action of this kind takes place.

It was in these circumstances that the Nigerian Government took the initiative in proposing a special Commonwealth conference on Rhodesia. As in the past, one of the objectives was to discuss differing opinions on how to deal with the Rhodesian issue so that these differing opinions should not result in a split in the Commonwealth along racial lines.

At the Lagos conference, Britain welcomed the proposal of Prime Minister Pearson which led to the establishment of two continuing Commonwealth committees. The most important of these, the Sanctions Committee, now chaired by the Canadian High Commissioner in London, is maintaining a review of the sanctions against Rhodesia and considering ways and means of making them more effective. Its tasks include co-ordinating aid to Zambia, which, of course, is an integral aspect of the Rhodesian situation. A second Commonwealth committee is planning a large-scale programme of training for Rhodesian Africans, which will come into effect when constitutional government is restored. This will help to prepare the ground for a viable independent state under a multi-racial administration by training for their new responsibilities leaders, officials, and technicians from the African majority. These committees are a new type of Commonwealth machinery, in that they have been established by the prime ministers for a limited and finite purpose and with some duties which are of a rather wider and less technical nature than those normally carried out by Commonwealth institutions.

Rhodesia is not, of course, of concern only to the Commonwealth and to Africa. World concern about Rhodesia has been expressed through the United Nations, and the Rhodesia problem has been before the General Assembly and Security Council of the United

Nations a number of times in the past three or four years. The issues involved must be understood in the light of developments in modern Africa, with its many new sovereign independent states.

After the unilateral declaration of independence, it was the British Government itself which raised the issue in the Security Council. Britain asked the members of the United Nations to join with her in making effective the economic measures taken against Rhodesia. It was obvious that the co-operation of other nations, particularly the principal trading nations of the world, was necessary if the economic sanctions were to be effective.

The experience of the international community with sanctions is very limited. In fact, I think this is the first instance where a programme of economic sanctions, even though on a non-mandatory basis, has been imposed, unless one were to include the decisions of the Security Council in August of 1963 urging member states of the United Nations to take action in regard to the situation in South Africa.

On November 20, the Security Council adopted a resolution by ten votes to none with one abstention recommending the severance of all economic relations between member states and Rhodesia, including an oil embargo.

Canada has acted in support of Britain's policy of ending the illegal situation by non-military means; and, as a member of the Commonwealth, has acted in concert with Britain and other members of the Commonwealth and through Commonwealth institutions. Canadian economic measures have been taken together with other major trading countries, including the U.S.A. and Western European nations, and in compliance with the Security Council resolution of November 20. This is in accordance with the basic Canadian policy of strong support for the UN in grave situations of this kind.*

The Canadian Government sincerely believed that Rhodesia should not become independent on the basis of the 1961 constitution unless it was substantially modified. In theory, the 1961 constitution could eventually produce majority rule in the country, when sufficient Africans reached the required property and educational level to obtain the franchise for election to 50 out of the 65 seats in the Rhodesian Legislative Assembly. These educational and property qualifications

---

* This basic approach to the Rhodesian problem remained largely unchanged over the years. See CHCD, December 1, 1971, for a restatement by Mr. Sharp in the light of developments at that time.

are so high in terms of conditions in Rhodesia that only a very small percentage of the Africans in Rhodesia qualify to vote for these 50 seats. The qualifications of the remaining 15 seats are lower, and all but one are now occupied by Africans. However, 14 seats out of 65 is a long way short of a majority. Mr. Smith and his followers have made it plain that they did not expect Africans to become the majority of the electorate in their lifetime. It seems clear that the Smith Government made its illegal declaration because Mr. Smith and his followers were unwilling to accept the basis which would assure the attainment of a fair political voice to the majority of the population within a reasonably short period rather than the very long and indefinite period desired by the illegal Government of Mr. Smith. They knew that the consent of the people of Rhodesia as a whole required by Britain would not be given to independence based on the 1961 constitution as it stood.

Another basic reason why Canada is applying economic sanctions to Rhodesia is that such means are much preferable to the use of force, which is always to be avoided if possible.

Military operations could have explosive effects on the whole of Africa and grave international repercussions. The British have not precluded the use of force to restore law and order in Rhodesia, but the British Government has declared that it is unwilling to use force in existing circumstances, and this is a matter where the British Government alone is constitutionally responsible.

The sanctions campaign against the illegal regime which has only been in operation for a relatively short time has not produced the swift results that some had expected, but there is no doubt that the sanctions are adversely affecting the Rhodesian economy. How long it would take for this campaign to produce the desired result I do not know. It is a field in which predictions are inherently difficult. In this case also, the result may well be obtained at a point well short of economic collapse. When Mr. Smith's followers realize that the growing economic dislocation resulting from the UDI is not a temporary phenomenon but rather that their trade will continue indefinitely and progressively to be damaged by sanctions and that their economic prospects are distinctly bleak, they should realize their mistake in backing his illegal action. It is therefore very important to keep up the economic pressure on the illegal regime to make clear to its supporters that there is to be no slackening but rather an increase in the efforts of countries applying the sanctions. We attach importance to the general embargo on exports to Rhodesia by the United States on March 18.

What action will be taken in the United Nations if the sanctions do not give evidence of greater success remains to be seen. Action under Chapter VII of the United Nations Charter could be confined to oil sanctions, or it could be confined to other sanctions.

Speaking for the Canadian Government and knowing what this means to the Commonwealth as a whole, we cannot in any way relent in our conviction and in our effort, within the limitations that we have prescribed for ourselves, to see this matter through. Nothing less than the interests of the Commonwealth is involved in this situation.

A major Canadian contribution, apart from the total embargoes on exports and imports that we have authorized, has been the Canadian contribution to the Zambia airlift. This airlift was necessitated by the action of the illegal regime in cutting off the supply of oil products to Zambia in December of last year after the embargo commenced against Rhodesia. Zambia was almost wholly dependent on Rhodesia for oil products from the refinery inside Rhodesia.

Now, far from being ineffective, this airlift has enabled Zambia to maintain and build up its oil stocks to the point where, with increased use of road transportation, the airlift itself may be reduced or become unnecessary in a few weeks' time. This has been a useful undertaking and one most effectively carried out by the Royal Canadian Air Force. Our participation was orginally intended for a period of one month, starting late in December. We subsequently agreed at the request of the British and Zambian Governments to continue the airlift until the end of April. The position now is being reviewed. I might say that the airlift has cost Canada up to March 31, $1,125,000.

B. SOUTH AFRICA

˜ Canadian policy regarding South Africa came increasingly under criticism, particularly at the time of the 1969-1970 foreign-policy review. This criticism can be epitomized in the question put at the time to Prime Minister Trudeau by a Carleton University student as to how Canada's policy of trading with South Africa could be reconciled with Canadian condemnations of *apartheid*. As quoted in the *Toronto Telegram* on February 25, 1970, Mr. Trudeau replied as follows: "I have a very poor answer to that. We are keeping on with our trade despite the fact that we condemn this policy (*apartheid*) in the United Nations. We are not very proud of this approach. It's not consistent. We should either stop trading or stop condemning." He hoped that the students would "bear with him" until the publication of the foreign affairs White Paper later that year "resolved this contradiction".

No separate White Paper on Africa as such emerged from the foreign policy review, although the subject was dealt with in part in Section 4 of the White Paper on the United Nations, as explained in the following document.* Generally, the Government opted for maintenance of the status quo. While this outlook still prevails on the whole (1977), consideration is being given to tightening up some of its practical approaches to South Africa, such as the phasing out of its commercial offices in Johannesburg and Capetown.**‾

39. Canadian Policy Towards Southern Africa

Extract from Foreign Policy for Canadians, *The United Nations Canadian objectives in Southern Africa, 1970.****

In its approach to this area, the Canadian Government has considered a wide range of options. These included, for example, the maintenance of its current posture, which has evolved steadily in recent years as the situation on the ground has itself evolved. Within this stance there are measures which can be adopted which would further demonstrate Canada's support for human rights and its abhorrence of apartheid in South Africa and of Portuguese colonialism, and its willingness to assist economically the independent African states in the area.

Alternative policy lines considered took two directions—toward an enhancement of economic relations with white southern Africa or toward an intensification of Canadian support of the principle of freedom. Taken to the extreme, these would have involved either (a)

---

* See also Documents 80 and 81 below.

** A group of Canadian academics, churchmen, and journalists produced in late 1970 *The Black Paper: An alternative policy for Canada towards Southern Africa.* See Issue No. 30, June 1, 1971, House of Commons, Standing Committee on External Affairs and National Defence for its full text. The "Black Paper" has also been reproduced by the CIIA in *Behind the Headlines,* XXX, September 1970.

*** *Foreign Policy for Canadians,* "The United Nations", 1970, Section 4, p. 20, Available from QP or DEA, Ottawa.

pursuit of economic benefit without regard for the consequences for Canada's reputation with the black African states and its position in the United Nations or (b) furthering its support of the aspirations of Africans and of the fundamental human rights involved, without regard to the bleak prospect of early practical results and without regard to the substantial economic cost of the severance of Canadian economic and political relations with the white regimes of southern Africa. It must always be borne in mind that economic and political sanctions are not ends in themselves, but are for the purpose of bringing about improvements in the racial policies of the regimes against which they are directed.

The Government has concluded that Canadian interests would be best served by maintaining its current policy framework on the problems of southern Africa, which balances two policy themes of importance to Canadians. The Government intends, however, to give more positive expression to the Social Justice policy theme. To this end, the Canadian Government will make available further economic assistance to black African states of the area to assist them to develop their own institutions and resources. It is also the Government's intention to increase its contribution to the UN Educational and Training Programme for southern Africa.

C. NIGERIA

During the autumn of 1967, civil war broke out in Nigeria. The eastern region of that country, peopled by the Ibos, seceded from the Federation, which had become increasingly wracked by internal dissension among the large ethnic groups making up this country of some 70,000,000 people—e.g. the Hausas in the North, the Yorubas in the Southwest, the Ibos in the Southeast, etc.

The Ibos named their country *Biafra* and launched a military offensive towards Lagos, the federal capital. At first they were generally successful but were eventually unable to consolidate their gains. In a war of attrition time was against them. Their situation—demographically, economically, militarily—was not unlike that of the South during the Civil War in the United States one hundred years before. The Biafrans fought valiantly under their leader, Colonel Odumegwu Ojukwu, but they were heavily outnumbered and the odds against them proved too much. Warfare ceased on January 11, 1970.

Like the South during the Civil War, Biafra sought to enlist outside support for its cause. It mounted an imaginative and highly successful public relations campaign in Western Europe and North America. The plight of its inhabitants as the war ground on evoked mounting sympathy in Canada. The Trudeau Government made large-scale deliveries of relief supplies to both sides. It was also urged to intervene in the conflict. It did not do so, as documented below.¯

40. The Conflict in Nigeria: Basic Canadian Policy

Statement in the House of Commons, November 26, 1968, by the Secretary of State for External Affairs, Mr. Mitchell Sharp.

The civil war in Nigeria has presented both human and political problems of a high order.* The humanitarian problem has been one of amassing vast quantities of food and other assistance for those in need as a result of the hostilities. A great effort, and I think this will be agreed upon on all sides, has been made by the International Red Cross and by other international and national bodies to alleviate the suffering. It is seldom that people of the world have gathered so much in a voluntary way, and amongst governments, for relief of the suffering in a country which has been torn by civil war. But more will be needed as long as the war continues. I can assure the House that Canada will continue to play an important part in this effort.

The political problem is more delicate because, as has been made clear, this is a civil war. There will have to be a readiness by all parties to compromise if a negotiated settlement is to be reached. We in Canada would of course be ready to facilitate the peace keeping if there were any indication whatever that this would help bring an end to the war. Let us be frank about this. What has been missing so far is not more mediators—there are lots of those—but an indication from both sides that they are willing to participate in meaningful negotiations. The Commonwealth Secretary-General, the Organization for African Unity, both stand ready at a moment's notice to assist in the negotiating process. All they are waiting for is word from both par-

---

* See SS 68/19 of November 26, 1968, for further background as presented to the House of Commons by Prime Minister Trudeau that day. See also his statement, CHCD, November 27, 1969, reaffirming the Government's decision not to intervene in the conflict. Hostilities came to an end on January 11, 1970. SS 69/21 of November 25, 1969, provides a chronology of Canadian efforts to help to ease the civil war.

ties that they are prepared to make the concessions necessary to get meaningful negotiations under way. As has been said by many speakers, action by outsiders in a situation such as exists in Nigeria is of no value whatever unless it is effective. As the Prime Minister himself said at the opening of this debate, unless the action is responsive to the wishes of those directly involved it can produce hostile reactions.

Canada's whole policy towards African and other newly emerging countries in recent years has been built on a spirit of co-operation rather than intervention. African history is ripe with examples of domination and intervention by peoples from other continents, and Africans are rightly sensitive about their hard-won sovereignty and their right to manage their own affairs.

Canada has earned a good name in Africa. Many speakers have mentioned this. They have said that Canada has a good reputation. Why do we have a good reputation? Because we observe these principles of co-operation and non-intervention. We have been able to make a positive contribution to developments on that continent. We have been welcome in the Commonwealth countries of Africa, and we have been welcome in the francophone countries of Africa. We have been welcome because our policy has been to assist Africans and not to tell them how to run their affairs.

Canada's policy has therefore been recognized as sympathetic and disinterested. This Government does not intend to change that policy regardless of emotional appeals, however well-intentioned they may be, because I believe, and so I believe do all Hon. Members of this House, that if we were to abandon that policy we would become unacceptable and ineffective in the vast task that remains on that continent to overcome the problems of underdevelopment and to create viable political societies on that continent.

The Government's responsibilities on the international scene are different from those of private organizations. In saying this I am not criticizing non-governmental groups operating in Nigeria or in other areas. The churches and other groups have done commendable work in bringing aid to the needy, and I join with many of the Members who have spoken in praising their work. I support it. I hope that everybody in this House and that all Canadians will support the work of the churches. What I am saying is that governments must act as governments. For example, the Canadian Government has chosen to funnel its food and transport aid in the Nigerian situation through the International Committee of the Red Cross, the traditional organization for the assembly and distribution of assistance in difficult situations of this sort.

The International Committee of the Red Cross has maintained working relations with the federal Nigerian authorities and with those in charge on the rebel side. It has the necessary support staff and organization on both sides. It has proven worthy of our support and continued co-operation.

The Standing Committee (on External Affairs and National Defence) has made a most commendable examination of the many complex factors involved in this difficult situation. Its report contains recommendations in nine areas, and it might be useful if I commented briefly on those recommendations. We shall, of course, be giving further study to the points made, and shall be pursuing them if this is feasible or desirable as the situation develops further. An indication of our views on them, however, may be helpful at this stage.

On the observer team the Committee noted that the initial invitation for the observers was for two months, and suggested the Government request the Nigerians to extend the duration of this invitation. In the interval since the Committee's report was presented the Nigerians have in fact extended the operation of the team for a further month. We have been able to extend our participation accordingly and would expect further discussion of this and related questions at an appropriate time with the Federal Military Government, and with those other countries and bodies participating in the observer team.*

To the extent that the Committee's second recommendation deals with continuing and future Canadian assistance to Nigeria, I can report that we are in regular contact with the World Bank and with interested governments. The World Bank currently has a team of experts in Nigeria studying economic projects and priorities, and we expect to have the benefit of the conclusions of this team when it returns. It is important to note that assessments of this kind in any country must be carried out with the concurrence of the government concerned, and I may add, Mr. Speaker, that in this respect the co-operation between Nigeria and the World Bank is proving to be very useful at this critical juncture.

Insofar as the Committee was referring to emergency food aid, the Government has had constant advice from the International Committee of the Red Cross both on the amounts needed and on the particular categories of food to be emphasized.

---

* Canada was a member of this team, along with Britain, Poland, and Sweden.

The question of land and sea corridors has been discussed in the Committee and in this House. It is one of those items on which it has not been possible for the two sides to agree, despite the best efforts of the relief agencies. I am sure we all regret this because it is quite clear, as was pointed out by one of the speakers in the far corner, who said, "It would take planes moving in at about one a minute to supply the food that will probably be needed", and what we need will probably be land corridors.

I regret, as I am sure do all Hon. Members, the fact that it has not been possible to work this out. I hope it still will be possible. Most of all I hope that the war will be over.

The Committee's proposal for international machinery to aid innocent civilian victims of hostilities is one I supported at the United Nations.

The Committee's third recommendation relates to the continuation of our emergency aid to the victims of the hostilities. The Government has intensified its efforts to be of assistance in the humanitarian sphere. I wish to announce, Mr. Speaker, that we have made a further allocation of food aid to Nigeria-Biafra in the amount of $1,600,000. A shipment will be made early in the new year.

This aid will be distributed, as the other food aid was, to both sides. As to the airlift into rebel territories, it is obvious that daylight operations would permit the delivery of much larger quantities of relief. The Prime Minister therefore appealed to the rebel authorities to agree to daylight flights. I earnestly hope that Colonel Ojukwu will give his consent without further delay. It is tragic that food should be waiting to be moved in to feed hungry children, and is being held up because the necessary authority has not been granted for the movement. As to relief operations on the Federal side, Canadian Caribou aircraft have been offered through the Canadian Red Cross Society, and we await confirmation from the Nigerian Red Cross that they can be put to effective use.

The Committee proposed that we should offer, in concert with other interested governments, to provide non-military assistance in building a civil airstrip for the exclusive use of relief flights. This is a useful proposal, which will be explored, along with others, in preparing further development of our aid program to Nigeria. For the immediate future we have considered it better to use the facilities already existing and, for example, just recently we offered the lighter *Caribou* aircraft for use in federal-held territory, since the *Hercules* is too heavy for the forward airfields. It has been said on a number of occasions that the Canadian Government would like to have the

Hercules aircraft fly into Nigerian territory and into Biafran territory. They are not flying to Biafran territory because we cannot obtain agreement from the rebels, and they are not flying into Nigeria because there are no airstrips suitable for that size of aircraft.

The Government heartily endorses the Committee's appeal to all Canadians to support the relief effort with their contributions. With the new allocation I have mentioned, the Government's contributions to relief and transport activities now come close to $3 million.

The Committee's sixth recommendation deals with assistance to children from stricken areas. The Canadian *Hercules* aircraft stationed on the island of Fernando Po has been authorized to transport refugees to other neighbouring countries which are ready to welcome them. These people have been brought out from the rebel area by the Red Cross in order that they can be given better care. The Government has been happy to assist the International Red Cross in moving them to other countries. As to bringing children from the rebel area to Canada, the Government does not think it wise to press this idea in the face of the adverse views of those directly concerned.

The Government accepts the Committee's view that Canada should not sell arms to either side in this conflict. Indeed, as Hon. Members know, that has been the Government's policy throughout.

In its eighth recommendation the Committee urged the Government to intensify its efforts to persuade the parties to accept mediation. The caution attached by the Committee to this point is sound: that we should not operate in such a way as to jeopardize the effectiveness of our relief efforts. There are, as we have said, limitations on the Government's action on this essentially political question; but I can assure the House that within these limits we shall work strenuously for a peaceful settlement of this dispute.

On the proposal that Canada should contribute to an eventual peace-keeping force in Nigeria, I think it is premature to offer comment before a settlement or cease fire has been achieved or before the terms of any peace-keeping operation are known. I may add this, however: As is well known, Canada has always taken a positive look at peace-keeping proposals, and I can assure the House that any proposals in respect of the Nigerian situation will be given prompt and careful consideration by the Government.

An amendment has been proposed to the Committee's report, Mr. Speaker, which would oblige the Government to take this question to the United Nations, to the General Assembly or to the Third Committee. As the Prime Minister explained this afternoon, and as has been made clear before, following intensive study of the matter we have come to the conclusion that this is neither a practical nor a useful initiative. Any proposal to have the matter discussed at the United Nations would not gain more than minimal support. For that reason alone an initiative would not be effective and would have no helpful influence on the situation. Moreover, if we were to press on regardless of the lack of support, Canada's position in the world body would be affected and the possibility of our taking useful steps on this or other matters would be seriously reduced.

The Prime Minister said that we would incur the hostility and opposition of African states, and that would jeopardize our policy of dealing with the situation effectively. We would probably be told that we were not welcome in providing relief assistance in Nigeria, and our observer would probably be told to go home.

And now may I comment on the suggestion that we should intervene to press Britain, the U.S.S.R. and others to cease their sales of arms to the participants in this war? I am sure this House would be gratified if all the countries currently supplying arms to the two sides would cease to do so, and, if I thought that action by Canada would accomplish this, I would not hesitate to propose it. This is, however, a matter of policy for each government to establish for itself. It is well known that the French Government has denied it provides arms to the rebels. Moreover I ask the Members of the House this question: Would the situation be improved if external pressure caused the British Government to cease all its arms supplies to Nigeria, leaving the field open to the U.S.S.R. to become its principal source?

I should like to refer again to the hope, widely felt by the Canadian people, that this civil war can be brought to an end. I said earlier that the achievement of a peaceful negotiated settlement does not depend on the provision of facilities or the making of proposals by outsiders. Canada stands ready to be of assistance if that would be helpful; and I hope that the responsible course we have followed enhances the possibility of our playing a useful role. Whether any progress can be made toward peace depends, however, on the parties to the dispute. In particular, in my view, it depends on the Nigerian Government providing sufficiently convincing guarantees to the Ibos of their security after the conclusion of hostilities, and on the willingness of the rebels to envisage a negotiated settlement short of complete independence from Nigeria. To advocate a negotiated settlement and secession is a contradiction in terms. I would therefore urge those Canadians who have influence with the rebel side, both in this House and outside, to press them toward conciliation, and thus toward a peaceful settlement.

In conclusion may I restate the basic principles which have guided the Canadian Government's policy in this matter and which will continue to guide that policy:

1. The Government will continue to provide assistance generously to meet the needs of the people of Nigeria as a whole.
2. We will maintain close liaison with the legitimate government of Nigeria in order to provide relief to the population under its control.
3. We will continue to urge the secessionist authorities to co-operate in arrangements acceptable to the Nigerian Government for the relief of the population under rebel control.
4. The Government will be ready, when this tragic conflict is over, to co-operate with the Nigerian Government in the important tasks of reconstruction and rehabilitation it will face.
5. We will work toward a better international legal framework within which humanitarian assistance can be provided to people affected by civil conflict.
6. The Government will not violate international law by supporting or endorsing any move, bilateral or multilateral, which will con-stitute intervention in Nigerian internal affairs.
7. We will continue to call upon both sides in the conflict to negoti-ate their differences.
8. The Government will vigorously support any conciliation effort which may develop under the auspices of the OAU, the Common-wealth Secretariat or any other body acceptable to the parties.
9. We will stand ready to assist, if so desired by both parties, in promoting a negotiated settlement.

D. THE COMMONWEALTH CARIBBEAN

ˉ Canadian relations with the countries now commonly grouped to-gether under the general heading Commonwealth Caribbean are of long standing. They go back to the sugar-rum-molasses for cod-cereals trade of the eighteenth and nineteenth centuries. Trade was followed by investments. Canadian banks and insurance companies gradually acquired an influential position in many of the islands, not only those with a Commonwealth connection, but elsewhere in the area as well. Canadian oil and aluminum interests have been prominent there also.

Recently, the pattern has been changing. Many Canadian banks, insurance, and mining companies have been nationalized by local governments, most of which became independent during the 1960s. Four sectors now dominate Canadian-Caribbean relations: aid, immigration, sugar, and tourism. Out of this mixture an unusual amalgam is emerging. Canada is beginning for the first time to acquire a reputation for paternalism. Local nationalists have criticized Canada sharply for some of its trade and investment-related practices—e.g., its sugar and immigration policies, labour relations in the tourist field, etc. Incidents, some fatal to Canadian visitors, have occurred.

Canadian aid allocations to the Commonwealth Caribbean have, per capita, surpassed by far those to all other areas. Mid-way during the decade they stood at $8.80 (U.S.) for Barbados and Belize, $6.30 (U.S.) for Guyana; $4.89 (U.S.) for Trinidad and Tobago; $2.64 (U.S.) for Jamaica. The next highest Commonwealth aid allocation per capita was Ghana at $0.84 (U.S.). India and Pakistan, of course, received far greater amounts overall, but not per capita.~

41. Canada and the Commonwealth Caribbean

Text of the communiqué issued at the close of the conference that took place in Ottawa from July 6 to 8, 1966, between Canada and the Commonwealth countries of the Caribbean, with the texts of the Protocol on the Canada–West Indies Trade Agreement and of the Canadian Government Proposal on Sugar:

During the past three days, substantial progress has been made on the process of closer consultation and co-operation among the Commonwealth countries of the Western Hemisphere. This development holds great promise for the future and will bring early practical benefits to all the participants. The Heads of Government participating in the present Conference are determined to continue and strengthen the fruitful collaboration among them which has been begun in Ottawa this week.

At the Conference, Antigua, the Bahamas, Barbados, Canada, Dominica, Grenada, Guyana, Jamaica, Montserrat, St. Kitts–Nevis–Anguilla, St. Lucia, St. Vincent and Trinidad and Tobago were represented by their Heads of Government and British Honduras by the Minister of Natural Resources and Trade. Britain was represented by an observer and, by special invitation, the University of the West Indies was also represented.

Trade

A review of the special trade and economic relations among the Commonwealth Caribbean–Canada group of countries was a central feature of the Conference. Ministers were unanimous in the great value they attach to maintaining and further strengthening the special trade ties between Canada and the Commonwealth countries of the Caribbean. To this end, a special Protocol to the 1925 Trade Agreement has been approved by the Conference and signed by all participating countries. This Protocol provides for continuing close consultation and co-operation within the Commonwealth Caribbean–Canada group of countries.

It was agreed that a study of the question of a free-trade area between the Commonwealth Caribbean and Canada might be made jointly by appropriate institutions to be designated by the Trade and Economic Committee.

Aid

The Heads of Government agreed that they shared an obligation in common to ensure the most effective use of the limited resources available in the Caribbean area and that an increased effort should be made to mobilize additional resources to accelerate the pace of economic development in the Commonwealth Caribbean area. The Canadian Government announced that it was Canada's intention to strengthen its aid efforts in the countries of the Commonwealth Caribbean, with which Canada had special links. These countries had demonstrated their ability to use available resources effectively to meet their urgent needs.

The Canadian Government indicated that its basic aid programme for the Commonwealth Caribbean countries will be generally made more flexible in its terms, and over each of the next five years will reach at least the level of the enlarged programme for the current fiscal year of a total of more than $65 million for the period. The proposals for special aid for the Universities of the West Indies and Guyana and for a Caribbean Broadcasting Service would raise the minimum figure to $75 million for the five-year period. With good and practicable projects, the Commonwealth Caribbean part of the expanding Canadian aid programme for all purposes will rise substantially above that figure.

Reference was made to the problem of mobilizing in the area adequate financial resources to meet all of the local costs associated with economic development, and Canada indicated its willingness, in appropriate cases, to finance a portion of local costs of development projects.

It was also agreed to study the possibility of establishing a financial institution for regional development which might be used as a method of financing projects of particular interest to the smaller areas, as well as projects which would benefit the region as a whole.

Transport and Communications

The Heads of Government discussed matters relating to transport and communications both between Canada and the Caribbean and within the Caribbean area. The needs of the area for improved regional air services were reviewed and the technical co-operation of the Canadian authorities in meeting these needs was offered. Many of the governments presented the need for improvement of airport facilities and the Canadian Government agreed that these were matters which would be examined. The need for multilateral discussion with a view to the conclusion of air-services agreements between Canada and the Commonwealth Caribbean countries was discussed and the desirability of consultation and the greatest degree of mutual co-operation in the negotiation of bilateral arrangements with other countries was stressed.

The restoration of direct shipping services between Canada and the Caribbean area was urged by several delegations and it was agreed by the Canadian authorities that this matter should be fully investigated in the light of its possible long-term contribution to the promotion of trade. Reference was made to the international telecommunication services within the islands; Canada would be pleased to provide technical training and advice within the context of the External Aid Programme. The Canadian Government offered to co-operate in working out and underwriting arrangements for first-class air-mail service at surface rates between Canada and the Commonwealth Caribbean countries to be established as soon as technical arrangements could be made.

Migration

In the discussion on migration, the Heads of the Caribbean Governments took note of the fact that immigrants from the Commonwealth Caribbean were eligible for entry into Canada on as favourable a basis as immigrants from any other parts of the world and that migration from the area to Canada had increased in recent years. However, they emphasized the need for continued and expanded migration opportunities for their people. The Canadian Government announced that Canada was prepared to keep its door open to qualified immigrants from the Commonwealth Caribbean on a completely non-discriminatory basis. The experimental movement of seasonal farm labour to Canada from Jamaica during the current year was reviewed and Canada indicated that, if the experiment proved successful and there was a continued need for outside labour in future years, consideration would be given to broadening the programme to include other Caribbean countries. Canada also announced a 100 per cent increase in the special household-service worker movement from the Caribbean to Canada, and the extension of the Canadian Immigration Assisted Passage Loan Scheme to immigrants from Commonwealth countries of the Caribbean.

Other Economic Questions

The Heads of Government considered ways of promoting private investment in the Commonwealth Caribbean. They noted that there were no restrictions on the flow of Canadian private capital to the area, but expressed concern at the effect which the absence of double-taxation agreements could have on that flow. In the context of the relations between Canada and the Commonwealth Caribbean countries, the Canadian Government indicated its readiness to enter into discussions leading to agreements with interested Commonwealth countries in the area to avoid double taxation.

They also discussed possibilities for developing the tourist industry in the Caribbean and, as part of the process, as indicated in the report of the Trade Committee, the Canadian Government undertook to give consideration to the suggestion that enlarged duty-free exemptions be allowed to Canadians entering from Commonwealth Caribbean countries.

International Questions of Common Interest

The Commonwealth countries in the Western Hemisphere emphasized the great value they attach to their relations with the United States and the many countries of Latin America which make up the membership of the Organization of American States. Those participants in the Conference whose countries would be eligible for membership in that Organization indicated their intention either to carry out a joint study of the question or to give one another the benefit of national studies which were being made. They also expect to consult together on this question in the months ahead.

There was a thorough discussion of the implications of the continuing situation in Rhodesia. The Heads of Government noted that, unless there was an early solution of this grave issue, the future of the Commonwealth as a multi-racial association would clearly be endangered. They expressed the hope that such an early solution will be announced by the British Government at the forthcoming meeting of Commonwealth Prime Ministers.

The Conference endorsed the resolution adopted by the Commonwealth Caribbean Heads of Government at their recent meeting in Barbados affirming their fullest support for the self-determination of British Honduras in accordance with the wishes of the people of the country.

Cultural Relations

The Conference recognized the desirability of further strengthening the cultural ties between Canada and the Commonwealth Caribbean. It was decided to establish appropriate machinery for strengthening such ties with a view to giving the Canadian public the opportunity of seeing in their own country the expression by West Indian artists of indigenous Caribbean art forms such as the dance and the steelband and to making the West Indian public familiar with Canadian artistic achievements, particularly in the field of the performing arts. The Government of Canada also indicated its willingness to assist with the establishment of broadcasting facilities serving the entire region of the Commonwealth Caribbean, and consultations will now take place among the broadcasting authorities of the participating governments.

Methods of Following up the Canada–Caribbean Talks

In keeping with the intention of Heads of Government that the consultations instituted at this Conference should be continued, it was agreed that a meeting of the governments represented should be held, at a date to be fixed and at an agreed venue in the West Indies, for a general discussion of Commonwealth Caribbean–Canada relationships and to review progress. In the meantime, to ensure that effective follow-up action is taken on the matters discussed at this Conference, it was agreed that, in addition to normal bilateral consultations, the High Commissioners of the Commonwealth Caribbean countries in

Ottawa should consult jointly with Canadian officials regarding the timing and location of the first meeting of the Trade and Economic Committee and the form of other consultative arrangements for the future.

Protocol on Canada–West Indies Trade Agreement

Recognizing the important changes which have taken place in their trade and commercial relations since the negotiation of the Canada – West Indies Trade Agreement of 1925;

Recognizing the desirability of close co-operation and collaboration in the development of their respective economies in order to facilitate the most efficient utilization of resources and the maximum development of mutually advantageous trade;

Taking into account the urgent economic development needs of the Commonwealth Caribbean countries and the key importance of trade to the raising of their standards of living and the progressive development of their economies;

Taking into account the common interest of the Commonwealth countries of the Caribbean and Canada in ensuring a fair and remunerative return at stable prices for exports of primary products of particular interest to them and the urgent need of these countries to diversify their exports:

Antigua, the Bahamas, Barbados, British Honduras, Canada, Dominica, Grenada, Guyana, Jamaica, Montserrat, St. Kitts–Nevis–Anguilla, Saint Lucia, Saint Vincent, Trinidad and Tobago agree as follows:

1. To examine the 1925 Canada–West Indies Trade Agreement in detail with a view to its further amendment or renegotiation in the light of the results of the "Kennedy Round" of trade negotiations under the General Agreement on Tariffs and Trade;
2. To continue the Canada–West Indies Trade Agreement of 1925 in force, *ad interim*, subject to the following:
   (i)   to the extent that it may be necessary in order to avoid conflict between the provisions of the Agreement and the provisions of the GATT, the obligations of the Agreement, after consultation, may be waived.
   (ii)   Canada will consult with the Commonwealth countries of the Caribbean before concluding any agreement in the "Kennedy Round" which would have the effect of reduc-

ing margins of preference bound under the Agreement and to take such reductions into account in any renegotiation of the Agreement.

(iii)   The direct shipment requirements of Article VII are waived.

(iv)   Part II of the Agreement relating to steamship services is recognized as being no longer in effect.

3.   To consult upon request with respect to measures to encourage economic development which might substantially affect the trading interests of the other parties, with a view to avoiding possible damage to those trading interests and to achieving the best use of resources, taking into account the scope for regional co-operation.

4.   To consult and co-operate on tourism and in establishing or improving transportation, communications and other facilities designed to promote mutually beneficial trade and other exchanges.

5.   To work together in international community discussions and arrangements, and particularly to seek to secure and maintain an appropriate and effective price range under a new International Sugar Agreement which will be remunerative to producers and equitable to consumers.

6.   To endeavour to revive the banana trade and to bring about increased sales of bananas to Canada from the Commonwealth countries of the Caribbean.

7.   To seek to secure acceptable conditions of access for wheat in world markets in order to bring about increased trade at prices which will be remunerative to efficient producers and fair to consumers, taking into account world food needs.

8.   The Commonwealth countries of the Caribbean undertake in the development of local flour mills to provide fair and equal opportunities for the Canadian industry to participate in their development and for Canada to have a fair and equal opportunity to supply the wheat requirements of such new mills.

9.   The Commonwealth countries of the Caribbean undertake to ensure that Canadian exporters of salted cod are given a fair and equal opportunity to supply the market requirements at prices which will be remunerative to efficient producers and fair to consumers.

10.   To accord fair and equitable treatment to individuals and enterprises of the other parties.

11. Canada undertakes to require that the origin and Canadian content of any rum marketed in Canada be clearly marked and to use its good offices with the provincial authorities to facilitate the marketing of rum from the Commonwealth Caribbean countries.

12. In pursuance of the foregoing to establish a Commonwealth Caribbean–Canada Trade and Economic Committee to consult on trade, financial and related matters, which shall meet from time to time at ministerial or senior official level as may be appropriate.

In respect of those territories for which the United Kingdom Government has a responsibility in these matters, this Protocol is being signed with the authority of the Secretary of State for the Colonies.

Canadian Government Proposal on Sugar

The Canadian Government proposal regarding raw sugar imports from the Commonwealth Caribbean countries and territories is to provide on a unilateral basis duty free entry for a quantity of raw sugar equal to the average of such imports for the last five years.

This would mean the abolition for such countries and territories only of the present British Preferential Tariff rate of approximately 29 cents a cwt. Any allocation of this tariff quota would be a matter for the Commonwealth Caribbean Governments.

This tariff quota would, of course, be a new tariff preference and could not therefore be implemented before a waiver was obtained from the no-new-preference provisions of the GATT. Releases would also be required from the Australian, South African and United Kingdom Governments with whom Canada has trade agreements involving obligations concerned the Canadian tariff on raw sugar. The Canadian Government will be prepared to use its best endeavours with the Canadian sugar refiners to ensure that the amount of the tariff free quota is in fact taken up each year and that the full benefit of the additional margin of preference is received by the West Indian producers.*

---

* This arrangement was terminated unilaterally by the Canadian Government on April 17, 1970. This led to a series of difficulties with the Commonwealth Caribbean countries concerned. As a result, Mr. Paul Martin, Government Leader in the Senate, was sent on a special mission to the Caribbean. During September and October 1970, he made two visits to the area. He admitted "frankly, both to the governments and to the public, that we should have handled the issue perhaps in a more tactful way". He also brought with him the Canadian Government's offer "to extend the sugar-rebate payments for the calendar year 1970 and the offer of a regional agricultural fund" to assist in improving sugar production. See his statement to the Senate, December 8, 1970, for a detailed account of the results of his mission. See also the Report of the Standing Committee of the Senate on *Canada-Caribbean Relations*, Ottawa, QP, 1970, for an in-depth analysis of the subject. In addition, SS 67/6 of February 27, 1967, by Trade and Commerce Minister Winters describes the basic patterns of Canada's trade with the Caribbean region. Fundamentally, the Commonwealth Caribbean sugar problems stem from high production costs and relatively low productivity in comparison with competitor countries. The 1925 Canadian—West Indies Trade Agreement was ended in 1976 when the Commonwealth Caribbean countries decided to adhere to the Lomé Convention of the European Economic Community.

VI. International Economic Policy

˜ This chapter deals with Canada's basic trade and tariff policies, balance-of-payments difficulties, trade with state-trading countries, relations with the European Economic Community, and problems of the international monetary system. It should be read in conjunction with the economic section of Chapter III on Canada—United States relations and with Chapter VII on international development.

The subjects dealt with concentrate on the Canadian approach which continued to favour international monetary stability and multilateral trading arrangements. It should of course be projected against the background of certain intractable economic problems affecting all countries in the world, and not just Canada—for instance, inflation and unemployment, rapidly rising energy costs with resulting food and fertilizer production problems, expanding populations, an increasingly polluted environment whose resources are being consumed on an unprecedented scale.˜

42. Basic Trade Policy for the Mid-1960s

Statement by Mr. Mitchell Sharp, Minister of Finance, to the Canadian Society of New York, November 4, 1966. (Extracts)

I shall talk about two areas of economic policy facing us in North America.

The first is: How are we to continue the attack on barriers to international trade over, let us say, the next decade and how should we deal with other issues of commercial policy? I want to consider, in particular, what ought to be our strategy for trade policy after the "Kennedy Round" has been brought to a conclusion next spring.

Second, I shall talk briefly about the problem of financing the growth of world trade.

First then, trade policy. I begin by saying that trade policy means a good deal more than tariff policy. For example, tariffs have very little to do with trade in agricultural products. Quotas, production subventions, and economic aid are much more important to the movement of agricultural products between countries than are conventional tariff barriers.

Nor have European countries or our own two countries depended upon tariffs to limit the impact of imports of certain manufactured products from new sources at highly competitive prices. This is the problem of "low-cost" or "disruptive" imports, which is being dealt with either by import quotas imposed by importing countries or export quotas negotiated with the governments of exporting countries.

A third example of commercial policy problems of our time that has little to do with conventional tariffs is how to trade with those economies of Eastern Europe and Asia in which exporters and importers are branches of the state.

Moreover, I am inclined to suspect that in the great modern market entities, such as the United States and the European Economic Community, the tariff plays a relatively small role in the shaping of the economy, or in the solving of real trading problems. In these big mature economies it is much more a taxing device.

But what about the role of protective tariffs in the smaller economies, such as, say, Canada and Australia? These countries have small national markets with industries which have been stimulated over the years by protective tariff systems. In such countries the tariff has a more decisive impact on the industrial structure and the allocation of resources.

In Canada, for example, our population is too small to provide large enough home markets to support the optimum scale of production for quite a wide range of manufactured products. At the same time, many of our potential export markets are fenced off by protective tariffs, so that we are often denied the foreign sales that for us, as distinct from the United States or the Common Market countries, we must have to manufacture competitively.

Canada has been a member and firm supporter of the General Agreement on Tariffs and Trade since its foundation. A nation so dependent on foreign trade must try to ensure that world trade is conducted on as wide and as free a basis as possible. It is easy enough to state this general orientation. The real problem is how to continue to move in this direction in a realistic manner. I believe it is important that in the "Kennedy Round", and in future trade negotiations, we ensure that the particular problems of the smaller economies are adequately taken into account. This is an objective we should share in common. Canada is still the United States' largest market. Our mutual interest lies in finding methods of freeing trade in which Canada can participate enthusiastically—methods which fit Canada's circumstances.

In devising our approach to tariff negotiations, we have always shied away from any simple mathematical formula. We adopted a more selective approach to the "Kennedy Round" than the United States did, and I expect we shall continue to favour the selective approach to tariff cutting in the future simply because this enables us to participate more effectively in negotiations.

What I mean by this is that we are bound to look for those opportunities where a significant tariff adjustment in the markets of the great economic entities would provide us with the opportunity to move out of the confines of our small national markets and produce and sell on the same continental or intercontinental scale as do the industries of the United States and the European Community.

The Canada–United States Automotive Products Agreement was one essay in such a policy. We realized that to improve the efficiency of our industry we had to make a smaller range of car parts and a smaller range of vehicles. This could only be done if we had free entry to a mass market; for these products and for this industry, this meant the market of the United States. At the same time, we were prepared to provide free entry in our market albeit with some conditions and limitations for an initial period.

The Automotive Products Agreement is working well from the point of view of both our countries, and I am satisfied that it has done no harm to the trade of any other country. It is a striking example of what can be achieved by a realistic selective approach to trade policy.

It is, I think, most important to understand two points. First, that the form of the automotive agreement—by which I mean the conditions we attached to free entry into Canada, and the understandings reached with each company—was peculiar to this industry. For other products, other arrangements. Second, for this industry it was free entry into the market of the United States which was essential for Canada. For other products, free entry elsewhere may be equally important.

Let me take an example. One broad sector for which there is obvious scope for a greater international division of labour is forest products—lumber, wood products, pulp and paper. But the great expansion of markets for these products will not be confined to North America. Much of it will be in Europe and Japan. A purely bilateral trade arrangement between Canada and the United States in this sector would be second best to a tariff arrangement involving all the industrial countries of the free world. Canada and the United States would both gain much more from a multilateral than from a bilateral arrangement.

Let me give another example. I believe that for all industrialized economies it would make a great deal of sense to provide for the free movement of basic materials—for example, nickel, aluminum, lead and zinc, and a variety of chemicals. I should like to see all the free world move to free trade in these products in a concerted fashion. We should all gain.

What does all this mean for future trade policy? It means, I believe, that legislatures must be bold and must be prepared to back up their governments in negotiations, not just to reduce tariffs by formulae but to eliminate them where that is a part of a sensible pattern.

I should not wish the remarks I have just made about possible trade policies for the future to imply any lack of Canadian support for the "Kennedy Round" of trade negotiations. Canada is participating actively in these negotiations and I am still confident that they will be substantially successful. But it is not too early to look ahead to the next stage of the continuing campaign for freer trade.

We must also recognize the potential importance for world trade of the state-trading economies of the Far East and of Eastern Europe. Mainland China, the U.S.S.R. and the Communist countries of Eastern Europe are becoming increasingly significant as traders. Certainly they are important customers for us in Canada. In our experience, the markets of the state-trading countries are difficult to cultivate. Often their willingness to buy is limited by the preoccupation of the governments of these countries with achieving bilateral balances with their individual trading partners in the West, as well as by their shortage of foreign exchange. In Eastern Europe, competition from traditional suppliers in the West—from Britain, France and Germany—is a powerful factor. These countries have been trading with Eastern Europe for many years. They know the markets; they are in a position to give effective after-sales service for their sales of capital equipment, and they are not hesitant about extending fairly generous credit facilities in order to make sales.

In cultivating these markets, much will depend on the initiative and imagination of our businessmen and financial institutions in developing trade with these countries. Recently there have been signs of a greater readiness, on the part of some of these countries, to pursue more independent trading policies and even to restore or create, at least to some degree, some features of the market economy. I believe we should stand ready to help them trade with the free world economies, if they wish to do so.

I turn now to the trade problems of the developing countries. The ending of colonial rule and the emergence of new nations in the less-developed parts of the world have raised acute problems for the continuance of the non-discriminatory multilateral trading system as embodied in the GATT. In the United Nations Conference on Trade and Development, these countries have pressed for special tariff preferences in our markets. They believe these new preferences would help them sell their manufactured products in greater volume and at higher prices. They have also pressed for international agreements to increase and to stabilize their earnings from primary products.

On the basis of our Canadian experience, I am inclined to doubt that new preferential tariff systems would be of much assistance to developing countries. On the other hand, I doubt that, if all of us scrapped our protective tariffs on goods imported from the developing countries, there would be many very serious problems of adjustment for our own industries. The real difficulty facing most of the developing countries is that their industries, by and large, are simply not efficient enough.

I find singularly unattractive the schemes now being elaborated in certain quarters in Europe for a system of tariff preferences for the developing countries limited and confined by import quotas and licensing schemes. If we must give preferences to the developing world (and I remain convinced that they would be helped very little if we did), then I don't see much to be said for attaching all sorts of conditions to such preferences and creating a vast new bureaucratic apparatus to regulate preferential entry to our markets. Such a development would be welcomed only by the protectionists among us.

There is a danger that the failure to find satisfactory solutions to the trading problems of the developing countries on a multilateral basis may result in a series of increasingly anarchic preferential arrangements between the metropolitan powers and their former colonial territories, and the establishment within the world of more clearly defined and antagonistic spheres of economic influence. This would have dangerous implications for international political relationships. I suggest, therefore, that the nations of the Northern Hemisphere are going to have to give more attention to the trading problems of the less-developed countries than we have so far.

Indeed, if all of us put as much effort into that as we devote to restraining their textile exports, we might achieve a good deal! Specifically, I should suggest we begin by making a renewed attempt to work out sensible agreements covering trade in sugar and in cocoa. Then, we ought to scrap all tariffs on so-called tropical products. The United States Government has authority to negotiate free entry into the United States for a wide range of these products. We in Canada are certainly prepared to do as much. Together we should press our European friends to be a bit bolder and more imaginative.

Further advance in the trade field must be accompanied by progress in improving the international payments system. There is not much point in pressing ahead with the removal of barriers to trade if the world financial system is not capable of supporting the increased volume of trade we hope to achieve, and of meeting the balance-of-payments problems that many countries face from time to time.

The present payments system came into being in the brave years of the mid-forties. With the chaos and confusion of the depression and war years still fresh in their minds, the governments of that period constructed a new system based on internationally agreed exchange rates, linked in value to gold, with reserves held in the form of gold and reserve currencies, supplemented by conditional credits. The administration of this new international system was entrusted to a new institution, the International Monetary Fund. This system has served us well in the whole post-war period. The Fund as an institution has won for itself a vital role in the development and management of the international payments system.

But in recent years it has become increasingly apparent that some improvements are required. In particular, it has been recognized that the growth of reserves in the form of gold and reserve currencies will probably be insufficient to satisfy the growing needs. This is not because either gold or reserve currencies are unacceptable as a form of reserves. For Canada, U.S. dollars are quite satisfactory and we have been converting some of our gold into dollars during the past year. The problem is essentially one of the total quantity available for all countries. Most countries would prefer to have these needs met by increases in the reserves they actually own rather than by increased access to lines of credit such as the Fund provides.

For the past two or three years continuous efforts have been made to develop a new form of international reserve asset to supplement gold and reserve currencies. We have sought methods of defining the form and of controlling the quantity and use of this new asset so as to avoid building either an inflationary or a deflationary bias into the system.

The international payments system has been subjected to severe strains in recent years as a result of pressures on the major reserve currencies. So far, these strains have been successfully met through the close co-operation of the monetary authorities of the IMF. But these have been essentially *ad hoc* measures. Their success has been due to the ability of the authorities to convince the international financial community that the management of the international system was in firm, competent hands. The longer governments take to settle their differences on basic improvements in the system, the more they leave the burden of short-term financing and adjustment to *ad hoc* arrangements.

Why have countries been unable to reach agreement on these vital questions? Differences over basic political objectives have quite clearly been a contributing factor. But they do not provide the whole answer. There is a genuine concern in Europe that the collective ability to create new international liquidity would constitute a temptation to many countries to postpone or evade actions that are needed to run their own economies properly.

We in North America tend to criticize Europeans for adhering to policies and arrangements which make it harder for us and for the less-developed countries to correct our balance-of-payments deficits. Many Europeans, on the other hand, believe that the English-speaking countries—and they include Canada in that category—have a basic inflationary bias and would press for the creation of excessive amounts of international liquidity in order to cover continuing balance-of-payments deficits that should be eliminated or financed on a long-term basis.

Despite these differences over the creation of new reserves, we have in recent years made progress in the Organization for Economic Co-operation and Development and in the Monetary Fund towards a better understanding of the means by which deficits or surpluses in international payments can and should be adjusted. The system of surveillance of each other's economic policies and balance-of-payments positions is laying the basis for further advances in this area.

43. Canadian Trade Policy with the Soviet Bloc

Statement by the Minister of Trade and Commerce, Mr. Mitchell Sharp, to the annual conference of the Canadian Importers Association, April 6, 1965.

Canada has a major stake in the development of trade relations with the Sino-Soviet bloc. On the one hand, we cannot afford to ignore the potentialities of trade with the planned economies. Nor, on the other hand, can we ignore the kind of competition that is bound to arise from such economies, both in export and domestic markets.

Except for wheat and flour, we do very little business with the Sino-Soviet group. The scope for East-West trade is severely circumscribed by the very nature of socialist planned economies and by the prevailing attitudes towards trade in both market economies and such planned economies. Access to the Canadian market is in general a matter of law: in other words an importer is free to bring in goods from any country on payment of the duties set down in the customs tariff. Apart from Commonwealth preferences, every member of the GATT and every country with which we have a most-favoured-nation treaty is subject to the same rates of duty. This includes all the significant trading countries with socialist planned economies, except Rumania and Albania.

As far as imports are concerned, our basic policy is non-discrimination. Access to a country with a socialist planned economy, on the other hand, is a matter of administrative decision as part of an overall plan.

Trade negotiations between countries with market economies and those with socialist planned economies differ greatly from negotiations between countries with market economies. That is why, in negotiating trade agreements with the U.S.S.R., Bulgaria and Hungary, Canada has insisted on minimum purchase commitments for Canada's produce in return for most-favoured-nation treatment in the Canadian market.

One of the special difficulties for any country with a market economy like Canada is the matter of valuing imports from countries with a planned economy. The general rule is, as you know, that imports shall be valued at their fair market value in country of origin. This rule was devised for imports from countries with a market economy like our own where competition prevails. In socialist planned economies, however, prices at home are fixed not by competition but on some other basis which may not be directly related to costs and may be quite different from the prices at which the same goods are offered for export.

It is by no means easy to build a bridge between East and West over which goods can move freely to the mutual advantage of both. I believe, however, that it is well worth making the effort. One way of reducing the barriers and of changing the attitudes that now prevail is to demonstrate the advantages of trading by mutually engaging in it.

As I have said, the Canadian market is open to goods on a non-discriminatory basis from practically all countries. Except for strategic goods, there are no limitations imposed by Canada on the sale of Canadian goods to any destination.* Accordingly, East-West trade is a field for Canadian importers and exporters to demonstrate their initiative and enterprise.

44. Canada and the Kennedy Round**

On June 29, 1967, the eve of the signing of the final act of the Kennedy Round, the Canadian Minister of Trade and Commerce, Mr. Robert Winters, made a statement to the House of Commons on the Kennedy Round and its importance to Canada. Excerpts from Mr. Winter's statement are given below.

The final act of the Kennedy Round is to be signed tomorrow morning in Geneva, thus bringing these negotiations to a formal conclusion. The resulting agreements, including the schedules of tariff concessions granted by all participating countries, can now be made public. I should make clear that these tariff cuts will not come into effect until January 1, 1968, and in many instances they will be staged over the next four years.

At the conclusion of my remarks I shall ask leave to table, on behalf of the Minister of Finance and myself, detailed information on the tariff and trade agreements of interest to GATT concluded during the Kennedy Round. Everything possible is being done to ensure that the Canadian business community is made aware of these results without delay....

Mr. Speaker, as has been indicated on numerous occasions, the Kennedy Round constitutes by far the most important trade pact in history, the most comprehensive in coverage and the most significant in the extent and depth of tariff reductions.

---

* See SS 72/7 of March 6, 1972, by Mr. Jean-Luc Pépin, describing Canadian trade objectives and problems with the Soviet Union and China during the early 1970s, which have remained much the same as those outlined above.

** See *External Affairs*, DEA, Ottawa, August 1967, pp. 306-10 for an account of the overall results of the Kennedy Round.

Over $45 billion of goods and hundreds of thousands of tariff items are effected by the concessions exchanged; all aspects of world trade, including tariffs and certain non-tariff barriers, and agricultural as well as industrial goods, were within the ambit of the negotiations. Never before have trade negotiations of this scope, magnitude and far-reaching impact taken place.

It is fitting, on this final day, to pay tribute once again to the statesmanship and farsightedness of the late President Kennedy. To his initiative were due in large part the ambitious objectives which these negotiations set themselves and which have to such a high degree been attained.

It was to be expected that the Kennedy Round would be exceedingly complex and difficult, involving a great deal of intensive bargaining; indeed, there were occasions, through the nearly four years of negotiations, when the obstacles appeared to some too great to be overcome. However, despite crises and delays, and due to the perseverance and basic goodwill of all countries concerned, the issues blocking agreement were resolved.

For Canada, the success of the Kennedy Round has wide-ranging implications, opening new broad perspectives of expanded trade and benefiting all sectors and regions of the economy. Indeed, a dramatic and sustained increase in Canadian export trade is essential if we are to deal effectively with the common issues confronting us as regards standards of living, balance of payments, jobs and the like. The concessions granted in our own tariffs to gain greater access to other markets must be regarded in the light of the very great benefits which can accrue to Canada from expanded exporting opportunities.

Many sectors of industry, where Canadian tariffs are being reduced are also the sectors which stand to benefit most from export gains. In many instances, the cuts in Canadian tariffs are in areas which will help reduce the costs of production for Canadian processors and manufacturers, as well as for consumers. That, Mr. Speaker, is important.

The export benefits obtained by Canada from its agreements with major trading partners cover, including wheat, over $3 billion of our current export trade. In the United States and the EEC, most industrial tariffs will be reduced to levels of 10 per cent or less. As a result of the across-the-board tariff cuts made by our major trading partners, trade opportunities will become available for the first time to a very wide range of manufactured goods—many of which will be Canada's exports of tomorrow. For Canada, therefore, the Kennedy Round could contribute to the solution of many of our basic economic problems and set in motion the process of adaptation and restructuring which could, in time, reshape the character of the economy. There are many areas where we need more values added, more up-grading of our raw materials, and this should help.

It may well be that the Kennedy Round will be regarded in the future as a crucial turning-point in the transformation of Canada from a resource-based economy to one of the most advanced industrial nations of the world.

I have commented, on previous occasions, in some detail on the significance of the new cereals agreement for Canada's wheat trade, for the Western Prairie Provinces, and for the economy and balance of payments as a whole. The International Wheat Council is convening a special negotiating session in Rome on July 12, with a view to revising the International Wheat Agreement so as to incorporate the cereals commitments agreed to in the Kennedy Round.

Canada welcomes the participation of all countries with a significant interest in wheat trade in these negotiations, and would like to see the new agreement completed and put into operation as soon as possible.

Now that the Kennedy Round is concluded, it is vitally important that every sector of the Canadian economy should exploit the new export opportunities before us. The main initiative must rest with private enterprise itself. The department is being geared to provide maximum assistance to the Canadian business community in their export efforts. There will, of course, be areas and sectors which may feel a sense of greater exposure to competition because of tariff reductions made to gain access on a wider basis to the markets of the world for a very broad range of Canadian products. There are bound to be some local, negative reactions. But, in the overall, this is a great, positive step, and it can mean a very large net gain for the Canadian economy. I am sure our dynamic Canadian enterprise will ensure that result.*

45. Basic Tariff Policy for the Mid-1960s

Statement by Mr. Robert H. Winters, Minister of Trade and Commerce, to the Ministerial Session of the GATT Meeting, Geneva, November 22, 1967.

I wish to refer to the main purpose of this meeting—prospects for the

---

* See also SS 67/23 of May 29, 1967, for a detailed account of the Canadian approach to the final phase of the Kennedy Round.

years ahead. I recognize that it is unrealistic to envisage any major new initiatives in the immediate future—governments, business and labour must be given a chance to adapt effectively to the new situation flowing from the Kennedy Round. On the other hand, there is no marking-time in the field of international trade—there is either progress or regress.

I should like to propose that the governments here represented take this opportunity to reaffirm their basic policy commitment to the cause of freer multilateral trade and their determination to ensure that the impetus to trade liberalization given by the Kennedy Round is maintained. To this end, broad directives should now be established for a future work programme in GATT, an agenda for future action towards freer trade. The Contracting Parties, working with the Director-General, would thus be in a position to explore, without commitment as to the timing, nature or scope of future trade negotiations, the items which this agenda might contain. The four-year experience of the Kennedy Round showed that intensive and prolonged advance preparation will be required in breaking new ground and that an early start in setting the machinery in motion is essential.

Canada's suggestions for future work of the Contracting Parties might conveniently be grouped under the following headings: Trade and Tariff Negotiations; Non-tariff Barriers; Trade in Agricultural Products; Trade Problems of the Developing Countries and Trade Relations with Countries with Centrally-Planned Economies.

(A) TRADE AND TARIFF NEGOTIATIONS

(i) Trade Liberalization by Sectors

A promising avenue for further trade liberalization on a multilateral basis may lie in the conception of "sectoral" negotiations. This would involve freeing trade not by geographical areas but by important commodity sectors, covering both the primary, semi-processed and manufactured forms of production within that sector, and dealing not only with tariffs but with all governmental and other measures that affect trade in that sector.

It became clear in the Kennedy Round that there are certain sectors which might lend themselves particularly well to this approach. Generally, these are industries characterized by high levels of capital investment, advanced technology, large-scale production and, not infrequently, widely dispersed international operations. Corporate policies, no less than governmental measures, can have profound effects on trade in these fields, and the position of multinational corporations is a factor which may need to be taken into account. In addition, attention must be given to those domestic industrial programmes that have similar effects to high tariffs in that they seriously distort the efficient allocation of resources.

This comprehensive sectoral approach would represent a new departure in international negotiations. It would require careful and detailed advance preparation, both in terms of the negotiating rules that should apply and with respect to the identification and selection of commodity sectors that warrant consideration. In the give and take of bargaining, the criteria for determining the balance of advantages between countries flowing from the selection of sectors would be of particular importance and complexity.

We consider, in this context, that the possibility of moving forward on a sectoral basis of "free-up" trade in aluminum semi-fabricated products should be positively considered. Other sectors which may merit similar investigations are forest products, nickel, lead and zinc.

(ii) Primary Industrial Materials

The desirability of world free trade in basic industrial commodities should, I believe, also be examined as a matter of high priority. This is an area where much of world trade already moves duty-free but where certain tariffs and restrictions still remain. The GATT should assess the post–Kennedy Round situation in these areas and consider ways and means of achieving world free trade for these commodities where this is not likely to be accomplished through the sectoral approach to which I have already referred. All countries would clearly stand to gain.

(iii) Low Duty Items

Building on the precedent of the recent negotiations, consideration should be given to the elimination of very low, or "nuisance", duties, which serve little protective purpose but which, in practice, have a disproportionate and unnecessarily hampering effect on trade because of the administrative burdens involved.

(iv) Other Tariffs

The GATT work programme should also examine possibilities and appropriate techniques for the future reduction of tariffs in those areas of trade not covered by the proposals already described.

(B) NON-TARIFF BARRIERS

Urgent consideration should also be given to ways and means of reducing the impact of non-tariff barriers. These cover such disparate measures as customs administration, surcharges and prior deposits, import licensing and subsidies, internal taxes, export and technical standards, governmental procurement policies, as well as certain types of corporate policies and practices which may frustrate the intent of tariff agreements.

The Kennedy Round achieved certain important results in this area, but the bulk of non-tariff obstacles to trade remain. Many of these obstacles would presumably be covered in any consideration of free trade by sectors. However, the Canadian Government considers that special attention should be given to the whole field of non-tariff barriers which can be no less effective than tariffs in thwarting the efficient international allocation of resources. Furthermore, as tariffs come down, these non-tariff obstacles will have a correspondingly greater impact on world trade. Indeed governments will need to be alert to resist pressures to increase such barriers.

I urge the Contracting Parties to undertake a detailed study of non-tariff barriers with a view to identifying their effects, examining the possibilities of the removal of such barriers on an international basis, and determining whether means can be found to impede their proliferation.

(C) AGRICULTURE

Canada was a strong supporter of the decision taken in 1963 to work for an improvement in the conditions of access to world markets for agricultural products as part of the Kennedy Round. The International Grains Arrangement, with its food-aid programme, represents a major achievement for exporters and importers, for developed and developing countries alike. There were significant gains for some other agricultural products but, for some basic commodities, including grains, governments pulled back from the difficult decisions on domestic support policies necessary to reduce the obstacles to trade in farm products. In relation to the extent of the problems facing agricultural trade, and to the objectives set out over four years ago, the outcome of the Kennedy Round is disappointing.

The recent negotiations focussed attention on the problems of world trade arising from agricultural protectionism. Most countries have adopted measures to support one or more sectors of their agriculture, to protect them from international competition, and to achieve a greater measure of self-sufficiency. But this has gone too far. Massive protection is not the answer. It is to be remembered that the GATT provides orderly procedures for dealing with cases of serious injury arising from imports on a temporary basis. Canada, like other countries, from time to time also faces such special problems.

Agriculture is a sector of trade relations marked by long-standing "waivers" from GATT obligations, by residual quantitative restrictions, by domestic programmes and devices which, while perhaps conforming to the letter of the law, in practice represent a serious and unjustifiable impediment to trade.

The cost of income support to inefficient producers and the cost of lost markets to efficient producers is an increasing burden on all countries. The significant liberalization of trade in industrial products achieved in the Kennedy Round, as compared with the relatively more modest results in agriculture, can only result in a further widening of the gap between the productivity and incomes in agriculture and in industry. This presents a major challenge to governments, but it is a challenge which must be faced.

While recognizing the special factors affecting production and trade in agricultural products, the Canadian Government considers that new and positive steps must be taken in liberalizing trade in agricultural products. Unless progress can be made in this sector also, trade liberalization in industrial goods will be much more difficult.

(D) TRADE WITH STATE-TRADING COUNTRIES

Canada warmly welcomes the presence of Poland as a full Contracting Party, as well as the attendance of Hungary and Bulgaria as observers.

In the Kennedy Round, Canada strongly supported efforts to establish a new multilateral framework for trade relations with countries with centrally-planned economies, There are opportunities to make further progress on a pragmatic basis with individual countries.

(E) DEVELOPING COUNTRIES

Of particular importance in the future work programme for the GATT will be the expansion of trade of the developing world. Almost ten years ago, the GATT report by a distinguished panel of experts on trends in international trade emphasized that the avoidance of business cycles and the maintenance of a steady rate of domestic growth are the most important contributions which the highly industrialized countries can make to the rapid economic growth of the LDCs. Nevertheless, it has long been recognized that we cannot rely solely on growth in the industrial world to solve the problems of the developing countries. Vigorous, imaginative and courageous measures, specifically directed to assist these countries, are also essential.

Much has already been done in the GATT in this regard. What further steps can and should the GATT take to meet this growing crisis? This is a time of challenge and decision, reminiscent of the period when the Marshall Plan was launched to deal with another set of urgent issues. I should like to mention some of the trade aspects which could form part of a new plan to assist in overcoming the problems of development.

The most important priority is improved access to the markets of industrialized countries. There is little logic in encouraging development in the LDCs through aid and at the same time imposing barriers against imports of the products that they can produce on a competitive basis. To this end, the Contracting Parties should examine:

1. the possibilities of free trade in tropical products, a proposal which Canada, with some others, put forward in the Kennedy Round;
2. the possibilities of further reductions of tariff and non-tariff barriers on products of special interest to developing countries; and
3. the possibilities of further action, e.g. through work of the GATT Trade Centre, to assist developing countries to take full advantage of the new opportunities offered by improved access to developed markets as the Kennedy Round results are implemented.

International commodity agreements have an important role to play in improving the trade prospects of developing countries, and international cooperation in this area of work should be continued and intensified.

Recent discussions of the trade measures to help the developing countries have centered on the question of a system of temporary generalized tariff preferences extended by all developed countries to all developing countries. It is clear that the Contracting Parties will need to address themselves to any consensus on this matter which may emerge at the UNCTAD Conference. If there is to be some special tariff treatment for exports of developing countries, we must ensure that its impact is equitable and that it does not impede or prejudice movements towards further trade liberalization on a non-discriminatory basis.

The expansion of trade opportunities for the LDCs must continue to go hand-in-hand with sustained high levels of aid.

46. Canadian Trade in the Early 1970s

Statement by Mr. Jean-Luc Pépin, Minister of Industry, Trade and Commerce, to the Brantford Regional Board of Trade, Brantford, Ontario, April 16, 1970.

Everything now changes at an ever-rapidly-increasing pace. Not too long ago, it used to be that stability was the rule and change the exception. Today, it is the opposite. That is true of trade in particular.

Looking back briefly over the last decade, it is reassuring, nonetheless, to see how much actually was accomplished, tradewise, during what have been called the "ten years of turmoil":

1. The value of world trade more than doubled, and is now approaching the $250 billion (U.S.) mark.
2. New trading blocks have been formed. We have witnessed the establishment of the EEC and its consolidation as a strong economic and commercial entity. The EFTA (European Free Trade Area) was created by the principal remaining European countries to counterbalance the EEC's power. Now the possible enlargement of the EEC to include Britain and other continental countries may bring about a common market embracing almost all of Western Europe, thus creating what would be by far the biggest import market in the world. Smaller trading blocks like the LAFTA (Latin American Free Trade Area) have also been set up. Tradewise, this "blockation" of the world is one of the major events of our time.
3. As the culmination of 20 years of world trade liberalization, the Kennedy Round of tariff negotiations led to a general and spectacular lowering of the tariffs affecting the greater part of world trade.

During this time span, Canada hasn't remained static—much to the contrary. Our own exports have in effect changed rather drastically, in value, in direction and in composition:

1. The value of our exports nearly tripled during that time, going from $5.4 billion to $14.9 billion—this represents an average annual increase in excess of 10 per cent, one of the best-sustained rates of growth in modern times. Few people, even in our own country, realize that, with our population of 20 million, we rank sixth among the world's trading nations.

2. The direction has changed also significantly, and continues to do so. Exports to the U.S.A., by far our most important customer, more than tripled during the last decade ($3.03 billion to $10.6 billion). In 1960, that represented 57 per cent of our total exports; last year's corresponding figure is equal to 71 per cent.

   These results carry with them some attenuating side effects. Our economy has grown more dependent on the U.S. market and consequently more vulnerable to its fluctuations.

   Automobiles and parts, as a result mainly of the Auto Pact, now account for close to one-third of our total shipments to the United States. Newsprint accounts for another 9 to 10 per cent. The levelling off in growth of the U.S. economy, combined with the slump in auto sales earlier this year, leads us to greater caution in trying to predict a growth rate for 1970. It is expected to be below the 8 to 9 per cent increase of 1969. For the first three months of this year, it was, in fact, only 6.4 per cent.

   Britain, our second most important export market, has dropped off considerably in its overall relative importance to us. In 1960, Britain took 17.2 per cent of our total exports, while last year its share fell to only 7.5 per cent. This can be explained partly by Britain's recent economic policies aimed mainly at strengthening its currency and redressing its economy but also, to some extent, by its progressive preparation for economic integration with continental Europe.

   The EEC, with a total population of 321 million and a combined gross national product of $530 billion (compared to the U.S. GNP of $756 billion), represents a large and growing market for Canada. Our exports to the Community have nearly doubled during the last decade, going from $438 million to $851 million, but the general feeling is that we could and must do much better. At the moment, our share of the EEC import market remains not only relatively low but, as a percentage of total imports, it actually dropped between 1961 and 1967 (1.9 and 1.22, respectively).

Japan is another market that is growing very rapidly and becoming increasingly important to us. At $624.8 million in 1969, our exports to that country were 3.5 times greater than in 1960. But the proportion of manufactured goods is low. Our imports last year from Japan amounted to nearly half a billion dollars. Over 95 per cent of these imports were either partially or highly manufactured goods. This compared with roughly 3.5 per cent for our own exports. We should be able to do better here also.

The overall growth of our exports to Latin America has not quite kept pace with the growth of our exports generally, but at $443 million for 1969, compared with $185 million in 1960, Latin America represents, nonetheless, an important market for us. Here, however, we can expect some changes in the composition of our exports. Our traditional newsprint markets there, while growing continuously, will face increasing competition from the developing Chilean newsprint industry and our exports of aluminum may decrease because of the establishment of an aluminum smelter in Argentina. Many interesting opportunities do exist, though, for Canadian engineering and equipment in infrastructural projects such as airport development, thermal and hydro-electric power generating stations and telecommunications. STOL aircraft (short takeoff and landing) also appear to offer good prospects.

When compared to $47 million in 1960, our exports to state-trading nations (including China) are also doing proportionately well, at $161 million for 1969, and wheat sales were low then compared to what they will be in 1970. Our peak year for trade with these countries was in 1964, when our imports reached $619 million. In 1968, they amounted to $308 million. We see promising opportunities in Eastern European countries for the sale of raw materials, live-stock, grains, industrial chemicals, synthetic fibres, electrical and electronic equipment, consulting service, etc.

3. Composition. If we now consider the extent of fabrication which our exports represent, again the picture has changed considerably during the last decade. For statistical purposes, the Dominion Bureau of Statistics classifies products in three broad categories according to their degree of manufacture—crude materials, fabricated materials and end products. The relative importance of each category as a proportion of our total exports has changed remarkably:

| | THOUSAND $ | | PERCENTAGE OF TOTAL | |
	1960	1969	1960	1969
Crude Materials	1,771,795	3,330,453	33.7	23.0
Fabricated Materials	2,874,262	5,344,902	54.7	37.0
End Products	609,518	5,766,201	11.6	39.9
Total Value of Domestic Exports	5,255,575	14,441,556		

For our own purposes, these statistics are among the most important because they give us a good indication of the transformation of our economy.

The Government's Role in the Changing Trade Environment

I have attempted to illustrate briefly the major developments which occurred on the scene of world trade during the last decade: the remarkable increase in the volume of world trade; how well Canada has done in this respect; how the direction of our trade shifted; and also how manufactured products are becoming increasingly important as a proportion of our total exports.

The Canadian Government has been quite active during this period. In fact, it sometimes likes to believe that it was instrumental in influencing some of these mutations, e.g., through its participation in the Kennedy Round; because of its having negotiated the Auto Pact; thanks also to its trade-promotion programs; its aid to export financing; its industrial-development schemes, etc.

I should like to outline for you now some of the main trade preoccupations currently facing Canada and how the Government envisages them.

MULTILATERAL MATTERS

Broadening of the EEC

Britain's latest bid to enter the EEC appears to have been more favourably received than were its previous ones. We are, of course, concerned about Britain's terms of entry and how they might affect our access to its market.

Some two-thirds of our exports to Britain would be subject to less favourable terms of access if Britain adopted the existing EEC import regime. Without knowing the actual terms of entry which the British may negotiate with the EEC it is difficult to be precise on what the effect would be on individual commodities. The impact would be mitigated, however, in the case of manufactured goods, by the implementation of the Kennedy Round concessions, which are resulting in a reduction of the EEC tariff. We have, nevertheless, been pressing the British for consultations before, during and after their negotiations with the Community.

Also of concern to us is the fact that Britain's entry into the EEC may open the door to a further enlargement of the Community. This could result in a major shift of world trade towards greater regionalization. In our view, therefore, the British EEC negotiations should be accompanied by parallel or consecutive multilateral negotiations to ensure that the enlarged EEC would result in trade creation rather than trade diversion.

Foreign Government-Assisted Export Financing

Canadian manufacturers of machinery and equipment are being adversely affected by imports financed abroad under foreign government-assisted export financing programs. Many representations have been made to us on that subject.

Government export-financing facilities have been made available by all major developed countries for many years. Until recently, however, the interest rates available under these facilities were generally equal to, if not higher than, the domestic lending rates. Its use was, therefore, confined almost entirely to support sales to the developing countries, which lack indigenous capital and the ability to attract it on the required scale from conventional sources.

With the increase in conventional rates of interest over the last two years, the situation has changed drastically. Conventional rates have increased considerably, while most governments held their export-financing rates at about their original levels, thus creating a rather wide discrepancy. The problem arose when some governments extended their export-financing facilities to developed countries. Canadian manufacturers have complained that they are sometimes denied the opportunity to bid on projects in Canada controlled or financed from abroad because financing arrangements require that all equipment be purchased in the financing country.

Britain has been the principal source of such export financing in Canada. Should the British practice be allowed to continue, other countries will be drawn into a credit race and this would have a serious adverse impact on Canadian interests.

Canada is the largest single importer of industrial machinery in the world. In 1968, our imports reached $24 billion, about 45 per cent of our domestic consumption. While our machinery-manufacturing industry has demonstrated some definite competitive strength in foreign markets, the domestic market is, nonetheless, very important to its future development.

Being a net importer of capital, Canada is hardly in a position to retaliate by itself embarking on a competitive credit race. On the other hand, we greatly depend on export markets of capital equipment to attain the scale of output necessary for an internationally viable operation. It is also pointed out that a number of the projects which benefit from this low rate of financing, especially those in the slower growth areas of this country, would not be economically viable without such aid. That, then, is the predicament in which we find ourselves at the moment.

Textiles

Textiles have been one of the most notable exceptions to the post-war pattern of trade liberalization on a multinational basis. For the past ten years, an International Textile Agreement provided a framework for the negotiation of export restraints on cotton products. While this approach has been adequate until now, it is no longer sufficient to deal with current Canadian problems.

The difficulty is mainly created by imports from low-cost countries. Most developed countries maintain strict restraints on textile imports from low-cost nations. Canada, however, has had a more liberal policy and the closing off of major industrial markets resulted in significantly increased pressures on us. The system of negotiated restraints is becoming increasingly difficult to administer because many low-cost countries are reluctant to limit themselves. The delays needed to negotiate restraint agreements, the lack of suitable means in Canada to prevent overshipments and the problems associated with unilateral action further complicate the problem. Add also the important export interests we have in some of the textile-exporting countries—e.g. Japan and Mexico—and the favourable trade balances we have with them, include in your analysis the particular interests

of our own textile workers and those of the domestic textile companies and you will begin to have a better idea of the tremendous
complexities involved.

BILATERAL MATTERS

The Automotive Products Agreement

A number of you no doubt are associated with companies which
have an interest in the current negotiations with the United States
on the Auto Products Agreement.

This Agreement, as you well know, is a limited free-trade arrangement with the United States. As provided in the terms of the Agreement, we started a joint review last autumn at the request of the
United States. These consultations are continuing with the U.S. Government, as well as with Canadian industry, labour and other unilateral groups. Our discussions are concerned not only with the various
problems which have arisen over the six years of the Pact but also
with a number of changes and improvements which have been suggested by both countries. These talks are continuing and I look forward to a constructive outcome.

Petroleum

Petroleum plays an important role in Canada's foreign trade. Last
year, petroleum (crude and products) worth $570 million was export-
ed to the U.S. from the Western provinces. This trade makes a significant contribution to the health of Canada's balance of payments
and is essential to the prosperity of the Western provinces.

In recent months, circumstances have been transformed by a number of major developments. These have presented serious short-term
problems of adjustment but hold the promise of important benefits
in the future. There was, for example, the major oil-strike in northern Alaska. As the press has extensively reported, this new discovery
led to the trial voyages of the super-tanker *Manhattan* through the
Northwest Passage to test this route as a new means of shipping
northern resources to Eastern markets. Another possibility being considered is a pipeline across Canada along the Mackenzie River route.
The Alaskan discovery also suggests excellent prospects for oil explo-
rations now under way in the Canadian Arctic, and, as a matter of

fact, indications to that effect already exist. The latter would also benefit from the establishment of these new transportation routes.

Meanwhile, the Canadian and the American Governments have been deeply engaged in comprehensive reviews of their respective oil policies, including our cross-border trade in petroleum. Although a report on proposed new U.S. policies has been published, it will be some time before any final decisions can be reached by either government, owing to the great uncertainties enshrouding the North American oil perspective. President Nixon has proposed discussion on the possibility of moving toward freer access for Canadian exports of petroleum and possibly other energy commodities to U.S. markets. Such arrangements could, in my view, be beneficial for both countries.

However, as an immediate measure, the President recently introduced a system of mandatory restrictions on imports of Canadian crude oil into the bulk of the U.S. market. This clashes with the unrestricted access Canadian oil has historically enjoyed and is viewed by Canada as a rather strange first step to freer trade. The Government has stressed its opposition to these measures and has requested the U.S. reconsider them. It is my hope that these restrictions will prove to be only temporary and that the U.S. will recognize the mutual benefits that could flow from freer trade in oil between our two countries. You may be assured that the Canadian Government will continue to work toward that end.

47. World Economic Problems: Food, Oil, Inflation — the Canadian Approach in the Mid 1970s

Statement by the Secretary of State for External Affairs, Mr. Mitchell Sharp, at the Sixth Special Session of the United Nations General Assembly, New York, April 11, 1974.

The international trade and payments system is under increasing strains, strains which have roots in the growing pressure of demand on the non-renewable as well as renewable raw materials of the earth. We have become starkly aware of a developing crisis in the most essential commodity of all—food.

This global economic situation touches each and every one of us in some way. None of us, as nation states or as individuals, is or can be insulated. It is, therefore, appropriate that we should come together here at the centre of the United Nations system to discuss our common problems and to consider how they can be dealt with most effectively by co-operative action.

Three aspects of the global situation, all of them related to raw materials and development, are of particular concern:

- the problem of food for those in greatest need;
- the effects of high energy costs;
- the impact of inflation on the international trade and payments system.

As a substantial exporter of certain raw materials, and a significant importer of others, Canada approaches these questions very much aware that importer and exporter interests are closely interrelated. It is seriously misleading simply to equate exporter and developing-country interests, or those of importer and developed countries. Indeed, the common interest of exporters and importers, of developed and developing countries alike, in an effective international trade and payments system, may be the most salient point to emerge from our discussions at this session.

Canada's approach is coloured by its own experience. Canada began its history as an exporter of primary commodities. That is what attracted the first explorers. The exploitation of our natural resources helped to promote both growth and development within our economy. Over the years, our economy changed to a more sophisticated structure, involving a balance between resource exploitation and industrial production.

Many factors have contributed to growth and development in Canada, including:

- substantial foreign investment;
- access to technology, mainly through commercial channels;
- access to markets for our products; and
- a general sharing of the rewards of resource production among Canadians.

The importance of these factors in our development has made Canada an outward-looking country, with high per capita exports and a heavy dependence on foreign trade. It has also persuaded us that a reasonably free international flow of the factors of production, whether capital, materials or technology, is of central importance to the process of industrialization and the raising of living standards.

Nor has our experience led us to believe that there are simple answers to the problems of development, or simple formulas that will ensure equity in the relations between developed and developing countries. We are reinforced in this scepticism about simple answers by our own efforts to reduce economic disparities between far-flung regions and to reconcile the conflicting interests of industrialized and raw-materials-producing areas within Canada. We find the problem infinitely complicated, requiring a wide variety of approaches to achieve results.

I can give assurance, however, that Canada has a strong interest in stable markets and a reasonable price structure for renewable and non-renewable raw materials, including foodstuffs:

- We support international commodity arrangements in which both exporters and importers are represented.
- We favour the establishment of machinery to ensure that the decisions of multinational business corporations are consistent with the national interests of the countries within which they operate.
- We defend the right of capital-importing countries to define the terms for the acceptance of foreign investment. We do so in Canada.
- We believe that raw-material-producing countries have a legitimate interest in upgrading their resources.

In short, Canada recognizes the right of resource-owning states to dispose of their natural resources in the interest of their own economic development and of the well-being of their people.

What has to be borne in mind is that the legitimate aspirations of resource-owning states can only be achieved within a healthy and dynamic world economy. The world may have to curb the rate of growth of its consumption of certain raw materials. But this should be done in a co-ordinated manner and not by acts that cause economic dislocation, unnecessary unemployment and declining incomes.

That is why reasonable security of supply for consumers is the counterpart of the rights of producers.

Abrupt and arbitrary actions affecting supply may seriously disrupt international economic co-operation. All of us, whether raw-materials producers or industrialized countries, whether developed or developing—or a bit of both—have a responsibility to exercise our sovereign rights in a manner that does not run counter to the interest of other countries and peoples in the maintenance of a favourable economic environment.

This is all the more important if the world is to exercise prudence in the consumption of finite resources. It is extremely difficult, if not impossible, to plan rationally for conservation of world resources within an unstable economic environment in which countries must constantly adjust to fluctuations in world prices and supplies.

I turn, then, to the three urgent problems I identified at the outset—food, energy and inflation.

In the final analysis, foodstuffs are the most essential of raw materials. We are acutely aware of this because the world faces a grave situation, already marked by famine and distress. The World Food Conference in Rome later this year was called in recognition of the need to find constructive international solutions to this most pressing problem. We attach particular importance to the work of that conference, yet the urgency of the matter justifies some further comments.

Canada has for years been a major exporter of food and a large contributor of food aid internationally. We shall maintain our food-aid contributions bilaterally and through the international mechanisms we strongly support. The expenditure of an additional $100 million was approved by the Canadian Government last week to meet the emergency needs of developing countries, particularly for food and fertilizer. The world food problem, however, cannot be met by the exporting countries alone. It requires concerted action by all those countries able to contribute, and firm support for existing mechanisms. Canada welcomes the recent contribution by Saudi Arabia to the World Food Program. Such contributions are essential if we are to meet the crisis in food supplies in a number of countries.

Let us hope that nature will bless the world with good crops this coming year. But we must never again, if we can avoid it, permit the margin between famine and sufficiency to become so narrow. I shall not at this time expand upon the steps that must be taken. That is more suitable to the World Food Conference. Let me leave this thought: that only if the heavily populated developing countries achieve a higher degree of self-sufficiency in food can the future be faced with reasonable equanimity.

The sharp rise in the price of oil and changes in supply and demand have had extraordinary effects around the world. As in the case of other raw materials, Canada has approached this situation as both a producer and consumer, as both an importer and exporter. Because we import as much petroleum into Eastern Canada as we export from Western Canada, we have gained no significant advantage in our balance of payments from these developments. We have not, of course, been insulated from international price increases. At the same time, in contrast to many less-fortunate countries, we have not suffered serious set-back.

In general terms, Canada favours an orderly framework for world trade in oil, which would provide for stable prices at a reasonable level. Such a framework would reflect the cost of bringing in new conventional and non-conventional sources of energy in order to meet rising demand. Prices should yield a fair return to the producer, without overburdening the consumer.

The energy question, of course, goes beyond that of oil. It involves other energy sources and the technologies needed to exploit them.

I realize that this session was not called primarily to deal with energy resources. They are, however, of such importance to the topics on our agenda that I wish to emphasize the need for a constructive dialogue to be engaged on energy and energy-related problems wherever appropriate. Such a dialogue is needed particularly between the principal consumers and principal exporters, whose decisions are crucial for the world as a whole, and especially for the energy-poor developing countries. Canada, for its part, is willing to develop mechanisms for consultation between importers and exporters of uranium.

If the energy situation has had little direct effect on our balance of payments, Canada, like other countries, cannot hope to escape the inflationary effects of rising prices at a time when inflation is already a serious international problem. The terms of trade have in recent months shifted significantly in favour of commodity producers, as the prices of minerals and agricultural products have risen to unprecedented levels. But we are all consumers—of raw materials and manufactured products—and it is as consumers that the impact of world inflation is brought home to us most forcibly. I can see no easy solutions to this problem.

Governments can help by pursuing responsible policies. It is inescapable, however, that current energy costs compel a restructuring of international markets, which will inevitably take some time to work out. Every country will face challenges in adjusting its economy to the changed situation.

Urgent international action to meet this situation must include: the liberalization of trade arrangements; the growth of development assistance; and the systematic and progressive reordering of the monetary system in the IMF, so as to subject the creation of international liquidity to accepted disciplines.

In the face of these compelling priorities, Canada has reviewed its own commitments. Subject to Parliamentary approval, the Canadian Government intends to take several steps to help alleviate the situation of the developing countries most seriously affected:

- We shall proceed with our own contribution of $276 million to the Fourth Replenishment of the International Development Association.
- We shall permit the advance commitment of our first two payments to IDA, if that seems desirable.
- As I mentioned earlier, the Canadian Government last week approved an additional $100 million, over and above its originally projected program, to meet emergency needs in developing countries—particularly for food and fertilizer. For the coming year, Canada's development-assistance expenditures are expected to reach $733 million, as against $571 million last year.
- We are also reassessing our entire program with a view to ensuring that our development assistance is directed to those in greatest need and in sectors where an urgent response is required. The immediate measures will include balance-of-payments support through quick disbursing grants and soft loans for essential commodities. Longer-term measures will include assistance for the development of energy sources. Such adjustments in development-assistance programs are difficult but necessary.

In this context, the Canadian Government believes that all countries with appropriate resources have a responsibility to examine their own situations closely and take steps to alleviate the plight of those countries which are hard hit by the present energy situation. There are promising signs that countries which have benefited most from oil-price increases will, in fact, be taking concrete steps to provide assistance on concessional terms.

A renewed effort of international co-operation is called for, in which full use should be made of those established and recognized international institutions which have experience and expertise in supporting development. The United Nations Development Program (UNDP), the International Bank of Reconstruction and Development (IBRD), the World Food Program, and the Regional Development Banks are repositories of technical skills available to the international community. As such, they offer a ready means of securing early and effective action.

Some of these institutions have already begun to adapt their operations to the new situation. There is every reason for them to carry forward this process of adaptation and to work out revised policies and criteria, new techniques and types of program, geared to present circumstances.

Finally, the Canadian Government has decided to bring into effect, on July 1, 1974, its system of generalized tariff preferences in favour of developing countries.

Mr. President, these are some steps Canada is taking to help with the problems of concern to this special session. But none of them is as important, to my mind, as our intention to co-operate fully with other countries:

- in needed adjustments to the international trade and payments system;
- in matters of commodity trade;
- in the reduction of trade barriers;
- in support for the established development-assistance institutions.

There are mechanisms of international co-operation already established and in good working order. Let us use them.

Without close consultation in the appropriate bodies, there is little hope of maintaining an effective network of international economic relations. Conditions of disarray and sustained confrontation may yield short-term benefits for a few, but in the long run the consequences would be wasteful and dangerous for all countries.

Modes of international co-operation need constant adjustment in order to reflect existing trends and realities. These adjustments may be small or great. We may expect a reordering and readjustment of international economic relations to emerge from a range of multilateral consultations, including:

- the current monetary negotiations and the multilateral trade negotiations;
- continuing discussions and consultations on commodities;
- the evolution of international codes of conduct in various areas;
- the creation of particular mechanisms to meet urgent needs, such as the proposed special facility in the IMF, which we have encouraged the Managing Director to explore; and
- the evolution of new techniques of resource management, including conservation policies.

48. The Dollar Floats Again

Statement by the Secretary of State for External Affairs, Mr. Mitchell Sharp, June 8, 1971, to the OECD Ministerial Meeting in Paris. (Extracts)

We meet at a time of considerable economic difficulty for many, if not most, of the members of our Organization. Problems of unemployment and inflation continue to plague us. The recent crisis in the international monetary system and its longer-term implications call for study and action by member governments if we are to bring about greater stability in the financial environment.

As a major trading nation, Canada attaches the highest importance to an orderly international system of trade and payments. While the current-account balances of some major countries moved some distance toward a better equilibrium in the light of stated objectives in 1970, I note the forecast that there will be little progress in 1971 toward a pattern of current-account balances that would support appropriate capital flows. The fact is, though, that the recent disturbances have come about primarily as a result of capital movements rather than current-account imbalances. The speculative flows early last month, which resulted in changes in a number of European exchange-rates, emphasized the need for improvement in the present system. This will not be a simple task.

Let me recall the circumstances that led to the freeing of Canada's exchange-rate just over a year ago. In 1969, Canada had a sizable deficit on current account and there was a large outflow of short-term capital in response to a rise in interest-rates abroad. These out-payments were offset by the traditional inflows of long-term capital and only minor changes occurred in our official reserves during the year. Substantial shifts, however, occurred in our balance of payments during the first five months of 1970 and, as a result, our overall reserves rose at an accelerated rate and increased by $1,200 million (U.S.) during that period. Our exports increased to a much greater extent than could be accounted for by the rebound from the effects of strikes late in 1969. In addition, short-term capital outflows declined in response to lower interest-rates abroad and this combination left Canada exposed as a target for speculative inflows. We decided to act promptly before speculation became too heavy—thereby, we believe, making a contribution to the stability of the international monetary system.*

---

* Canada was considered by the IMF to be something of a "maverick", when it decided to allow the dollar to float. (The IMF regime called for fixed

Our situation in May 1970 was not quite comparable to that faced by others last month. In the first place, we had moved comparatively quickly from a deficit to an unexpectedly large surplus on current account. Secondly, our trading and financial relations with the U.S.A. are very close. Finally, the extreme openness of our economy to the movements of goods and capital causes us to experience unusual difficulty in maintaining a fixed exchange-rate within the margins prescribed by the IMF (International Monetary Fund).

The classic prescription would have been to seek the concurrence of the Fund to a new and higher par value. Our problem was to determine a rate that would be sustainable for a reasonable period.

In taking the decision to move to a floating exchange-rate, we made clear our intention to resume our obligations under the par-value system as soon as circumstances permit. This remains our firm determination and, while we have reviewed the situation from time to time during the past year, the underlying situation, both internal and external, has not seemed to us sufficiently settled to re-establish a par value that could be defended over the foreseeable future. In terms of payments, we have been confronted by a need to bring about an adjustment in our capital account in line with changes that have occurred in our current account. Expansionary financial policies, which our domestic economic situation required, have been helpful, but we have had to reinforce the effect of these policies by appeals to Canadian borrowers to seek the funds they required in the Canadian market to the maximum possible extent. At the same time, we felt a sense of uncertainty about the impact of international developments— a sense that would appear to have been justified by recent events.

---

parities generally at the time.) Canada's "float" has some tradition behind it, viz., in the 1950s and even as far back as the 1930s when the Canadian dollar—then a relatively minor currency not linked directly with any major currency—floated with reasonable stability in relation to the U.S. dollar and the pound sterling. The Canadian dollar reached its lowest ebb vis-à-vis the U.S. dollar in the early 1930s, e.g. $0.826 in 1933 and even lower (near $0.80) in 1931, although it rose to $0.90 in 1932. At the outset of the Second World War it was devalued by 10% in terms of the U.S. dollar, after having been close to par with the U.S. dollar since 1934, when the price of gold was revalued from $20.67 U.S. to $35.00 U.S. per ounce. See CHCD, June 1, 1970, for the Minister of Finance's statement explaining the decision to allow the dollar to float. Not long after the Canadian decision, the currencies of six other major industrial countries were also afloat (Austria, Britain, Italy, Japan, Switzerland, and the U.S.A.). Float and the world floats with you!

The extent of departures from the fixed-rate regime that have taken place raises very large issues. Our experience and that of others has underlined the inherent difficulties involved in combining a system of fixed exchange-rates and free capital flows internationally with the imperative demands placed upon our control instruments by the objectives of high employment and price stability domestically. There are a number of different ways of escaping from the dilemma— greater exchange-rate flexibility, greater control over the international flows of capital, greater international harmonization of monetary poli- cies—but all these alternatives raise difficulties of a practical and policy nature.

49. Canada, Britain, and the Common Market

Statement in the House of Commons by Mr. Jean-Luc Pépin, Minister of Industry, Trade and Commerce, December 1, 1970.

On behalf of the Government and accompanied by officials of the Departments of External Affairs, Finance, Agriculture, and Industry, Trade and Commerce, I visited Geneva, London and Brussels in October to put forward Canadian interests in the current negotiations for enlargement of the European Economic Community.

In my conversations, I highlighted four main themes:

1. Our concerns about the negative effects of EEC enlargement on Canada's access to the markets of the United Kingdom and Western Europe and its repercussions on the framework and patterns of world trade.
2. Our conviction that in some instances mutuality of interests ex- ists between Canada and Britain and the EEC, offering scope for adjustments.
3. Our intention to bring into play at an appropriate stage the contractual rights and obligations, under bilateral arrangements and under the GATT, which would be affected by EEC enlarge- ment.
4. Our views as to the importance of developing new initiatives for freeing of trade on a multilateral basis during the period of European negotiations.

Some Effects of Enlargement

In discussing the direct impact EEC enlargement would have on Canadian trade, I drew a statistical picture of the changes in access terms which our exports to Britain would face if that country adopted the EEC Common External Tariff and the Common Agricultural Policy unchanged. Only about 36 per cent of these exports would continue to receive free entry, compared with some 94 per cent at present. The remainder would face tariffs, loss of Commonwealth preferences and reverse preferences in favour of our EEC competitors. Our agricultural exports would be in an even more difficult position as the inward-looking Common Agricultural Policy makes use of levies, subsidies and other special protective devices.

The actual effects on the volume and profitability of Canadian sales would, of course, vary considerably from one item to another. However, it was important to ensure that the parties to the negotiations were fully seized of the fact that almost 70 per cent of our exports to Britain would be adversely affected under the present Common External Tariff and Common Agricultural Policy.

I underlined that Britain is Canada's second-largest export market, accounting for about one-quarter of our overseas sales. It has been purchasing more than $1 billion of Canadian goods annually in recent years and, in 1970, its purchases will exceed this level by a considerable margin. Our exports to the EEC and other applicant countries are approximately of the same magnitude as our sales to Britain. Some of these would also be adversely affected by EEC enlargement.

As regards the more general implications, we emphasized the danger of a polarization of the world trading community into inward-looking rival blocs. The EEC is already the world's largest trading entity. Enlarged, it would account for more than one-quarter of world trade, that is, not including intra-Community trade—compared with about 20 per cent for the United States. About 50 of the 91 members of the GATT could be either members of the EEC or countries associated with it.

I urged that the EEC use its influence to facilitate and encourage continued expansion of trade on a world-wide basis and not only within its own grouping of member and associated countries. The world trading community and the EEC itself would have much to gain from such an outward-looking policy. On the other hand, if EEC enlargement mainly has the effect of limiting and diverting trade from third countries, the Community is itself bound to lose over the longer run in terms of consumer and producer costs. Moreover, outside suppliers could not remain indifferent to the loss of important traditional markets for their goods in the EEC and in the countries associated with it.

Enlargement Negotiations and Canada

Britain has already told the EEC that it is prepared in principle to accept the Common External Tariff and the Common Agricultural Policy.

As regards accommodation for outside interests, the only specific issues Britain has raised in the negotiations relate to access for New Zealand butter and lamb and Commonwealth sugar and to relations between Commonwealth developing countries and the enlarged Community.

Certain arrangements which Britain is seeking in its own interest could help some of our exports. For example, as I have already told the House, nine of the 12 industrial materials for which Britain has requested special arrangements are of interest to Canada. These are aluminum, lead, zinc, newsprint, wood pulp, plywood, phosphorus, ferro-silicon and silicon carbide. Together they account for more than one-fifth of our sales in the British market.

There would also be, in case of enlargement of the EEC, a transitional period during which Canadian exporters could adjust to the new situation. The British have proposed that the application of the common tariff on industrial goods be staged over three years and that there should be a transitional period of six years for agriculture.

On the basis of my discussions with European leaders, I can say that Britain and the EEC are prepared to explore with us areas where their interests may to some extent coincide with our own. They are also willing to maintain a two-way flow of views and information with Canada throughout the negotiations. We hope that their agenda will not be too rigid to allow them to do these things in a meaningful way.

It would, however, be misleading for me to suggest that there is a prospect of any major accommodation of Canadian trade interests in the short term. Apart from whatever possibilities may exist for adjustments based on mutuality of interests, we must assume that, if the negotiations succeed, Canadian exports to Britain will eventually be subject to a Common External Tariff and a Common Agricultural Policy.

The general situation as far as access for Canadian goods is concerned would be significantly improved if the trading countries of the world undertook, during the enlargement negotiations or before the end of the transitional period, a broad negotiation to reduce tariffs and non-tariff barriers to trade. This would mitigate the trade-diverting effects of EEC enlargement in much the same way as the Dillon and Kennedy Rounds eased the impact on third countries of the original formation of the EEC.

For the present, however, European energies are being concentrated on the reshaping of Europe. In Brussels, it was emphasized that *élargissement* is only one of the current preoccupations of the EEC— the other being *approfondissement*, the progressive transformation of the Community from a customs union into a full economic and monetary union. We suggested that they should give more thought to the need for a *mondialisation*—or adaptation of the results of the enlargement negotiations to the requirements of world trade.

European Views

In both Brussels and London, there was a tendency to agree that the Canadians were exaggerating the impact of EEC enlargement on their trade. I was told that many of our exports would benefit from the dynamics of growth of the enlarged Community and its rapidly expanding import needs. Reference was made to the fact that the EEC's imports have more than doubled since 1958, when the Community came into being. It was also pointed out that the average level of the Common External Tariff on industrial goods was lower than that of the United States. Other favourable factors, including inter-company arrangements, could, some Europeans believe, ensure continued exports to an enlarged Community of some of our industrial goods.

In our meetings in London, the British sought to convince us that there would always be a large market for Canadian hard wheat in Britain because it was needed to maintain the right balance in milling operations.

We were repeatedly assured by all that the policy of the EEC (and perhaps even more so of an enlarged EEC) would be responsible and outward-looking. In fact, all said Europe "would not be comfortable with an inward-looking orientation".

We listened carefully to these reassuring assertions. I said we sincerely hoped that events would bear out the assumption of faster European economic growth, following enlargement. This would not help us, however, we emphasized, in those cases where their tariffs or other trade barriers were highly restrictive, as in the agricultural sector.

If Europeans are going to continue to need our industrial materials to sustain efficient economic growth, why impose on themselves the burden of paying significant customs duties on some of these products? If the enlarged Community will continue to need our wheat, should not the relevant regulations of the Common Agricultural Policy be adjusted to facilitate such trade?

I welcomed their predictions that an enlarged Community would be outward-looking and said that we hoped to see this reflected in the progress of the GATT work program and in future initiatives toward trade liberalization.

Canadian Strategy

What will be the Canadian attitude in the months and years to come? We shall continue, as I indicated, to keep considerations of this kind before our trading partners in Europe throughout the negotiations. We shall continue to seek areas of mutuality of interests. We shall continue to urge the EEC and the applicant countries, when they are weighing the merits of alternative solutions, to include in the balance the interests of their countries and the future of the world trading community.

Our discussions will be pursued in the coming months with all present and prospective members of the Community. In our consultations with them, we are placing considerable emphasis on the kind of relations an enlarged Community would have with Canada and other countries and trading groups.

As the negotiations in Europe proceed, we shall be considering how our important contractual rights and obligations can be put into play most effectively. We shall also be reviewing the implications of EEC enlargement for Britain's preferential access to the Canadian market.

In the meantime, we shall use our influence in the GATT to maintain the momentum of trade liberalization efforts and press in particular for a major round of negotiations before the results of the enlargement negotiations are put into effect. We shall continue to urge the United States to provide, with the EEC and other major world traders, the leadership and support which is essential if these efforts are to succeed. We had the opportunity to discuss these matters recently with members of the United States Administration when the Joint Canada–United States Committee on Trade and Economic Affairs met on November 23 and 24 in Ottawa.

We shall have no illusions, however, that we can safely leave the protection of Canadian interests to others. As a major trading partner of Britain and a significant market for the EEC and the applicant countries, Canada is not without bargaining power. These countries all wish to do more business with us; we shall insist that the terms on which we trade are fair to us as well as to them.

It will continue to be a key objective of Canadian policy to intensify our trading relations with Europe as a whole. There will be adjustments to be made because of enlargement, but in view of the magnitude and variety of Europe's import needs there should be many opportunities there for Canadian trade. We must strive to gain a share of European markets, which is more in line with our role in world trade generally.

In the first ten months of this year, our exports to the Community were 43 percent above those in the corresponding period of 1969. In 1970, the EEC will be, for the first time, a considerably more than $1-billion market for Canadian goods.

We shall be continually seeking ways of improving the effectiveness of our trade-development activities in the EEC and associated countries. I hope that Canadian exporters will also ask themselves whether there is anything more they could do to expand their sales to this dynamic trading group.

The public and private sectors in Canada will have to work closely together in order to minimize the adverse effects of EEC enlargement on our trade and to maximize its positive elements.

50. Canada and the European Economic Community

Statement by the Secretary of State for External Affairs, Mr. Mitchell Sharp, to the Canadian Institute of International Affairs, Toronto, November 18, 1972. (Extracts)

For the purposes of today's discussion, I am setting aside political considerations. But the economic stakes alone justify the most careful reflection. By 1980, the imports of the enlarged EEC from the outside world could soar to $130 billion. Canada—the world's fourth exporter after the EEC, the United States and Japan—must take the Common Market very seriously. The ten countries already form what is by far the world's largest trading unit; they imported over $70-billion worth of goods from the outside world last year. Of these $70 billion worth, over $2,000,700,000 worth of goods came from Canada. They represented 17 per cent of our total exports and about half of our exports outside North America, making the EEC our second-largest trading partner by a considerable margin.

Yet we can do much better. We shall have to do much better. Since 1958, Canadian exports to the EEC have increased greatly. They have not, however, kept pace with the increase in total EEC imports from the outside world. Our share of those markets has declined. Just as important, our exports to the EEC have not followed the trend in EEC imports toward manufactures and processed goods and away from primary materials and commodities. It is here, particularly in sectors of intensive technology, that we shall have to improve greatly.

It has not been easy to assess the cause of our difficulties in this category of exports to the EEC. Access has been a problem for a number of products, including some of interest to Canada. But this problem should not be exaggerated. By and large, the common tariff of the European Community is low. In spite of protective policies in the agricultural sector, the Community remains a large agricultural importer. Other world traders have done very well in this EEC market. Certainly the Americans have, with their export of sophisticated manufactures to the EEC, although they have been helped by their massive investment in Western Europe. Much of the difficulty probably lies with our industrial structures and trading habits themselves. We can't sell too well what we don't make, obviously. For this reason, we are thinking about our general policies toward the EEC very much in terms of policies on which we are working in other areas: energy policy, investment policy, industrial policy generally—including policy on secondary industry and policy on research and development—and other related policy studies. Our success in realizing our own potential could well be related to some extent to the EEC's success in doing the same thing. We should develop a degree of interest in this expanding but difficult market in keeping with its potential and with what we are doing, say, in the United States market.

We can also find a basis for understanding with the Europeans in the fact that we share some of the same problems. Many of you will have read the book by Jean-Jacques Servan Schreiber of a few years ago which has by now become something of a classic, *Le Défi Américain*.

You will recall that *Le Défi Américain* documents the difficulties the Europeans have had in building big enough companies in technologically sophisticated fields to generate sufficient capital, to finance sufficient research and development, to permit the innovation in technology, to make these companies competitive. Meanwhile, European firms have shown a tendency to sell out more often to American multinationals than to a European competitor. Put in these terms, the

Europeans have a problem with which we have had some experience.

Common problems don't necessarily make partnerships. We should all, I'm sure, prefer to choose our bedfellows on some basis other than misery. Moreover, I think that both the EEC—which has wrought an economic miracle—and Canada—which last year led the world in growth in industrial production—are buoyant in terms of economic expansion. But there are problems. To the extent that these are common to both the EEC and to Canada, we can help each other to develop solutions to our mutual benefit. This is the basis for partnership and this is the time to make the effort required.

In recent years, we have also been trying hard to develop closer economic relations in the field of sophisticated manufactured goods. We have sent technological missions and trade missions to Europe. We have had some good results. But now I think that we shall begin to get better results. I don't know if the Europeans have had the political will in the past to make the effort necessary. They may have been inhibited by reservations about the degree to which Canadian interests were nationally distinct, and about our wish to co-operate in the future.

The Government decided several years ago that it was necessary to have no doubt in European minds on these points. Furthermore, the Canadian case had to be presented with particular persistence and force because the Europeans were understandably preoccupied with the task of internal consolidation. We had to rap firmly but politely on the table to get their attention. We had to make plain, to take only one example, that, with Britain's entry into the EEC, over 48 per cent of our 1971 exports to Britain—trade valued at more than $1,300 million—would face more difficult entry. We wanted to explain that we had no quarrel with the British decision, which was for Britain to take; on the contrary, we rejoiced in the success of the EEC. But the parties to the enlargement had to understand that the burden of adjustment thrown upon Canada was greater than that placed upon any other country outside the enlarged Community. There were other issues as well. We had, above all, to change the attitude—which for a variety of reasons had been common in the EEC countries—that the view they took of their relations with the United States would do more or less for their relations with Canada.

In all this, we have had an encouraging measure of success. In June, a mission of senior officials held discussions with all the member countries of the EEC, as well as with Britain, Ireland and the EEC Commission. The mission found that the Europeans recognized the unique impact enlargement of the Community was going to have on Canada and welcomed Canada's constructive, matter-of-fact approach to British entry. The Europeans generally were open to a Canadian proposal that Canada and the EEC should examine the long-term development of relations, including the possibility of concluding a bilateral most-favoured-nation (MFN) agreement between Canada and the enlarged Community. There were useful discussions of what would be involved in bringing up to date the various bilateral trade and economic agreements Canada already had with member countries, to take account both of the enlargement of the Community and of its internal consolidation. The Europeans were assured that the Canadian objective was to reinforce bilateral relations with the member countries of the Community through creating an appropriate framework linking Canada and the EEC as such. The mission emphasized that what Canada had in mind would complement the GATT and other multilateral institutions, not substitute for them. It was also recognized that, since the Community was still evolving, any agreement negotiated in present circumstances would have to be flexible enough to accommodate itself to future changes in the powers of the Commission itself.

It was in part because of careful efforts like this that, when the European summit meeting took place in the autumn, the question of the EEC's relations with countries outside the Community was on the agenda. And because we had worked hard to prepare the ground, the European leaders affirmed in the summit communiqué that they wished "to maintain a constructive dialogue with the U.S.A., Japan and Canada and the other industrialized Community partners, in an outward-looking spirit and the most appropriate form". If the summit had taken place, say, two years ago, I very much doubt that it would have seemed natural to the leaders of the EEC countries to single out Canada in this way along with the United States and Japan.

I am happy to say that the constructive dialogue mentioned in the summit communiqué is continuing. A delegation of senior EEC officials will begin a four-day round of talks with their Candian counterparts in Ottawa next week. These talks will provide an opportunity to review certain world economic problems, like inflation. They will also provide for further examination, in considerable detail, of the substance of Canada's relations with the EEC. While the talks remain exploratory in nature, it will provide some indication of how thoroughly the matter is being pursued if I list some of the subjects we have said we want to discuss. They include the possibility of negotiating a bilateral MFN agreement with the Community itself, the modernization of agreements relation to goods in transit, the question of state-purchasing policies, of countervail, cabotage, export subsidies, concessional financing, security of supplies of energy and raw materials, copyright, consumer protection, protection of the environment, standards and quality control.

These are not the only subjects we have mentioned, and the representatives of the Community will not necessarily be in a position at this stage to pursue even subjects I have listed. But there is no question that the dialogue is well and truly launched. And there is no question that it proceeds from a clear understanding on the part of the EEC Commission and of the EEC governments that the problems posed for Canada by the enlargement and consolidation of the Community merit serious and separate consideration.

51. The Contractual Link—a Canadian Contribution to the Vocabulary of Co-operation

Statement by the Prime Minister, Mr. Pierre-Elliott Trudeau, at the Mansion House, London, England, on March 13, 1975. (Extracts)

I am in Europe to meet with heads of government of member states of the European Economic Community. I have conveyed to each of them, as I did to the European Commission in Brussels, the desire of Canada to enter into a contractual relationship with the Community—one that would ensure that both the Community and Canada would keep the other informed, would engage regularly and effectively in consultations, would not consciously act to injure the other, would seek to co-operate in trading and any other activities in which the Community might engage.

We have described our goal as the attainment of a contractual link. Because we do not know—indeed Europe does not know—how far or how fast its experiment in integration will take it, or what form it will assume on arrival, no overall agreement can be laid in place at this time. But what can be done is to create a mechanism that will provide the means (i.e., the "link") and the obligation (i.e., "contractual") to consult and confer, and to do so with materials sufficiently pliable and elastic to permit one mechanism to adapt in future years to accommodate whatever jurisdiction the European Community from time to time assumes.*

In each of the capitals I have visited I have been heartened by the willingness of governments to examine such a conception. Nowhere have I found it necessary to emphasize that Canada is not seeking preferential treatment or special advantages—for this would be contrary to the GATT—but only a guarantee of fair treatment at the hands of an economic unit rapidly becoming the most powerful in the world. In the interim since my visit to Europe last autumn, a series of exploratory talks has commenced with the object of constructing a framework within which formal negotiations will take place.

---

* The Canada-European Communities Framework Agreement for Commercial and Economic Cooperation entered into force on October 1, 1976. As a result, a Joint Cooperation Committee was formed. It is responsible for promoting and reviewing commercial and economic activities between Canada and the Community.

VII. International Development

‾It was in the aid sector that the Trudeau Government made a major effort—indeed, in the opinion of many, its main contribution—in the foreign affairs field. Aid budgets, which in 1965-66 were hovering around $300,000,000 per annum, had by 1975-76 reached the vicinity of $1,000,000,000. In addition, the emphasis had changed. Programs had become more concentrated, with efforts expended mainly in the forty poorest countries of the world. Bilateral aid had become less tied to procurement from Canadian sources and therefore more flexible. In addition, CIDA is now authorized to pay all shipping costs. More than a third of the assistance program is now channelled through multilateral organizations, completely untied. In fact, 57% of the total program is untied today (1977). During a period of economic difficulty and restraint at home, especially at a time when aid allocations in certain other donor countries either remained static or dwindled, these are notable achievements. In addition, the International Development Research Centre (IDRC) was founded in 1970. It was funded by the Government ($30,000,000 for its first five years of operation) and has an international board of directors.‾

52. Aid: General Policy—1966

(A) *Statement by the Secretary of State for External Affairs, Mr. Paul Martin, at the Consultation "Focus on Africa", sponsored by the Canadian Council of Churches, Queen's University, Kingston, June 17, 1966. (Extracts)*

In November 1963, the Government decided to embark on a phased expansion of its economic assistance programmes over a period of three years. It decided to make substantial quantitative and qualitative improvements which would enable Canada to assist the developing countries more effectively.

In the current fiscal year, appropriations for economic assistance will come close to $300 million. In the last four years approximately, our appropriations have almost tripled. I am glad to confirm the Government's intention to continue making substantial increases in aid allocations. We are working towards levels of aid activity which will enable us to play our full part in the development effort while taking fully into account:

(a) the recommendations of competent international organizations;
(b) our own special position as a net importer of capital; and
(c) the need to develop programmes which will be of a type and of a quality that will most effectively assist development in the nations concerned.

This is a very broad picture of Government policy. I do not want to present too much detail which might obscure the main lines of our activities. I should remind you, however, that carrying out an economic assistance programme is not simply a matter of making allocations—writing a larger cheque each year as it were. That is only the beginning. The agency concerned must then proceed on the basis of parliamentary authority to implement the plans. This involves a very considerable effort of discussion and negotiations, the movement of people and supplies, the introduction of new programmes, the criticism and revision of existing programmes and the effective central administration of public funds.

International organizations are, of course, involved in the use of some of the funds we allocate. For the most part, however, our aid is carried out by Canadians, by the Government and by the agencies and individuals whose services are enlisted. In considering the expansion of assistance in recent years, therefore, we must not think only of total allocations but consider also the significance, in terms of time and effort, of the increased levels of activity and of new departures in aid techniques.

There is, of course, a considerable debate going on among economists and political scientists about foreign-aid motivation. It seems invariably to be carried on in terms of the thinking and interests of donor nations. Perhaps we should approach the question differently. So far as I am concerned, Canada is responding to the requests of developing nations. I am interested in their thinking on the subject.

When African states drew up a charter of unity in Addis Ababa in 1963, they naturally devoted a good deal of attention to economic problems. They noted, among others, the considerations that "economic development, including the expansion of trade on the basis of fair and remunerative prices, should tend to eliminate the need for external economic aid, and that such external economic aid should be unconditional and should not prejudice the independence of African states".

This statement expresses some of the chief concerns of developing nations in Africa or elsewhere. It is clear that they want to derive the benefits of trade under the conditions which we in the developed nations consider normal. They want to obtain for their peoples the standard of living which technology, education, hard work and political stability can obviously, under contemporary conditions, produce. They want to bolster a highly cherished political independence with economic strength.

The responsibility of initiating this drive for better conditions, of defining the goals and of providing the greatest amount of the effort, is that of the developing nations. But if, in undertaking this drive, they turn to the developed nations for some of the credits, the grants, the technical knowledge and advice which are extremely important in achieving the initial momentum of economic growth, then we can only say that the efforts which they are willing to undertake on their own behalf have self-evident value in terms of our interest also, and that we shall help. No developed country which attributes any importance to its acceptance of the United Nations Charter could, so far as I am concerned, do otherwise.

There is an abundance of reasons supporting this view, ranging all the way from instinctive humanitarianism to political realism. I might remind you of some of the considerations of realism. If the independence of nations should be threatened by extreme poverty leading to anarchy, there would be a considerable temptation to those with greater power to intervene, with all the threats which intervention would pose to world peace. If the solution of some problems of frontiers, of lines of communication and of resources are not sought through regional and world economic co-operation, they will become the sources of brooding resentments and conflicts. If the relationship between races which characterized earlier eras of industrial revolution and colonialism is not clearly altered by new conditions of economic co-operation and political respect, then resentments, misunderstanding, ideological clashes and the formation of political blocs will impede diplomacy, international co-operation and trade.

(B) *Statement by the Secretary of State for External Affairs, Mr. Paul*

Martin, on July 20, 1966, to the Ministerial Meeting of the Development Assistance Committee in Washington, D.C. (Extracts)

In our assessment, the needs of developing countries for aid on appropriately "soft" terms remain one of the essential problems. The Canadian Government has, therefore, decided to make further adjustments in the terms on which Canadian development assistance is to be made available. To "soften" further our long-term, interest-free loans, the Canadian Government has decided to abolish the service charge of three-quarters of one per cent. This will mean that the bulk of Canadian development lending will be interest-free at 50-year maturities and ten-year grace periods. There are, of course, certain countries which can accept harder terms, and it has been decided to introduce an intermediate lending facility under which we would, in these few cases, be able to lend on 30-year terms, including a seven-year grace period and an interest rate of 3 per cent *per annum*. These intermediate loans would be used only in cases justified by the current and prospective economic and balance-of-payments situation of the recipient.

In mentioning the need for appropriate terms of aid, I should also point to the Canadian view that more is required to achieve harmonization of terms so that donors can pursue similar lending policies in specific cases. There is accumulating evidence that the terms on which aid is being extended to a number of developing countries, including India and Pakistan, are considerably harder than those which their economic circumstances would demand. As an example, the weighted average interest rate in the consortium for India has climbed from 2.8 per cent to 3.1 per cent. The Canadian average rate of interest in the case of India is below 2 percent. It is our belief that DAC countries as a group could make more rapid progress in achieving their stated objective of harmonization, particularly within the framework of consortia and consultative groups.

In summary, more aid, on softer terms with better techniques, is required. It is, of course, for each member to determine its share of the collective aid effort and the terms on which its share is extended. We have noticed with regret, as I have mentioned, that the volume of aid provided by certain countries has been decreasing and that terms have been hardening. So far as we in Canada are concerned, however, the terms as well as the volume of our aid will be determined less by what other DAC countries are doing and more by our assessment of the needs of the developing countries.

(C) *Lecture by Mr. Paul Martin, Secretary of State for External Affairs, in the First Series of the Jacob Blaustein Lectures, Columbia University, New York, April 28, 1967. (Extracts)*

Canada maintains the policy of insisting that its aid be given in the form of Canadian goods and services, of tying our aid funds, in other words, to procurement in Canada. We do this of economic necessity, rather than by conviction, because our sympathies lie with the terms of the recommendation adopted by the Development Assistance Committee in July 1965, which said, in part:

> [Tying of aid] can bring about cumbersome limitations on the freedom of the recipient to choose freely the most suitable sources of supply on the international market. With regard to bilateral assistance, member countries should jointly and individually endeavour, unless inhibited by serious balance-of-payments problems, to reduce progressively the scope of aid-tying, with a view ultimately to removing procurement restrictions to the maximum amount possible.

A significant proportion of Canadian aid is channelled through the multilateral agencies and is, of course, already untied. In respect of our bilateral aid we are willing, indeed anxious, to move from our position in concert with our fellow donors, particularly those whose economic influence in the world is so much greater than that of Canada. To be realistic, I cannot visualize early international agreement on this question, considering the disparate nature of aid programmes and donor economies. I am, however, hopeful that it will be possible to arrive at a formula which would permit gradual movement towards the objective.

53. A New Approach to Aid

Statement by the Prime Minister, Mr. Pierre-Elliott Trudeau, to a Convocation Ceremony marking the Diamond Jubilee of the University of Alberta, Edmonton, Alberta, May 13, 1968. (Extracts)

Never before in history has the disparity between the rich and the poor, the comfortable and the starving, been so extreme; never before have mass communications so vividly informed the sufferers of the extent of their misery; never before have the privileged societies possessed weapons so powerful that their employment in the defence of privilege would destroy the haves and the have-nots indiscriminately. We are faced with an overwhelming challenge. In meeting it, the world must be our constituency.

I can find no better words to express this view than those employed in General Principle Four of the Final Act of the 1964 United Nations Conference on Trade and Development: "Economic development and social progress should be the common concern of the whole international community and should, by increasing economic prosperity and well-being, help strengthen peaceful relations and co-operation among nations".

Pope Paul VI in his fifth encyclical was even more concise: " . . . the new name for peace is development . . . "

These references to assistance and to co-operation relate not only to economic assistance. They relate to assistance in any form that will create the political, economic and human climate most conducive to the nurturing of human dignity. International activities of this breadth are a far cry from the earlier and more primitive concepts of direct financial assistance. In their impact and in their value, they are also a long way from charity and philanthropy. If the Canadian goal is to assist other states in this way, then we are involved with humanity. And we are involved for our mutual benefit.

I emphasize this because when one benefits from an activity one is less likely to object to its cost. How do we benefit? In several respects:

(a) A world community of nations freely co-operating should result in a lessening of international tension. This would lead to a world less susceptible to war. Canada and Canadians would become more secure, and in this troubled world, that would be benefit beyond measure.

(b) A multiplicity of nations possessing expanding economies would mean that standards of living would rise and world markets would multiply. Canadian products would find more purchasers, and for a trading nation such as Canada, that would be a benefit of great value.

(c) In times of peace, men have turned their attention towards the development of their cultures, and the enrichment of life. Canadians live more meaningfully by enjoying the works of artists and scholars of whatever national source, and that is a benefit of unquestioned value.

These interests and these benefits submit to no national boundaries. The social, economic, and political betterment of any man anywhere is ultimately reflected in this country. If at the same time our consciences—our humanitarian instincts—are served, as they are and as they should be, then so much the better. Unquestionably the concept of international assistance is appealing because it is one of the most uplifting endeavours in which man has ever engaged. But we must never forget that in this process Canadians are beneficiaries as well as benefactors.

Any discussion of development assistance tends to lead eventually to a complex of issues which can conveniently be grouped under the word "strings". The very mention of this word prompts cries of "foul" from those whose interest in aid programmes is essentially philanthropic since it suggests Machiavellian political motivation on the part of the donor. The situation, as with any problem which has defied final solution over the years, is very complicated. A frank and open discussion of it by the Canadian public could do nothing but good. Our assistance programme, and the way in which it is conducted, must respond to the wishes and wisdom of those upon whose support it depends.

Canadians, I think, expect a certain selectivity in these programmes. We all feel instinctively that our help should go to those in the direst need, to those who will make the best use of it and to those making an honest effort to promote democratic institutions and personal liberties. Beyond this, however, difficult questions arise. Should aid be given unconditionally or should it be dependent on some concept of performance? For example, if land reform or tax revision are in our view necessary for economic or social development in the recipient country, should this "string" be attached to our aid? More difficult, perhaps, in domestic terms at least, is the problem of "Canadian content". It is widely held that "tied aid" diminishes the real value of development assistance by increasing costs. Yet an element of tying, with the immediate benefit it implies for Canadian production, may be an important factor in assuring wide domestic support for the aid programme.

These are difficult matters of judgment, not absolutes, and informed attention to them by people such as yourselves can help us to make choices more intelligently and more closely attuned to the deepest feeling of our people.

The long-range benefits cannot be over-emphasized. As Canadians we must realize that international co-operation, particularly in the field of economic assistance, in order to remain effective must take on a new form. From the present pattern of commodity and food assistance, of gifts of manufactured goods and loans of money, we must, in response to the economic needs of the developing countries, turn more and more to preferential trade arrangements. The two United Nations Conferences on Trade and Development have made clear that economic aid, in order to be effective, must increasingly take the form of trade.

The Secretary General of the United Nations, U Thant, concisely described this change in 1962. He said:

> The disappointing foreign trade record of the developing countries is due in part to obstacles hindering the entry of their products into industrial markets, and in part to the fact that production of many primary commodities has grown more rapidly than demand for them. It is appreciated that "disruptive competition" from low income countries may be felt by established industries in high income countries. Yet, precisely because they are so advanced, the high income countries should be able to alleviate any hardship without shifting the burden of adjustment to the developing countries by restricting the latters' export markets. A related problem to be solved is that of stabilizing the international commodity markets on which developing countries depend so heavily. Progress could certainly be made if the main industrial countries were to devote as much attention to promoting as to dispensing aid.

This kind of aid, these preferential trade arrangements, have no glamour attached to them. They cannot be illustrated by stirring photographs of rugged Canadian engineers posing before massive dams in remote places. This kind of aid doesn't offer a ready market to Canadian manufacturers, nor does it reduce our base metal or other commodity surpluses. In short, this kind of aid is competition, and bears little evidence of the sweet philanthropy which we have sometimes employed in the past to coat the cost of our aid "pill". Unless Canadians are aware of the vital goal our aid is seeking to achieve, they may not be sympathetic to a change of this sort. It is my opinion that Canadians will understand, and will accept the challenge. Economic aid, unless effective, will be useless. In order to be effective it will, in all likelihood, be costly. Yet we and the other developed nations have no alternative. The world cannot continue to accommodate mutually exclusive blocs of rich nations and poor nations.

We must recognize that, in the long run, the overwhelming threat to Canada will not come from foreign investments, or foreign ideologies, or even—with good fortune—foreign nuclear weapons. It will come instead from the two-thirds of the peoples of the world who are steadily falling farther and farther behind in their search for a decent standard of living. This is the meaning of the revolution of rising expectations. I repeat, this problem is not new. But its very size, involving some two-and-a-half billion people, makes it qualitatively different from what it has been in the past.*

54. Aid and Trade with Developing Countries

Statement by Mr. Jean-Luc Pépin, Minister of Industry, Trade and Commerce, University of Windsor, November 6, 1970.

Two-thirds of mankind lives in countries defined as "developing".

World peace cannot be established on relatively firm ground unless the economies of these countries are strengthened, unless these countries are brought into the normal world trading patterns ... (this is only one condition of peace, but it is an important one). Much of the success of the United Nations is predicated on the need to achieve international co-operation to eliminate the social and economic gaps between the developed and developing countries.

Developed countries have now generally assumed a responsibility in this respect—for moral, political, or straight economic considerations.

Developing countries not only expect to be admitted in these world trading patterns, they claim it a right to be.

Three main economic instruments are available to bring about this objective: aid, investment and trade.

Aid

Developing countries are now receiving some $7 billion annually in official development assistance from the industrialized countries. Canada has been expanding its total assistance program, which will reach $380 million this year.

Our own bilateral aid program (exceeding $280 million this year) of grants, loans and food aid is directed to Colombo Plan countries in Asia, Commonwealth Caribbean, francophone Africa, Commonwealth

---

* Many of the thoughts broached in this statement are to be found in the White Paper on "International Development", one of the six booklets which emerged from the foreign policy review of 1968-70 in *Foreign Policy for Canadians*, available from the QP or DEA, Ottawa.

Africa, and Latin America and has involved more than 50 countries at various times.

We are major contributors to such multilateral agencies as the World Bank, the International Development Agency, the UN Development Program and to the regional development banks in Latin America, Asia and the Caribbean as well as to such international organizations as the World Food Program.

A lot of debate amongst ourselves has centred on the value of these programs. They have received criticism but it is not without pride that we make contributions in the field of international development.

Investment and Trade

However important aid can be, investment and trade are more so. Eighty per cent of the foreign-exchange earnings of the developing countries are accountable to international trade.

Mr. Pearson once said:

> There is little logic in encouraging growth in developing countries through aid and other measures while imposing barriers against imports of products they can appropriately produce on a competitive scale.

This is generally accepted. There is a growing awareness and understanding in Canada and in the international community of the degree to which developing countries are dependent upon their export earnings to pay for their imports of capital equipment.

The goal of the international development effort should be to put the developing countries in a position where they can realize their aspirations with regard to economic progress without relying on foreign aid. Trade must provide the missing link in their evolution from poverty to affluence.

The question is how? How can trade and its extension, investment, contribute in bridging the development gaps between developed and developing countries?

This is not an easy question to answer. Let us assess some of the difficulties.

The complexity of the development process was underestimated by the classical approach to economic growth as a simple operation of capital injection. This was the pattern followed in Canada. But all the countries which face these tasks now cannot benefit from the same economic base, resource potential or educational levels. Repeatedly,

African and Asian leaders have pleaded with advisers from the developed countries to gain a better understanding of the physical and cultural environment of their countries, before suggesting programs for development.

The problem is also oversimplified by the convenient shorthand which consists in classifying countries as "developed" or "developing" countries.

In fact, a wide spectrum in degree of development exists both among and within each group:

(a) Some "developed" countries include those that have not yet achieved balance between the manufacturing, raw-material processing, and primary-resource extraction sectors. In some ways, Canada is one of those. It could be very well said that some regions of Canada are developing.

(b) The group of "developing" countries includes some with essentially agricultural economies of subsistence (e.g. most of Africa and Asia), but there are others outside the market economy close to take-off points of self-sustained growth, with modern industrial sectors and cosmopolitan cities with high standards of living (e.g. most of Latin America).

CANADA AND DEVELOPING COUNTRIES IN WORLD TRADE

A. Volume

While developing countries' exports have not grown as fast as trade among industrialized countries, their growth rate (6.5 per cent) in the last decade was better than predicted.

World trade in 1969 reached the level of $272 billion (U.S.). Of this, developing countries accounted for about $50 billion. (This represents 18 per cent of world trade as opposed to 21 per cent in 1913, 31 per cent in 1948 and 22 per cent in 1960).

Canada's share of world trade in 1969 was 5 per cent; although this looks modest, it is nevertheless equal to the contribution of the whole of Latin America. It was also more than the share of Africa or Southeast Asia taken separately.

There were projections some years ago that the trade-account deficit ($1.5 billion) of the developing countries (1960) might rise to more than $10 billion by 1970. Yet by 1969, the size of this deficit had not grown ($48.5 billion in exports and $50 billion in imports). The fear of the gap widening never materialized.

Developed countries take over 75 per cent of the exports of developing countries. Yet in 1969 Canada only took 2 per cent of their total exports. This still represents over $1 billion, or 8 per cent of total Canadian imports. In 1969, developing countries took about $900 million, or 7 per cent of total Canadian exports.

So who has been benefiting on the exchanges in recent years?

Since 1966, the balance of trade between Canada and developing countries has been in favour of the developing countries (last year by over $100 million).

B. Direction

Canada's trade to developing countries has not changed direction significantly in the last decade. In 1969, as in 1959, Latin America still led in volume with 50 per cent, Southeast Asia with 26 per cent, the Commonwealth Caribbean with 13 per cent, the Middle East with 7 per cent, and Africa with 4 per cent.

C. Composition

Developing countries still obtain over 80 per cent of their foreign-exchange earnings from exports of primary commodities. These include food, raw materials, ores and minerals, and fuels.

For many years ahead, favourable conditions for the international marketing of primary commodities will remain a basic prerequisite of the modernization and industrialization drive of the developing countries.

It is not surprising therefore that *Canadian imports* from developing countries are largely composed of tropical foodstuffs and raw and semi-processed materials. The remainder is made up of miscellaneous manufactured products, textiles, and chemicals.

The composition of *Canada's exports* to developing countries is largely made up of foodstuffs (70 per cent) and manufacturers' industrial materials (25 per cent), for which there is continuing demand by developing countries whatever their degree of economic development.

However, as many of the developing countries make significant progress towards industrialization there are now significant sales of capital equipment and technical services.

In the years to come we expect Canada to be particularly well qualified to provide the necessary equipment and expertise in such fields as telecommunications, grain-storage facilities, hydro-electric equipment, port-handling equipment, pulp and paper machinery, specialized aircraft, road and rail equipment, nuclear reactors, airport construction, aerial surveys, consulting engineering services and educational equipment.

Recently, we have sold quantities of hydro-electric turbine equipment to Brazil ($5.6 million), oil-well production equipment to Saudi Arabia ($1 million), locomotives to East Africa ($14 million) and highway-construction equipment to Indonesia ($28 million).

To appreciate fully Canada's trading position *vis-à-vis* developing countries it is useful to review the basic elements of the Canadian approach to trade. Since the Second World War, Canada has adhered to the rules and principles of multilateralism, freer trade, and reciprocity as embodied in the General Agreement on Tariffs and Trade (GATT). This has been reflected in the full support that successive Canadian Governments have extended to six different rounds of GATT trade negotiations, which culminated in the Kennedy Round in 1967.

We have followed this policy because Canadian farms and industries need the widest possible markets of the world in order to take advantage of specialization and economies of scale, in so doing providing better employment in Canada.

Freer international trade also serves the interest of the Canadian consumer in providing him with goods and services of wider variety and at a lower cost.

How does this GATT-oriented policy apply to our trade relations with developing countries?

Since the large majority (70) of developing countries have become members of the GATT—it is no longer a rich man's club—Canada exchanges the most-favoured nation (MFN) treatment with them through the GATT. With countries such as Mexico, Colombia and Venezuela, which have not acceded to the GATT, we have bilateral arrangements of non-discrimination.

As for our Commonwealth trading relations (which predates GATT), the GATT obligations have meant a freezing of the margins of tariff preferences exchanged on a contractual basis with countries such as the West Indies at the levels existing in 1949, when the GATT was formed. Multilateral tariff reductions have tended, over the years, to erode the significance of the Commonwealth preferences.

The ground rules of the GATT have also emphasized reciprocity as a major feature of international trade. The significance of this rule for developing countries has, in fact, been considerably diluted over the years, to the point where the GATT obligations tend to be applied unilaterally to the developed members. Indeed, the non-reciprocity principle has been incorporated in 1965 into Chapter IV, added to the GATT to deal with development problems.

A policy of freer international trade as it applies to Canada has completely eliminated tariffs on almost 70 per cent of imports from developing countries.

1. PRIMARY COMMODITIES

How can developing countries market their primary products in the best possible way?

As an important commodity trader, it has been Canada's experience that an expansion of this traditional type of supply is geared to the industrial activities in the industrialized countries. This applies to the exports of industrial materials of developing countries as well.

a) Freer access for industrial materials

i) Canada has strongly pressed for multilateral free trade in industrial materials and resource-based industries, such as forest products and non-ferrous metals, in both primary and processed form. We continue to support this objective.

ii) A sound international allocation of these resources would require that access to world markets be freed on a world-wide basis. Such a concerted move would provide the greatest benefits to all concerned, whether developed or developing, exporters or importers.

iii) Access to the markets of the U.S.A., the EEC, Japan and Britain is already free for products such as bauxite, tin and iron ore, but not generally so for products like unwrought aluminum, copper, lead and zinc.

Progress has been made and Canada has made significant contributions, but more must come.

b) Freer access for tropical products

i) Because of their geographical position, developed countries do not as a general rule grow tropical products. The existence of import duties is not, therefore, intended to protect domestic growers but to maintain a competitive advantage of preferential developing suppliers.

ii) Tariffs on several tropical products (e.g. coffee, tea, cocoa) were significantly reduced as a result of the Kennedy Round negotiations, but import duties still remain, mainly because of unreadiness of preferential suppliers to share their markets with other competing developing countries.

iii) Most of Canada's Kennedy Round reductions on tropical products were implemented in one stage on January 1, 1968. This means that Canada provides duty-free access for products such as cocoa beans, cocoa butter, green coffee, coconuts and peanuts.

Canada continues to support freer access for tropical products in the markets of advanced temperate countries by calling for the avoidance of fiscal duties on such commodities by importing countries, which tends to reduce the free flow of goods.*

iv) If all industrialized countries were to move in that direction, existing preferential suppliers (i.e. developing countries of the Commonwealth and those associated with the EEC) would be adequately compensated for the sharing of their preferences through improved access in other markets.

This would be another step forward towards duty-free non-discriminatory trade.

c) International commodity agreements

Canada believes that international commodity arrangements can play an important role in the trade prospects of primary-commodity producers by stabilizing price fluctuations at levels remunerative to efficient producers and fair to consumers. In some cases, commodity arrangements may be necessary to ensure adequate supplies of particular commodities.

---

* On July 1, 1974, Canada implemented a system of tariff preferences for developing countries covering most industrial products and a number of agricultural and food products. The Tokyo Declaration of September 1, 1973, which initiated the current Multilateral Tariff Negotiations, stated that priority should be given to product areas of specific interest to developing countries and a special negotiating group was set up to deal with tropical products. Canada has participated in the activities of this group within the Multilateral Trade Negotiations and has agreed that it will work towards the implementation of its tropical-products offer.

Commodity arrangements may also take the form of international agreements involving contractual obligations in which exporters and importers, developed and developing alike, accept reciprocal commitments regarding price levels and supply commitments, as in the case of the wheat and tin agreements.

There are other commodity arrangements involving informal price agreements (e.g. hard and soft fibres), or intergovernmental arrangements consisting merely of regular international consultations on the market situation and outlook (e.g. olive oil, tea).

Canada is a member of all the major international commodity agreements. In so doing Canada fosters the mutuality of interests and benefits in international trading.

a) In the case of the International Grains Arrangement, Argentina benefits from commercial sales at price levels fixed under the Arrangement. Developing importing countries benefit through the Food Aid Convention, which provides 4.5 million tons of wheat annually. By the way, the experience under the Grains Arrangement points to the difficulties of maintaining prices at agreed levels when there is a substantial surplus.

b) In the International Sugar Agreement, several developing countries are exporting members who benefit from a higher and more stable price for raw sugar (e.g. the West Indies, Mauritius, Cuba), while importing members like Canada benefit from supply commitments and quota increases at specific price levels.

c) In the International Coffee Agreement, all exporting members are developing countries and, in some cases (Brazil, Colombia) a large percentage of their export earnings come from sales of coffee at higher and more stable prices. The Agreement contains a diversification fund for inefficient coffee producers, which is raised through a premium of exports above agreed annual export quotas. There is also a device for controlling production.

d) The International Tin Agreement, through a buffer stock mechanism, greatly assists its developing members (e.g. Malaysia and Bolivia).

e) Canada has also actively participated in efforts to negotiate an International Cocoa Agreement, which would be of particular benefit to Ghana and Nigeria. It is interesting to note that since cocoa prices have risen and stabilized at higher price levels, developing countries are not as anxious to obtain an early agreement. In addition, the developing producing countries cannot agree on which countries should be entitled to export quotas under any agreement or how the quotas should be divided amongst them.

Canada is also a member of various international study groups on a wide range of primary commodities of interest to developing countries (e.g. rubber, lead and zinc, vegetable oils). There have been suggestions for more commodity agreements (e.g. iron ore, oilseeds, oil and fats).

Obviously the system is a good "gimmick". The technique offers great possibilities. But it is not a panacea. Each case must be studied on its own merit, taking into account the particular characteristics of the commodity involved. In some cases (e.g. oilseeds), the difficulty could lead to the use of substitutes, in others (e.g. rubber), it is the risk of encouraging the development of synthetics which would limit the volume of the natural products traded internationally. In still other cases, where world trade in a commodity is growing very rapidly (e.g. iron ore), a formal agreement might stimulate vast surpluses, encourage inefficient production, or discourage new investment ventures, depending on the price level fixed.

Needless to say, in assessing the need for such agreements, Canada must take into account its own industrial development interests, its competitiveness by international standards, and the conditions of trade in the world market. I think I've demonstrated that our conduct has to take into account the interests of the developing countries.

2. MANUFACTURED PRODUCTS

Developing countries cannot be left to primary exports. They are also entitled to industrialize.

Because of the limited size of domestic markets in most developing countries and because of the relatively weak purchasing power even in countries such as Brazil, industrialization cannot proceed on the appropriate scale and with the necessary specialization unless the countries can sell their manufactures in world markets.

Developing countries also have to find new market opportunities in industrialized countries in order to obtain foreign-exchange earnings to pay for their growing requirements of industrial equipment and capital goods from abroad.

If this could be brought together it would accentuate the trade flows.

A) Regional blocs

What are the techniques available to increase trade flows? The formation of regional markets is a technique often used to achieve the benefits of rationalization and large production scale.

Canada has taken a generally positive position towards the formation of customs unions or free-trade areas among developing countries (e.g. Latin American Free Trade Area, Central American Common Market, Caribbean Free Trade Area). We have been anxious to ensure, however, that these regional trade groupings remain outward-looking and are not used simply to extend national import substitution policies on a regional or a non-competitive basis.

Canada is not attracted by the formation of special regional trading arrangements encompassing developed and developing countries of the northern and southern hemispheres. For example, we are concerned about the proliferation of special preferential trade deals negotiated by the EEC with a large number of African and Mediterranean countries. There are serious risks that the eventual accession of Britain to the EEC will lead to similar discriminatory arrangements with many Commonwealth developing countries. Trade discrimination along hemispheric lines would lead to a polarization of the world into economic blocs with their economic spheres of influence. This kind of arrangement, which could result in old-time protectionism within wider borders, will inevitably generate resentment and political confrontation between trading blocs. Developing countries should be aware of these dangers to international trade and consequently to themselves.

B) Freer access through MFN liberalization

It is Canada's conviction that it would be in the long-term interest of the smaller trading nations, both developed and developing alike, to open up new markets for industrial products of developing countries on the basis of equal opportunity for all. The erosion of basic trading rules through discriminatory arrangements could only benefit the strong rather than the weak.

We are concerned about current protectionist pressures in the U.S.A., since it takes about one-fifth of developing country exports. A shift toward more protectionism would have substantial negative effects on the economies of the Third World and would lead to pressure on countries like Canada to take more or to go the same way (pressure is twofold).

Another major source of great concern arises from the negotiations for EEC enlargement. Unless such a powerful trading bloc in Europe adopts an outward-looking attitude, particularly with respect to its Common Agricultural Policy, it could have substantial adverse effects on the interests of third-country suppliers of agricultural products, developed and developing alike.

C) Tariff preferences

Trading conditions should be further substantially improved as a result of the institution of a temporary and non-reciprocal "generalized preference scheme" of tariff preferences for manufactured and semi-manufactured goods of developing countries in the markets of all Western industrialized countries. As we see it, such a scheme should facilitate an expansion of trade and not create an obstacle to further trade liberalization on a multilateral basis, and this is being done by being temporary.

The offer of tariff preferences which Canada recently submitted to UNCTAD should provide maximum trading advantages to developing countries consistent with the objectives of Canadian industrial policy.

Under this offer, Canada is prepared to extend tariff reductions equivalent to the lower of either the British preferences or one-third off the MFN rates for manufactures and semi-manufactures except for a limited list of sensitive low-cost products. Tariff reductions of varying magnitude are also offered on a selected list (45 tariff items) of agricultural products of special interest to developing countries.

The importance of this offer has to be seen in perspective, since almost 70 per cent of developing-countries exports to Canada are already duty-free. The offer will further substantially improve this situation by adding more than 300 tariff items on the duty-free list and by extending more than 50 per cent tariff reductions on about 100 more items.

This preference offer does not impose any quantitative limit on preferential imports. We have put it as a first step toward liberalizing tariff treatment for developing countries. Further reductions will be considered in the light of experience.

The extension of the British preferential rates—except in a few cases of particular interest to the West Indies, e.g. bananas, rum, citrus fruit —to all developing countries entitled to MFN treatment in Canada is an additional step forward in line with our general trade policy of non-discrimination.

How does Canada's tariff-preference offer compare with that of other countries? Let's have a look at some of the main features of other offers.

The U.S.A. has offered duty-free treatment but has excluded most textiles, footwear, and petroleum products. Our approach is much more selective and is based on the injury conception. It is still possible that preferential treatment will be denied in the U.S.A. to developing countries extending preferential access to countries of the Commonwealth or the EEC unless these are gradually phased out.

The EEC has also offered duty-free treatment but has put quantitative ceilings on the volume of preferential imports. Japan has adopted a similar approach.

Canada has no quantitative ceiling. So we think we have a good liberal offer.

D) Non-tariff barriers

In a world where tariffs have gradually come down, non-tariff barriers (e.g. export subsidies, government purchasing, standards, valuation procedures, quantitative restrictions) have become relatively more important. The GATT work program designed to identify these problems and to prepare the way for their future multilateral negotiations could also bring substantial direct benefits to the developing countries. We have been actively campaigning for rapid progress in this area.

E) Freeing of trade by sectors of industry

In the GATT, Canada has also proposed that further trade liberalization on a multilateral basis be explored through sectoral negotiations. This approach for freeing trade with respect to tariffs and non-tariff barriers, and covering both primary, semi-processed and manufactured forms of production within the same sector, is particularly appropriate at a time when developing countries are endeavouring to export more of their primary industrial materials in processed forms.

As resource industries are characterized by high levels of capital investment, advanced technology, large-scale production and often by multinational corporations, the sector approach would also allow developing countries to deal with problems arising from corporate and governmental policies affecting trade in these fields.

F) Low-cost imports

Action on tariffs does not necessarily answer problems of market disruption caused by low-cost imports, in certain sectors in which developing countries have already significant competitive advantages such as textiles.

The situation with regard to international trade in textiles is very difficult because of the restrictions maintained by a number of importing countries—and we all know the pressures in the U.S.A. for more restrictive measures. In these circumstances, the relatively open Canadian market is rather inviting for suppliers who are constantly seeking out alternative markets.

This highly restrictive world environment has had a double impact on the Canadian industry. Firstly, the restrictions by other industrialized countries have led to increased pressures from "low-cost" competition on the relatively open Canadian market. *Per capita*, overall penetration by "low-cost" textile products is more than double the level reached in the U.S.A., and many times more than the degree of penetration in the countries of the EEC. Canada can hardly be accused of not having done its share to accommodate "low-cost" suppliers. Secondly, the tariffs of other countries have severely limited the access for Canadian textile and clothing exports, thus limiting the attainment of full competitive potential for the Canadian industry.

It is for this reason that some established Canadian sectors of the textile industry are particularly vulnerable and are being seriously damaged. Plants are often located in slow-growth areas, where Canada too has problems of industrial development.

In the recently announced textile policy, I indicated that Canada is prepared, indeed anxious, in step with others, to move toward a more liberal international trade regime in textiles. In the meantime, however, Canada could not be expected to leave its established industry unreasonably exposed. In the current period, therefore, while Canada has not sought comprehensive limitations on textile exports to Canada, we have found it necessary to seek protective arrangements on a relatively narrow range of specific items.

We look forward to the transformation and restructuring of some of Canada's traditional industries into internationally viable industries, but this could only take place gradually. We've got to have the right mix of trade and industrial policies and we are moving in that direction.

In fields where we have already experienced problems of adjustment caused by low-cost imports, we must press other industrialized countries to do their share so that we can look ahead to a continuation of a progressive liberalization and orderly growth of international trade.

Such a restructuring of developed economies is already taking place as a result of a continuously changing pattern of world trade and swift changes in technology.

For a country like Canada so dependent on world trade, this would mean to specialize deliberately some research and science-based industries where we can.

G) Assistance in export-promotion techniques

Progress in export-promotion techniques and better knowledge of market conditions in both developed and developing regions are also conditions for successful international marketing of products produced in developing countries. Canada sees assistance in export promotion as a good way to ensure that developing countries will not experience new frustrations by losing export opportunities provided by better access to world markets.

Experience gained by the ministerial mission to Latin America in 1968 has confirmed that problems such as the lack of direct shipping lines or of appropriate contacts between businessmen result in loss of trading opportunities.

The assistance provided by the GATT-UNCTAD International Trade Centre and the Inter-American Export Promotion Centre is an effective means to help developing countries to market their products in industrialized countries. In addition to market surveys, the International Trade Centre offers developing countries training programs for their trade experts to familiarize them with modern marketing techniques.

We also extend technical assistance in trade promotion bilaterally. For example, in recognition of the need for Latin American countries to increase their export trade, CIDA recently undertook the financing of a survey of the potential for Mexican and Brazilian products on the Canadian market.

3. THE PRIVATE SECTOR

Better access to industrialized markets could by itself be of limited practical value to developing countries, particularly in non-traditional sectors. Consequently, foreign private investments have an important contribution to play if production facilities are to be set up to take advantage of new export opportunities, particularly for capital-intensive industries.

Canadian business and industry have a growing role to play in the development-assistance program. Canadian experience with small-scale and medium-scale industrial enterprises, and in such sectors as food-processing, wood products and raw-material processing, is often particularly relevant to the requirements of a number of recipient countries at this stage of their development.

Direct investment in developing countries by Canadian business is not negligible. Examples include: electronics plants in Turkey, Greece and the Philippines; mining developments in the Dominican Republic and Brazil; and bauxite-mining and alumina-processing plants in Jamaica and Guyana.

Investment brings with it some of the best managerial talents and know-how, and transfer of technology badly needed in these areas. It also paves the way to new trading connections in a part of the world which, if development efforts succeed, could become the fastest-growing market in the world before the turn of the century.

Foreign investments now make up 45 per cent of the total transfers of financial resources from developed to developing countries ($5.8 of $12.8 billion).

The flow of private investment largely depends on the attitude of the developing countries themselves. They must create a "sound" climate—for not only foreign but also domestic private capital.

Under the Export Development Corporation there is now available to Canadian investors an insurance facility against some of the special risks inherent in productive ventures in developing regions (e.g. expropriation, inability to repatriate earnings or capital, revolution). The Corporation encourages local participation in the investment.

This Investment Insurance Program of the EDC is in addition to its more established functions of (1) insuring credit extended in connection with exports from Canada, and (2) making direct long-term loans to foreign buyers of Canadian capital goods in particular. While both activities are designed to improve the access of Canadian goods to world markets, they also help developing countries to acquire needed capital goods. All but $3 million of the $395 million of loans outstanding have been made to developing countries. As for export credit insurance, over 40 per cent of this covers exports to developing countries ($103 million out of $241 million as of December 1969).

The Canadian International Development Agency has recently introduced a pre-investment incentives program to assist Canadian firms undertaking "starter" studies and feasibility studies of investment possibilities in developing countries. This program should encourage Canadian business and industrial firms to increase their participation in the economic growth of developing countries.

In the event the company decides not to proceed with an investment following examination of the results of the study, CIDA will reimburse the company to 50 per cent of the approved costs of the study on condition that it becomes the property of the Government. In such cases, the study will be made available to other potential investors.

55. Oil and the Less-Developed Countries

Statement by the Secretary of State for External Affairs, Mr. Mitchell Sharp, to the House of Commons Standing Committee on External Affairs and National Defence, Ottawa, March 19, 1974.

Since last I spoke to this Committee on the estimates of the Department of External Affairs and of CIDA, there has occurred a series of related events with far-reaching and widespread consequences for the world as a whole and inevitably, therefore, for Canada. The major event of this series is, of course, what has been called the energy crisis. In fact, the problems of the supply and price of oil are only the currently most acute symptoms of a much wider problem: the increasing demands made by mankind on the world's food and industrial resources.

When I spoke to you last May,* I mentioned the increasing preoccupation about a prospective energy shortage and associated balance-of-payment questions. At the time, it was clear that the world would have to think hard and rapidly about its energy resources in view of the tremendous annual increase in demand upon these resources, which has been the pattern in recent years. What was not

---

* Standing Committee on External Affairs and National Defence, May 15, 1973. See also SS 73/15.

foreseen at that time was that this situation would suddenly become acute with respect to both supply and price, particularly of oil.

The sharp and sudden rise in the price of oil has had extraordinary effects throughout the world. Unless measures are taken to insure continued growth of the world economy, the world trading system could as a result be seriously undermined.

The main industrialized countries, which are large users of energy, have a major responsibility, because of their importance in world trade, to try to prevent this from happening. It was with this end in view that Canada attended the Washington Energy Conference in early February and has co-operated in the follow-up to that conference, which is aimed essentially at identifying the economic facts of the situation and trying to ensure that appropriate steps to correct the situation are being taken in the various international institutions and to lay the groundwork for an early and meaningful dialogue with the oil-producing countries on problems of mutual concern.

Another broad area of agreement in Washington was on the necessity for research into and development of the world's untapped sources of energy. These include the known deposits of the more complex forms in which oil is found, such as heavy oil and oil-sands in Western Canada, and the oil-shale deposits in the U.S. There is also the longer-term problem of the smooth transition to other forms of energy, such as nuclear power, about which quite a bit is already known, and the longer-term quest for geothermal and solar power.

As both producer and consumer, Canada occupies a rather different position from a good many of the other industrialized countries. While the net effect of oil-price increases on our balance of payments is very small, we cannot hope to escape the inflationary effects of still rising prices in an already serious world inflationary situation. Nor can we as a country heavily dependent on foreign trade afford to ignore the possible adverse effects on world trade caused by the run-down of foreign-exchange reserves and the general destabilization of world production.

Canada, therefore, has supported vigorously efforts to maintain the world pace of economic activity and to encourage the newly wealthy oil-producers to play a role in international financial institutions commensurate with their new financial status.

We have learned with great interest that the producing countries are actively seeking ways in which to share with other developing countries some of their new-found wealth. Canada welcomes this positive step. Most of these countries are themselves in the process of development and in the earliest stages of industrialization. They have made clear their desire to use these funds for the rapid development of their economies, as well as for a large range of social purposes.

A number of these countries have made known to Canada their wish for closer relations for the mutual benefit of both sides. We have, therefore, begun a program of extending our representation in the Middle East to assist this process. The opening of a Canadian embassy in the Saudi Arabian capital of Jeddah was announced on December 21. At that time, I said that the Government would shortly be considering the opening of other missions in the Middle East, such as in Baghdad and elsewhere.

Apart from the opening of embassies, the earlier step of establishing formal diplomatic relations with Bahrain, Qatar, Oman and the Federation of Arab Emirates was announced on February 2. The Canadian Ambassador resident in Tehran will be the Canadian representative accredited to these states.

We have also agreed to establish diplomatic relations with the two Yemens: the Arab Republic and the People's Democratic Republic. We had already established commercial relations with these two countries. This now completes the formal establishment of relations with all countries of the Middle East.

At the intergovernmental level we shall wish to encourage discussion:

- to ensure the dependability of world oil supply;
- to discourage the use of oil and other commodities for political purposes; and
- to achieve some stabilization of oil prices at levels which are reasonable from the point of view of both producers and consumers.

Oil prices did indeed remain low for a good many years, and there was room for upward movement to reflect the cost of bringing on new conventional and non-conventional sources of energy.

We are particularly concerned to ensure that action is taken to prevent the economic collapse of those developing countries heavily dependent on imports of oil. An overall increase in the flow of development aid, bilaterally and through multilateral institutions, is urgently required from major traditional donors and from those who have benefited from increased oil revenues, together with a reassessment of the geographic allocation and the composition of aid programs, both bilateral and multilateral, in the light of the differing effects on developing countries of those higher oil prices.

The current uncertainty as to the prospective level of world oil prices makes it, of course, extremely difficult to extrapolate the effects of the situation even over a one-year period. However, certain inescapable facts confront us. Almost three-quarters of the developing countries do not produce their own energy supplies. Based on oil-demand projections calculated prior to October 1973, those countries might expect to pay for their oil imports in 1974 triple the amount they paid for oil imports in 1973. The resulting foreign-exchange costs could surely not be borne without cutting back severely on other essential imports or running down already limited exchange reserves.

The amount of aid extended to all developing countries was approximately twice their estimated oil-import bill in 1972. By contrast, in 1974 the oil-import bill for all LDCs could approach twice the 1972 aid level. In dollar terms, the 1972 oil-import bill for these countries was $3.7 billion. In 1974 they will have to pay at least $15 billion. In some individual cases, such as that of India, the added costs will completely offset the flow of development assistance from all quarters. It is, of course, misleading to generalize on the effects of increased oil prices on the 70 odd oil-importing LDCs. These effects will vary depending on the nature of their economies and the movement of other import and export prices. Certain major fast-growing exporters may be better able to withstand increased costs. Populous countries of slow export growth, yet with a growing industrial base catering to domestic needs, will be particularly hard hit. The gravest indirect effect of the oil situation is likely to be in the agricultural sector of developing countries. Fertilizers and pesticides, which have been so necessary for the success of the "Green Revolution", are energy-intensive products, and there is already a growing shortage of fertilizer.

For some time now, fertilizer production has been inadequate to meet demand and new capacity has not been built at a sufficient rate. This shortfall, combined with growing demand for food, means that food grains are almost certain to remain in short supply, and the developing countries will have to spend considerably more for their imports of a number of essential commodities. To cite a few examples: the price of wheat has increased sharply over the past two years from $86 a metric ton in 1972 to $210 today—an increase of 146 per cent. Rapeseed went up from $130 a ton to $300. Prices of other commodities and products, and of services such as transportation, have shot up as well. Potash fertilizers have gone up 71 per cent in one year. Prices of lead and zinc have almost doubled in the last 12 months, and fabricated steel has risen to $800 a ton from $500 a year ago.

The full significance of these price increases is only apparent when actual quantities likely to be shipped are taken into account. A few years ago, for example, we shipped roughly 600,000 tons of wheat to India at a cost of $40 million. A similar shipment today would cost $128 million. Looking at our food-aid program as a whole, the cost of providing the identical quantity (roughly 750,000 tons) of food that was made available to developing countries two years ago under our program has risen by 123 per cent—from $81 million in 1972-73 to $181 million in 1974-75, without taking account of shipping costs, which have also risen by over 100 per cent during the same period.

Canada is already on record as being against any cutback in aid-flows. At the energy conference in Washington in February, my colleagues and I went still further, taking a leading part in getting the conference to endorse a statement in the official communiqué that a strenuous effort must be made "to maintain and enlarge the flow of development aid bilaterally and through multi-lateral institutions, on the basis of international solidarity embracing all countries, with appropriate resources".

Here in Canada, the Government is exploring several approaches:

1. The use of our membership in the various multilateral institutions, including the regional development banks, to encourage and support a reassessment of lending programs, enabling a redirection of resources to those developing countries that are most severely affected by the increases in oil prices.
2. We have requested legislative authority for Canada's contribution to the fourth replenishment of the funds of the International Development Association (IDA). This is the arm of the World Bank on which the very poorest countries depend for development assistance. It provides loans on the most concessional terms, usually at zero interest.
3. Bilaterally, CIDA programs will be adapted to the new situation wherever appropriate. Some countries have already stated their most pressing needs, and the World Bank has also identified some areas where assistance is urgently needed.

Clearly, CIDA will need not only more money but also a great deal of adroitness in adapting Canada's development assistance to offset some of the adverse effects of recent dislocations, while continuing to maintain the momentum of development in those countries of the Third World with which we have well-established relationships.

World Food and World Population Conferences

The relationship of resources, food and population is obvious. Within a space of 25 years, the world's population is expected to reach a figure of 6 billion. To underline the common concern about this problem, 1974 has been designated World Population Year. A World Population Conference will be held in Bucharest in August. The conference will examine the relations between population and economic and social development, resources and environment. These are questions of the first importance to all countries. The Government has initiated major preparations for Canada's participation. The CIIA, in conjunction with the Family Planning Federation and the Inter-Church Project on Population, will be holding a series of meetings across Canada beginning this week. The provinces will also be consulted in the final preparations for the Canadian delegation's brief.

Changing demand and consumption patterns and the aggravation of the supply situation by natural causes are already such that food reserves are being run down at an alarming rate and starvation conditions already exist in some parts of Africa. The shortfall in production in the Asian subcontinent is this year expected to reach serious proportions. Shortages of fertilizer and the high cost of other agricultural inputs can only serve to aggravate the situation, particularly in the developing countries, which have struggled to attain some measure of self-sufficiency.

Canada will look to the World Food Conference to marshal opinion and forces for a concerted and coherent attack on the problem.

Canada is an important food producer and exporter, and we have in the past been a major provider of emergency supplies in times of world need. Although we are in effect a marginal supplier of world food requirements, we shall continue to do our part in improving production and providing emergency aid. But the real nub of the problem lies in capitalizing on the food-production potential of the developing countries, where the worst food-supply situations will arise. The Food Conference must place its main emphasis on the building of agricultural productivity in the developing countries.

The role and the financing of future food aid will also have to be re-examined in the light of rising commodity prices and short supply.

We shall have to aim at greater co-ordination of food stocks on the international plane, which would encourage growth of these stocks outside the food-exporting countries.

56. Food Aid

Statement by the Secretary of State for External Affairs, Mr. Allan J. MacEachen, to the Commonwealth Ministerial Meeting on Food Production and Rural Development, London, England, March 4, 1975.

With the increasing attention being paid to food production and rural development throughout the world—especially in the wake of the World Food Conference*—this meeting must ensure that any activity undertaken through our Commonwealth supplements and reinforces— and does not duplicate—activities being undertaken elsewhere.

Let me turn now, briefly, to the World Food Conference and review the follow-up action that is being taken internationally and by Canada.

It was understandable that many delegates to that conference from developing countries were preoccupied with the urgent short-term problems arising from a rapidly deteriorating world food situation. This made it difficult to place proper emphasis on the resolution of longer-term food problems and of increased agricultural production— especially in developing countries—that represented a major objective of that conference.

Nevertheless the conference did achieve agreement on a number of important institutional issues:

1. The establishment of a World Food Council.
2. The establishment of the FAO Committee on World Food Security.
3. The setting-up of a Committee on Food Aid Policies and Programs.
4. The creation of a global information and early warning system.
5. The establishment of a consultative group on food production and investment of the IBRD, FAO and UNDP.

---

* Rome, November 1974. See SS 74/13 by Mr. MacEachen for an account of its deliberations and the Canadian approach. The statement by Madame Jeanne Sauvé, Minister of the Environment, to the World Population Conference, Bucharest, August 20, 1974, carries useful related information.

6. The creation of the framework for an international fund for agricultural development.

Discussions are now taking place or are scheduled in the very near future to advance each of these matters. In keeping with Canada's role at the conference, we intended to take part in these discussions in the spirit that was developed at the Rome Conference. In the three months or more since the conference, we, in Canada, have been occupied translating our pledges into realities.

We did pledge one million metric tons of food grain annually for each of the next three years to help overcome the short-term food shortages. Plans are nearly completed for the allocation of this grain to bilateral recipients and multilateral organizations. In keeping with our pledge to channel at least 20 per cent of our food-aid through multilateral agencies, a significant portion of the one million tons will be made available to the World Food Program.

We also pledged to make available immediately $50 million of aid funds to assist some of the most seriously distressed countries. This total sum has been fully committed to the provision of fertilizers, and food-aid shipments are now being made. We are deeply aware that measures of this kind are but the first steps on a long road. This conference is a further step down that road to improving the economic well-being of the developing world. I think this conference must concentrate on the basic long-term priorities—the increase in food production, the improvement of nutrition, and the advance of rural development. This conference is concerned with efforts to improve the lives of the rural poor who represent some 40 per cent of the total population of developing countries—about 750 million persons. Canadian efforts will concentrate on increasing the productivity of rural people by enhancing the means of production at their disposal.

To help meet demands of this magnitude we have been engaged in Canada in developing a new broad strategy for Canadian development assistance, which is now in its final stages. It is intended to provide, among other things, new guidelines that should result in a greater capacity to respond to the changing priorities of developing countries.

In addition, other policies of government that affect Canada's relations with developing countries are also being re-examined with a view to ensuring a consistent approach to the development of a stable and equitable world economic environment.

Within the broad dimensions of this strategy, we have been reassessing our development-assistance programs in order to enlarge them and make them more effective in the renewable-resources sector. Through our bilateral and multilateral aid programs, we have been involved in a wide range of activities in this sector—for example, the provision of fertilizer, research in dryland farming, water-resources evaluation, the development of wheat farming and beef and dairy projects, and the development of storage and bulk-handling facilities. We can also extend our activities in fisheries and forestry.

In agriculture, Canada is strong in the production of cereals such as wheat, oats, rye, barley and maize, and in oil-seed crops such as rapeseed, sunflower seeds and soy-beans, as well as starch crops like potatoes. We have a strong technology in dryland agriculture.

Most of our cereal crops are grown in areas with under 20 inches of annual rainfall. In other agricultural technologies, we are good in the soil sciences, animal-breeding, animal nutrition, and crop storage and processing. We are using these strengths as a back-up for our international development work. There are many projects and programs drawing upon our expertise in these areas. Here are just a few examples:

In India, there are Canadian scientists working with their Indian colleagues adapting Canadian dryland technology to a variety of Indian soil and climatic conditions. They are also working on scaling down large-sized Canadian minimum-tillage implements to small mechanical or ox-power systems. In Tanzania, Canadian scientists and practical farmers are opening new lands to wheat farming. In Lesotho, we are helping to sort out areas suitable for a variety of oil crops and, if successful, we shall help with the technology for growing, harvesting and processing.

But we have our limits. We manufacture relatively few agricultural implements and practically no tractors. One of our biggest constraints is the fact that we do not have many professional agricultural personnel available for development work, even though we are placing more emphasis on training and recruiting for work abroad. Specialized manpower is a great lack, though perhaps we may yet find a way to tap the extensive knowledge that exists among our farmers. Finally, although we are the largest per capita donors of food aid in the world, there are clear limits to the amount of agricultural land in Canada located in a climate suitable for crop or animal production.

In fisheries, Canada has a highly developed capability in biological research, exploratory fishing, resource management and quality control. Fisheries-development planning and resource management are two particular areas in which Canada has been involved in projects in several Commonwealth countries in Asia, the Caribbean and Africa.

We know there are limitations not only to our food production capability but to the extent to which Canadian experience is immediately relevant to the problems of rural development in developing countries. From Canadian experience, we have learnt that rural development is damnably difficult. As I have indicated, we are re-examining our international assistance operations in an effort to make them meet more effectively the needs of our partners in development. What we hope to hear at this conference from our developing-country partners is some plain talk about their priorities. We want to match our response more closely to their needs.

57. North-South Confrontation

Statement by the Secretary of State for External Affairs, Mr. Allan J. MacEachen, at the Seventh Special Session of the United Nations General Assembly, New York, September 3, 1975.

The sixth special session of this General Assembly in April 1974 posed a grave challenge to the international community. The proposals for a new international economic order involve a far-reaching transformation of the world's economic relations. Let there be no doubt that a challenge of this magnitude demands from all of us a considered and forthcoming reply.

Thirty years ago, against a background of war, misery and economic collapse, a remarkable group of internationally minded and far-sighted statesmen also faced the challenge of creating a new economic—and political—order. We owe the United Nations to their creativity and daring. We also owe to them those economic institutions whose existence and operations have done so much to increase economic growth and human well-being, such as the International Monetary Fund, the World Bank and the General Agreement on Tariffs and Trade.

It is easy now to lose sight of the magnitude of these achievements. We have grown too familiar, perhaps, with the institutions these men created and, in recent years, we have become increasingly conscious of their shortcomings. But let us not forget that, with scant precedent to guide them, these remarkable statesmen created institutions and arrangements that provided a unique basis for international co-operation and economic growth. Now the challenge of the new international economic order is for us to apply a similarly innovative spirit to the changed circumstances of the present.

As I understand it, the new economic order is based upon two propositions:*

1. that developing countries do not derive sufficient benefits from the existing system of international trade, investment and finance;
2. that monetary instability, lagging economic growth, inflation and the impact of price increases of petroleum and other essential imports have demonstrated the shortcomings of the world economic system and the need for changes which will benefit developing countries.

Canada accepts the validity of these propositions and recognizes the need for changes in international economic relations to reduce disparities that we consider intolerable between rich and poor nations.

International development assistance

One—indeed the most established—of the ways of closing this gap between rich and poor, between developed and developing, is development assistance. This conception is one that we owe to the first generation of postwar leaders. Novel in 1945, it has since become firmly established as an instrument of international co-operation through the creation of the International Development Association (IDA), UNDP, the regional development banks, and the extensive network of bilateral development assistance programs.

But the proposals for a new economic order call for a fresh approach to development assistance. Its purpose, scope and character must be altered to fit the new circumstances of the Seventies.

Canada's response is contained in a new *Strategy for International Development Co-operation for 1975-80*, which was made public by the Canadian Government yesterday in Ottawa. Allow me to mention the main features of our new *Strategy*, which is designed to meet these new demands:

---

* To a great extent the North-South dialogue regarding the new economic order has been centered in the Conference on International Economic Cooperation (CIEC), of which Mr. MacEachen is Co-Chairman. The other Co-Chairman is from Venezuela. CIEC arose out of the oil crisis of 1973-1974. The first CIEC meeting was called by President Giscard d'Estaing of France and was held in Paris.

1. We pledge to continue and to increase our programs of development assistance. This year our disbursements will exceed $900 million, and they will grow significantly in the years ahead.
2. We are determined to achieve for official development assistance of the official UN target of 0.7 per cent of our GNP and to move toward it by annual increases in proportion to GNP.
3. We intend to place major emphasis on fostering economic growth and the evolution of social systems in such a way that they will produce the widest distribution of benefits among the population of developing countries.
4. We plan to concentrate the bulk of our bilateral assistance on the poorest countries and on the poorest sectors of their economies.
5. We plan to develop new forms of co-operation to meet the needs of middle-income developing countries in order to strengthen their potential for more self-reliant development.
6. We pledge to maintain a degree of concessionality in our bilateral programs of not less than 90 per cent. The grant component of Canada's development assistance is at present 95 per cent.
7. We intend to untie bilateral development loans so that developing countries will be eligible to compete for contracts.
8. We reiterate our pledge made at the World Food Conference to provide a minimum of one million tons of grain a year as food aid for each of the current and the next two fiscal years.
9. We plan greater emphasis on programs of agricultural and rural development in developing countries.

But aid alone is not the answer. It must be supplemented by measures in the areas of trade, investment and finance from which developing countries can derive greater benefit. Development assistance tends to be concentrated on the poorest countries. Broader measures of international economic co-operation will bring greater benefit to those countries that have advanced further towards self-reliant growth. In this respect we must be ready to consider new ideas and new approaches.

Basic Canadian response

The Government has reached certain broad conclusions on its approach to co-operation with developing countries:

1. We agree that there must be adjustments in the international economic system that will lead to a more rapid reduction in the disparities between developed and developing countries.

2. We consider that the transfer of resources that these adjustments would entail can best be achieved in the context of a growing world economy.
3. We believe the reform of existing institutions, where possible, is preferable to the establishment of new ones.
4. We believe positive co-operation rather than confrontation is required to solve difficulties, particularly in the area of commodities and other raw materials, including energy resources.

The discussions and negotiations now under way will establish the framework of world trade and finance in the 1980s. There is much at stake for both developed and developing countries. I wish now to turn to three areas of particular concern to developing countries—commodities, trade liberalization and industrial co-operation.

Commodities

The area that has been accorded the greatest attention of late is commodities. This attention is undoubtedly justified. As both an importer and an exporter, Canada regards the instability of the international commodities market as a major weakness of the international trading system.

How can we best deal with the "boom or bust" phenomenon in commodity trade?

1. We believe commodity arrangements involving both producers and consumers constitute the most practical approach to the problem. Canada was an early supporter of commodity arrangements, including formal agreements on a commodity-by-commodity basis. We are one of the few countries that have adhered to all the major commodity agreements.
2. We are prepared to examine positively the idea of negotiating arrangements for a wide range of products, including, but not limited to, those listed in UNCTAD's Integrated Approach.
3. We recognize that the use of buffer stocks and alternative stock mechanisms may be an appropriate stabilizing technique for a number of commodities.
4. The conception of a common fund for financing such stocks is certainly worth examination. We are prepared to consider this conception sympathetically, along with other potential donors, including both producers and consumers.

5. We recognize that commodity prices cannot be determined without reference to market forces. At the same time, we are well aware that no one's interest is served by commodity prices that are so low as to discourage production.
6. We believe new features in commodity agreements to take account of international inflation and exchange rate changes should be explored.
7. We wish to pursue these issues in the context of UNCTAD's Integrated Approach.*

Trade liberalization

On trade liberalization, we believe that improved access to markets can yield significant benefits to developing countries:

1. At present, 78 per cent of Canada's imports from developing countries enter duty free, and we have proposed in the trade negotiations the removal of all duties on tropical products by industrialized countries.
2. We are prepared to consider deeper tariff cuts and advance implementation on an MFN basis of other tariff cuts of particular interest to developing countries in the trade negotiations now taking place in Geneva.
3. We are also reviewing our generalized system of tariff preferences for developing countries in light of their suggestions for improvements.
4. We recognize the importance that developing countries attach to the further processing of their commodities prior to export. Indeed, we share with them a common interest in the removal of tariff escalation and non-tariff barriers that impede the establishment of efficient processing facilities in the resource-exporting countries. In our view, the "sector" approach is the most effective technique for achieving this goal in the multilateral trade negotiations.

Industrial co-operation

The further industrialization of developing countries is an essential element in any concerted attack on the disparities between rich and

---

* See CHCD, June 10, 1976, for results of UNCTAD IV, Nairobi.

poor. In shaping the world of the 1980s, we must aim to bring about faster and more balanced industrialized growth in the developing countries. We recognize that developed countries must contribute to this process.

Two of the elements essential to more rapid industrial growth—investment and technology—are primarily available from the private sector in industrialized countries; accordingly, we believe there is an urgent need to reconcile the legitimate interests of developing countries their need for capital, their right to sovereignty over their natural resources, their control over their own economic destinies—with the role of the private sector in providing capital and technology.

Industrial co-operation on a bilateral basis may be an effective means of reconciling these interests. It might incorporate a variety of instruments, including investment, technical assistance, management training and counselling, and at the same time provide a legal framework within which the private sector can operate to the benefit of both participating partners.

We believe that a model industrial co-operation agreement might be drawn up internationally as a guide to governments and the private sector.

We favour the provision of information and expertise to developing countries as the means whereby host countries can identify and articulate their national priorities concerning transnational corporations.

We are prepared to put our own experience in the establishment of screening mechanisms, statistical methods, and techniques of taxation at the disposal of developing countries. We support international efforts to enable developing countries to assess their own interests more clearly and to negotiate effectively the terms of the entry of transnational corporations in a manner consistent with their national goals.

The Commonwealth expert group's report

We have stressed the need for concrete measures to assist developing countries in sharing more equitably in the world's wealth and resources. In the past four months we have been involved in productive discussion with our partners in the Commonwealth on practical measures that contribute to closing the gap between developed and developing countries.

The report entitled *Towards a New International Economic Order*, prepared by a Commonwealth group of experts on the instructions of the Commonwealth heads of government, I understand is being made available to members of this Assembly. Last week at the Commonwealth finance ministers' meeting in Georgetown, Commonwealth countries (and I quote from the communiqué) "gave general endorsement to the report and agreed that the early implementation of these proposals would constitute a first step towards achieving the progressive removal of the wide disparities of wealth now existing between different sections of mankind". The report does not represent the full answer to our problems. Certain of its recommendations present a challenge to existing Canadian policy. However, we consider this report a most valuable document because of its practical nature and the high degree of consensus that exists on its provisions, a consensus that extends to countries from all six continents. We believe the report can provide an aid to the conduct of negotiations and to the national formulation of policy with the ultimate aim of closing the gap in living standards. I commend its practical approach and its emphasis on concrete measures to this Assembly.

Over the course of the past several months, as well as in the debate here, we have heard some important and imaginative proposals both from developed and developing countries. They all deserve careful study. The atmosphere, as I see it, is conducive to progress and change. We must seize this opportunity. During the next ten days, we must work through the *Ad Hoc* Committee and through informal consultations and negotiations, to achieve a result in this session which will launch us in the right direction for dealing with the challenges of the future.

Conclusion

I have outlined in broad terms the position of the Government of Canada on the principal issues confronting this session. I wish to stress again the need for real and not imagined progress, for plans and negotiations, and not paper and rhetoric. We are determined to play a positive role, to invest our resources and our influence, in renewed efforts to bring about constructive change in the international economic system and thereby reduce the glaring disparities between rich and poor nations. It is our hope that this session will be a constructive step in that direction.

58. Strategy for International Development (1975-80)

Statement to the Diplomatic Corps by Mr. Allan J. MacEachen, Secretary of State for External Affairs and Minister Responsible for International Development, Ottawa, September 2, 1975.

Allow me, first, to thank you for attending this unveiling of Canada's new strategy for international co-operation.* As you know, it is somewhat unusual in Ottawa for the Government to invite the heads of diplomatic missions or their representatives to the Pearson Building to receive officially a policy document and to be briefed on it. We are far from secretive about our activities, especially in the field of international affairs; but we generally rely on more informal contacts to convey to you and to your authorities some substance of Canada's foreign policy as it unfolds, under the pressure of changing needs and expectations in this country and abroad. Similarly, we are usually able to deal with the very large number of bilateral issues that arise between Canada and each of your countries without resorting to the formal instruments of diplomacy.

During my first year in this portfolio, I have had the pleasure to meet, privately or socially, most of you; but only on rare occasions have I felt the need to call in an ambassador and, reciprocally, have your governments deemed it necessary to convey directly their views to the Secretary of State for External Affairs. The channels of communication are open, information is readily exchanged at all levels, differences are smoothed out, by and large, before they become contentious. These are the facts of diplomatic life in Ottawa; and these facts are a tribute to the effectiveness of your missions and of the various bureaus in the Department of External Affairs.

Therefore, if we have invited you here this afternoon, it is not only so that you may take cognizance, and apprise your governments as swiftly and thoroughly as possible, of the new strategy that CIDA and other government agencies will strive to implement in the next five years; it is rather to emphasize the importance, indeed the very high

---

* See *Strategy for International Development Co-operation*, 1975-1980. Ottawa, QP, 1975. For an account of the Government's aid priorities in the early 1970s, see the proceedings of the House of Commons Standing Committee on External Affairs and Defence, February 4, 1971 (International Development Assistance Sub-Committee). In résumé, these were, as outlined by the President of CIDA:

1. Taking fuller account of the local and social impact of our assistance;
2. Placing further emphasis on multilateral assistance and co-operating in international moves to make the terms of aid more liberal;
3. Putting greater impetus behind assistance to Francophone Africa and Latin America;
4. Speeding up the progress of projects in general;
5. Awakening the interest and involvement of the Canadian people.

priority, that the Government of Canada attaches to its international development policy. It is for the same reason that we have chosen to make this policy document public on the opening day of the seventh special session of the United Nations General Assembly, convened precisely to deal with the nexus of development issues and problems that, in my view, will remain the major challenge faced by the international community during the last quarter of this century.

Diplomats have become somewhat immune to catchwords, slogans and slick phrases; I shall, accordingly, be restrained in qualifying the policy document you have before you.

I shall not call it a radically new departure, although it unquestionably inserts Canadian development assistance into a novel and wider perspective and contains a number of proposals whose potential implications for reducing the economic and social disparities between the peoples of the world could be quite radical, were they to be implemented with the active co-operation of other countries, both developed and developing. May I mention, for example, our intention to develop new forms of co-operation with developing countries not deriving substantial earnings from raw material exports and to engage in tripartite or multipartite development co-operation with countries at varying stages of development. But I could claim, with some justification I think, that a radical departure was not really needed, given Canada's historical record in the field of development assistance.

Similarly, I shall resist the temptation to call this document an agonizing reappraisal of Canada's international development policy, although I can assure you that the Cabinet, as well as CIDA and other departments involved, went through quite a bit of soul-searching—and some agony—as they progressed from one draft to another. It was not the easiest of policy reviews, being undertaken at a time when the world economy plunged into its worst recession in more than 30 years, suffered through the worst bout of inflation since the twenties and struggled to overcome the trauma of quite unprecedented increases in energy costs. From one draft to the next, we had to beware of a new set of myopic—and therefore excessively pessimistic—predictions about the world's economic future. From one month to the next, we were bombarded with new facts—yet another formulation of the rising expectations of developing countries, yet another twist in the response of industrialized countries. All this while, negotiators were attempting to establish a new international monetary framework and to launch the third postwar reform of the international trading system.

In the final analysis, we have felt that a cautious optimism was justified. We have banked on a resumption of growth, on more comprehensive and international co-operation, on increases in resource transfers from rich to poor countries, on gradual reforms of world economic institutions, deliberately introduced to bridge the gap and redress the balance between one group and the other. In the matter of details, we expect some of our assumptions to be superseded by events. Consequently, in unveiling this international development strategy, we are not laying down the tablets of the law, come what may in the next five years. CIDA experts and other Government officials will continue to monitor the world situation, be it with respect to food production, terms of trade, industrialization, or foreign-exchange earnings and indebtedness. The Cabinet will stand ready to alter, even as early as 1976, the thrust of Canada's international development policy, if new circumstances warrant it.

For this policy document was not conceived in a vacuum.* As you well know, it has been in the works for quite some time; its drafting has been enlightened by a wide-ranging debate on developing assistance; and a number of recent Canadian initiatives have been influenced by these strategic orientations even before these were made public. For example, coming after the pledges we made to the Rome Food Conference and Canada's growing involvement in renewed international efforts to dispel, once and for all, the threat of famine in the world, the emphasis we intend to place in the next five years on food production and rural development will not come as a surprise to you; but this should not detract from its significance.

I turn now to other features of the new strategy. In international development, as in other fields, the attraction of novelty is such that the elements of continuity, in a policy review such as this, tend to be taken for granted. Yet what is retained of past policies is often at least as important as what is changed or added to these. Consequently, I thought it appropriate to point out that the Canadian Government remains committed to the United Nations target for official development assistance of 0.7 per cent of the gross national product and to reach this goal through gradual increases in annual appropriations. Secondly, the terms of Canadian assistance will retain in the future the very high degree of "concessionality" that has become, to a very real extent, the trademark of Canada in this field. At a time when some donors, faced with economic difficulties that Canadians also

---

* See SS 75/15 of May 20, 1975, by Mr. MacEachen, for aspects of the conceptual background and the role of aid with respect to the new international economic order.

experience, are curbing their aid programs and shifting towards more commercially attractive forms of assistance, these renewed commitments, I should think, are worthy of some notice. I also draw your attention to the continuing Canadian support that is pledged in the document for regional co-operation among developing countries, as well as research institutions and programs focusing on major development issues and programs. Similarly, we have decided not only to maintain but to increase the substantial food-aid component in our development-assistance effort and to bear the commercial costs that this decision entails at a time when most foodstuffs are in short supply; and we have allowed for a gradual increase in Canadian assistance through multilateral institutions—in effect, the component in our program that is completely untied to Canadian procurements.

Before drawing attention to some of the specific innovations put forward in the document, I should like to emphasize the two pervasive themes that run through it and that, as they are put into practice in coming years, will really give a "new look" to Canada's international development policy; one is "multidimensionality", the other is "flexibility".

In deciding to rely in the future on multiple instruments to accelerate international development, the Government is attempting, in effect, to end the "splendid isolation" that has tended to characterize the development-assistance program, within the spectrum of international economic policies, and the consequent reduction of Canada's international development policy to its aid program. In other words, the Canadian perspective on world development is being widened. While continuing to attach a high priority to the volume, quality and effectiveness of development assistance, the Government intends to introduce, more systematically and more forcefully, developmental considerations in policy planning in other fields, such as trade and monetary reform, domestic and international investment and transfers of technology. Perhaps I should caution you against too great expectations on this score. Canadian interests have always loomed large and will continue to loom large in the shaping of this wider range of economic policies. A more coherent effort will be made, in the future, to reconcile Canadian interests with the interests of the developing world. In my view, the scope for such reconciliation is much greater than is often realized; but the extent to which we shall succeed will depend on the co-operation of developing countries, their flexibility, their willingness to negotiate transitional measures—in effect, to engage to some extent in joint development planning with industrialized countries such as Canada.

As the document states: "Movement towards the use of non-aid instruments establishes a direction of overall change that will take several years to implement fully. The first steps of what may be called a 'multidimensional approach' would be necessarily investigative and exploratory, given the need to assess carefully the impact of all initiatives on the Canadian economy and to plan where necessary compensatory measures. These first steps eventually will lead to specific policy recommendations."

In fact, the Government has already moved beyond the exploratory stage. Following the initial studies of the Interdepartmental Committee on Economic Relations with Developing Countries, established at the end of 1974, we have defined a number of positions that, if they were found acceptable by other countries, would give substance to our new multidimensional approach to international development. I shall have more to say on this score tomorrow in New York, during my intervention at the seventh special session of the United Nations General Assembly.

The other pervasive theme of the new strategy—flexibility—is a necessary corollary of the first one; it is also a necessary response to recent changes in the world's economic structure. One of the paradoxes of our times is that, while developing countries have managed to achieve in recent years a much more effective degree of political solidarity within international institutions, the dynamics of the world economy have revealed, sometimes glaringly, significant material differences and discrepancies among them. Some developing countries are fantastically rich in natural resources; others are almost completely bereft of them. Some have a considerable agricultural potential or are surrounded with seas teeming with marine life, while the territory of others is land-locked or covers mostly arid lands. Climate, topography, culture, political traditions, literacy, public health, technology, initial capital, "resource mix"—all these factors make the permutations of the developmental equation almost infinite. It follows that international development policies will have to be much more flexible in the future if they are to be more effective; and, hence, the intent of the new Canadian strategy is to ensure that each development program or project will be tailored to the specific needs of each recipient country.

Naturally, this flexibility will be exercised within a general framework—one whose "parameters" will be more explicit, perhaps, than in the past. Thus there has never been much room, in the Canadian assistance program, for the "frills" of development, as evidenced by the considerable investments we have made in social infrastructure such as roads, hydro-electric or irrigation projects. Yet we have deemed it useful to restate our basic priorities: food production and rural development, energy, basic education and training, public health, demography, shelter—in other words, the most crucial, and also the most intractable, problems of international development. Similarly, you are all aware that the world-wide economic difficulties of recent years have inflicted inordinate hardships upon precisely those countries least able to cope with them, so that our commitment to direct the bulk of our resources and expertise to the poorest countries should surprise no one and be supported by all. Again, to achieve greater flexibility as well as to add to the developmental impact of our assistance, we shall untie partially bilateral loans by allowing developing countries to compete for contracts and by selectively seeking procurement in other donor countries when this practice will bring demonstrable and significant benefits. Finally, we have become increasingly aware that the pattern of bilateral assistance in past decades—the often uncoordinated "sprinkling" of both financial and technical resources on a large number of recipient countries by most donors—has been somewhat ineffective. It should surprise no one, therefore, that Canada has decided to concentrate its assistance on a limited number of countries to achieve a greater geographic concentration of its programs—and thus greater efficiency.

But, lest some of you be concerned about impending cut-backs to existing bilateral programs, I hasten to add that these new guidelines will be implemented with the flexibility that pervades the new strategy, and that all present commitments will be honoured. Indeed, too sharp a break with current practices would defeat the essential purpose of this policy review. Interdependence, after all, is not limited to relations between developed and developing countries; and the poorest countries of the world would hardly be better off if too brutal a shift of Canadian assistance from their slightly more affluent neighbours were to weaken the latter's ability to contribute to overall development through regional trade and cooperation.

Consequently, I invite all of our partners in international development to read this policy document carefully and to discuss in coming weeks its long-range implications for their countries with the appropriate officials in CIDA and External Affairs. I should add that we should also welcome discussions with other donor countries on the new strategy's basic orientations and implementation, as well as on the more general problem of co-ordinating bilateral assistance programs.

VIII. The Environment

˜ Domestic and international concern about environmental problems intensified between 1965 and 1975. Massive oil spills in the oceans have served to galvanize public attention, as has the deteriorating quality of the atmosphere and the water in many countries of the world.

This concern has embraced such fields as: population growth and housing; the protection of the living resources of the land and of the sea; food and water supplies; the cleanliness of the atmosphere; the preservation from pollution of the Arctic and Antarctic regions, the oceans, outer space.

These questions have been dealt with mainly at large-scale international conferences conducted under the auspices of the United Nations. Canada has been at the forefront of such conferences since the very beginning. The main Canadian international activities in this sector during the decade under review are documented in this chapter. Owing to provincial experience and expertise in many of these fields, arising out of constitutional responsibilities as apportioned under the British North America Act, provincial participation in Canadian delegations attending international environmental conferences has become a matter of course. ˜

59. The Environment: Canada's Approach

Statement by the Secretary of State for External Affairs, Mr. Mitchell Sharp, to the Twenty-Sixth General Assembly of the United Nations, New York, September 29, 1971. (Extracts)

Canada has a special interest in environmental questions if only because we occupy such a large part of the earth's surface. Despite its vast extent and relatively small population, Canada has serious air—and water—pollution problems of its own. It also, inevitably, is a recipient of the pollution of others through the Great Lakes system and oil-spills on its coast-lines, to name only two examples. This is why Canada is concerned about the inadequacy of existing international law relating to the preservation of the environment in general and the marine environment in particular.

Canada is working toward the development of an adequate body of law in this field. At the national level, the Canadian Government has adopted laws for the protection of fisheries from the discharge or deposit of wastes, for the prevention of pollution disasters in Canada's territorial waters and fishing zones, and for the preservation of the delicate ecological balance of the Arctic. At the twenty-fifth General Assembly, and last month in a resolution jointly submitted with Norway to the preparatory committee for the Third Law of the Sea Conference, Canada invited other states to take similar measures at the national level to prevent and control marine pollution as a move toward the development of effective international arrangements.

Canada is working towards a multilateral treaty regime on safety of navigation and the prevention of pollution in Arctic waters with other countries having special responsibilities in the Arctic region.

In a wider multilateral context, Canada is participating actively in the preparations for the Stockholm Conference on the Human Environment, the IMCO Conference on Marine Pollution and the Third Law of the Sea Conference. These three conferences, taken together, present a unique opportunity for the development of a comprehensive system of international environmental law. As the first and widest-ranging of the three, the Stockholm conference will be of particular importance in helping states to come to grips with the apparent conflict between environmental preservation on the one hand and economic development on the other.

Canada is properly classed as a developed nation, but is still in the course of development, still importing capital and know-how, still engaged in building its industrial base. This makes Canadians aware of the conflict between the need to develop—essential to economic growth—and the need to preserve, and where necessary recapture, a viable natural environment—essential to the survival of life.

For this reason Canada has a special understanding of the dilemma seen by the developing nations, where the highest priority must be given to economic and social development as the means to achieve a standard of living that will offer dignity and opportunity to all their citizens and where the preservation of the physical environment, however desirable in itself, would seem to come second. But I would suggest that this dilemma is wrongly posed.

Technology has now reached a stage where the industrialization needed for economic development need not disturb the environment to an unacceptable extent, and it is by no means the rule that an ecologically sound industrial or other project must be more costly than one that is not. With far-sighted planning and careful attention to design and ecological considerations, there need be little or no added cost. The pollution befouling the Great Lakes system largely results from wasted opportunities, from dumping into the water by-products that in themselves have value if properly recovered. The Canadian Government is working with the governments of the United States of America and of the American states and Canadian provinces bordering on the Great Lakes system to establish water-quality standards, achieve them in the shortest possible time and see to it that they are maintained.

The discussions now going on between the various levels of government of Canada and the United States will set in motion a program for the rehabilitation and preservation of the Great Lakes which will cost billions of dollars and call upon vast human and technological resources. These astronomical expenses would not have been incurred had we and our neighbours been able to foresee and forestall the damage we have done to the largest fresh-water system on earth.

I urge my friends in the developing nations to balance the costs of anti-pollution measures against the cost of pollution and the mindless waste of limited resources it so often represents. Everyone in this room is looking and working for the day when the prosperity now enjoyed by the few can be shared by all. Economic and social development is the route to prosperity. We should all take advantage of the fact that advances in technology mean that we can follow this route without poisoning the air we breathe, the water we drink and the soil that gives us sustenance, without disturbing the ecological balance that supports all life.

60. Law of the Air

Statement by Mr. Paul Martin, Secretary of State for External Affairs, to the Second International Conference on Air and Space Law, McGill University, Montreal, November 3, 1967.

Your meetings today must have prompted you to reflect on the work of those nations which met in Chicago in the winter of 1944.* That

---

* The meetings led to the creation of ICAO, whose headquarters are located in Montreal.

was a time when those with foresight were preparing for peace and were recognizing the urgency of radical changes to meet the immediate needs of a vastly different world. Perhaps in no single industry had the effects of war been felt more strongly than in aviation. The war proved beyond doubt the tremendous potential of the airplane, both as an awesome and devastating carrier of destruction and a swift and reliable means of transport. It is said that the Second World War telescoped a quarter century of normal peacetime technological development in aviation into six years. If anything, the pace of this development is accelerating. Due to the ingenuity of the scientist, engineer and businessman, the airplane is now a major instrument of commerce and—what is significant for the lawyer—a creator of major international problems.

Aviation today is mainly an international activity requiring, for safety's sake alone, the most complex co-ordination of techniques and laws. Air law is the result of a compromise between national drives and international imperatives. It is a conglomeration of specific branches of national and international law, both private and public.

Aircraft of one nation travelling through the air space of several states, landing in others and carrying large numbers of passengers, create many problems of conflicting legal systems. Without determined and imaginative efforts on the part of those concerned with air law, it will be increasingly difficult for the law to keep pace with social and technological development.

But I am not saying anything startling, or even new. The facts are obvious. Nevertheless, the extent of the danger due to the unprecedented growth of the industry has been seriously underestimated.

The Chicago Convention of 1944 was a major step towards international legal standardization. It is often called "the Constitution of Air Law" or "The Charter of the Air". At Chicago, the strong Canadian delegation, headed by C. D. Howe, then Minister of Reconstruction, played an active role in support of an international air authority. We were strong proponents of the "freedoms of the air"—a term which the Honourable Adolf A. Berle, then head of the American delegation, attributed to Canada. In fact, "Freedom of the Air", the title of your present meeting, is what the late Mayor LaGuardia referred to at Chicago as the "meat" of the Convention, for it lay at the very centre of the problem of the number of services that ought to be permitted on a particular route and the share each country should have in these services.

The Chicago Convention was but the first chapter, albeit a successful one, in the work of international co-operation which Franklin

Roosevelt described then as part of "a great attempt to build enduring institutions of peace". The Canadian Government continues to subscribe fully to this ideal, for as C. D. Howe said, "if we cannot devise a working system of co-operation and collaboration between the nations of the world in the field of air transport, there will be a smaller chance of our enjoying peace for the remainder of our lives".

What are the problems of the future of aviation to which we should all address ourselves? The trend today is towards greater aircraft productivity and more and longer passenger trips. This means larger, faster, costlier and more complex aircraft flying more often over greater distances. Foreseeable technological developments include "jumbo" jets, supersonic transports, hovercraft, vertical and short take-off aircraft and, eventually, hypersonic vehicles propelled partially by rocket motors with speed and performance characteristics akin to those of spacecraft. Large investments will be required by all governments and airlines, not only for these more sophisticated vehicles but also for related facilities to accommodate the expected increase in traffic. In Canada, we are acutely aware of these problems and are having to revalue estimates we made only a few years ago. The new Canadian Transport Commission is part of our general effort to improve methods of study and co-ordination in the whole field of transportation, including aviation.

The Chicago Convention was a dual-purpose treaty. It contained an international civil aviation code and it established the International Civil Aviation Organization (ICAO). There are now over 115 member states in ICAO. It is a continuing source of pride to Canadians that ICAO should have its headquarters in this city. Every day ICAO assists in matters of co-ordination, technical assistance and education, to help its members with difficulties which are often beyond their individual ability to overcome. Considerably more could be done, however, to utilize ICAO for the general benefit. Greater use of ICAO machinery for the settlement of disputes should be actively encouraged. The economic necessity of using the large and costly aircraft to their fullest capacity, and therefore of international airlines obtaining traffic rights in as many places as possible, underlines the desirability of having impartial means of arbitrating disputes and a larger degree of standardization and unification in the rules, regulations and laws governing the international use of air space. The international legal implications of aircraft now in the drafting and experimental stages of development also require our urgent attention. Take the hovercraft, for example. Is it a surface vessel or an airplane? The legal arguments need resolution since this vehicle has a potential for international commerce.

In 1964, Canada faced domestically something similar to what is now a common international problem: the competing claims and interests of large airlines. The Government decided that the international air services provided by Canadian airlines should be integrated into a single plan which would avoid unnecessary competition or conflict. This means that outside Canada neither of our two major airlines (Air Canada and Canadian Pacific Airlines) serves any point served by the other. The Government also made it clear that any development of competition in domestic main line services must not put the Government airline, Air Canada, "into the red". In addition, Canadian regional air carriers were given an enlarged role in relation to domestic main line carriers. The application of these three principles has strengthened Canada's position in world aviation. For instance, since 1964 there have been successful negotiations with several countries, designed to achieve international route extensions and improvements for both Air Canada and Canadian Pacific Airlines.

Projecting this domestic example onto the international scene, would be to suggest that perhaps the logical course for public and private international air law is in the direction of one set of rules to govern all flight at whatever altitude.

If international air law is to abandon the techniques of bilateral negotiation, with its jungle of complicated agreements based on the narrow application of national sovereign rights, then it could probably take a lesson from developments in the law of outer space. A new frontier for the law of the air figuratively and literally lies at the fringe of outer space. In 1963, the UN Declaration of Legal Principles Governing Activities by States in the Exploration and Use of Outer Space marked the end of the speculative phase in which the "general pundits" conjectured on whether certain maritime and air-law principles of national sovereignty and freedom of the seas were applicable in outer space. Events since then, such as the recent Outer Space Treaty, suggest that a new legal order is emerging—that of the world community acting for the common good and welfare of all mankind.

The main provisions of the Outer Space Treaty are that outer space, the moon and other celestial bodies shall be explored and used for peaceful purposes only. Like the Limited Test Ban Agreement of 1963, it is part of a series of international agreements leading towards general and complete disarmament. Hopefully, more agreements are on the way—a non-proliferation treaty and, interestingly, an item now before the General Assembly calling for a treaty on the peaceful use of the sea-bed and the ocean floor and their resources in the interests of mankind. First outer space, now the sea-bed and ocean floor. What environment will be next? Air space? What a blessing it would be if by universal agreement the use of the air were reserved exclusively for peaceful purposes, in the common interest of all men.

The main thrust of outer space law is today towards two conventions—one on assistance and return of astronauts and space vehicles, the other on liability for damage caused by the launching of objects into outer space. The implications of these conventions for air law are obvious. Considerable attention is also being given to defining outer space in legal terms. Again, this cannot but affect the law of the air for, apart from drawing a boundary between air and space, there is the related problem of defining spacecraft and hybrid-air-and-space-craft in legal terms and of co-ordinating international regulations for their use in air space. We must avoid the confusion of having different and possibly conflicting regulations for space vehicles and aircraft flying in the same environment. In this regard, it seems a pity that there is not more contact between air lawyers and space lawyers.*

Let us look for a moment at a few problems which will require international legal action. A major problem facing us all in this machine age is noise. We are continually bombarded with noise, and despite our increasingly elastic thresholds of tolerance, jet aircraft have multiplied this attendant disturbance to the point of nuisance. Unless there are some major technological improvements, the larger and faster jets with their greater power take-offs and shallower landing paths will compound this problem. There are several possible solutions: airport curfews, to enable some quiet periods; relocation of airports and runways and restrictions on building near them; and better insulation of dwellings and offices—but each of these national solutions will require some kind of international agreement to be made completely effective. I hope that the fifth Air Navigation Conference of ICAO, starting in Montreal soon, will succeed in agreeing on an international standard unit for noise measurement as the first step towards an international agreement on aircraft noise. Perhaps international air lawyers could then produce regulations and provisions for their world-wide enforcement. The time may come when all new

---

* See also "Canadian Participation in Space Programmes", by Mr. C. M. Drury, President of the Treasury Board, Canadian Aeronautics and Space Congress, Montreal, November 17, 1970.

aircraft will be required to demonstrate that they do not exceed a set of internationally accepted noise levels.

One of the agreements signed at Chicago was the International Air Services Transit Agreement—commonly known as "the two freedoms agreement"—in which freedom of mutual overflight was guaranteed. Such flights, if at supersonic speeds, promise to disturb and annoy those on the ground under the SST's flight path. Consequently, if overflight is to be permitted, international agreements will have to be reached on the level of the noise from the sonic boom to be tolerated.

Domestically, old common law conceptions of property ownership from the soil upwards *usque ad coelum*, have been limited legislatively and judicially to meet the requirements of country-wide air travel. To have recognized private claims to air space would have interfered with development of aviation in the public interest. The extent to which airlines will be able to take advantage of technological progress in aviation, will depend upon the willingness of countries to exchange "freedom of the air" on a multilateral basis.

Another specific problem is that of liability. In 1965, the United States denounced certain provisions of the Warsaw Convention of 1929 limiting the liability of air carriers for personal injury or death of passengers in international air carriage. This denunciation was withdrawn last year when most of the world's major airlines entered into an agreement in which they accepted considerably increased limits of passenger liability. It would not seem advisable, however, that a matter of this nature, which is really one of governmental responsibility, should continue to function for too long as an agreement between carriers. It is time some fresh attempts were made to draft new protocols, perhaps introducing some flexibility in the amount of the limits of liability. I might mention that the draft convention on liability now under active consideration in the UN Legal Sub-Committee on Outer Space will probably adopt criteria of absolute liability for damage caused on earth or in the air space. Urgent thought should, therefore, be given by air lawyers as to how this may affect private international air law.

Still another problem which may require action internationally is that of integration. There is a growing tendency towards private arrangements for international co-operation. There are pooling arrangements, airline unions and various regional efforts at multilateralism, such as the Scandinavian Airlines System and Air Afrique and the proposed Air Union in Europe. The enormous cost of the next generation of aircraft will accelerate the merging process and, in turn, cause further difficulties in the negotiation of traffic rights, particularly if each of these new organizations considers its individual members to be one entity. Many bilateral agreements will become obsolete and require complicated renegotiation. On the brighter side, however, these same joint operational arrangements may well be regarded as useful precedents for future, far-reaching multilateral conventions.

The airplanes of the past will serve the common interests of the future no better than will the law of the past. Therefore, we must effect a breakthrough in legal attitudes every bit as impressive and functional as the everyday wonders in which we fly. More effort should be made by governmental policy makers, by the academic community and the legal fraternity, to insure that international civil aviation realizes its full potential for the economic and cultural development of our world.

There is a requirement for multilateral agreements regulating the scheduled commercial operation of international civil aviation. A serious attempt was made at Chicago in the International Air Transport Agreement and in the forthright proposal by Australia and New Zealand, supported I understand by France, to plan for the internationalization of civil aviation. We should not, nor if the predictions are accurate can we, continue to say that the time is not yet ripe for such a development. Nevertheless, whatever international arrangements are made, they must, ideally, be both fair and functional and allow for profitable commercial operations and future expansion. Moreover, they should bring to the industry a far larger amount of certainty than that which exists today, thereby enabling airlines and governments to effect more orderly planning and programming to avoid such troublesome matters as excess capacity.

61. Law of the Sea: I. Sovereignty in the Arctic

On April 8, 1970, the Prime Minister, Mr. Pierre-Elliott Trudeau, announced in the House of Commons the Government's intention of introducing two bills concerning Canada's marine environment and the living resources of its territorial seas.

Mr. Trudeau tabled at this time a copy of a letter that had been delivered to the Secretary General by the Canadian Ambassador to the United Nations, in which a reservation was submitted to Canada's acceptance of the compulsory jurisdiction of the International Court of Justice. The Prime Minister stated that this reservation was meant to

obviate any litigation of certain features of the two new bills.
The text of the letter follows.

Your Excellency,

On behalf of the Government of Canada,

1. I give notice that I hereby terminate the acceptance by Canada of the compulsory jurisdiction of the International Court of Justice hitherto effective by virtue of the declaration made on September 20, 1929, and ratified on July 28, 1930, under Article 36 of the Statute of the Permanent Court of International Justice, and made applicable to the International Court of Justice by paragraph 5 of Article 36 of the Statute of that Court.

2. I declare that the Government of Canada accepts as compulsory *ipso facto* and without special convention, on condition of reciprocity, the jurisdiction of the International Court of Justice, in conformity with paragraph 2 of Article 36 of the Statute of the Court, until such time as notice may be given to terminate the acceptance, over all disputes arising after the present declaration with regard to situations or facts subsequent to this declaration, other than:

   (a) disputes in regard to which parties have agreed or shall agree to have recourse to some other method of peaceful settlement;

   (b) disputes with the Government of any other country which is a member of the Commonwealth of Nations, all of which disputes shall be settled in such manner as the parties have agreed or shall agree;

   (c) disputes with regard to questions which by international law fall exclusively within the jurisdiction of Canada;

   (d) disputes arising out of or concerning jurisdiction or rights claimed or exercised by Canada in respect of the conservation, management or exploitation of the living resources of the sea, or in respect of the prevention or control of pollution or contamination of the marine environment in marine areas adjacent to the coast of Canada.

3. The Government of Canada also reserves the right at any time, by means of a notification addressed to the Secretary-General of the United Nations, and with effect as from the moment of such notification, either to add to, amend or withdraw any of the foregoing reservations, or any that may hereafter be added.

It is requested that this notification may be communicated to the governments of all the States that have accepted the Optional Clause and to the Registrar of the International Court of Justice.

Accept, Excellency, the assurances of my highest consideration.

Yvon Beaulne,
Ambassador.

His Excellency U Thant
Secretary-General of the United Nations
New York, New York

In his statement to the House, the Prime Minister said:

Canada strongly supports the rule of law in international affairs. Canada has made known to other states that it is prepared to participate actively in multilateral efforts to develop agreed rules on the protection of the environment and the conservation of the living resources of the sea.

Canada is not prepared, however, to engage in litigation with other states concerning vital issues where the law is either inadequate or non-existent and thus does not provide a firm basis for judicial decision. We have, therefore, submitted this new reservation to Canada's acceptance of the compulsory jurisdiction of the International Court relating to those areas of the law of the sea which are undeveloped or inadequate.

It is well known that there is little or no environmental law on the international plane and that the law now in existence favours the interests of the shipping states and the shipping owners engaged in the large-scale carriage of oil and other potential pollutants. There is an urgent need for the development of international law establishing that coastal states are entitled, on the basis of fundamental principle of self-defence, to protect their marine environment and the living resources of the sea adjacent to their coasts.

In spite of this new reservation, Canada's acceptance of the compulsory jurisdiction of the Court remains much broader than that of most other members of the United Nations, and it is the hope of the Government that it will prove possible to reach agreement with other states on the vital need to develop the law to protect the marine environment and its living resources so as to make it possible for Canada again to broaden its acceptance of the court's jurisdiction.

The following background notes on the two bills were provided:

The first of these bills reflects the policies of the Government as stated by the Prime Minister in the Throne Speech debate on October 24, 1969, on the need for legislative action to protect the delicate ecological balance of the Canadian Arctic by laying down stringent anti-pollution measures. The second bill would extend Canada's territorial sea to 12 miles and provide for the establishment by the Government of new fisheries zones.

The Prime Minister stated, on October 24 last year, that Government policy "will reflect Canada's proposed interests not only in the preservation of the ecological balance . . . but as well in the economic development of the North, the security of Canada and our stature in the world community". The two bills are directed towards the maintenance of these interests and together form a part of a comprehensive approach to the Canadian North, the protection of the Canadian environment and the conservation of the fisheries and other living resources of the sea.

These bills are evidence of Canada's determination to discharge its responsibilities for Canada's offshore marine environment. The Canadian Government has for some time been concerned about the inadequacies of both international law and domestic law to give adequate protection to the environment and to ensure the conservation of fisheries resources. The two bills are part of a series of related measures to cope with these problems.

The effect of this new legislation would be to make clear that the Northwest Passage is to be opened for the passage of shipping of all nations subject to necessary conditions required to protect the delicate ecological balance of the Canadian Arctic.* Canada seeks to preclude the passage of ships threatening pollution of the environment. Commercially owned shipping intending to enter waters of the Canadian Arctic designated by the Canadian Government as shipping safety control zones would be required to meet Canadian hull, construction and navigation safety standards. These zones may extend up to 100 miles offshore. The owners of shipping and cargoes would be required to provide proof of financial responsibility and will be liable for damage caused by pollution. This liability would be limited but would

---

* For background, see *1st Report*, December 16, 1969, House of Commons Standing Committee on Indian Affairs and Northern Development. See also CHCD, April 16, 1970, for a comprehensive outline—with historical background—of the Arctic Waters Pollution Prevention Act by Mr. Sharp.

not depend upon proof of fault or negligence. In the case of shipping owned by another state the necessary safety standards would be given effect by arrangement with the state concerned. Similarly, protective measures would apply to exploration and exploitation of the submarine resources of Canada's northern continental shelf.

The main provisions of the Arctic Waters Pollution Prevention Bill are set out in the attached summary. The second bill, amending the Territorial Sea and Fishing Zone Act of 1964, would have the effect of replacing the three-mile territorial sea and nine-mile exclusive fishing-zone by a 12-mile territorial sea. (Over 50 maritime states now claim a territorial sea of 12 miles or more.)

The bill would also enable the Government to draw fisheries closing lines across the entrances to bodies of waters in special need of fisheries conservation protection. Canada pioneered in the development of the concept of exclusive fishing-zones distinct from the territorial sea and this proposed legislation takes a step further Canada's attempt to contribute to the development of international law both by state practice and by multilateral negotiations.

State practice, or unilateral action by a state, has always been accepted as one of the ways of developing international law. There have been many such instances; for example, the 1948 Truman Proclamation on the Continental Shelf, which became established in international law a few years later.

The proposed anti-pollution legislation is based on the overriding "right of self-defence" of coastal states to protect themselves against grave threats to their environment. It is widely accepted that existing international law does not adequately recognize the need of coastal states to protect themselves against such dangers, which are real and present, as recent experience has shown. Traditional principles of international law concerning pollution of the sea are based largely on ensuring freedom of navigation to shipping states engaged in the large-scale carriage of oil and other potential pollutants. These principles are of little or no relevance to an area having the unique characteristics of the Arctic, where there is an intimate relationship between the sea, the ice and the land, and where the permanent defilement of the environment and the destruction of whole species could take place. There is an urgent need to develop both domestic and international law directly related to the special economic, social and environmental needs of the Canadian North.

These bills are the first of a series of related provisions with regard to the Canadian marine environment and offshore fisheries resources off Canada's East and West Coasts. Legislation now being prepared will protect that environment against the kind of pollution caused by the wreck of the oil tanker *Arrow* in Chedabucto Bay.

The Government is pledged to the development of the use of Canada's Arctic waters to encourage expansion of Canada's northern economy. The Government intends to open up the Northwest Passage as a waterway for innocent passage by ships of all states, by laying down conditions for the exercise of such passage; by establishing that the passage of ships threatening pollution will not be considered innocent; by ensuring against the Northwest Passage becoming, through the process of customary usage, an uncontrolled international strait; and by adopting a functional and constructive approach which does not interfere with the activities of others and reflects the Government's responsibility to its own people and the international community to preserve the ecological balance of Canada and its marine environment.

62. Law of the Sea: II. The Territorial Sea and Fishing Zones Act

On April 17, 1970, Secretary of State for External Affairs Mr. Mitchell Sharp took up, in the following statement in the House of Commons, the subject of the second of the two bills announced on April 8 by Mr. Trudeau.

Mr. Speaker, the proposed amendments to the Territorial Sea and Fishing Zones Act contain two major provisions: the first would establish the territorial sea of Canada at 12 miles in substitution for the present limit of three miles, and as a result would eliminate the present nine-mile fishing zone which would become incorporated within the 12-mile territorial sea; the second would authorize the Government, by Order in Council, to create exclusive Canadian fishing-zones comprising areas of the sea adjacent to the coasts of Canada.

There are a number of reasons why the Government is proposing to extend its territorial sovereignty from three to 12 miles. Basically, the reason is that the limited fisheries jurisdiction which Canada at present exercises over the outer nine-mile zone is no longer sufficient to protect the full range of Canada's vital coastal interests. The 12-mile territorial sea would have the following advantages: (a) It would provide the comprehensive jurisdictional basis which Canada requires to enforce anti-pollution controls outside Arctic waters off Canada's East and West coasts up to 12 miles from the baselines of Canada's territorial sea, rather than merely three miles as at present. (b) It will permit Canada to expedite the conclusion of negotiations with the European countries which have been permitted to continue their fishing activities in Canada's nine-miles fishing-zone. (c) It will further protect Canada's security interests by permitting Canada to exercise greater control over the movement of foreign ships.

The legal regime of the territorial seas permits the coastal state to determine whether a particular passage is innocent. This bill extends that right for Canada up to a distance of 12 miles from the territorial sea baseline. All the reasons why a state requires a three-mile territorial sea apply with equal vigour to the 12-mile territorial sea. From the point of view of security, the danger is removed farther offshore and the coastal state can take all measures open to it on its own territory within a wider belt of 12 rather than three miles. Then (d), since the inner limit of the continental shelf is measured from the outer limit of the territorial sea, the 12-mile territorial sea will have the effect of pushing the inner limit of Canada's continental shelf seawards a distance of nine miles.

Mr. Speaker. The U.S. Government has made clear its willingness to accept a 12-mile territorial sea provided this is achieved by multilateral agreement and not by the continuing development of customary law through state practice. The Canadian Government sympathized with the U.S. desire for agreed rules of law on these questions. Canada has repeatedly shown its good faith in the multilateral approach to these questions by participating vigorously and constructively in every effort in the last 40 years to achieve agreed rules of law on the breadth of the territorial sea and the nature and extent of contiguous zones.

I shall now turn to the question in which all parties have expressed great interest—namely, the implications of the establishment of a 12-mile territorial sea for Canada's Arctic sovereignty. I should like to emphasize that there is no difference of views concerning Canada's sovereignty over the islands of the Arctic archipelago or Canada's sovereignty rights to explore and exploit the mineral resources of Canada's northern continental shelf. There is no need even to comment concerning Canada's long-established and universally accepted sovereignty over the land.

What, then, is the effect of the 12-mile limit with respect to the Northwest Passage? It is known that the United States regards the waters of the Northwest Passage beyond three miles from shore as high seas. I think I have already demonstrated the weakness of the legal basis for such an assertion. The 12-mile territorial sea is far too widely recognized for it to be ignored by any state. Indeed, a state that refuses to recognize the 12-mile territorial sea of another state is itself unilaterally opting out of a developing rule of law.

Since the 12-mile territorial sea is well established in international law, the effect of this bill on the Northwest Passage is that under any sensible view of the law, Barrow Strait, as well as the Prince of Wales Strait, are subject to complete Canadian sovereignty. Whether or not those who disagree with us wish to allege that other waters are not Canadian, they cannot realistically argue any longer concerning these two bodies of water.

The question was asked whether Canada will admit a right of innocent passage through such waters, since the right of innocent passage pertains in the territorial sea but not in internal waters. There is considerable misunderstanding on some of the technical legal questions involved here. Firstly, it is incorrect to argue that there can be no right of innocent passage in internal waters. The 1958 Geneva Convention on the Territorial Sea and Contiguous Zones makes specific provision for the right of innocent passage through internal waters where such waters have been established as such by means of the straight-baseline system. I do not cite that rule as now applicable to these waters but merely so as to point out that the difference between the regime of internal waters, over which a state has complete sovereignty, and the regime of the territorial sea, over which a state's sovereignty is subject to the right of innocent passage, is not as clear-cut as is alleged.

There is a school of thought, for example, that the status of the waters of the Arctic archipelago fall somewhere between the regime of internal waters and the regime of the territorial sea. Certainly, Canada cannot accept any right of innocent passage if that right is defined as precluding the right of the coastal state to control pollution in such waters. The law may be undeveloped on this question, but if that is the case we propose to develop it. Mr. Speaker, I hope I have said enough about the implications of this bill for the Arctic to allay any fears, real or imagined, about its effect upon our sovereignty.

The fisheries provisions of this bill will provide the Government with greater flexibility for completing the delimitation of Canada's exclusive fishing-zones in those coastal areas where straight baselines have not so far been drawn from headland to headland. These provisions are enabling only; the creation of the proposed new Canadian fishing-zones will require executive action by way of Order in Council.

Under the existing legislation, Canada could not exercise exclusive fishing rights within such bodies of water as the Gulf of St. Lawrence, Bay of Fundy, Dixon Entrance, Hecate Strait and Queen Charlotte Sound. With the proposed amendment, Canada could now, where appropriate, draw what might be called "fisheries-closing lines" across the entrances to these bodies of water and thereby establish them as exclusive Canadian fishing-zones. In this way, Canada would have the required domestic legal basis for managing the fisheries resources of these areas.*

The new fishing-zones will be established only where Canada's primary interests relate to fisheries, and in areas where Canada has historic claims. In such areas, the bill would, in keeping with the Government's approach to the question, enable us to separate fisheries jurisdiction from the complete sovereignty which states exercise in their territorial sea and internal waters. This separation of fisheries jurisdiction from sovereignty already underlies the concept of the contiguous fishing-zone which has become an established principle of customary international law, owing in good measure to the pioneering activities of Canada.

Before concluding, Mr. Speaker, perhaps I might refer to the note which was delivered to our Ambassador in Washington on April 14 and the reply which he delivered yesterday on behalf of the Canadian Government. When the question was raised two days ago, I made clear that we had already requested U.S. consent to dispense with the usual diplomatic practice of declining to publish exchanges of notes, but that I should, nonetheless, raise the question again. Our Ambassador has since stressed to the State Department the importance of publishing the exchange so as to lay at rest, once and for all, the misinformation appearing in some American newspapers to the effect that the United States note contained threats. I have already assured the House that the note contained no such threats and that the summary of the note published by the State Department accurately summarized its substance.

We have today received the response of Secretary of State Rogers to my proposal that the text of the diplomatic note of April 14 be published. His response is as follows:

---

* The fisheries closing-lines were brought into effect in early 1971. See notice in the *Canada Gazette* of December 26, 1970, and also SS 70/26 of December 18, 1970.

The Secretary of State regrets that he cannot agree to the proposal of the Canadian Government that we depart from the usual diplomatic practice of not publishing exchanges of notes between governments in the case of our note of April 14, 1970, relating to the introduction by the Canadian Government of legislation on pollution in the Arctic, fisheries and the limits of the territorial sea. Because of the public interest in the matters discussed in the note, the United States did include the substance of its note in its press statement of April 15, 1970.

Therefore, Mr. Speaker, I am now tabling—with the suggestion that it be appended to Hansard—a summary of the Canadian note. This is not the note itself but a summary of its contents.*

63. Law of the Sea: III. The 200-Mile Exclusive Economic Zone

*Statement by the Secretary of State for External Affairs, Mr. Allan J. MacEachen, to the Halifax Board of Trade, Halifax, February 25, 1975. (Extracts)***

There was, as you all know, a first substantive session of the Law of the Sea Conference last summer in Caracas. For ten weeks, 138 sovereign nations—each with one vote, let me stress—attempted to draft an all-encompassing convention to regulate all of man's activities in, below, and above the sea—that is, 70 per cent of the earth's surface. What is important, therefore, is to assess the general direction of the conference and relate it to Canada's essential objectives.***

---

* See *External Affairs*, DEA, Ottawa, May 1970, pp. 154-60, for the texts of the U.S.A. Press Release and the summary of Canada's reply.

** SS 74/7 of May 3, 1974, provides much useful historical background regarding the evolution of the concept of the 200-mile exclusive economic zone.

*** The World Population Conference examined in August 1974, for the first time, the implications of the tremendous growth of the world's population during this century, and especially since the Second World War. A related conference, on world food problems, took place in Rome in November 1974. The United Nations special session on resources (1974) looked at the problem of food and other raw materials from another viewpoint: the impact on development of the disruption of the international trade and monetary system due to the recent sharp increases in the prices of a number of commodities, especially oil. All these conferences were concerned with one fundamental problem: the growing pressure of demand on the finite resources of the world, with which the 200-mile exclusive economic zone is also closely related.

There is a clear trend towards the acceptance of a three-tier concept —that is, an economic zone out to 200 miles, an international area beyond the economic zone reserved for the benefit of all mankind, and the application throughout the oceanic space of sound management principles for the use and preservation of the sea.

First, the economic zone—that is certainly the area where progress was most evident at Caracas. I believe I can safely say that, whether or not the conference is altogether successful, the economic-zone concept is here to stay. That is to say that, within 200 miles of its coasts, a coastal state will have very substantial rights over the mineral and living resources of that zone and more extensive rights than it now possesses over marine pollution and scientific research.

For Nova Scotians and Canadians in general, that is a most encouraging development. It means that in the very near future Canada will be able to exercise full control over the most important economic activities now taking place or that may take place in the future in our offshore waters. To be realistic, I must point out that this does not amount to an automatic remedy to all the economic ills of our coastal areas. Such a panacea does not exist. But it does mean that we shall have the legal means and the necessary tools to put into effect sound management and conservation practices for the benefit of our own citizens, a power we have not had.

Let us consider for a moment what a 200-mile zone would do for Canada as far as fishing is concerned.

First, we shall acquire the exclusive right to manage all living resources within 200 miles from our shores. We shall have the final say in determining maximum or optimum sustainable yields for each species. We shall have the final say in establishing quotas, closed seasons, the size and nature of gear and the numbers, sizes and types of fishing vessels that may be used. We shall have the final say in licensing foreign fishermen, fishing vessels and equipment. In short, we shall have the exclusive power to prescribe any terms, conditions or regulations we consider necessary to govern the harvesting of all living resources and their proper management and conservation.

Secondly—and this is perhaps the most important feature of the conception for the future development of our fishing industry—we shall have the right to reserve to our own fishermen that portion of the total resource they have the capacity to catch in any given year. In practice, this means that, as our capacity increases, so does our percentage of the total catch. In principle, this percentage could reach 100 per cent.

We shall, therefore, manage the whole and be guaranteed our fair share of the proceeds. It does not mean, of course, the immediate exclusion of all foreign fishing vessels from our 200-mile zone. That would simply mean a waste of close to 70 per cent of the living resources now being exploited. It does mean, however, control of foreign fishing on Canadian terms. Of course, we shall continue to use international bodies such as the International Commission for Northwest Atlantic Fisheries (ICNAF) to exchange scientific data and catch statistics, as well as for the establishment of joint research programs. But Canada, with respect to the resources of its zone, will have the last word as to who gets what, and who does what. The Government is now studying the ways and means to put into place, when the time comes, the proper mechanisms to exercise this widely increased jurisdiction. Undoubtedly, for a long time to come, we shall have to enlist the co-operation of all nations fishing near our shores, particularly in respect of data-gathering. Indeed, such co-operation will be a condition of their continued operations within our zone.

We are also actively considering how to improve our surveillance and inspection capabilities. Already some use has been made of our naval units on the East Coast and contracts are out for new inspection vessels. We all agree that more has to be done in this field and we shall spare no effort to ensure the best use of all resources available.

Such are some of the benefits that can accrue to Canada if the 200-mile economic zone is accepted. That is good news. That is progress. But a 200-mile limit does not fully cover the Canadian case.*

We must obtain recognition of our rights and needs beyond that limit if we want to protect adequately our natural resources in three particular situations. A strict 200-mile limit would leave out over 400,000 square miles of continental margin, mostly on the East Coast, 10 per cent to 15 per cent of our fish stocks, also on the East Coast, and would leave all of our salmon unprotected during that part of their lives they spend in the open sea.

We have an uphill battle to fight on these three issues. We have many allies, our negotiators have made great efforts to promote our legitimate cause and we are still confident of ultimate success as part of the overall accommodation the conference will, it is hoped, produce. But let us be realistic enough to see our main difficulties.

A second major trend has also emerged at the conference in favour of establishing the international area of the oceans as a zone reserved for the benefit of mankind. Almost all nations agree that the exploita-

---

* The 200-mile economic zone off Canadian shores went into effect in January 1977.

tion of manganese nodules—those potato-shaped rock formations that lie all over the ocean seabed at depths of 15 to 20,000 feet and are rich in nickel, copper, cobalt and manganese—should be carried out for the benefit of the whole world and not solely for the advantage of the technologically advanced states. That is a concept Canada whole-heartedly supports. Unfortunately, the conference has not gone very far beyond accepting this very basic concept. The practical implemen-tation of the concept—that is, the creation of a new international authority—has given rise to a most serious confrontation between developed and developing nations.

This may seem to some Canadians a controversy so far removed from our essential preoccupations that it should not cause us to worry. There are, on the contrary, two very basic concerns that trouble us: One is that the two opposing factions on this issue attach such impor-tance to its resolution that failure on this item might undo the whole conference. Our second concern is that, if a proper international legal regime is not established over the international area, we shall not only find ourselves faced with conflict between developing and developed states but we, as Canadians, might also suffer from an uncontrolled exploitation of mineral resources—in particular of nickel—which con-stitute a good part of our hard-minerals exports and on which entire Canadian communities depend.

Both for reasons of world-wide equity and our own domestic inter-ests, we must do everything we can to set up a strong and economic-ally viable international authority.

Finally, the third major trend at the conference can be expressed in terms of a growing realization by all states that the oceans must be managed in a rational manner as opposed to the laissez-faire attitudes of the past. While it is desirable to maintain the ocean as a major thoroughfare for commerce, communications and general exchanges between nations, the time of unfettered freedom that has so often led to abuse is over. Navigation, fishing, research and exploration must be permitted and encouraged, but they must also be made subject to appropriate controls, rules and standards.

64. Law of the Sea: IV. The Seabed

Statement by Mr. Mitchell Sharp, Secretary of State for External Af-fairs, to the International Law Association, Toronto, November 5, 1969. (Extracts)

Among the various types of legal regime for the seabed which have been suggested so far, those which involve dividing up the entire seabed and ocean-floor among the coastal states already appear to have been rejected by the international community. Those theoretical systems that do not involve national appropriation can be broadly summarized as follows:

1. Systems under which states and their nationals would exploit seabed resources subject to an agreed body of rules but without any international control agency or machinery beyond a simple registration procedure;
2. systems under which an international agency, or the United Nations itself, might act as a trustee in controlling exploitation of the seabed by states and their nationals;
3. systems under which sovereignty over the seabed might be granted to the United Nations, which could itself carry on exploitation activities.

There appears to be general agreement that the regime to be adopted should ensure exploitation of the seabed in the interests of humanity and for the benefit of mankind, having regard to the special needs and interests of the developing countries. The provision concerning the special needs and interests of the less-developed countries has been written into all United Nations resolutions on this subject. Accordingly, many developing countries favor a regime or system which would be based on strong control or ownership by an international agency or by the United Nations itself.

On the question of establishing international machinery, the nature of the regime would determine whether any machinery is required and what its nature and scope should be. Even the most *laissez-faire* regime would probably require at least a central registry of licences for exploration and exploitation. Control or ownership by an international agency or the United Nations would imply the creation of international machinery of an extensive kind for which no precedent exists.

Those states that favour a supra-national approach to a seabed regime tend to press for strong international machinery, while states which favour a national approach tend to resist anything but the most limited machinery. On this issue there is a rather extreme polarization of views between many developing countries and certain developed countries—the Soviet Union in particular. The U.S.S.R. strongly opposes the supra-national overtones of the seabed question, and has resisted the study of international machinery in the United Nations.

The Canadian Government's position on these matters is still developing. We agree that there is an area of the seabed beyond national jurisdiction. We want this area to be reserved for peaceful purposes. We consider that a workable legal regime must be developed if the seabed is to be exploited in an effective, equitable and orderly manner. And we assume that some form of international machinery will be required. In our view, the seabed regime and machinery should provide some revenue for international community purposes, while protecting the legitimate interests of *entrepreneurs* and coastal states. We intend to be flexible and open-minded in examining all possible systems, but we have serious reservations about the more extreme proposals for international ownership and control.

I should now like to turn to the question of reserving the seabed exclusively for peaceful purposes. The basic Canadian position is that the widest possible range of arms-control measures should be extended to the widest possible area of the seabed and ocean-floor.

We have argued from the beginning that this objective should be understood in the light of the United Nations Charter and other principles of international law. Use of the seabed for offensive military uses should be prohibited, and especially the deployment of nuclear weapons and weapons of mass destruction. However, its use for purely defensive purposes, especially in areas adjacent to the coast, should not be precluded. We were the first country to call for the widest possible area of the seabed to be reserved for peaceful purposes, irrespective of the area which will eventually by subjected to an international legal regime.

The Conference of the Committee on Disarmament which has been considering this question reached an early consensus on the desirability of extending arms-control measures to the continental shelf as well as the area beyond national jurisdiction. There was also early agreement that there should be a narrow coastal band to which the proposed seabed arms-control measures would not apply, largely on the grounds that states have sovereignty over their territorial sea. The United States and the Soviet Union, co-chairmen of the Disarmament Committee, eventually agreed on a limit of 12 miles for this coastal band. This corresponds to the breadth of the territorial sea claimed by the U.S.S.R. and some 55 other states.

The United States and the U.S.S.R. also agreed that this coastal band, or "maximum contiguous zone", should be measured in the same way as the territorial sea. Allowance will be made for the use of the straight-baseline system which Canada has applied to long stretches of its coast, and for the status of historic waters such as Hudson Bay.

The results so far of negotiations on arms control on the seabed have now been incorporated in a draft treaty by the United States and the Soviet Union. The major achievement reflected in the draft treaty is prohibition of the emplacement of nuclear weapons and weapons of mass destruction on the seabed and ocean-floor. We warmly welcomed this bilateral self-denying agreement by the two great nuclear powers on the most important requirements for a seabed arms-control treaty. In other respects, however, the draft treaty falls short of our expectations and those of many other countries.

In the Disarmament Committee, Canada advanced a group of interrelated suggestions for disarmament of the seabed. In summary, these suggestions involved:

1. The prohibition not only of nuclear weapons and weapons of mass destruction, but also of conventional weapons and military installations which could be used for offensive purposes, without, however, banning installations required for self-defence;
2. the establishment, beyond the 12-mile coastal band, of a 200-mile security zone to which the proposed arms prohibitions would apply in full but where the coastal state could undertake defensive activities;
3. the elaboration of effective verification and inspection procedures to assure compliance with the terms of the treaty, together with an international arrangement making such verification possible for countries with a less developed underwater technology.

With the exception of the prohibition of the emplacement of nuclear weapons and weapons of mass destruction, these Canadian suggestions are not reflected in the draft treaty put forward by the U.S.A. and U.S.S.R. The co-chairmen's draft does recognize the existing right of states to observe the seabed activities of other states and it does incorporate an undertaking to consult and co-operate in removing doubts concerning compliance with the treaty. It does not, however, provide for the right of inspection and access on the model of either the 1959 Antarctic Treaty or the 1967 Outer Space Treaty.

Non-nuclear coastal states like Canada wish to be sure that there is nothing on the seabed which could threaten their security and that even permissible defensive activities on the continental shelf are limited to the coastal state concerned.

The provision in the draft treaty limiting the prohibition to nuclear weapons and weapons of mass destruction only in our view intensifies the need for the recognition of a broad coastal-state security zone.

Demilitarization of the broadest possible area of the seabed would make such a zone much less necessary, since *no* state would then have any right to make *any* military use of the continental shelf. With only nuclear and mass-destruction weapons prohibited, the possibility arises that states may attempt to emplace conventional weapons or military installations on the continental shelf of another state. Obviously, no coastal state could accept with equanimity the emplacement of offensive installations near its shores. If any state has the right to make any military use of the continental shelf, even for defensive purposes, it is the coastal state and the coastal state only. The exclusive sovereign rights of the coastal state to explore the continental shelf and exploit its resources are not compatible with any degree of freedom of military activity on the shelf by other states. The possibilities of conflict between foreign military activities and the coastal state's exploration and exploitation of the shelf are only too obvious.

65. Stockholm Conference: Declaration on the Human Environment

Statement on June 14, 1972, to the Plenary Session of the United Nations Conference on the Human Environment, Stockholm, concerning the Draft Declaration on the Human Environment, by Mr. J. A. Beesley, Legal Adviser to the Department of External Affairs. (Extracts)

I shall now summarize briefly the view of the Canadian delegation concerning the conceptions embodied in the Draft Declaration.

We consider that there is a fundamental need for an environment that permits the fullest enjoyment of the basic human rights reflected in the universal Declaration of Human Rights, including, in particular, the right to life itself. This conception is reflected in the Draft.

We recognize that life on the planet Earth is dependent on the land, the earth, the water and the sun and upon other forms of life on earth. This conception is reflected in the Draft.

We are aware that human life is also dependent upon the maintenance of the ecological balance of the biosphere. This conception is reflected in the Draft.

We are increasingly aware that human life is affected by environmental processes and influences, which are in turn affected by human activities. This conception is reflected in the Draft.

We are equally aware that human beings require and utilize the resources of the biosphere for their physical, mental, social and economic development. This conception is reflected in the Draft.

We are conscious that economic and social development and the quality of the environment are interdependent. This conception is reflected in the Draft.

We accept that the limited resources of the biosphere, including, in particular, land, air and water, require rational utilization. This conception is reflected in the Draft.

We recognize that there is cause for concern that irrational utilization of these resources is posing an accelerating threat to the environment. This conception is reflected in the Draft.

It is the firm position of the Canadian Government and people that environmental problems are the concern of all human beings and all peoples irrespective of their social or political systems, geographic situation or state of economic development. This conception is reflected in the Draft.

It is the further position of the Canadian Government and the Canadian people that all human beings and all peoples have equal rights to an environment adequate to their needs. This fundamental principle is also reflected in the Draft.

I have spoken of the importance of this Draft Declaration as an instrument laying down the foundation for the future development of international law. I should like to take advantage of the unusual opportunity presented to us by this Conference, which we regard as of historic importance, to make the following statement of interpretation. It is not, I should like to stress, a statement of reservations. On the contrary—it is an affirmation.

The Canadian Government considers that Principle 21 reflects customary international law in affirming the principle that states have, in accordance with the Charter of the United Nations and the principles of international law, "the sovereign right to exploit their own resources pursuant to their own environmental policies, and the responsibility to ensure that activities within their jurisdiction or control do not cause damage to the environment of other States or of areas beyond the limits of national jurisdiction".

The Canadian Government considers that the secondary consequential Principle 22 reflects an existing duty of states when it proclaims the principle "that States should cooperate to develop further the international law regarding liability and compensation for the victims of pollution and other environmental damage caused by activities within the jurisdiction or control of such States to areas beyond their jurisdiction".

The Canadian Government considers also that the tertiary consequential principle contained in the Draft Declaration on the Human

Environment as it first came before us in plenary (former Principle 20 not now contained in the Draft) on the duty of states to inform one another considering the environmental impact of their actions upon areas beyond their jurisdiction also reflected a duty under existing customary international law, when it proclaimed in essence the principle "that relevant information must be supplied by States on activities or developments within their jurisdiction or under their control whenever there is reason to believe that such information is needed to avoid the risk of significant adverse effects on the environment in areas beyond their national jurisdiction".

These legal principles, taken together with the important and closely related marine-pollution principles and the draft articles on a proposed dumping convention, on which we have already taken action, together provide us with an opportunity to work together in a co-operative spirit of conciliation and accommodation (accommodation not only as between differing national interests but as between national interests and the interests of the international community) to elaborate laws that will protect us all by protecting our environment.*

---

* See SS 72/16 of June 8, 1972, for the statement made by Dr. Victor Goldbloom, Minister of Environment, Quebec, regarding human settlements and the results of the UN Conference on Pilot Projects in Human Settlements (Habitat), Vancouver, May 1975.

IX. The Provinces and Foreign Policy

~Provincial interest in Canada's external relations increased and broadened during the decade, ranging from Quebec's concentration on education in the French-speaking world to Alberta's concern about energy exports to the United States and Ontario's about investments and energy supplies.

Quebec's early moves abroad are documented in the previous volume. They were given a good deal of impetus as a result of President de Gaulle's visit to Quebec during the summer of 1967 and the growing support he gave to Quebec's overseas ventures until he left office in 1969.

The invitation received and accepted by the Quebec Government to attend a meeting of the French-speaking Education Ministers at Libreville, capital of Gabon on the west coast of Africa, in January 1968 accelerated the deterioration in Ottawa's relations with Quebec and with France. The federal government had not been invited to attend the Libreville meeting. Quebec was present with all the trappings of an independent state. Ottawa proceeded to suspend diplomatic relations with Libreville, but these were resumed later after things had quieted down. Canada's aid program in Gabon was maintained. Quebec participated in the second phase of the Education Ministers' meeting, which took place in Paris in April 1968. Again, Ottawa was ignored. Concurrently, France's cultural activities among the French-speaking minorities in New Brunswick and Manitoba were stepped up. The French Government's official presence in Quebec, through increased consulate strength and activity, was greatly intensified.

These developments constitute the political backdrop to the two White Papers published by the Federal Government during the first half of 1968.* These two White Papers give the federal position on the constitutional demarcation line in this sector and convey suggestions

---

* See *Federalism and International Relations,* Ottawa, QP, February 1968, and *Federalism and International Conferences on Education,* Ottawa, QP, May 1968.

regarding provincial participation at international meetings. Extracts are given below.

As documented below, Ottawa's suspension of relations with Gabon was essentially a warning, partly to France which was believed to be behind the Gabonese invitation to Quebec, but also to the other French-speaking African states, to tread warily in this area. If the federal government had ignored the matter, it would have implied that it was prepared to countenance repetitions of the incident. This would have served as an encouragement both to Quebec and to others to continue. Acceptance of participants at international conferences constitutes a form of diplomatic recognition. A series of precedents established by Quebec participation in intergovernmental meetings of the Francophone states could have led to eventual recognition of its independence: hence the importance of a federal response to the Gabonese gesture.

Ottawa was determined that Canada and not just Quebec should be invited to the next meeting of the French-speaking Education Ministers, scheduled to be held at Kinshasha in January 1969. It was also determined that Canada should be present at the international conference where the foundations of a French-speaking Commonwealth—*la Francophonie*—were soon to be laid. This conference was slated to take place at Niamey, capital of Niger, in February 1969.

Sustained approaches to the countries concerned—particularly in Francophone Africa—ensued. Urgent consultations with the provincial authorities in Quebec were undertaken. These measures were accompanied by increased Canadian aid activity in Francophone Africa, of which the Chevrier Mission during the late winter and early spring of 1968 is an example. It was authorized to approve aid projects and to commit funds on the spot.

These steps were successful, as documented in the following pages. Attention is drawn, in particular, to the voting procedures and to the evolution of arrangements for the chairmanship of Canadian delegations agreed upon by the federal government, Quebec, and other interested provinces for the two types of meetings concerned. In essence, for the Education Conferences, when a vote is called for and the Canadian delegation cannot agree on an issue, it abstains. In addition, delegations to such meetings are headed by the Quebec Minister of Education (with federal advisors in the foreign policy field). At Kinshasha, a co-chairmanship arrangement between the federal and Quebec governments had obtained.* For the *Franco-*

---

* Zaire had recently been the scene of difficulties connected with the Katan-

phonie Conferences where the mandate is broader than for the Education Conferences (aid, cultural exchanges, etc. are also included), only when disagreement occurs within the delegation on a matter affecting strictly provincial jurisdictions is abstention to take place. Canadian delegations to *Francophonie* Conferences are chaired by the federal government, the Vice-Chairman being from Quebec as detailed below. Other interested provinces are also represented at *Francophonie* meetings. These arrangements tend to make Canadian delegations to such conferences by far the largest and most colourful of all, since Ottawa and each province have the right to be identified by plaques, flags, etc. These manifestations of Canadian tribalism are said to amuse the Africans no end.

As a result of the second conference of Niamey, held in March 1970, *la Francophonie* came into official being. It took the form of an international organization called the *Agence de Coopération Culturelle et Technique*, with some 30 member states. Its headquarters are located in Paris. France contributes 45% of its budget; Canada 35%, of which slightly more than 2% comes from Quebec; Belgium 12%; the remainder comes from the other member states. The *Agence*'s activities are concentrated mainly in the technical assistance and cultural exchange fields.

With the departure of President de Gaulle from the political scene in 1969 and the two electoral victories of Premier Bourassa in 1969 and 1973 respectively, relations between Ottawa and Quebec as well as between Ottawa and Paris improved. Participation in the programs of the *Agence* at the federal and provincial levels became less politicized, more pragmatic and routine. By virtue of the *Agence*'s constitution, notably article 3(3), Quebec became—with Ottawa's blessing—a *gouvernement participant* in the *Agence*. This special arrangement is documented below. It remains to be seen what effects the Quebec elections of November 15, 1976, which brought the *Parti Québécois* to power, will have on the work of the *Agence* and on Quebec's international activities.

---

gan (now Shaba) secessionist movement. Its government was therefore more aware than those of most other Francophone African countries, largely unitary states, of the complexity of federal systems arising out of the distribution of powers between different levels of government. It invited the Federal Government to attend the conference. Quebec received, and accepted, a separate invitation from the secretariat of the conference shortly before it opened. It was alleged at the time that France had threatened to withdraw from the meeting unless such an invitation were issued.

While Quebec has been in the forefront of federal-provincial inter-national relations, there have been substantive developments—al-though of a quieter nature—initiated by other provinces as well, nota-bly Alberta, British Columbia, Ontario. Alberta has been active in the international energy field. British Columbia has developed important trade links with Japan. Ontario has a far-flung network of agencies abroad, standing at 12 currently, to foster its interests. Quebec now has 12 such offices also; Alberta 3; British Columbia 3; Nova Scotia 3; Manitoba and Saskatchewan, 1 each. Ontario and Quebec recently closed three agencies each as an economy measure.

PROVINCIAL OFFICES ABROAD, 1977		(By year of opening) (Since 1943)					
LOCATION	ONT.	QUE.	N.S.	ALTA.	B.C.	SASK.	MAN.	TOTAL
Europe:								
London	1945	1962	1969	1948	1973	1949		6
Paris		1961						1
Brussels	1969	1972						2
Milan	1963	1965						2
Dusseldorf		1970						1
Frankfurt	1970							1
Vienna	1969							1
Stockholm	1968							1
United States:								
New York	1956	1943	1971					3
Los Angeles	1967	1970		1964	1964			4
Boston		1970						1
Chicago	1953	1965						2
Cleveland	1967							1
Minneapolis							1975	1
Dallas		1970						1
LaFayette		1970						1
San Francisco					1961			1
Portland		1972						1
Others:								
Tokyo	1969	1973		1970				3
Mexico	1973							1
TOTAL (1977)	12	12	3	3	3	1	1	35
OPENED AND CLOSED								
1967-1977	3	3	1	0	0	0	0	7

New Brunswick, Prince Edward Island, and Newfoundland have no offices abroad.
New Brunswick maintained an office in London from 1970 to 1975.

SOURCE: By courtesy of Prof. D. M. Page, Deputy Director, Historical Divi-sion, DEA, Ottawa, from a presentation made to the Canadian Studies Panel on Quebec's Future at the Western Social Science Association meeting, Denver, Colorado, April 22, 1977.

It is not possible in a book of this size to document all the external activities of all the provinces. As an example of the interest of provinces other than Quebec in foreign affairs, the last document in this chapter gives Premier Lougheed's vigorous views about Alberta's position on oil diplomacy. As for the province of Ontario, see "The Role of the Provinces in International Affairs", Ronald G. Atkey, *International Journal*, Toronto, CIIA, Vol. XXVI No. 1, Winter 1970-71, pp. 249-73.

Provincial co-operation has become increasingly essential to ensure that Canada is appropriately represented at international conferences dealing with energy, environmental affairs, education, immigration, highways, transport, and so on, where the provinces have well defined responsibilities.* Provincial co-operation is also required to implement many international agreements, for instance, in the field of education, culture, human rights, and others. As a result, a series of complex linkages in the implementation of Canadian foreign policy affecting provincial interests has now come into being.

On the federal side, the Department of External Affairs has created comprehensive mechanisms and procedures to ensure that the provinces are kept informed of international developments of significance to them and that, conversely, sight is not lost in Ottawa of corresponding provincial interests. These arrangements are centred mainly in the Department's Bureau of Co-ordination, which is in close contact with the various provincial departments of inter-governmental affairs. Many other federal government departments and agencies which deal with the provinces in their respective areas of jurisdiction have also set up similar units of co-ordination or consultation.

On the provincial side, government external activities are now widespread and serve to project an image abroad of Canadian regional realities. This fact of Canadian life increases the need for co-operation between the two levels of government; otherwise, the coherence and impact of Canada's external relations could be seriously hampered, even stymied. This need is recognized. Accordingly, Canadian foreign policy has—for all practical purposes—become a shared jurisdiction, constitutionally, where provincial interests are concerned. In co-operating with the provinces, the federal government has of course striven to preserve its leadership and primacy, while stressing its co-ordinating role, so as to ensure that Canada speaks with one voice on the international stage.⁓

---

* See Swanson, Roger F., *State/Provincial Interaction*, prepared for the U.S. State Department, Washington, D.C., 1974.

66. Vive Le Québec Libre

Discours de Charles de Gaulle, le 24 juillet 1967, à l'Hôtel de Ville, Montréal.

C'est une immense émotion qui remplit mon coeur en voyant devant moi la ville de Montréal française. Au nom du vieux pays, au nom de la France, je vous salue de tout mon coeur.

Je vais vous confier un secret que vous ne répéterez à personne. Ce soir, ici, et tout le long de ma route, je me suis trouvé dans une atmosphère du même genre que celle de la Libération.

Et tout le long de ma route, outre cela, j'ai constaté quel immense effort de progrès, de développement et par conséquent d'affranchissement vous accomplissez ici, et c'est à Montréal qu'il faut que je le dise, parce que s'il y a eu au monde une ville exemplaire par ses réussites modernes, c'est la vôtre. Je dis: c'est la vôtre, et je me permets d'ajouter: c'est la nôtre.

Si vous saviez quelle confiance la France, réveillée après d'immenses épreuves, porte maintenant vers vous! Si vous saviez quelle affection elle recommence à ressentir pour les Français du Canada! Et si vous saviez à quel point elle se sent obligée de concourir à votre marche en avant, à votre progrès! C'est pourquoi elle a conclu avec le gouvernement du Québec, avec celui de mon ami Johnson, des accords pour que les Français de part et d'autre de l'Atlantique travaillent ensemble à une même oeuvre française. Et d'ailleurs, le concours que la France va tous les jours un peu plus prêter ici, elle sait bien que vous le lui rendrez parce que vous êtes en train de vous constituer des élites, des usines, des entreprises, des laboratoires qui feront l'étonnement de tous et qui un jour—j'en suis sûr—vous permettront d'aider la France.

Voilà ce que je suis venu vous dire ce soir, en ajoutant que j'emporte de cette réunion inouïe de Montréal un souvenir inoubliable. La France entière sait, voit, entend ce qui se passe ici et je puis vous dire qu'elle en vaudra mieux.

Vive Montréal, vive le Québec, vive le Québec libre, vive le Canada français, vive la France!

67. Canada, Quebec, and France

Statement by the Prime Minister, Mr. L. B. Pearson, in the House of Commons, November 28, 1967.

Mr. Speaker, I should like to make a short statement commenting on one made yesterday in Paris by General de Gaulle.

I said in my statement of July 25, 1967, Mr. Speaker, commenting on some earlier remarks of the President of the French Republic, that Canada had always had a special relationship with France, which was the motherland of so many of its citizens. I said we attached the greatest importance to our friendship with the French people; that it had been and remained the strong purpose of the Government of Canada to foster that friendship. I should like to confirm those words today.

I do not propose to deal in any detail with General de Gaulle's statement of yesterday, a statement very carefully prepared and made to the press. General de Gaulle's statement will obviously arouse discord in Canada. I am sure the people of this country will be restrained in their response to it, as I am in mine today, so as not to serve the purposes of those who would disunite and divide our country.

I believe the statement distorted some Canadian history, misrepresented certain contemporary developments and wrongly predicted the future. This statement was not merely a commentary on Canadian domestic or foreign policies, which could have been ignored; it was an intervention in those policies by the head of a foreign state. As such it remains unacceptable. Indeed, Mr. Speaker, in this case it is intolerable that a head of a foreign state or government should recommend a course of political or constitutional action which would destroy Canadian Confederation and the unity of the Canadian state.

The future of Canada, Mr. Speaker, will be decided in Canada, by Canadians.

I have confidence, and I know all members of this House have confidence, in the ability and good sense of all Canadians, French-speaking or English-speaking, to make the right decision. They will do it in their own way and through their own democratic process. I believe this decision will require further constitutional changes to bring our federalism up to date and to ensure, among other things, that French-speaking Canadians who form one of our two founding cultural and linguistic groups, or societies if you like, will have their rights accepted and respected in Canada.

I agree also that the Federal Government—any Federal Government—should encourage and promote special and close cultural relations between French-speaking Canadians and France and other French-speaking countries. Indeed, Mr. Speaker, we are doing that. There should be no argument on this score, except with those who wish to use these relations to destroy the Federal Government's responsibility for foreign affairs, and that we do not accept.

Canada is a free country and its people govern themselves. Canadians in Quebec and elsewhere in Canada have the right to exercise fully their political rights in federal and provincial elections. Self-determination is no new discovery for us.

We do not need to have it offered to us. To assert the contrary is an insult to those who discharge their democratic privileges as Canadian voters and to those who serve their country in this House or in provincial legislatures.

To those who would set us free, we answer: "We are free". To those who would disunite us, we answer: "We remain united, in a federal system which is being brought into line with the requirements of our time and of our origins and history". On April 19, 1960, the gallant and illustrious head of another state, speaking in Ottawa, had this to say; I quote from his speech:

"And now, how do you Canadians appear to us? Materially, a new country, of vast size, mighty resources, inhabited by a hard-working and enterprising people. Politically, a state which has found the means to unite two societies, very different in origin, language and religion; which exercises independence under the British Crown and forms part of the Commonwealth: which is forging a national character even though spread out over three thousand miles alongside a very powerful federation; a solid and stable state".

Mr. Speaker, I agree with those words of General de Gaulle in 1960. I disagree with his words in November 1967.

68. The Chevrier Mission to Francophone Africa

*Statement by the Director General of the External Aid Office, Mr. Maurice F. Strong, February 14, 1968, to the Senate Standing Committee on External Relations.**

Senator Croll:　Mr. Chairman, may I ask a question at the outset? Mr. Strong, the newspapers report that the Honourable Mr. Chevrier, along with a group of other people, has been visiting what was formerly colonial France with the idea of ascertaining their needs there with the idea in mind, I suppose, of giving them some assist-

---

* The External Aid Office is now known as the Canadian International Development Agency (CIDA).

ance. The reports are rather sketchy and I wonder if you could tell us what it is all about.

Mr. Maurice F. Strong, Director General, External Aid Office: Mr. Chairman, honourable senators, this mission to which Senator Croll has referred left several days ago to visit French-speaking states in West Africa. The purpose of their visit is to ascertain the present status of discussions we have had over a period of some months with a number of these countries concerning specific aid projects and aid programs and to make known to the governments of these countries the various areas in which Canadian assistance is available and again to determine from them the specific needs to which these Canadian resources can best be applied.

I think I referred in some of my earlier comments to the fact that in the French-speaking states of Africa there had been some difficulties in developing a program of the size which is considered to be desirable from the point of view of its relationship to the total Canadian aid program, the reason for this simply being that these countries have been closely linked with France in the past and have not been closely linked with Canada, and therefore it takes time for them to be properly informed about the kind of projects with which Canada can best help them. So the constraint in the growth of our program in French Africa has been a kind of institutional restraint rather than a limitation in the amounts of money.

Senator MacKenzie: Do you think that this is something that should go under your auspices?

Mr. Strong: This is something in the nature of a high level technical mission. Mr. Chevrier has senior officers accompanying him from the External Aid Office and from the Department of External Affairs as well as local officers from our missions in the countries concerned and they are having discussions now with regard to the implementation of Canadian aid programs. This is part of a continuing process whereby we have been attempting to identify specific projects and specific programs in Francophone Africa which would recommend themselves to the application of Canadian assistance.

Senator Croll: In other words a fact-finding group?

Mr. Strong: Fact-finding—I would prefer to use the word "facilitating" in the sense that it is a situation where Mr. Chevrier actually has authority to commit Canadian funds to projects, some of which have been in a state of development for some months, and some for even longer than that, because some are complicated projects that require some time to develop and a number are at the stage where, subject to being assured that conditions are such that they can be processed, the mission is armed with specific authority to commit itself.

Senator Croll: This is similar to the one that Humphrey took for President Johnson and he committed himself as he went along.

Mr. Strong: Well, it was designed. This one has been in the mill, we have been preparing for it in Canada and in our missions abroad for more than six months.

Senator Croll: All right, I have all the information I wanted on it.

69. The Gabon Affair—Libreville

Text of Statement issued by the Prime Minister, Mr. L. B. Pearson, Ottawa, March 4, 1968.

The Ambassador of Canada in Washington has delivered to the Ambassador of Gabon a note protesting the fact that the Gabonese Government acted in a manner incompatible with international law and the maintenance of close and friendly relations between our two countries in connection with the Libreville meeting of February 5-10. In the following note the Canadian Government expresses its hope that the Gabonese Government will reconsider its attitude, but states that in the present circumstances the Canadian Ambassador designate to Gabon will not proceed with the presentation of his credentials.

The Canadian Government also regrets that on the occasion of the Libreville meeting it was not possible to reach agreement between the Federal and Quebec Governments on sending a Canadian delegation to that meeting.

Quebec as a Francophone province having exclusive domestic jurisdiction over education was clearly and particularly interested in the matters to be discussed at this conference. The Federal Government was prepared to make appropriate arrangements to ensure the fullest representation of provincial and francophone interests on a Canadian delegation, and our willingness to do so was made clear on more than one occasion to the Quebec authorities and to the countries involved in organizing the conference. Indeed it was suggested that the Quebec Minister of Education could head a Canadian delegation. It was also made clear to all concerned, however, that the Canadian Government was the only authorized spokesman of all Canadians at the international level, and the only one entitled to receive such an invitation.

The policy of the Canadian Government to develop agreed procedures for provincial participation, as a part of Canadian delegations to international meetings of interest to the provinces, is explained in detail in a document submitted to the recent Constitutional Conference entitled "Federalism and International Relations". The document also contains proposals for strengthening existing mechanisms for facilitating provincial participation in such meetings. In view of these proposals and the statements of the Government of Quebec at the Constitutional Conference and elsewhere that it is their desire to discuss these and related matters with the Federal Government, it is my hope that Quebec will agree that there should be such discussions before decisions are taken in this field.

Following is a copy of the note handed to the Ambassador of Gabon in Washington.

The Secretary of State for External Affairs of Canada presents his compliments to the Minister of Foreign Affairs of the Gabonese Republic and has the honour to refer to Note No. 161 of January 30 from the Ambassador of the Gabonese Republic in Washington in which the Government of Gabon confirms information previously given to the Canadian Government by the Foreign Minister of Gabon that the invitation addressed to the Minister of Education of the Province of Quebec to attend the Libreville Meeting of February 5-10 was of a strictly personal nature, and in which the Government of Gabon makes certain comments on the Canadian constitution.

The Government of Canada wishes to inform the Government of Gabon of its deep concern about the actions of the Gabonese Government and in connection with Canadian representation at the Libreville meeting of February 5-10. The Canadian Government considers that, in disregarding the representations of the Canadian Government and their own assurances that no invitation to an international conference would be addressed to a Canadian province, in failing to address to the Canadian Government, in accordance with international law and practice, the invitation to attend the conference, in treating the Minister from Quebec and his suite in a manner incompatible with the statement by the Gabonese Government that he was attending in a purely personal capacity, and in attempting, in its note of January 30, to make certain interpretations of the Canadian constitution, the Government of Gabon has acted in a way which is neither in conformity with the principle of international law nor with the maintenance of close and friendly relations between our two countries.

The Canadian Government regrets, therefore, that the actions of the Government of Gabon are incompatible with the wishes expressed in its note to reinforce relations between the two countries on the basis of mutual respect, sincere friendship and active cooperation. The Canadian Government shares this wish and hopes that the Government of Gabon will reconsider its attitude. In present circumstances, however, the Government of Canada deems it appropriate to instruct its Ambassador designate to Gabon not to proceed with the presentation of his credentials.

The Secretary of State for External Affairs of Canada avails himself of this opportunity to renew to the Minister of Foreign Affairs of the Gabonese Republic the assurances of his highest consideration. February 19, 1968.

70. The Provinces and Foreign Policy

Extract from the White Paper, Federalism and International Conferences on Education, *QP, Ottawa, May 8, 1968.*

The issues raised by the question of provincial attendance at intergovernmental conferences are not related merely to form or protocol, as has sometimes been suggested. In fact, they raise two fundamental policy questions, which go to the heart of our Canadian federal system:

First, can Canadian foreign policy and foreign relations be divided?

Second, if foreign policy is indivisible, and Canada must speak with one voice, is the Federal Government willing to promote the interests of all Canadians, of both major linguistic groups?

The answer to the first question is "no".

The answer to the second is "yes".

The central problem at issue concerns the very nature of foreign policy in the modern world. What precisely are external relations and foreign policy? Can some relations with states be considered to be part of the foreign policy of a country while others can be considered to be outside this sphere?

The question involved is one of principle: who is responsible for Canadian representation abroad, whether in matters of education or any other matters within provincial jurisdiction?

The second question posed at the outset remains to be considered: if foreign policy is indivisible, is the Government of Canada willing to promote all Canadian interests the interests of Canadians of both major linguistic groups, and of all provinces and regions?

The answer is "yes".

It is, in fact, because the Government is fully conscious of its responsibilities to all of Canada and to all Canadians that it has given a bilingual and bicultural character to its foreign policy. The Government's policy in this respect has been described in some detail in the paper *Federalism and International Relations.**

The principles developed in connection with attendance at, and participation in, Commonwealth education meetings and international organizations such as UNESCO are also applicable, in the Government's view, to Canadian representation in *la Francophonie*. The establishment of specific procedures for federal-provincial co-operation in the latter field, particularly in respect of educational conferences, will require further consultation between the Federal Government and the provinces, but there can be no doubt that Canada's bilingual character entails a lasting interest on the part of all Canadians in close and harmonious relations with the French-speaking world.

Thus far, there have been no general conferences of all French-speaking states in respect of educational matters. However, for several years there have been meetings of the Conference of African and Malagasy Ministers of National Education which have brought together representatives from France and a number of French-speaking African states. These conferences are essentially regional in nature and deal with questions relating to educational exchanges between France and countries of the area. Thus, countries from outside the area which use French as an official or working language—for example, in North Africa, Asia and Europe—are not participants. However, Quebec received an invitation to attend, and was present at, the sessions held in Libreville in February 1968 and was also present at the resumed session held in Paris in April 1968. Canada's attempts to obtain an invitation to these sessions, which would have allowed all of Canada to be represented, were not acted upon.

As will be seen below, the Federal Government has put forward

---

* Published in February 1968. Available from QP or DEA, Ottawa.

certain proposals, of both a general and specific nature, concerning Canadian participation in intergovernmental meetings of *la Francophonie*. The Government considers that, although these proposals may require further elaboration, they provide in broad outline for procedures which take full account of the interests of Quebec, as the province in which the great majority of French-speaking Canadians live, as well as provinces with large French-speaking minorities such as New Brunswick and Ontario, and which at the same time respect the requirements of Canadian unity.

In accordance with the Government's policy toward *la Francophonie*, and its desire to ensure that Canada should play a significant role in this movement, consultations were begun with the Province of Quebec in the late autumn of last year with a view to determining the nature of Canadian participation. Following initial indications that Quebec might be invited to attend the next session of the Conference of African and Malagasy Ministers of National Education, to be held early in 1968, and that a general conference of *la Francophonie* might be held later in the year, the Prime Minister wrote to the Prime Minister of Quebec on December 1, 1967, to suggest that arrangements be agreed upon between the two governments with respect to *la Francophonie* generally, which would allow for full Quebec participation in Canadian representation. The Government's proposals were based upon an extension of the principles underlying arrangements worked out between the Federal Government and the provinces for attendance at Commonwealth and UNESCO conferences on education. The Prime Minister's letter read as follows with respect to delegations to conferences of *la Francophonie*:

The composition of the Canadian delegation will, of course, be dependent on the subject matter of the meeting. If such a meeting, for instance, should deal with questions of a general character, or with external aid, it would then seem desirable for the Secretary of State for External Affairs to lead the Canadian delegation; which I would hope would also include strong representation from Quebec. If, on the other hand, the purpose of the conference was, for example, to deal exclusively with education, it would then be appropriate for the Minister of Education of Quebec to be a member of the Canadian delegation, if such was your wish. Needless to say, he should occupy within this delegation a place appropriate to his position, taking into account the nature of the conference. In certain cases, the Quebec Minister might well be the head of the Canadian delegation.

Discussions were subsequently arranged between senior federal officials—acting under the Prime Minister's instructions—and the Quebec authorities. During these discussions, the Federal Government proposed that the Federal and Quebec governments should agree that the Quebec Minister of Education should head any Canadian delegation to the meeting of education ministers to be held in Libreville, Gabon, and that this arrangement should be communicated by the Canadian Government to the organizers of the conference with a view to an invitation being issued to Canada. The reaction of the Quebec authorities was non-committal, and no agreement was reached on the composition of a Canadian delegation.

The conference took place in Libreville from February 5 to 10, and was attended by France, Quebec and 15 independent francophone African states. Delegations were represented at the ministerial level. The Minister of Education of Quebec was accompanied by a delegation of three officials from the Quebec government.

Following the failure to reach agreement on the composition of a Canadian delegation to attend the Libreville conference, the Government again communicated with the Quebec authorities with a view to arriving at an understanding on future meetings. In a letter of March 8 to the Prime Minister of Quebec, Prime Minister Pearson re-emphasized that the Federal Government's purpose was to find arrangements which "would allow the Province of Quebec to make a full contribution to the development of *la Francophonie* and to be represented in discussions concerning various matters of interest to the French-speaking world in a manner which would be compatible with the continued existence of a sovereign and independent Canada".

With regard to education meetings, the Prime Minister summarized the Federal Government's position as follows:

I would envisage that at meetings of ministers of education held within the context of *la Francophonie*, the Minister of Education of Quebec would as a general practice, represent Canada as chairman of the Canadian delegation, a possibility to which I referred in my earlier letter and which was followed up in subsequent discussions. At such times, I think it would be desirable and compatible with their responsibilities that ministers or officials from other provinces, particularly those with large French-speaking populations, should be added as appropriate to the delegation. I refer in particular to Ontario and New Brunswick. There would be occasions, no doubt, when it would be appropriate for a minister from another province to be chairman of the delegation. If there were advisers from the Federal Government on the Canadian delegation, they would not, of course, involve themselves with questions of education but rather with aspects of these conferences which relate to the federal responsibility for international relations.

In view of the effective role which the Council of Ministers of Education has played in providing provincial nominations for Canadian delegations to Commonwealth, UNESCO, and IBE meetings, the Prime Minister also made the suggestion in the letter that one way to work out suitable arrangements in respect of *la Francophonie* would be to request the Council "to recommend the general composition of the delegation for each education conference".

The Prime Minister went on to underline the Government's conviction that:

We can find a way to work out among ourselves and without aid or interference of outside powers an acceptable method of representation in *la Francophonie* which would give your government and others concerned the opportunity of playing a full and active role without weakening the structure of Canada or its presence in the world.

He concluded by again emphasizing that Canada's structure and its presence abroad:

Would certainly be weakened—and ultimately destroyed—if other countries invite Canadian provinces to international conferences of states. If these provinces accept the invitation, and if the provincial delegates are treated formally as representatives of states while the Government of Canada is ignored.

A sovereign state—and Canada is one—must maintain responsibility for foreign policy and for representation abroad, or it ceases to be sovereign. I know you do not wish this fragmentation of our country before the world to happen. That is why I am writing to you again on this matter and why I earnestly hope that discussions between our two governments may lead to arrangements in the conduct of international affairs which will be satisfactory to both.

As the Libreville ministerial meeting was soon to resume in Paris, and as no reply had yet been received to these letters, the Prime Minister, in view of the gravity and increasing urgency of the situation, wrote a further letter (dated April 5, 1968) to Prime Minister Johnson in order to emphasize to the Quebec authorities the importance of finding a mutually acceptable solution. Prime Minister Pearson suggested that the proposal put forward earlier, that Canada as a whole should be represented at *Francophonie* education conferences, would be particularly appropriate in the case of the Paris meeting.

During the period of consultation with the Province of Quebec, the Government was also in touch with the Province of New Brunswick regarding the development of cultural links with France and participation in meetings of *la Francophonie*. In recent statements the New Brunswick authorities have made clear that they hope to take full advantage of opportunities open to them in this field and to be represented in Canadian delegations to international conferences on education which are held by French-speaking states. The Province of Ontario has also expressed an interest in developing exchanges with France and discussions have been held between the federal and provincial authorities, and between Ontario and French officials, with this end in view.

On April 9, 1968, Prime Minister Johnson sent a personal letter* to Prime Minister Pearson which constituted the only reply received to the three letters cited above. This reply was received the day before the Minister of Education of Quebec publicly announced his government's decision to attend the conference. The meeting was held from April 22 to April 26.

The Canadian Government was never officially informed of the status of the Quebec delegation at the Paris meeting. While there had been indications in connection with the earlier session at Libreville that the Quebec Minister of Education had been invited in a strictly personal capacity, it appears from the proceedings of the conference that he participated on the same basis as other delegates. In the case of the Paris session, the Quebec Minister stated after the conference that Quebec had participated on the same basis as other delegations.

71. The Kinshasa Conference

Exchange of telegrams between Prime Ministers Bertrand and Trudeau, January 8-10, 1969.

A.   Au Premier Ministre Trudeau (via M. Hellyer, Premier Ministre intérimaire), 9 janvier 1969.

Ai pris connaissance du message que vous m'avez fait parvenir hier concernant la Conférence des Ministres de l'Education à Kinshasa . . .

Comme j'ai eu l'occasion de le dire à Monsieur Trudeau lors d'une conversation au téléphone hier, le Ministre de l'Education du Québec a reçu une invitation pour cette conférence. Cette invitation a été acceptée et le Gouvernement du Québec a formé une délégation qui

---

* Prime Minister Pearson's letter of April 5, 1968, and Premier Johnson's letter of April 9, 1968, were not published in the White Paper.

se rendra à la conférence. La délégation sera dirigée par l'Honorable Jean-Marie Morin, Ministre d'Etat à l'Education et il sera accompagné de Messieurs Yves Martin (Sous-Ministre adjoint), Julien Aubert (Directeur du Service de Coopération), Jean Tardif (Service de Coopération au Ministère de l'Education), et Gilles Loiselle (Conseiller à l'Information à la Délégation Générale à Paris).

Les négociations qui se sont poursuivies à ce sujet entre nos fonctionnaires au cours des dernières semaines devront être continuées lors de la Conférence Constitutionnelle en vue d'arriver à un accord sur les modalités de la représentation canadienne à de telles conférences des Ministres de l'Education francophones. Pour résoudre le problème immédiat qui se pose à nos gouvernements, la délégation du Québec, dûment identifiée, se joindra sur place aux autres représentants de la fédération canadienne. De la sorte, il me semble que les prérogatives de nos deux gouvernements seront respectées.

Nous devons nous rendre compte qu'il devient essentiel de discuter en profondeur de cette question dans le cadre des négociations constitutionnelles globales.

Pour notre part, nous croyons sincèrement que nous devons innover dans ce domaine. La solution que je propose dans le cas de la Conférence de Kinshasa découle, je crois, de cet esprit de renouvellement dont nous devons tous faire preuve.

Jean Jacques Bertrand
Premier Ministre du Québec.

B.   A l'Honorable Jean-Jacques Bertrand, 10 janvier 1969.

Je vous ai informé le 23 décembre de l'invitation qu'a adressée la République Démocratique du Congo au Canada par l'entremise du Secrétariat Technique de la Conférence des Ministres de l'Education de participer à la prochaine conférence qui doit s'ouvrir à Kinshasa le 13 janvier. Je vous avisais en outre que j'avais informé le Congo que j'espérais que la délégation du Canada représenterait tous les éléments francophones de notre pays et qu'il me semblait indiqué que le Président de la délégation canadienne soit un Ministre ou un fonctionnaire de votre gouvernement.

J'ai de même fait part de cette invitation aux gouvernements des autres provinces. L'Ontario et le Nouveau Brunswick m'ont alors fait connaître leur intention de participer à la délégation canadienne.

Par ailleurs des discussions nombreuses et suivies eurent lieu entre les fonctionnaires de nos deux gouvernements en vue d'assurer une participation québécoise à la délégation canadienne qui soit à la mesure de l'importance et de l'intérêt que le Québec attache à cette conférence. Pour faire suite à ces discussions je vous ai adressé le 8 janvier le télégramme suivant proposant les normes selon lesquelles la participation québécoise à une délégation canadienne pourrait être acceptable à nos deux gouvernements:

A l'Honorable Jean-Jacques Bertrand, 8 janvier 1969.

Le Gouvernement du Canada ayant reçu une invitation d'assister à la Conférence des Ministres de l'Education à Kinshasa le 13 janvier 1969, a l'intention d'accepter cette invitation et de former une délégation représentant les intérêts de tous les Canadiens aux questions d'éducation en langue française et particulièrement ceux du Québec.

Comme suite aux entretiens qui ont eu lieu récemment à cet égard entre nos représentants respectifs, je désire maintenant proposer formellement que les normes suivantes concernant la participation du Ministre de l'Education du Québec à une délégation canadienne soient acceptées par nos deux gouvernements.

1. Le Québec déléguera à la conférence de Kinshasa son Ministre de l'Education ou son mandataire qui sera le Président ou le co-Président de la délégation canadienne. La délégation du Canada se composera des Ministres de l'Education des provinces désireuses de participer à la conférence, ou de leur mandataire, et de toutes autres personnes nommées par le Gouvernement Canadien.

2. Le Ministre du Québec parlera au nom du Québec sur toute matière du domaine de la compétence constitutionnelle du Québec. Les délégués des autres provinces parleront de même. Quant à la délégation canadienne en tant que telle, elle s'exprimera par la voix de son Président ou de ses co-Présidents.

3. La présence du Québec pourra être identifiée de la façon suivante: Lors des séances d'ouverture et de clôture, le président de la séance ou les autres orateurs pourront identifier le Québec et les autres provinces par des mentions appropriées.

Les documents déposés par le Québec ou les autres provinces sur toute matière de leur compétence constitutionnelle le seront en leur nom et porteront leur marque distinctive; ces documents seront cependant déposés à la conférence par la délégation canadienne dans un cahier émanant de la délégation canadienne et contenant tous les documents soumis par les provinces.

La voiture des délégués du Québec portera une plaque avec la double mention Canada et Québec, et un fanion consistant en un drapeau miniature du Québec.

Le drapeau du Québec pourra flotter sur l'hôtel où logera le Ministre québécois.

A la salle de conférence, ou à l'extérieur de cette salle, où flotteront les divers drapeaux, celui du Québec sera déployé pourvu qu'il le soit en association avec celui du Canada, la préséance étant donnée à celui-ci.

Dans le cas d'un vote éventuel à la conférence, le Canada, y compris le Québec, n'aurait qu'un seul vote. Si les membres de la délégation ne s'entendaient pas, le Canada s'abstiendrait.

Les arrangements décrits ci-dessus s'appliqueront aussi bien à la deuxième session de 1969 de la Conférence des Ministres de l'Education des Etats d'expression française d'Afrique et de Madagascar.

Ces propositions ont été élaborées avec le souci de tenir compte dans la mesure du possible du point de vue du Gouvernement du Québec et de concilier ses responsabilités en matière d'éducation et celles du Gouvernement du Canada en matière de politique extérieure.

Etant donné la date prochaine de la conférence en question, je vous serais obligé de me faire savoir le plus tôt possible si votre gouvernement est d'accord sur les propositions énoncées ci-dessus.

Je vous ai subséquemment appelé de Londres pour poursuivre nos discussions. Ces propositions constituaient une innovation importante dans ce domaine et répondaient, je crois, au désir d'innover que nous partageons. Il va sans dire que toute autre province pourrait se prévaloir de ces dispositions.

Je regrette qu'il ne vous ait pas été possible de répondre autrement que par votre décision d'accepter l'invitation adressée ces jours derniers à votre Ministre de l'Education de la part du Secrétariat Technique de la Conférence.

Vous comprendrez qu'il est essentiel pour le Gouvernement du Canada d'assurer qu'il n'y ait qu'une seule délégation canadienne à des conférences intergouvernementales comme celle qui se tiendra à Kinshasa le 13 janvier. Le Gouvernement du Canada ne saurait accepter sans qu'il soit porté gravement atteinte à la personnalité internationale du Canada et à son unité que des invitations à de telles conférences soient envoyées à des provinces canadiennes. Le Gouvernement du Canada ne saurait non plus accepter que des provinces soient représentées de leur propre chef à de telles conférences. Nous continuons d'espérer que le Gouvernement du Québec participera à la délégation canadienne à Kinshasa selon les normes énoncées dans mon télégramme et lors de notre conversation téléphonique. Ces normes prévoient une identification appropriée des provinces.

Dans votre télégramme du 9 janvier vous avez déclaré que pour résoudre le problème immédiat qui se pose à nos gouvernements, la délégation du Québec dûment identifiée se joindra sur place aux autres représentants de la délégation canadienne. Tenant compte des principes énoncés ci-dessus, la délégation canadienne sera évidemment heureuse d'accueillir en son sein le Ministre d'Etat à l'Education et ses collaborateurs.

Je voudrais vous laisser savoir que la délégation canadienne en plus de l'Honorable Jean-Marie Morin et des autres représentants que vous avez annoncés hier sera présidée par l'Honorable Louis Robichaud, Premier Ministre du Nouveau Brunswick, et comprendra en outre Monsieur Armand Saint-Onge, Sous-Ministre de l'Education du Nouveau Brunswick, Monsieur Jean-Marc Tessier, Surintendant adjoint des Programmes Scolaires pour la province de l'Ontario. Des conseillers fédéraux seront en outre attachés à la délégation.

Pierre-Elliott Trudeau
Premier Ministre du Canada

72. Conférence des Ministres de l'education: Paris, 1 au 4 décembre 1969

Echange de lettres entre les Premiers ministres Bertrand et Trudeau.

Ottawa, le 26 novembre 1969

Monsieur le Premier ministre,

Vous êtes déjà au courant que le gouvernement du Canada enverra une délégation à la deuxième session de la Conférence des Ministres de l'Education d'expression française, qui se tiendra à Paris du 1er au 4 décembre 1969.

A la suite d'entretiens qui ont eu lieu récemment entre nos représentants respectifs au sujet de cette Conférence, les fonctionnaires québécois concernés ont transmis à mes représentants le texte d'arrangements *ad hoc* qui se rapportent à la participation du Québec à la délégation canadienne à cette Conférence. Je crois savoir que ce texte, qui nous est parvenu le 24 novembre, a déjà reçu votre assentiment.

Je me félicite que ces arrangements *ad hoc*, dont je joins copie pour mémoire, permettront une présence québécoise importante au sein de la délégation canadienne. Je demande donc au ministère des Affaires extérieures de prendre des dispositions immédiates en vue d'une réunion de la délégation avant son départ. Des agents du ministère se mettront sans délai en rapport avec vos représentants à cette fin.

Veuillez agréer, Monsieur le Premier ministre, l'assurance de ma haute considération.

(P. E. Trudeau)

le 21 novembre 1969

"Sommaire des arrangements *ad hoc* concernant la deuxième session de la Conférence des ministres de l'éducation d'expression française à Paris, du 1er au 4 décembre 1969.

1. Le Québec déléguera à la Conférence de Paris son ministre de l'éducation qui agira comme président de la délégation canadienne.

   Celle-ci comprendra, en outre des délégués du Québec, des délégués des autres provinces s'il en est, et des conseillers en affaires étrangères de l'administration fédérale.

2. Une réunion des participants aura lieu avant le départ pour Paris.

3. Le ministre de l'éducation du Québec parlera au nom du Québec sur toute matière du domaine de la compétence constitutionnelle du Québec. Les délégués des autres provinces parleront de même. La délégation canadienne s'exprimera par la voix de son président, ou à défaut, celle de son vice-président.

4. La présence du Québec pourra être identifié de la façon suivante:

   —lors de la séance solennelle d'ouverture de même qu'à la séance de clôture, le président de la séance, ou les autres orateurs, pourront identifier le Québec au sein de la délégation canadienne par une mention appropriée;

   —la voiture des délégués québécois portera une plaque avec la double mention Canada et Québec, et des fanions consistant en des drapeaux miniatures du Canada et du Québec;

   —le drapeau du Québec pourra flotter sur l'hôtel où logera le ministre québécois;

   —à la salle de conférence ou à l'extérieur de cette salle, si l'on fait flotter les divers drapeaux, celui du Québec sera déployé pourvu qu'il le soit en association avec celui du Canada, la préséance étant donnée à celui-ci.

5. Dans le cas d'un vote éventuel à la Conférence, la délégation canadienne n'aurait qu'un seul vote. Si les membres de la délégation ne s'entendaient pas, le Canada s'abstiendrait.

6. Dans la salle de conférence, la délégation canadienne sera identifiée par une plaque se lisant "Canada". Des plaques placées derrière la plaque "Canada" identifieront les provinces représentées au sein de la délégation comme suit: "Canada-Québec", "Canada – Nouveau Brunswick", etc. Les lettres indiquant les noms des provinces seront de dimension comparable à celles indiquant le nom du Canada.

7. La liste officielle de la délégation canadienne sera présentée à la Conférence selon le format suivant:

Délégation du Canada
  Québec: Honorable Jean-Marie Morin, Président

  _____

  _____

Québec, le 27 novembre 1969.

Monsieur le Premier ministre,

Je réponds aux lettres que vous m'avez transmises par télex hier et aujourd'hui. L'une portait sur la conférence des ministres de l'Education et l'autre sur la conférence des ministres de la Jeunesse et des Sports. Ces deux conférences ont lieu à Paris la semaine prochaine.

Je suis d'accord avec les arrangements *ad hoc* auxquels nous en sommes arrivés à la suite des consultations qui ont eu lieu entre les représentants de nos deux gouvernements. Ces arrangements sont en substance semblables à ceux qui ont prévalu à Kinshasa en janvier dernier, et j'estime qu'ils permettront une collaboration heureuse de la délégation québécoise avec les délégations des autres provinces intéressées ainsi qu'avec les conseillers de l'administration fédérale qui seront sur les lieux, constituant tous ensemble la délégation canadienne.

J'ajoute toutefois que cet accord étant fait de nuances et de choix de termes, j'aurais souhaité que la correspondance échangée sur le sujet reflète avec autant de précision que possible l'esprit qui y préside. Vous dites dans votre lettre concernant la conférence des ministres de l'Education que "le gouvernement du Canada enverra une délégation" à cette conférence. Dire plutôt qu'il y aura une délégation canadienne composée des délégations d'un certain nombre de provinces et de conseillers en affaires étrangères de l'administration fédérale me paraîtrait plus conforme au texte des arrangements conclus et au concept recherché.

Je vous prie d'agréer, monsieur le Premier ministre, l'expression de mes sentiments les meilleurs.

(J. J. Bertrand)

73. Canada and La Francophonie

Statement by the Prime Minister, Mr. Pierre-Elliott Trudeau, on the occasion of the signing of agreements with the President of Niger, Mr. Diori Hamani, Ottawa, September 19, 1969. (Extracts)

Canada, with six million French-speaking citizens, is naturally a part of the francophone family. For Canada, the active participation in *la Francophonie* that is being organized is a necessity. In the North American setting, our country intends to reinforce its French characteristics and to spread their influence far afield. To that end, Canada must enter into close relations with all the peoples of the world who express themselves and assert themselves in the French language.

This is true for the French-Canadian people in the Province of Quebec, which is the home *par excellence* of French culture in Canada. It is also true for the one million French Canadians in other Canadian provinces.

This participation in *la Francophonie* is, moreover, an extension of Canadian bilingualism on an international scale. It is thus a fundamental element, and a permanent one, in our policy. I say further that our bilingualism should be expressed not only through co-operation among French-speaking people but also in all of our foreign policy, especially within international organizations.

Co-operation with the French-speaking world has existed for some time through a whole network of bilateral relations, first of all in Europe, then in Africa and Asia. We shall continue to further systematically these relations as new prospects for multilateral co-operation open before us.

You are especially known in Canada, Mr. President, as one of the most important builders of *la Francophonie*. You will succeed, I am sure, in providing it with the structures envisaged at the Niamey Conference.

The Niamey Conference marked a turning-point, because it was decided at the time to study the possibility of establishing an agency for "cultural and technical co-operation". Co-operation among French-speaking nations will thus be placed on an organized basis—multilateral and intergovernmental. Canada has promised its full support in this project; we have already made a financial contribution to the agency's provisional secretariat. We shall maintain our support.

We view this agency not as a political community but as an instrument for multilateral aid in cultural and technical matters between French-speaking countries. We are prepared to recognize it as an agency for co-ordination, promotion and implementation, an agency that will evolve and expand in the light of experience. The agency will have to pioneer in unexplored or neglected areas. In short, Mr. President, we hope that the agency will play a major role in the organization of *la Francophonie*.

The Canadian Government intends to support African efforts towards economic expansion and social development. Considerable sums have been devoted to this end. Since 1960 it has been promoting a program of aid to French-speaking Africa by means of a fund that has almost doubled each year, reaching a total of $30 million in 1969. And this is only a beginning. Canada wants to see a strong, prosperous Africa, whose peoples are truly forging ahead.

74. Conference de Niamey, mars 1970*

Article 1: Sommaire des Arrangements ad hoc pour la Deuxième Conférence des Pays Francophones

A. Un Ministre ou Haut Fonctionnaire du Gouvernement Québécois sera désigné pour faire partie de la délégation canadienne dont il sera le Vice-Président. La délégation comprendra des membres du Gouvernement et de l'administration fédérale et des délégués en provenance des provinces.

B. La délégation se réunira en temps utile, avant son départ, pour coordonner la participation canadienne à la conférence;

C. La délégation canadienne s'exprimera par la voix de son Président ou, à défaut, de son Vice-Président. Le Ministre ou Haut Fonctionnaire du Gouvernement Québécois pourra parler au nom du

---

* Communiqué, Ministère des Affaires extérieures, Ottawa, 24 mars 1970.

Québec sur toute matière de la compétence constitutionnelle du Gouvernement Québécois. Les délégués en provenance des autres provinces pourront faire de même. Il y aura consultation préalable sur les points de vue à mettre de l'avant à la conférence.

D. Dans le cas d'un vote éventuel à la Conférence, la délégation canadienne n'aura qu'un seul vote. Si les membres de la délégation ne s'entendaient pas sur une matière relevant de la compétence législative exclusive des provinces, la délégation s'abstiendrait.

E. La signature du Canada sera apposée comme suit: A la place qui lui est réservée et sous la signature du Président de la délégation apparaîtront immédiatement la signature du Ministre ou Haut Fonctionnaire du Gouvernement Québécois ainsi que celles d'un délégué en provenance de chacune des autres provinces. On s'en tiendra pour ces signatures à la formule suivante: "Gérard Pelletier, Secrétaire d'Etat du Canada"; "Julien Chouinard, Secrétaire Général du Gouvernement du Québec".

F. La présence du Québec pourra être identifiée comme suit, à la lumière des usages locaux. Il en sera de même des autres provinces.

1. Lors de la séance solennelle d'ouverture, de même qu'à la séance de clôture, le Président de la séance, ou les autres orateurs, pourront identifier le Québec au sein de la délégation canadienne par une mention appropriée.

2. La voiture des délégués québécois portera une plaque avec la double mention Canada et Québec, et les fanions consistant en des drapeaux miniatures du Canada et du Québec.

3. Le drapeau du Québec pourra flotter sur l'hôtel où logera le Ministre Québécois.

4. A la salle de conférence ou à l'extérieur de cette salle, si l'on fait flotter les divers drapeaux, celui du Québec sera déployé pourvu qu'il le soit en association avec celui du Canada, la préséance étant donnée à celui-ci.

5. Dans la salle de conférence, la délégation canadienne sera identifiée par une plaque se lisant Canada. Une plaque placée derrière la plaque Canada identifiera le Québec au sein de la délégation, comme suit: Canada-Québec. Les lettres indiquant le nom du Québec seront de dimension comparable à celles indiquant le nom du Canada.

G. La liste officielle de la délégation canadienne sera présentée à la conférence selon le format suivant:

"Délégation du Canada

M. Gérard Pelletier   Secrétaire d'Etat du Canada
                        Président et Chef de la Délégation.

M. Julien Chouinard
Québec: Secrétaire Général du Gouvernement du
                                 Québec et Vice-Ministre du Conseil exécu-
                                 tif; Vice-Président de la délégation.

Ontario: M ....
Nouveau-Brunswick: M ....
Manitoba: M ....
Conseillers: M ....
                               .... ,,

*Article II: Arrangements Relatifs au Rôle du Gouvernement Québécois
dans la Participation canadienne à l'Agence*

A. Conférences Générales

Un membre ou haut fonctionnaire du Gouvernement Québécois sera
normalement Vice-Président de la délégation. On pourra s'entendre
sur la présidence d'un Ministre ou Haut Fonctionnaire du Gouvernement Québécois, selon les circonstances et la nature des intérêts en
cause à chaque conférence. Pour que la délégation comprenne un
nombre satisfaisant de représentants québécois et autres, on proposera
que le nombre de délégués par pays ne soit pas limité à cinq. Cependant, les frais de délégués supplémentaires pourraient ne pas être à la
charge de l'agence.

Il y aura une présence adéquate de représentants québécois dans les
commissions et comités, compte tenu des règlements de la conférence
générale.

Les arrangements *ad hoc* pour la conférence constitutive s'appliqueront aux conférences générales en ce qui concerne les réunions de
la délégation avant les conférences, l'expression des points de vue
fédéraux et provinciaux, l'identification du Québec et la liste de la
délégation. Si des modifications étaient requises par les circonstances,
les autorités fédérales et provinciales intéressées verraient à s'entendre
à ce sujet.

B. Conseil Executif

Le Québec occupera un des postes disponibles pour le Canada au
conseil exécutif.

C. Secrétariat Général

Il y aura consultation à l'intérieur de la délégation au sujet d'une candidature canadienne au secrétariat général.

D. Finances

La contribution canadienne aux frais de l'agence sera présentée de la façon suivante dans les rapports de l'agence: "Contribution du Canada: $ ——, dont le Gouvernement Central a contribué $ ——, le Québec $ ——, l'Ontario $ ——, etc. ... "

Tout en notant que les contributions nationales seront versées globalement au budget général de l'agence, le Québec entend computer sa participation à la contribution du Canada sur les bases suivantes:

(A) Frais d'opération du Secrétariat:
—participation du Québec jusqu'à concurrence d'un montant égal à celui que contribuera le Gouvernement fédéral;

(B) Programmes d'action de l'agence:
—la contribution canadienne au coût des programmes de l'agence sera en principe fournie par le gouvernement fédéral, mais le Québec pourrait accroître sa participation à la contribution canadienne selon l'intérêt qu'il portera à ces programmes.

Les autres provinces peuvent évidemment participer à la contribution si elles le souhaitent.

75. Modalités selon lesquelles le Gouvernement du Québec est admis comme Gouvernement Participant aux Institutions, aux Activités et aux Programmes de L'Agence de Coopération Culturelle et Technique, Convenues le 1ᵉʳ octobre 1971 entre le Gouvernement du Canada et le Gouvernement du Québec.*

L'article 3.3 de la Charte de l'Agence de Coopération culturelle et technique prévoyant que:

Dans le plein respect de la souveraineté et de la compétence internationale des Etats membres, tout gouvernement peut être admis comme gouverne-

---

* Communiqué, Ministère des Affaires extérieures, Ottawa, le 8 octobre 1971.

ment participant aux institutions, aux activités et programmes de l'Agence, sous réserve de l'approbation de l'Etat membre dont relève le territoire sur lequel le gouvernement participant concerné exerce son autorité et selon les modalités convenues entre ce gouvernement et celui de l'Etat membre,

les modalités suivantes selon lesquelles le gouvernement du Québec est admis comme gouvernement participant aux institutions, aux activités et aux programmes de l'Agence sont convenues.

Participation aux Institutions

Article 1
Le gouvernement du Québec participe aux institutions de l'Agence:

Conseil d'Administration
Comité des Programmes
Conseil consultatif
Autres comités et commissions
Secrétariat général
Groupe d'experts en gestion administrative et financière
Conférence générale

Des modalités sont prévues à cet effet pour chaque institution.*

76. Alberta and Oil Diplomacy

Statement by Mr. Peter Lougheed, Premier of Alberta, Ottawa, November 7, 1971, as reported in the Toronto Globe and Mail, *November 8, 1971.*

OTTAWA—Alberta Premier Peter Lougheed said yesterday that his province should participate with the Federal Government in establish-

---

* There follow here the articles of the agreement (two to nineteen inclusive) describing the precise way in which Quebec participates in the activities of each body mentioned in Article 1, as well as the manner in which Quebec takes part in the programs and activities of the Agency. By virtue of Article 17, the Government of Quebec contributes 50% of the Canadian share of the operating costs of the Agency's secretariat, headquartered in Paris. Canada's overall contribution to the Agency's total annual budget (staff and other administrative and operating costs, programs, and related development activities and assistance) amounts to 35%, of which Quebec pays 2%. The full text is available from the DEA, Ottawa.

ing a national energy policy, and that Alberta should have official observer status at federal meetings with other countries over energy matters.

Interviewed on the CTV public affairs program *Question Period*, Mr. Lougheed said that if Alberta were allowed to participate directly in discussions relating to the sales of natural resources and domestic energy policy, he would reconsider a decision to open a "listening post" in Washington.*

Mr. Lougheed first suggested opening a provincial office in Washington during the Alberta election campaign last summer. The federal government is known to be opposed to such a move.

According to Mr. Lougheed, however, gas and oil installations in Alberta are extensive and important enough to warrant giving his province a direct voice in sales and policy negotiations.

He said yesterday: "I think it would be quite in order for the government of the province of Alberta to have an official observer, of our choosing, sitting there at the discussions—be they at the ministerial level or at the official level between Canada and the United States—if energy is to be one of the major subjects discussed".

Mr. Lougheed described the role of a provincial official in Washington as being essentially that of a lobbyist who would also keep his government informed, and protect Alberta's oil interests.

---

* This was not followed through and at this writing (January 1977) no Alberta Government representative has been stationed in Washington. Quebec has an Education Counsellor attached to the Canadian Embassy in Abidjan.

X. Foreign Policy Review: 1968-1970

> The foreign policy of this country is so obvious that it does not require much discussion. (R. B. Bennett, February 9, 1937)

Foreign policy is not created in a vacuum. Possibly the most fundamental influence on the formulation and implementation of a country's foreign policy is its geographical location. A country's site tends to give to its external policies a degree of continuity frequently more consistent and longer lasting than its internal policies. The foreign policy of the Czars and the Commissars, for instance, had much in common; that of pre-Mao and post-Mao China also. History, traditions, culture—and those of a country's neighbours—are also basic components. Canada and Poland both have powerful neighbours. Yet how different their histories and foreign policies are.

For 20 years after the Second World War, Canada's foreign policy was remarkably stable. If one compares the basic principles outlined by Secretary of State for External Affairs St-Laurent in the Gray Lectures of 1947 at the University of Toronto* and Mr. Paul Martin's outline of 1967, given as the first document below, the similarities are striking. Domestic policies during that 20-year period changed much more.

In his reflections on the basic principles underlying Canadian foreign policy, Mr. Martin stressed development and social justice more than Mr. St-Laurent did two decades earlier. It is interesting to note that these two themes are given even greater prominence today as a result of the Trudeau Government's foreign policy review of 1968-1970. In a way, they served as a link between the two eras.

New themes such as the environment and the quality of life, which constitute two of the six basic aspects of the conceptual framework of Canada's current approach to external relations, reflect concerns which were not so much at the forefront during the previous decades. In the foreign policy review of 1968-1970, a hexagon was used to depict this conceptual framework and background. This hexagon is illustrated below.

---

* See R.A.M., p. 388.

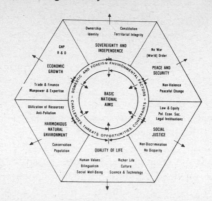

THE FOREIGN-POLICY HEXAGON*

In each segment the 'key words' in small print indicate the kind of policy questions that may arise, though not always under the same theme necessarily.

The straight arrows indicate the relationship between basic national aims and external functions. The one-way arrows in the inner circle indicate the everchanging environmental factors: the two-way arrows in the outer circle signify the interrelationships among the policy themes.

The decision to review Canada's foreign policy was one of the first taken by the new administration during the spring of 1968. The background, evolution, and at times turmoil occasioned by the review, as well as the responses it drew, are ably presented in the books of Bruce Thordarson and Peter Dobell.**

The review took the form of six booklets entitled *Foreign Policy for Canadians*, which were released on June 25, 1970. Extracts are given below.

Relations with the United States were not dealt with directly in the booklets, although the subject permeated all of them. This topic was the subject of a separate study in 1973, presented in a special issue of *International Perspectives*, the bi-monthly journal published by the Department of External Affairs. It has become known as the "Third Option" and is documented in Chapter III.

---

*Canada. House of Commons. The Standing Committee on External Affairs and National Defence. "Fourth Report respecting 'Foreign Policy for Canadians'." June 1971. p. 48.

** *Trudeau and Foreign Policy*, Bruce Thordarson (Toronto: Oxford University Press, 1972); *Canada's Search for New Roles*, Peter Dobell (Toronto: Oxford University Press, 1972).

To round out this Chapter, a special section on Canadian relations with the Soviet Union has been included. Although nowhere near as prominent or as important as relations with United States, Western Europe, or Japan, their growth in recent years reflects the Government's desire to diversify Canada's foreign policy.

In conclusion, mention should be made of an in-house review of Canadian foreign policy undertaken by the Department of External Affairs in late 1967. It was conducted by a former Under-Secretary, Norman Robertson, with the assistance of two senior foreign service officers, Geoffrey Murray and Geoffrey Pearson. It was concluded early the following year and was circulated to the Prime Minister, the Secretary of State for External Affairs, and senior Departmental officers. While the existence of this review is well known, its contents have not been released.* In *Trudeau and Foreign Policy*, Bruce Thordarson deals with its background and certain of its facets, which presage some of the results of the 1968-1970 review, thereby illustrating the continuum characteristic of the evolution of foreign policy generally.⁻

77. Canadian Foreign Policy, 1967

Statement by Mr. Paul Martin, Secretary of State for External Affairs, at Waterloo Lutheran University Convocation, May 22, 1967. (Extracts)

Early in 1947, shortly after he had been appointed Secretary of State for External Affairs, the Right Honourable Louis St-Laurent gave a lecture at the University of Toronto in which he set out to define the principles underlying Canadian foreign policy. As Mr. St-Laurent pointed out in his lecture, a policy in world affairs, to be truly effective, must have its foundations laid upon general principles which have been tested in the life of the nation and which have secured the broad support of large groups of the population.

The principles which Mr. St-Laurent distinguished were as follows:

1. national unity;
2. political liberty;
3. the rule of law in national and international affairs;
4. the values of Christian civilization;
5. the acceptance of international responsibility in keeping with our conception of our role in world affairs.

---

* The Robertson review may be consulted on request at the Historical Division, DEA, Ottawa.

Twenty years have passed, but I think the principles listed by Mr. St-Laurent would still be widely accepted in Canada as guidelines in the conduct of our foreign policy. However, it seems to me that they may need to be expanded somewhat, if they are to reflect the realities of the modern world.

In particular, I believe that we must now acknowledge that national security is a vital factor underlying our foreign policy. The survival of Canada is necessarily our primary objective.

To the conception of political liberty, I think we should now want to add that of social justice, for it has become increasingly evident that the freedom we so rightly prize can flourish only when there is a social order characterized by a fair distribution of wealth and equal opportunity for all. Hand in hand with this principle would go another—namely, economic development, both in Canada and in the world at large.

We might also rephrase the last principle, or guideline, as the acceptance of international responsibility in accordance with our own interests and our ability to contribute towards the building of a peaceful and secure international system. While it is not inappropriate to speak of our role in world affairs, it may be misleading, in that it can lead to the belief that there is some particular role that we are predestined to play. As with other countries, Canada's foreign policy must ultimately reflect its national interests, the foremost of which is, of course, the maintenance of world peace.

In summary, then, it appears to me that the basic principles, or guidelines, underlying our foreign policy could be listed as follows:

1. national security;
2. national unity;
3. political liberty and social justice;
4. the rule of law in national and international affairs;
5. economic development in Canada and the world;
6. the values of Christian civilization;
7. acceptance of international responsibility, in accordance with our interests, and our ability to contribute towards the building of peace.

In 1947, it was possible for Mr. St-Laurent to discuss the practical application of the principles which he had listed under a limited number of headings: the Commonwealth, relations with the United States, traditional ties with France, and support for constructive international organization. None of these applications has diminished in importance, but circumstances have so changed as to require a much broader view now than was either possible or necessary 20 years ago. Indeed, there is now no part of the world which lies outside the scope of Canadian foreign policy.

In the period since the war, there have been two particularly significant changes in the nature of international affairs which have had major implications for our foreign policy. The first is the very great increase in the number of sovereign, independent states during the last 20 years, resulting from the dissolution of the old European empires in Africa and Asia. This change has, of course, been most strikingly illustrated in the continent of Africa, where the number of independent countries has increased from four in 1945 to 37 today.

The emergence into the mainstream of world affairs of so many newly independent states has had implications far beyond the increase in absolute numbers. For many of the new nations, independence has been only the first step in the often difficult and agonizing process of nation-building. In the great majority of them, standards of material well-being have been extremely low, and the complex technological and industrial society which we now almost take for granted in the older, Western countries was virtually unknown. Under the circumstances, it was only to be expected that instability and uncertainty would characterize the newly independent states as they embarked on the enormous and challenging task of simultaneously building modern economies and modern national societies.

The second major change in the nature of international affairs which deserves special mention is the greatly increased complexity and diversity of economic relations between states. While trade has traditionally been one of the first and most important factors in bringing peoples and nations into contact with one another, trade is now only one aspect of the economic relations between states, and even it has grown immensely both in volume and complexity over the years. Other, newer aspects of international economic relations include those in the fields of monetary management and of development assistance.

The evolving nature of economic relations between states has given rise to the establishment of a whole range of influential international organizations, such as the International Monetary Fund, the World Bank, the General Agreement on Tariffs and Trade, and the Organization for Economic Co-operation and Development. There is also, of course, the United Nations itself, which, through the United Nations Development Program and the various Specialized Agencies, has assumed major responsibilities in the economic field. The importance of this is underlined by the fact that four-fifths of the financial and manpower resources available to the United Nations system are now applied to the tasks of economic development.

The international effort which is now being made to assist the economic development of the developing countries is perhaps the most clear-cut, practical illustration of the widespread realization that nations are not rivals in their efforts to grow and prosper but necessary partners. The responsibilities of governments for human welfare arc no longer limited by national boundaries. This represents a marked, indeed a revolutionary, change from conceptions that prevailed even two or three decades ago.

As one of the major developed countries, Canada has a clear responsibility to participate fully in the task of international development. Canada's programmes of development assistance began when the Colombo Plan was established in 1950, and have now grown to approximately $300 million a year. The Government has taken the decision to increase its contributions to international development to the level of one per cent of our national income by the early 1970s.

Canada's aid programmes are but one example of the way in which our foreign policy has evolved in recent years in accordance with the guidelines set out by Mr. St-Laurent in 1947. Another example can be found in our developing association with the "Francophone" countries.

It is true now, as it was 20 years ago, that our foreign policy must reflect both our French and English heritages if it is to contribute to national unity. There are now many more French-speaking countries than there were in 1947, and the scope for valuable associations based on our French heritage has greatly increased. I am convinced that all Canada stands to benefit from this development.

Our efforts to establish the rule of law in international affairs are concentrated now, as they have been since 1945, in the United Nations. Canada has been ready to contribute to United Nations peacekeeping operations, and to support the United Nations in other ways, in the firm belief that through this international organization we are helping build a firm structure of international order.

Like any forum embracing different members, and reflecting different viewpoints, the United Nations is only as strong and as effective as its members choose to make it. For this reason, I believe it is of vital importance that the United Nations be made truly universal, and that the power to make decisions within the United Nations context be clearly related to the responsibility which ultimately devolves on member states for their implementation. It is also, I believe, most important that the nations of the world realize that the effectiveness of the United Nations, and, in the final analysis, their own security, depend on their willingness to accept modifications in the conception of national sovereignty in accordance with the interests of the wider international community.

78. Canada and the World, 1968

Statement by the Prime Minister, Mr. Pierre-Elliott Trudeau, issued on May 29, 1968. (Extracts)*

There is no reason for running down Canada's post-war record in international affairs. In many respects it was a brilliant record, for which we owe much to the inspiring leadership of the Right Honourable Lester Pearson, both as External Affairs Minister and as Prime Minister.

Reassessment has become necessary not because of the inadequacies of the past but because of the changing nature of Canada and of the world around us.

All of us need to ponder well what our national capacity is—what our potential may be—for participating effectively in international affairs. We shall do more good by doing well what we know to be within our resources to do than by pretending either to ourselves or to others that we can do things clearly beyond our national capability.

Canada's position in the world is now very different from that of the post-war years. Then we were probably the largest of the small powers. Our currency was one of the strongest. We were the fourth or fifth trading nation and our economy was much stronger than the European economies. Ours were among the very strongest navy and air forces. But now Europe has regained its strength. The Third World has emerged.

It is for us to decide whether and how we can make the best use abroad of the special skills, experience and opportunities which our political, economic and cultural evolution have produced in this rich and varied country.

Realism—that should be the operative word in our definition of international aim; realism in how we read the world barometer; realism in how we see ourselves thriving in the climate it forecasts. For we must begin with a concrete appraisal of the prevailing atmosphere—

---

* This document should be read in conjunction with the Prime Minister's statement of April 3, 1969, to which it is the backdrop. (See Chapter II above, Document No. 14).

conscious always that rapid change is likely to be its chief characteristic.

What are some of the salient features we face?

The peace which we value most rests mainly on a balance of nuclear terror. Fortunately, the two super-powers have kept the terror firmly within their grasp and have been showing increasing responsibility about unleashing it. The threat of a major military clash has measurably receded, but not the need to ensure that the intricate power balance is maintained by a wide variety of means.

International tension is sustained in various regions and in varying degrees because of localized hostilities, latent disputes, racial discrimination, economic and social distress. Whatever comfort we can take from the most recent developments in Vietnam, we dare not disregard the dangers inherent in the Middle East impasse, the race conflicts in the southern half of Africa, the heavy pressure of urgent needs in the developing world. In Europe there remains the lingering threat of an unresolved German problem, which must be resolved if that continent is to capitalize on its growing desire to draw together and not turn once again down the dangerous road to aggressive nationalism.

It is no longer realistic to think in terms of a single model of organization and development in Eastern Europe or of a monolithic Communist unity such as Stalin could impose. There has been a perceptible *détente* in East-West relations. There has been a growing recognition in Eastern European countries of the need through economic reforms to adapt their economies to national needs, rather than adhere in a doctrinaire way to an economic model inspired largely by nineteenth century conceptions. Although it remains true that there are some fundamental and far-reaching differences between us and the Communist countries, it is no longer true to say that the Communist world is monolithically and implacably hostile to us.

Economic and social development continues to pose a major international problem, and it will increasingly engage the initiative, energy and resources of the world community far into the future. The essential needs of the developing countries require a vigorous, comprehensive and co-ordinated response from all the organizations, agencies and individual nations seeking to alleviate the areas of want in the world. The realities of this North-South relation are such that humanity as a whole cannot rest easy until a steady and solid progress toward a better balance between have and have-not nations has been assured.

The international institutions and methods which have been adopted for dealing with the demands of the contemporary world situation have to be brought into closer alignment with actual developments, and especially with the revolutionary desires of rising generations in all parts of the world. If man is to become the master rather than the victim of his restless genius for material progress, he must radically reduce the distance between his ever-advancing attainment in science and technology and the rather sluggish evolution of international instruments for maintaining political and economic order.

All round the earth, nations suffer the nervous exhaustion of living in an atmosphere of armed threat. It is risky enough that two superpowers, armed even now for "overkill", continue their competition for the most advanced weaponry. It does not help that secondary powers have embarked on nuclear-arms programmes. But, even if it becomes possible to contain the nuclear competition, the world will still have to face what almost amounts to an unrestrained, and perhaps uncontrollable, traffic in conventional arms of all kinds, which, far from adding to security, tend to induce insecurity and increase tension.

In most of these international contexts, China continues to be both a colossus and a conundrum. Potentially, the People's Republic of China poses a major threat to peace largely because calculations about Chinese ambitions, intentions, capacity to catch up and even about actual developments within China have to be based on incomplete information—which opens an area of unpredictability. Mainland China's exclusion from the world community stems partly from policies of non-recognition and of seeking to contain Chinese Communism through military means, and partly from Peking's own policies and problems. Yet most of the major world issues to which I have referred will not be resolved completely, or in any lasting way, unless and until an accommodation has been reached with the Chinese nation.

Those are the broad lines of the international environment in which Canada finds itself today. What are we proposing to do about it? We are going to begin with a thorough and comprehensive review of our foreign policy which embraces defence, economic and aid policies. Policy review is part of the normal process of any government, but we wish to take a fresh look at the fundamentals of Canadian foreign policy to see whether there are ways in which we can serve more effectively Canada's current interests, objectives and priorities.

Our approach will be pragmatic and realistic—above all, to see that our policies in the future accord with our national needs and resources, with our ability to discharge Canada's legitimate responsibilities in world affairs.

Our progressive involvement in international development and relations during two decades or more have given this country a position of prominence and distinction. The policy area to be reviewed is broad and complex. In our review, we shall be giving special attention to certain areas.

We as a Government must discharge our duty to the people of Canada in meeting the needs of national security. In the narrowest sense, this could mean the strengthening of North American defence arrangements in a manner calculated to safeguard our national sovereignty and at the same time to make the best use of resources allocated to national defence. But the defence strategies of our time are neither static nor restricted in scope. NATO and NORAD, though not linked organizationally, are complementary in their strategic importance and implication. They are an integral part of the delicate balance of power on which the peace of the world has rested during a long and difficult period. We shall take a hard look, in consultation with our allies, at our military role in NATO and determine whether our present military commitment is still appropriate to the present situation in Europe. We shall look at our role in NORAD in the light of the technological advances of modern weaponry and of our fundamental opposition to the proliferation of nuclear weapons.

Canada continues to have a very large stake in Europe, perhaps not so much in the military sense of two decades ago but in political, commercial and cultural terms. We have been fascinated and greatly encouraged by the marked improvements in the political and economic situation in Europe as a whole, in both the Eastern and Western sectors. It seems almost axiomatic that, far from relaxing them, Canada should seek to strengthen its ties with the European nations, whose many and varied cultures contribute so much to our own. We should seek to join with them in new forms of partnership and cooperation in order to strengthen international security, to promote economic stability on both sides of the Atlantic and in other regions of the world, to balance our own relations in the Western Hemisphere.

We have a major aim of maintaining mutual confidence and respect in our relations with the United States. We have to sort out the dilemmas which that complex relation poses for us so as to widen the area of mutual benefit without diminishing our Canadian identity and sovereign independence.

We have to take greater account of the ties which bind us to other nations in this Hemisphere—in the Caribbean, Latin America—and of their economic needs. We have to explore new avenues of increasing our political and economic relations with Latin America, where more than 400 million people will live by the turn of the century and where we have substantial interests.

We accept as a heavy responsibility of higher priority Canada's participation in programmes for the economic and social development of nations in the developing areas. We shall be exploring all means of increasing the impact of our aid programmes by concentrating on places and projects in which our bilingualism, our own expertise and experience, our resources and facilities make possible an effective and distinctively Canadian contribution. We see Africa as an area of growing activity, but not to the exclusion of other regions in which Canada's aid effort is well established. We intend, moreover, to combine these efforts with initiatives, policies and leadership relating to trade which will enable the developing nations to attain lasting improvement in their economies.

We shall be guided by considerations such as the foregoing in sustaining our support for international organizations—and especially the United Nations family. We believe that Canada's contribution to the co-operative efforts of those organizations may benefit from some shift of emphasis but there will be no slackening of our broad policy of support. In making our reappraisal, we shall be looking for realistic means for making multilateral organizations as effective as possible and, correspondingly, Canada's participation in their endeavours.

We shall be looking at our policy in relation to China in the context of a new interest in Pacific affairs generally. Because of past preoccupations with Atlantic and European affairs, we have tended to overlook the reality that Canada is a Pacific country too. Canada has long advocated a positive approach to mainland China and its inclusion in the world community. We have an economic interest in trade with China—no doubt shared by others—and a political interest in preventing tension between China and its neighbours, but especially between China and the United States. Our aim will be to recognize the People's Republic of China Government as soon as possible and to enable that Government to occupy the seat of China in the United Nations, taking into account that there is a separate government in Taiwan.

As I suggested earlier, in reviewing the international situation and our external policies, we are likely to find that many of the problems are the same ones which Canada has faced for many years—global and regional tensions, under-development, economic disruptions. Our broad objectives may be similar, too—the maintenance of peace and security, the expansion and improvement of aid programmes, the search for general economic stability. But what we shall be looking for —systematically, realistically, pragmatically—will be new approaches, new methods, new opportunities. In that search we shall be seeking the views of Canadians, and particularly of those with expert knowledge in the universities and elsewhere.

We shall hope, too, to find new attitudes, for ourselves and in others, which will give us the latitude to make progress in the pursuit of those objectives. There is much evidence of a desire for this kind of change in most countries of the world. Our need is not so much to go crusading abroad as to mobilize at home our aspirations, energies and resources behind external policies which will permit Canada to play a credible and creditable part in this changing world.

To do this we need not proclaim our independence. We need not preach to others or castigate them. What we do need is to be sure that we are being as effective as we can be in carrying out our own commitments and responsibilities, which will be commensurate with our growing status and strength, with our special character.

What is our paramount interest in pursuing this kind of foreign policy? Well, the foreign policies of nations are grounded in history and geography and culture. There are very obvious major interests for most nations today—peace, prosperity, and progress of all kinds. There is always a substantial element of self-interest. In this general sense, Canada is no exception.

But at the present time (it may have always been so and certainly will be so far into the future) our paramount interest is to ensure the political survival of Canada as a federal and bilingual sovereign state. This means strengthening Canadian unity as a basically North American country. It means reflecting in our foreign relations the cultural diversity and the bilingualism of Canada as faithfully as possible. Parallel to our close ties with the Commonwealth, we should strive to develop a close relation with the *francophone* countries. It means the development of procedures so that Canada's external relations can take even more into account the interests of provincial governments in matters of provincial jurisdiction.

There are many ways of serving that paramount interest. Some of them are already abundantly apparent in the policies and methods which the Government has been promoting for some time. I have indicated throughout this statement our determination to explore every opportunity for applying such policies with maximum effect. They will be projected in the world of today and tomorrow.

Our search, our exploration, our reassessment, are motivated and directed by a desire not for new approaches for the sake of novelty but for better policies and better methods which will keep Canada effectively in the forefront of those international endeavours which realistically lie within our national resources—active and potential.

While this broad review has been set in motion by the Government, we have taken some immediate steps which will give the Canadian people an indication of the direction the Government will follow and these are:

We have decided to send before the end of 1968 a special mission at the ministerial level to tour Latin America. This mission will be designed to demonstrate the importance the Government attaches to strengthening our bilateral relations with leading Latin American countries.

In order to exploit more fully the opportunities inherent in our bilingual country, it is our intention to open five new missions by 1969 in French-speaking countries. A substantially increased share of our aid will be allocated to *francophone* countries as an important investment both in improving bilateral relations and in contributing to national unity.

Within the general review, we have set up a special task force on our relations with the countries of Western and Eastern Europe. Its purpose is to prepare detailed recommendations concerning ways in which co-operation could be further strengthened with European countries, from which so many Canadians have originated. It will study the whole range of our economic, political and cultural ties with Europe, together with the presence of Canadian military forces in Europe.

In order to stress the true objectives of our aid programme, we shall change the name of the External Aid Office to Canadian International Development Agency. Aside from removing the resentment that might be felt by some recipient countries, this change will illustrate that our preoccupation is with co-operative international development, not aid as such. In addition, we shall give speedy and favourable consideration to the creation of an International Development Research Centre. This would be an international institute established in Canada to apply the latest advances in science and technology to the problems of development and to ensure that Canadian and other aid moneys are put to the most effective use possible.

Such, then, is our liberal approach to foreign policy and Canada's position in the world. We should not exaggerate the extent of our influence upon the course of world events.

79. The Relation of Defence Policy to Foreign Policy

Statement by the Prime Minister, Mr. Pierre-Elliott Trudeau, to the Alberta Liberal Association, Calgary, April 12, 1969.

Our decisions of last week in the area of foreign policy, in the area of our defence policy and the announcement we made about NATO* are very important and very far-reaching.

Our foreign policy, the one we are defining for Canada, is also very important for another reason. Our defence budget as you know is one-sixth of the total budget. That's a lot of money—$1,800 million for defence. And it's a lot of money especially when you realize that it's accompanied by a great deal of uncertainty on the part of Canadians. There is a tendency in the past few years, when more money is needed for housing or more money is needed for anti-pollution schemes or more money is needed for social welfare legislation, for every form of expenditure in Canada (a project here, a research grant there), on the part of individuals, on the part of institutions and on the part of provincial governments, to say to the Federal Government, "Spend less on defence, you'll have more for this other worthwhile project"—whether it be education or health or housing or urban growth. There is a tendency on the part of all Canadians to say, "Take it away from defence, you will have more money for the worthwhile things"—implying, I suppose (and this comes, as I say, from many institutions, and even from provincial governments), that the money we spend on defence is not well spent.

Now this may be so, and if it is so, it is important that we correct it. It is important that we realize that the sixth of our national budget which is spent on defence is not an expenditure which is accepted as justifiable by a significant proportion of the Canadian people—and even the military themselves.

Well, what should we do about it? Are we spending too much money or are we spending too little? This is the kind of question we have been asking ourselves in Ottawa, this is the kind of question that during the election, last spring, I said that we should deal with in this Government. And we are doing it now. Our first decision we announced last week, and I want to explain to you the significance of it.

These decisions in the area of foreign policy are extremely important then for these reasons, and they are important also because of the objectives. What we want to do with this $1,800 million is to defend Canadian sovereignty and to contribute towards world peace. Why

---

* See Chapter II above.

else would Canadians want to spend money on defence? We don't want to go to war with anybody. These are the aims then of our foreign policy, to serve our national interests, and when I say national interests I am not thinking in any egotistical sense of just what's happening to Canadians. It's in our national interest to reduce the tensions in the world, tensions which spring from the two-thirds of the world's population who go to bed hungry every night, the two-thirds of the world's population who are poor whereas the other third is rich, and the tensions which spring from this great ideological struggle between the East and the West. This is the aim of our foreign policy; it is to serve our national interest and to express our national identity abroad so that other countries know us. They know what we stand for, they know what our interests are and what our values are, in the economic sphere, in the cultural sphere, in the social sphere, in the ideological sphere. This is what our foreign policy is all about.

And this is what we have been examining in the past several months in Ottawa. And some people think it is taking too long. But it will take longer, because you only re-examine your foreign policy once in a generation. You can't switch every year, you can't switch after every election.

We promised during the last election to re-examine our foreign policy, because the data, because the objective situation, have changed, because the Canadian requirements have changed over the past generation. We're beginning to realize now that we're not a one-ocean country, not an Atlantic country, not even a two-ocean country, an Atlantic and a Pacific. We're a three-ocean country. We're beginning to realize that this Pacific seaboard is more important to Canadians than we realized in the past. We're beginning to realize that countries like Japan, like China, like Australia, and those on the Pacific coast of South America are as important partners for Canadians as the nations across the Atlantic. And we're beginning to realize that in the Arctic Canadian interests are very great and that there are not only ice and barren lands up there but that there is oil and there are minerals and there is untold wealth.

And we're beginning to realize, too, in the cultural sphere that *la Francophonie* is important and that part of our national identity is having a bilingual country, and that if it is important that we remain in the British Commonwealth of Nations it is important also that we express our identity in the French-speaking countries, those that form *la Francophonie*.

And we are realizing too that the strategic factors making for peace or threatening war have changed immensely in a generation, and that the existence of ICBMs which are pre-targeted on all the major European and North American cities and which can spell immediate destruction if they are ever unleashed is a new factor. And that there is a very delicate balance, a balance of deterrent forces, between the two poles of military strength on this planet of today, and this is a new factor.

And we realize that all these factors are "inputs" in our foreign policy, and that we can't go on as we did in the past with the same foreign policy. Before the Second World War, it is said, we practically had no foreign policy, we were too small a country in terms of population and in wealth, and our foreign policy wasn't very different from that of the United States or of the United Kingdom, providing they had the same foreign policy, and when their interests diverged or were divergent, well, we tacked onto one or onto the other. So before the Second World War we didn't have a very distinct foreign policy.

After the Second World War, we were faced with a Europe which was divided into two power blocs, hostile, a Europe which had been impoverished and destroyed by war, and we realized that the tensions in Europe could be the most destructive ones for a lasting peace. And it's at that time that Canada, along with other countries, realizing the principal threat to peace was Soviet aggression, helped set up NATO as an answer to that possibility of aggression. And it's at that time that NATO was developed as a very important policy for peace in the world because Europe at that time, a Europe which had been destroyed, I repeat, by the war, had to be strengthened and had to be fortified against the danger of aggression. And as a result of that, NATO became practically all of our foreign policy. Until then our foreign policy was that of the United States or of the United Kingdom. But since '49 our foreign policy has taken on a new dimension. That was the dimension of NATO, a dimension wherein we could talk to other countries in Europe which had more or less the same values as us but which had the same interest in stopping any possibility of Soviet aggression.

Twenty years later, today, Europe has been rebuilt. The gross national product of the NATO countries in Europe is over $500 billion. The population, 300 million people. Canada's contribution to this Europe, important though it has been and important though it remains, is marginal—20 million people against 300 million. Our defence policy, which flowed from this foreign policy of NATO, now was more to impress our friends than frighten our enemies. Our contribution in Europe which was brought in in the early years after the Second World War was very important then; it is marginal now in terms of strict military strength—one mechanized division against perhaps 80 or 55, depending on how you count them. This is our contribution. It is important; I am not trying to belittle it. But we have to remain free to decide our own foreign policy. And when we are told that we shouldn't be taking a free ride to peace in the world, when we are told that if we withdraw from NATO even in any degree this will lead other countries to withdraw from NATO, I don't admit this. I don't admit that Europeans or even Americans won't follow their own wisdom, that they don't have their own foreign policy. And I don't admit that our friends and allies will be guided in their decisions and determined in their actions by what Canadians do, and, if they think we are doing the wrong thing, that they will imitate us just because we have done it. I don't believe this. I believe that each country must have its own foreign policy. And in our case, where our contribution to Europe, I repeat, is marginal, but where we still believe that NATO is an important force in the world, we are entitled, we have a right, to ask questions about our participation in NATO.

In 1949, when we set up NATO, I think it was true that we could not wait for political settlements in order to meet the security issue, because the security issue was the number-one issue. But 20 years later I should be inclined to say that we can't wait until all the problems of security have been settled before we tackle the political issues of peace in the world. And it so happened that NATO after 20 years in our opinion had developed too much into a military alliance and not enough into a political alliance, not enough into an alliance which is interested not only in keeping the balance of deterrence of tactical power in Europe but into an alliance which is interested in arms control and de-escalation.

And I am afraid, in the situation which we had reached, NATO had in reality determined all of our defence policy. We had no defence policy, so to speak, except that of NATO. And our defence policy had determined all of our foreign policy. And we had no foreign policy of any importance except that which flowed from NATO. And this is a false perspective for any country. It is a false perspective to have a military alliance determine your foreign policy. It should be your foreign policy which determines your military policy.

So all we have done (and it is pretty important), last week in Ottawa, was to stand the pyramid on its base. It was standing on its head. We have decided to review our foreign policy and to have a defence policy flow from that, and from the defence policy to decide which alliances we want to belong to, and how our defences should be deployed. And that is why we gave a series of four priorities. In our statement last week, we said that the first priority for Canadians was not NATO, important though it is, and we have said that we wanted to remain aligned in NATO with those countries who believe in deterring the Soviet aggression in Europe. But this is not our first priority. Our first priority is the protection of Canadian sovereignty, in all the dimensions that it means.

And I don't accept the criticism of those who say this is a return to isolationism, or this is a return to the "fortress America" conception. This is not our purpose and this is not our aim.

What we are doing in our foreign policy, and what we are doing in our defence policy, we shall do by discussing with our allies, and we shall explain to them that our contribution is in order to promote the values which they are promoting in NATO—values of freedom and of liberty. And this is what we are aiming for first.

But it is false to talk of isolationism when you think of Canada, which is territorially one of the largest countries in the world, second in terms of its land space, and which has a very small population in terms of the middle and great powers. It is absurd to say that this is isolationism because we are not on all the fronts of the world, political and military, fighting with other people. You can't talk of isolationism of Canadians because, with the small manpower we have, with the economic means we have, we say we want to use the first part of it in terms of our own sovereignty, the second part of it in terms of the defence of our territory and of the continent, and the third part of it in defence of other alliances such as NATO, such as peace-keeping operations which we will embark upon and we have embarked upon through the United Nations. We need our armed forces in order to perform these roles, but in degrees determined by our foreign policy. We don't want a military alliance or a defence policy to pre-empt all our choices.

That is why we decided last week to announce what I call Phase One of our defence policy, saying that we were not neutralists and we were not pacifists, that we believed in aligning ourselves with countries who wanted to protect the same kind of values as we in the world but we wanted to do this by leaving also our military options open to these four priorities. And that is why we shall not say, until our foreign policy has been determined and presented to Parliament and presented to the country, in a final way, what forces we shall put into NATO and what forces we shall draw out of NATO. It is our foreign policy which must come first, and not the defence policy and not the military alliance.

That is why last week, because of the deadlines, because there was a meeting of the foreign ministers of NATO countries in Washington, we had to then state our general position. And we did. We stated we were remaining in NATO but we would not be pressed into making decisions now about our contributions to NATO, which I repeat we shall only make after our foreign policy has been determined overall. This is going apace. We have made several announcements. We have talked about recognizing Peking; we have talked about our policy in South America; we have even talked about the Vatican, to the scandal of a lot of people. We have talked of a lot of areas where we are reassessing our foreign policy. But until this policy has been presented, I repeat, to the Canadian people, we shall not close our options and say that all of our military strength will be oriented towards NATO.

We have a right to ask questions of our allies. If they want to keep us on these terms we shall be very happy because, our friends in NATO, we want to keep them. We want to continue "dialoguing" with them in the political sense. We want to keep these channels of communication open. We want to keep friends in Europe. But we don't want their military policy to determine our foreign policy. That's why we shall ask questions. It's right now, I believe, that we ask questions of ourselves about NATO and we ask questions of our allies about NATO.

Is an armoured brigade the right kind of contribution Canadians should make to Europe, could make to NATO? Is an armoured brigade, which can only be used in the plains of northern Germany, the right kind of contribution for Canadians to make? Is our squadron of CF-104s, which can be armed with conventional bombs or with nuclear bombs, the right kind of contribution? And what is the scenario for using nuclear arms in Europe, in our bombers, in our CF-104s? Do we want to participate in this way in an alliance without knowing in which way these so-called tactical weapons will be used? And has the scenario ever been explained to you, to the Canadian people, as to under what conditions our aircraft would fly nuclear weapons and unleash them on Europe? Will it only be as a second strike, will it only be as a deterrent? Are these 104s, are they soft targets? In the eyes of the Soviets, in the eyes of the Warsaw Pact countries, are they not entitled to ask themselves: "Well, what are these 104s flown by Canadians going to serve? Are they going to be first strike or second strike? Is it likely that they will be second strike? They are soft targets, they are on the ground, we know where the airfields are. Isn't it likely that they might be used to attack us first?" These are the questions that our enemies, the Soviets, are asking themselves, and these are the questions we are asking of our allies.

Our contribution in the naval area to our anti-submarine warfare – is this the right contribution? Should we be having the kind of naval force which is prepared to destroy the Soviet nuclear-armed submarines, which are a deterrent for them as the *Polaris* is a deterrent for the United States? The United States has *Polaris* submarines in the oceans and it will use them if it is attacked first, and if the American cities are destroyed the Americans know that they have their submarines as a second-strike capacity. And this strengthens the second-strike capacity of the United States. This is part of the balance of terror. This permits the Americans to say to the Soviets: "If you start first, we can still destroy you with our submarines." But the Soviets say the same thing: "If you Americans start first with your ICBMs, we can still destroy you with our submarines." The submarines are by nature, I suppose, in this capacity – they are second strike, they are deterrent. Is our policy right to be armed essentially against them?

These are the questions we want to ask of our allies, and we want to decide what our contribution in NATO will be. I am not promising any revolutionary changes. There may be some and they may not be very great. But I say that whatever our contribution will be in a military sense will flow from our foreign policy. And that is the purpose that our Government, your Government, is pursuing in Ottawa. It is an attempt to redefine our policies in all spheres. We have done it in the cultural, in the constitutional, in the trade spheres. We are doing it in the area of our foreign policy and of our defence policy.

80. Foreign Policy for Canadians

*Extracts from the General Paper.**

The ultimate interest of any Canadian Government must be the progressive development of the political, economic and social well-being of all Canadians now and in future. This proposition assumes that for

---

* On June 25, 1970, Mr. Sharp tabled in the House of Commons six booklets on *Foreign Policy for Canadians*. There are one "General" paper, of which brief extracts are printed here, and five "Sectoral" papers, of which a résumé appears below. The sectoral papers concern the United Nations, Latin America, Europe, the Pacific, and International Development. On

most Canadians their "political" well-being can only be assured if Canada continues in being as an independent, democratic and sovereign state. Some Canadians might hold that Canada could have a higher standard of living by giving up its sovereign independence and joining the United States. Others might argue that Canadians would be better off with a lower standard of living but with fewer limiting commitments and a greater degree of freedom of action, both political and economic. For the majority, the aim appears to be to attain the highest level of prosperity consistent with Canada's political preservation as in independent state. In the light of today's economic interdependence, this seems to be a highly practical and sensible evaluation of national needs.

Basic National Aims

In developing policies to serve the national interests, the Government has set for itself basic national aims which, however described, embrace three essential ideas:

  that Canada will continue secure as an independent political entity;
  that Canada and all Canadians will enjoy enlarging prosperity in the widest possible sense;
  that all Canadians will see in the life they have and the contribution they make to humanity something worthwhile preserving in identity and purpose.

These ideas encompass the main preoccupations of Canada and Canadians today: national sovereignty, unity and security; federalism, personal freedom and parliamentary democracy; national identity, bilingualism and multicultural expression; economic growth, financial stability, and balanced regional development; technological advance, social progress and environmental improvement; human values and humanitarian aspirations.

September 18, 1970, Mr. Sharp gave a lengthy outline, at the University of Toronto, of why and how these papers came to be written. His remarks on that occasion are well worth reading. See SS 70/12 of September 18, 1970, for the text of his statement. See also Mr. Sharp's comments of January 5, 1969, to a group of prominent academics regarding how the foreign policy review was conducted. The six booklets are available from DEA or QP, Ottawa, and are also to be found in university and public libraries across the country.

Pursuit of Canadian Aims

Much of Canada's effort internationally will be directed to bringing about the kinds of situation, development and relationship which will be most favourable to the furtherance of Canadian interests and values. As long as the international structure has the nation state as its basic unit, the Government will be pursuing its aims, to a substantial degree, in the context of its relationships with foreign governments. While Canada's interests might have to be pursued in competition or even in conflict with the interests of other nations, Canada must aim at the best, attainable conditions, those in which Canadian interests and values can thrive and Canadian objectives be achieved.

Canada has less reason than most countries to anticipate conflicts between its national aims and those of the international community as a whole. Many Canadian policies can be directed toward the broad goals of that community without unfavourable reaction from the Canadian public. Peace in all its manifestations, economic and social progress, environmental control, the development of international law and institutions – these are international goals which fall squarely into that category. Other external objectives sought by Canada, very directly related to internal problems (agricultural surpluses, energy management, need for resource conservation) are frequently linked to the attainment of international accommodations (cereals agreements, safeguards for the peaceful uses of atomic energy, fisheries conventions) of general benefit to the world community. Canada's action to advance self-interest often coincides with the kind of worthwhile contribution to international affairs that most Canadians clearly favour.

Canada's foreign policy, like all national policy, derives its content and validity from the degree of relevance it has to national interests and basic aims. Objectives have to be set not in a vacuum but in the context in which they will be pursued, that is, on the basis of reasonable assumption of what the future holds. The task of the Government is to ensure that these alignments and interrelationships are kept up-to-date and in proper perspective. In no area of policy-making is this whole process more formidable than foreign policy. . . .

The world does not stand still while Canada shapes and sets in motion its foreign policy. The international scene shifts rapidly and sometimes radically, almost from day to day.

The problem is to produce a clear, complete picture from circumstances which are dynamic and ever-changing. It must be held in focus long enough to judge what is really essential to the issue under consideration, to enable the Government to act on it decisively and effectively. That picture gets its shape from information gathered from a variety of sources—public or official—and sifted and analyzed systematically. The correct focus can only be achieved if all the elements of a particular policy question can be looked at in a conceptual framework which represents the main lines of national policy at home and abroad.

The Framework

Broadly speaking, the totality of Canada's national policy seeks to:

    foster economic growth
    safeguard sovereignty and independence
    work for peace and security
    promote social justice
    enhance the quality of life
    ensure a harmonious natural environment.

These six main themes of national policy form as well the broad framework of foreign policy. They illustrate the point that foreign policy is the extension abroad of national policy. The shape of foreign policy at any given time will be determined by the pattern of emphasis which the Government gives to the six policy themes. It is shaped as well by the constraints of the prevailing situation, at home and abroad, and inevitably by the resources available to the Government at any given time.

Interrelationships

The conceptual framework serves particularly well to emphasize the various interrelationships which enter into the consideration and conduct of Canada's foreign policy. These include, for example:

    the relationship between domestic and foreign elements of policy designed to serve the same national objective (The utilization of energies and resources in Canada is related to international agreements on their export, both elements being pursued to promote economic growth.);

    the relationship between basic national aims and intermediate objectives for furthering their attainment (National unity is related to the external expressions of Canada's bilingualism and multicultural composition.);

    the relationship between activities designed to serve one set of objectives and those serving other national objectives (Cultural and information programmes are related to trade promotion activities.);

the relationship between and among the six main thrusts of policy (Ensuring the natural environment is related to enhancing the quality of life; both are related to the fostering of economic growth; which in turn relates to the promotion of social justice.)

Hard Choices

Most policy decisions—certainly the major ones—involve hard choices which require that a careful balance be struck in assessing the various interests, advantages and other policy factors in play. As in so many fields of human endeavour, tradeoffs are involved. For example:

In striving to raise national income through economic growth, policies may be pursued which adversely affect the natural environment by increasing the hazards of pollution or by depleting resources too rapidly. Such policies might also cause infringement of social justice (because of inflation, for example) and impair the quality of life for individual Canadians.

In seeking social justice for developing nations, through trade policies which offer them concessions or preferences, the Government's policy may adversely affect the domestic market opportunities for certain Canadian industries, or it might involve parallel policies to curtail or reorient their production.

Similarly, if international development assistance programmes require a substantial increase in Canadian resources allocated, the trade-off may be some reduction of resources allocated to other governmental activity, like the extension of Canadian welfare programmes or the attack on domestic pollution.

Reductions in military expenditure may lead to results difficult to gauge as regards Canada's capacity to ensure its security, to safeguard its sovereignty and independence, and to make a useful contribution to the maintenance of peace, though resources might thereby be freed for other activities.

The most difficult choices of the future may result from seeking to recapture and maintain a harmonious natural environment. Such policies may be essential to enhance the quality of life (if not to ensure human survival) but they may well require some curtailment of economic growth and freedom of enterprise and a heavy allocation of resources from both public and private sources.

From this whole review a pattern of policy for the seventies emerges. None of the six themes—Sovereignty and Independence, Peace and Security, Social Justice, Quality of Life, Harmonious Natural Environment or Economic Growth—can be neglected. In the light of current forecasts, domestic and international, there is every reason to give a higher priority than in the past to the themes of Harmonious Natural Environment and Quality of Life. Canadians have become more and more aware of a pressing need to take positive action to ward off threats to the physical attractions of Canada, and to safeguard the social conditions and human values which signify Canada's distinct identity. They are increasingly concerned about minimizing the abrasions of rapidly evolving technologies, conserving natural resources, reducing disparities regional and otherwise, dealing with pollution, improving urban and rural living conditions, protecting consumers, cultural enrichment, improving methods of communication and transportation, expanding research and development in many fields. All of these concerns have international ramifications. To enlarge external activities in these fields and to meet ongoing commitments such as development assistance (Social Justice), disarmament negotiations, the promotion of détente and peace-keeping (Peace and Security), it will be essential to maintain the strength of Canada's economy (Economic Growth).

Policy Patterns

To achieve the desired results, various mixes of policy are possible. For example, priorities could be set as follows: In response to popular sentiment, which is concerned with the threats of poverty and pollution and the challenge to national unity, the themes could be ranked beginning with (i) Social Justice; (ii) Quality of Life; (iii) Sovereignty and Independence.

or

In order to meet growing environmental problems the emphasis could be (i) Harmonious Natural Environment; (ii) Quality of Life; (iii) Social Justice.

or

In order to deal with economic crises the policy emphasis could be: (i) Economic Growth; (ii) Social Justice.

After considering these and other alternatives, and having in mind its determination to emphasize what Canada can do best in order to promote its objectives abroad, the Government is of the view that the foreign policy pattern for the seventies should be based on a ranking of the six policy themes which gives highest priorities to Economic Growth, Social Justice and Quality of Life policies. In making this decision, the Government is fully aware that giving this kind of emphasis to those themes of policy does not mean that other policies and activities would or indeed could be neglected. Policies related to other themes (Peace and Security, Sovereignty and Independence) would merely be placed in a new pattern of emphasis. Emphasis on sovereignty and independence, in any event, primarily depends on the extent to which they are challenged or have to be used at any given time to safeguard national interests. Peace and Security depend mainly on external developments. On the other hand, the survival of Canada as a nation is being challenged internally by divisive forces. This underlines further the need for new emphasis on policies, domestic and external, that promote economic growth, social justice and an enhanced quality of life for all Canadians.

Inevitably, sudden developments, unanticipated and perhaps irrational, could require the Government to make urgent and radical readjustments of its policy positions and priorities, at least as long as the emergency might last. Flexibility is essential but so too is a sense of direction and purpose, so that Canada's foreign policy is not over-reactive but is oriented positively in the direction of national aims. This is one of the main conclusions of the policy review.

Emerging Policy

While the review was going on, while the conceptual framework was taking shape, the Government has been taking decisions and initiating actions which reflect a changing emphasis of policy and Canada's changing outlook on the world.

The pattern has now been set, the policy is in motion. The broad implications for the future are becoming apparent. If the seventies do present Canada with anything like the challenges and conditions foreshadowed in Chapter IV, prime importance will attach to internal conditions in the country and steps taken by the Government—at home and abroad—to improve those conditions. Sound domestic policies are basic to effective foreign relations. The most appropriate foreign policy for the immediate future will be the one:

Which strengthens and extends sound domestic policies dealing with key national issues, including economic and social well-being for all Canadians, language and cultural distinctions, rational utilization of natural resources, environmental problems of all kinds;

Which gives Canadians satisfaction and self-respect about their distinct identity, about the values their country stands for, about shouldering their share of international responsibility, about the quality of life in Canada; and, which helps Canada to compete effectively in earning its living and making its own way with the least possible dependence on any outside power.

81. Foreign Policy for Canadians

Résumé of the five "Sectoral" papers as conveyed in an explanatory note released by the Department of External Affairs on June 25, 1970, after Foreign Policy for Canadians *had been tabled in the House of Commons by the Secretary of State for External Affairs.**

The Pacific

The Government's intention to enlarge its interests and activities in the Pacific was made known from the outset of the policy review. The Pacific sector study is largely concerned with ways and means of doing this effectively. The study notes measures already taken by the Government, such as the opening of negotiations with Peking for the establishment of diplomatic relations, and outlines future intentions for increased aid and development assistance.

A major emphasis is on the prospects for expansion of trade relations. The Pacific area is Canada's third largest market and third largest supplier. With a vast and varied potential it offers great challenges and opportunities for the growth of trade and investment. Western Canada enjoys a favoured position in this economic exchange. Of the 54 principal Canadian commodities selling in Japan, for example, no fewer than 48 are of Western Canadian origin.

Latin America

The Government has stated its intention that Canada should accept its full responsibility as a part of the Western Hemisphere and as an American nation. This paper examines the means whereby this responsibility should be discharged. It sets out the Government's option—to undertake a set of co-ordinated programmes designed to strengthen systematically Canadian links with the Latin American countries while at the same time playing a larger part in the Inter-American System without becoming a full member of the Organization of American States in the immediate future. A series of programmes for the strengthening of bilateral ties with Latin American countries is set out in Chapter IV. These include increased development assistance, incentives for greater trade and investment and enlarged technical, scientific and educational exchanges. Canada's relationship to the Organization of American States is discussed in Chapter III.

---

* For further useful background, see the report to the House of Commons respecting "Foreign Policy for Canadians", June 1971, by the Standing Committee on External Affairs and National Defence.

Europe

The expansion of Canada's activities in the Pacific and Latin America does not imply any lessening of Canada's traditional and active involvement in Europe. Canada values as never before its relationship with the Western European nations in terms of cultural and scientific exchanges, collective security, trade and investment; as a source of skilled immigrants and for the diversification of relationships it offers to a country faced with the predominant power and influence of the United States. The dynamic changes in Europe, both Eastern and Western, present challenges and opportunities that must be met if full advantage is to be taken of Canada's historical connections with Europe.

International Development

In this paper the Government acknowledges that international development is a long-term commitment requiring a steady and increasing flow of resources. To provide this stability and to recognize the priority of the development assistance programme, the Government will endeavour to increase each year the percentage of national income allocated to official development assistance. In the fiscal year 1971-72 the level of official development assistance will be increased by $60 million from the level of $364 million in the fiscal year 1970-71.

United Nations

The paper indicates the major objectives Canada will be pursuing at the United Nations. They include some that are long-standing in Canadian foreign policy such as working to stop the arms race, promoting peace-keeping and peace-making, contributing to the progressive development of international law. Others have to do with international issues of more recent origin—the peaceful uses of satellite systems, co-operation in the use of the seabed, measures to prevent deterioration in the human environment. The inclusion of southern African questions which receive attention at the United Nations emphasizes their importance to the future of the United Nations.

CANADA-U.S.S.R. RELATIONS

¯ Canada established diplomatic relations with the Soviet Union in 1942 at the height of the Second World War. A trade treaty, arising out of increasing Russian grain requirements, was signed in 1956, as documented in the previous volume. Trade, never extensive, has tended to favour Canada over the years largely as a result of our cereal exports.

Arising out of the Foreign Policy Review of 1968-1970 and following the shock of the Nixon Doctrine of August 15, 1971, with its accompanying surcharge on exports to the U.S.A., relations between Canada and the U.S.S.R. drew somewhat less distant. Mutual experiences in the Arctic, advanced Russian technology and progress there were the catalyst and common denominator. Mr. Trudeau visited the U.S.S.R. in 1973. He was the first Canadian Prime Minister to do so while in office. He described his visit as follows: "Pour nous (cette visite fut) un pas important vers l'établissement d'une politique étrangère la plus autonome possible. Chacun sait que les Canadiens se sentent passablement dominés par la présence américaine et c'est important pour nous d'avoir d'autres interlocuteurs.... Je pense que c'est important pour nous, comme nation canadienne, d'avoir des ouvertures sur un pays qui, comme l'Union Soviétique, est certainement l'une des deux superpuissances". (CBC interview, Moscow, May 20, 1971).

82. Canada and the Soviet Union*

Statement by the Prime Minister, Mr. Pierre-Elliott Trudeau, in the House of Commons, May 28, 1971. (Extracts)

Canada has long had treaty arrangements with the Soviet Government. Our first trade agreement was signed in 1956. Since that time, in every year except 1969, we have enjoyed a favourable and often substantial balance of trade in our favour. I might add that while in Moscow our trade in wheat was reviewed, including the Soviet assurance that, when the U.S.S.R. has requirements to import wheat, it will in the first instance apply to Canada as a preferred source of supply. In January of this year, the Minister of Industry, Trade and Commerce concluded an important agreement with the U.S.S.R. on the industrial application of science and technology, an agreement that

---

* This should be read in conjunction with material on relations with the United States provided in Chapter III above, notably on the "Third Option".

reflects the recognition in the U.S.S.R. of Canada's increasing stature as the owner of important, advanced technology and of our awareness of the important progress made by the Soviets in a number of fields.

This increasing interest in the Soviet Union has not been confined to the Government. A wide range of contacts has been established in recent years by persons who recognize the Soviet Union as a near neighbour, as a country of great influence, as a marketplace and trading partner of immense potential, as the home of wide cultural attainments and as a fascinating land. I believe we have much to gain in this process of increasing awareness.

Against this steadily developing background, it was only natural that steps be taken to place Canadian-Soviet relations on a more "structured" and orderly basis, and this was the purpose of the protocol which was signed in Moscow last week and tabled in this House by the Secretary of State for External Affairs on the same day.*

This document, which I believe to be an important one, goes some distance toward placing Canadian-Soviet consultations on the same basis as has existed for a number of years with Britain, the United States and Japan. A similar arrangement was entered into with Mexico as part of the work of the ministerial committee which travelled to Latin America, and agreements for regular consultation with both New Zealand and Australia were reached during my visits to those countries last May.

This process of broadening Canadian relations is an ongoing one and was spelled out in the foreign policy review. The principles of that review have been discussed widely in Canada and were studied at length by a Parliamentary committee. The foreign policy of this Government has been to contribute where it can to a peaceful world and to strengthen our relations with a number of countries. In both respects this policy is designed to serve basic Canadian values and interests. The Canadian-Soviet protocol is a natural manifestation of that policy.

As the communiqué tabled this morning reveals, the protocol will ensure continuing consultations at a variety of levels on matters of the kind discussed by me and the Soviet leaders, President Podgorny, Premier Kosygin and Secretary-General Brezhnev.

While in no way diluting our friendship or our contacts with those countries, such as the United States, Britain, France and others, with which we have had traditional and friendly relations, we have taken a

---

* Its text is provided at the end of this document.

fresh look at the world and at the Canadian interests in it. Areas of the world which have not in the past figured prominently in Canada have been sought out consciously as friends, as prospective trading partners, as sources of information and advice, as contributors to an independent Canada; a Canada not overwhelmingly dependent upon or dominated by any one state or group of states; in short, a Canada with a singular identity and well recognized as such both by Canadians and by citizens of other countries.

We have been active in the world in those areas where we could contribute positively and usefully: economic and technical assistance, through the creation of the Canadian International Development Research Centre; fresh juristic concepts for the prevention of pollution in waters off our shores and for the conservation of fisheries; studies and proposals in the fields of disarmament and arms control. We have looked to Latin America and are seeking permanent observer status in the Organization of American States; we have expressed our many-faceted interest in the countries of the far "rim" of the Pacific; we have adjusted our defence posture to remove from it any elements that could be regarded as provocative, and to ensure that our policy adequately but truly reflects the needs of Canada for national defence, we have been successful in establishing useful and official contacts with the most populous nation in the world, the People's Republic of China; we have entered wholeheartedly the new Francophone organization.

All this has been done while retaining Canadian membership in NATO and NORAD, while strengthening our relations with such economic associations as the OECD and GATT, while contributing in an effective and constructive fashion to the UN and to the Commonwealth.

These activities are good in themselves, are good for Canada and, I am convinced, are supported strongly by the majority of Canadians.

It is in this context that my visit to the Soviet Union should be viewed. As we have looked traditionally south to the United States and east to Europe and, more recently, west to Asia, so should we not disregard our neighbour to the north. The relations between Canada and the Soviet Union in the postwar years have not all been of a wholesome or a desirable nature. I harbour no naive belief that as a result of this protocol our two countries will find themselves suddenly in a relation that will reflect nothing but sweetness and tender feelings. As I stated in my speech in the Kremlin, there remain many fundamental differences between us: differences relating to deep-seated concerns springing from historic, geographic, ideological, economic, social and military factors.

But, surely, the only way to resolve these differences and eliminate these concerns is by increased contact and effort at understanding. That is what the protocol proposes. That is what, in a different way, is achieved by prime ministerial visits. Through them an opportunity is created by the pens of journalists and the cameras of photographers for the people of both Canada and the Soviet Union to learn much more about one another—their respective histories, their sufferings, their aspirations.

Because tolerance and good will are nowhere so evident as they are in Canada, Canadians are possessed of an uncommon opportunity to urge all men everywhere to pursue these universal goals. I attempted to do so while in the Soviet Union, where I expressed to Premier Kosygin the widespread concern in Canada over the alleged refusal of the Soviet Government to permit its Jewish citizens to emigrate to Israel or to other countries of their choice. I was assured by Mr. Kosygin that these allegations were not well-founded and that, in particular, his Government had permitted the exit to Israel for many months of significant numbers of Soviet Jews. I might add that Mr. Kosygin's statement has been corroborated by the Canadian Government from other, independent sources.

I seized the opportunity to urge Mr. Kosygin to permit persons of all ethnic origins with relatives in Canada to come here and thus reunify the many families which have been split tragically for many years.

He assured me that his Government would not place unjustifiable barriers in the way of those persons and he promised that he would give personal attention to the list of names of such persons which I took with me to Moscow.

In another area entirely, I was able to discuss with Mr. Kosygin the concern and fear expressed by our East Coast fishermen over the practices of the Soviet Atlantic fishing fleet. I pointed out to him the immense increase in recent years of the Soviet catch, the decrease in the Canadian catch and the vital need for conservation of this important food resource in the interests of both our countries. Mr. Kosygin observed that the Soviet Union was a party to the North Atlantic fisheries convention and had a profound interest in a long-lasting and healthy fish stock. We agreed that this issue was deserving of further talks.

Only time will tell whether the warm welcome which was accorded me in the U.S.S.R. reflects the commencement of an era in Canadian-Soviet relations as advantageous as we all hope will be the case. I prefer to be optimistic and I am urging all government departments to exploit these new openings. I urge Canadian businessmen to accept the new challenge. For our part as Canadians, I assured the Soviet leaders that there was no impediment in our desire for better and more mutually beneficial relations.

U.S.S.R. – Canada Protocol on Consultations

Inspired by a desire to develop and strengthen relations of friendship, good neighbourliness and mutual confidence between the two countries,

Expressing a desire for co-operation in the interests of maintaining international peace and security in accordance with the purposes and principles of the Charter of the United Nations, and

Conscious of the responsibilities of the Soviet Union and Canada as members of the United Nations to promote the preservation of peace,

Believing that the Soviet Union and Canada can contribute toward the above goals by acting in a spirit of co-operation, mutual respect and reciprocal benefit,

Endeavouring to improve and further develop relations between the two countries by means of high-level contacts, expanding ties and exchanges in the fields of economy, trade, science, technology, culture and northern development,

Noting with satisfaction the conclusion of the Soviet-Canadian Agreement on Co-operation in the Industrial Application of Science and Technology,* and the development of trade on the basis of the 1956 Trade Agreement,

Conscious of the responsibility of the two sides to preserve and protect the environment of the Arctic and the sub-Arctic areas,

Fully determined to go on developing political and economic co-operation,

The Prime Minister of Canada and the Soviet leaders have agreed on the following:

1. The Soviet Union and Canada shall enlarge and deepen consultations on important international problems of mutual interest

---

* This Agreement was signed on January 27, 1971. See SS 71/8 of February 4, 1971, for background.

and on questions of bilateral relations by means of periodic meetings. Such consultations will embrace:

- questions of a political, economic and cultural nature, environmental questions and other subjects concerning relations between the two countries;
- international questions, including situations causing tension in various parts of the world, with a view to promoting détente, furthering co-operation and strengthening security;
- problems which are the subjects of multilateral talks, including those considered at the United Nations;
- any other subjects in respect of which the parties may find it useful to have an exchange of views.

2. In the event of a situation arising which, in the opinion of the two governments, endangers the maintenance of peace or involves a breach of the peace, the two governments will make contact without delay in order to exchange views on what might be done to improve the situation.

3. The provisions set forth in paragraphs 1 and 2 above do not affect obligations previously assumed by the parties in respect of third states and are not directed against any of them.

4. The conduct of such consultations between the Soviet Union and Canada is designed not only to promote the welfare of their peoples and develop relations between them but also to contribute towards better relations among all countries.

5. These consultations, at levels to be determined by mutual agreement, will have a regular character. The Ministers of Foreign Affairs or their representatives will meet whenever the need arises and, in principle, at least once a year. Either party is free to recommend the holding of such consultations, including the time and level at which they should be held.

Moscow, May 19, 1971.

Chairman of the Council of
Ministers of the U.S.S.R.

Prime Minister
of Canada.

Suggested Reading

GENERAL

Apart from the basic bibliographies on Canadian foreign policy and external relations mentioned on page 421 of the preceding volume, attention is drawn to the 1971-75 sequel (Toronto, CIIA, 1977) to Dr. Donald Page's *Bibliography of works on Canadian Foreign Relations 1945-70*. The second edition of Professor Granatstein's bibliography, *Canada since 1867: A bibliographical guide* edited with Paul Stevens (Toronto: Hakkert, 1977), should also be consulted. This *Guide*, Professor Page's two bibliographies, and the three volumes of documents on Canadian external relations now available in the Carleton Library constitute the most comprehensive survey of source material currently available on the formulation and evolution of Canadian foreign policy over the last three decades.

The following general books covering aspects of Canadian external relations during the 1965-1975 decade should also be consulted: John W. Holmes. *Canada: A Middle-Aged Power*, Carleton Library No. 98 (Toronto: McClelland and Stewart, 1976);

Also Holmes' *The Better Part of Valour*, Carleton Library No. 49 (1970);

S. Clarkson, *An Independent Foreign Policy for Canada?* (Toronto: McClelland and Stewart, 1968);

Peter C. Dobell, *Canada's Search for New Roles* (Toronto: Oxford University Press, 1972);

J. Eayrs, *Diplomacy and its Discontents* (Toronto: University of Toronto Press, 1971);

J. Granatstein, *Canadian Foreign Policy since 1945: Middle Power or Satellite?* (Toronto: Copp Clark, 1969);

Peter C. Newman, *The Distemper of Our Times*, (Winnipeg: Greywood Publishing Limited, 1968). In addition, *The Canadian Annual Review of Politics and Public Affairs* includes useful material on Canadian foreign policy in its yearly editions.

The regular publications of the CIIA such as *Behind the Headlines, International Canada, International Journal, Etudes Internationales* are basic to any study of Canadian external affairs during the decade. The various publications of the Department of External Affairs such as *External Affairs* (before 1971) and, more notably, its sucessor *International Perspectives* are helpful sources, as are the White Papers documented in the body of the text.

CHAPTER I—THE UNITED NATIONS

E. L. M. Burns, *A Seat at the Table: A Struggle for Disarmament* (Toronto: Clark Irwin, 1972).

William Eppstein, *Disarmament: 25 Years of Effort* (Toronto: CIIA, 1972)

William Eppstein, *Nuclear Proliferation and Control* (New York: Free Press, 1976).

Granatstein, Taylor, and Cox, *Peace-Keeping: International Challenge and Canadian Response* (Toronto: CIIA, 1968).

DEA, *"Where is the UN Heading?"* (Ottawa: May 1977).

CHAPTER II – NATO

H. Cleveland, *NATO: The Trans-Atlantic Bargain* (New York: Harper and Row, 1970).
John Gellner, *Canada in NATO* (Toronto: Ryerson Press, 1970).
Colin Gray, *Canadian Defence Priorities* (Toronto: Clarke Irwin, 1972).
L. Hertzmann, *Alliances and Illusions – Canada and the NATO-NORAD Question* (Edmonton: Hurtig, 1969).
Albert Legault, "La Nouvelle Politique de Défense du Canada" (Montréal: *Le Devoir*, 25-26 Novembre 1969).
Albert Legault, "La Position Stratégique du Canada et la Décennie 1970", *International Journal*, Winter 1970-71.

CHAPTER III – THE UNITED STATES

Kari Levitt, *Silent Surrender: The Multi-National Corporation in Canada* (Toronto: Macmillan of Canada, 1970).
John Sloan Dickey and Whitney H. Shepardson, *Canada and the American Presence*, (New York: New York University Press, 1975).
John Fayerweather, *Foreign Investment in Canada: Prospects for National Policy* (Toronto: Oxford University Press, 1974).
J. H. Redekop, *The Star-Spangled Beaver* (Toronto: Peter Martin Associates, 1971).
Dennis Smith, *Gentle Patriot: A Political Biography of Walter Gordon* (Edmonton: Hurtig, 1973).
John Warnock, *Partner to Behemoth* (Toronto: New Press, 1970).

CHAPTER IV – THE FAR EAST

J. M. Gibson and D. M. Johnston, *A Century of Struggle: Canadian Essays on Revolutionary China* (Toronto: CIIA, 1971).
Keith A. G. Hay, *Canada's Economic Ties with Japan* (Toronto: McClelland and Stewart, 1977).
Lorne Kavic, "Canada-Japan Relations", *International Journal*, Vol. XXVI, Summer 1971.
Maureen Appel Molot, "Canada's Relations with China since 1968", in N. Hillmer and G. Stevenson, *Canada: A Foremost Nation* (Toronto: McClelland and Stewart, 1977).

CHAPTER V – THE COMMONWEALTH

Andrew Brewin and David MacDonald, *Canada and the Biafran Tragedy* (Toronto: James Lewis and Samuel, 1970).
Robert Chodos, *The Caribbean Connection* (Toronto: James Lorimer, 1977).
Robert O. Matthews, "Canada and Anglophone Africa", in P. V. Lyon and T. Y. Ismael, *Canada and the Third World* (Toronto: Macmillan of Canada, 1976).
Kari Levitt and A. McIntyre, *Canada–West Indies Economic Relations* (Montreal: Private Planning Association, 1969).

CHAPTER VI–INTERNATIONAL ECONOMIC POLICY

G. E. C. Brierley, "International Trade Arbitration, the Canadian Viewpoint", in R. St. J. Macdonald, *Canadian Perspectives on International Law and Organization* (Toronto: University of Toronto Press, 1974).

John G. Crean, "The Coming Negotiations under GATT" (Toronto: CIIA, *Behind the Headlines*, June 1973).

H. Edward English, Bruce W. Wilkinson, and H. C. Eastman, *Canada in a Wider Economic Community*, published for the Private Planning Association of Canada (Toronto: University of Toronto Press, 1972).

Fred Lazar, "Trade and Investment", in *Canadian Annual Review of Politics and Public Affairs*, 1975.

A. F. W. Plumptre, *Three Decades of Decision: Canada and the World Monetary System, 1944-1975* (Toronto: McClelland and Stewart, 1977).

A. Rotstein, *The Precarious Homestead* (Toronto, New Press, 1973), especially Chapters 4, 6, 9, and 10.

In addition, Chapters 2, 4, and 5 of Hillmer and Stevenson, *Canada: A Foremost Nation* (Toronto, McClelland and Stewart, 1977) provide useful essays on Canada and the European Economic Community, transnational corporations, and world energy problems.

CHAPTER VII–INTERNATIONAL DEVELOPMENT

Irving Brecker, "The Continuing Challenge of International Development, a Canadian Perspective", *Queen's Quarterly*, Autumn 1975.

Canadian International Development Agency, *Taking Stock, a Review of CIDA Activities, 1970-74* (Ottawa: QP, 1974).

L. B. Pearson, *Partners in Development* (New York: Praeger, 1969).

Escott Reid, "Canada and the Struggle Against World Poverty", *International Journal*, Winter 1969-70.

Clyde Sanger, "Canada and Development in the Third World", in P. V. Lyon and T. Y. Ismael, *Canada and the Third World* (Toronto: Macmillan of Canada, 1976).

Note: *Canadian Annual Review of Politics and Public Affairs* contains a chapter by R. B. Byers on international development assistance in each recent yearly volume.

CHAPTER VIII–THE ENVIRONMENT

J. A. Beesley, "Canadian Approach to International Environmental Law", *Canadian Yearbook of International Law*, 1973.

Maxwell Cohen, "The Arctic and the National Interest", *International Journal*, Winter 1970-71.

D. M. Johnston, "International Environmental Law, Recent Developments and Canadian Contributions", in R. St. J. Macdonald, *Canadian Perspectives on International Law and Organization* (Toronto: University of Toronto Press, 1974).

CHAPTER IX – THE PROVINCES AND FOREIGN POLICY

Ronald G. Atkey, "The Role of the Provinces in International Affairs", *International Journal*, Vol. XXVI No. 1, 1970-71.

T. A. Levy, "Provincial International Status Re-Visited", *Dalhousie Law Journal*, Vol. III, 1976.

G. L. Morris, "Canadian Federalism and International Law", in R. St. J. Macdonald, *Canadian Perspectives on International Law and Organization* (Toronto: University of Toronto Press, 1974).

CHAPTER X – THE FOREIGN POLICY REVIEW: 1968-1970

Andrew Brewin, "Foreign Policy for Canadians: Comments on the White Paper", *Behind the Headlines* (Toronto: CIIA, August 1970).

Peter C. Dobell, "The Management of a Foreign Policy for Canadians", *International Journal*, Winter 1970-71.

Ivan L. Head, "The Foreign Policy of the New Canada", *Foreign Affairs*, Vol. 50 No. 2, January 1972.

Peyton V. Lyon, "A Review of the Review", *Journal of Canadian Studies*, May 1970.

Garth Stevenson, "For a Real Review", *Current Comment* (Ottawa: School of International Affairs, Carleton University, 1970).

D. C. Thompson and R. F. Swanson, *Canadian Foreign Policy: Options and Perspectives* (Toronto: McGraw-Hill Ryerson, 1971).

Bruce Thordarson, *Trudeau and Foreign Policy* (Toronto: Oxford University Press, 1977).

There are several general books on subjects which had to be omitted from this volume. The following could be usefully consulted:

J. C. M. Ogelsby, *Gringos from the Far North* (Toronto: Macmillan of Canada, 1976).

C. Pestieau and C. I. Brandtford, *Canada and Latin America: the Potential for Partnership* (Montreal: CALA and the Private Planning Association, 1971).

Léon Mayrand, *Vers un Accord Américano-Cubain* (Québec Collection *Choix*, Centre Québécois de Relations Internationales, Université Laval, 1974).

In addition, the White Paper on Immigration published in 1966 and the Green Papers issued (in four volumes) by the Department of Manpower and Immigration (Ottawa: QP, 1974) should be consulted. Attention is also drawn to Mr. MacEachen's statement of May 22, 1969, in the House of Commons, on Canada's immigration policies and practices as applicable to members of the armed forces of other countries, who seek permanent entry to Canada. This issue troubled Canadian – United States relations during the decade but dwindled in importance when the Viet Nam War came to an end. *Canada and Immigration* by Freda Hawkins (Montreal: McGill-Queen's University Press, 1972) provides useful coverage of immigration generally. *Canadian Treaty Making* (Toronto: Butterworth, 1968) and *Human Rights, Federalism and Minorities* (Toronto: CIIA, 1970), both by Allan E. Gotlieb, should be consulted regarding these foreign-policy-related fields.